MW00901935

e3 Chemistry

Guided Study Book

High School Chemistry

with

NYS Chemistry Regents Exams
The Physical Setting

2018
Home Edition

E3 Chemistry Books
Student and Teacher-friendly High School Books to:
✓ *Excite* students to study
✓ *Engage* students in learning
✓ *Enhance* students understanding

E3chemistry
Guided Study Book

2018 Home Edition

© 2017 by E3 Scholastic Publishing.
All rights reserved. No part of this book may be reproduced or transmitted in any form or by any means, electronic, mechanical, photocopying, recording, or otherwise, without prior written permission of E3 Scholastic Publishing.

ISBN-13: 978-1981186310
ISBN-10: 198118631X

Printed in The United States of America

excite   engage   enhance

E3 Scholastic Publishing

E3chemistry.com
(877) 224 – 0484
info@e3chemistry.com

Table of Contents

Table of Contents

Table of Contents

Also available:

Guided Study Book 2018 - School Edition: ISBN: 978-1979088374

No answers in the book. Free Answer Key Booklet for teachers with a class order.

Topic 1
Matter, Energy and Changes

Lesson 1: Classification of Matter

Lesson 2: Phases of Matter and Temperature

Lesson 3: Heat and Heat Calculations

Lesson 4: Gas Laws and Calculations

Lesson 5: Physical and Chemical Properties

Lesson 1: Types of Matter
Elements, Compounds, Mixtures

Chemistry is the study of matter: its composition, structures, properties, changes it undergoes, and energy accompanying these changes.

Matter is anything that has mass and takes up space. Matter, in other words, is "stuff." Matter can be grouped and classified as pure substances or mixtures.
In this lesson, you will learn about the different types of matter.

Pure Substances
Elements and Compounds

Pure substances are types of matter composed (made up) of particles that are the same. The composition and properties of a pure substance are uniform and definite in every sample. Elements and compounds are classified as pure substances.

Examples of Pure Substances

Elements	Compounds
Na (sodium)	H_2O (water)
Al (aluminum)	CO_2 (carbon dioxide)
H_2 (hydrogen)	NH_3 (ammonia)
He (helium)	$C_6H_{12}O_6$ (sugar)

Practice 1
Carbon dioxide, CO_2, is classified as a pure substance because
1) its composition can vary
2) its composition is fixed
3) it cannot be separated
4) it can be separated

Practice 2
Which list consists only of chemical pure substances?
1) Soil and salt water.
2) Air and water.
3) Iron and sodium chloride.
4) Sugar and concrete.

Elements
Composed of the Same Atom. Cannot be Broken Down.

An atom is the most basic unit of matter.
Elements are pure substances that are composed of identical atoms with the same atomic number. Elements cannot be decomposed or broken down into simpler substances by physical nor chemical methods. Calcium (Ca) and bromine (Br_2) are examples of elements. All known elements are listed on the Periodic Table. The structure of an atom is covered in Topic 3.

Examples of Elements

Mg (magnesium)	Br_2 (bromine)
Au (gold)	F_2 (fluorine)

Practice 3
Which cannot be decomposed by physical or chemical methods?
1) HBr   3) K_2O
2) Ni   4) CO

Practice 4
Lithium is classified as an element because it is composed of atoms that
1) have the same mass
2) have different masses
3) have the same atomic number
4) have different atomic numbers

 ©2017 E3 Scholastic Publishing. All Rights Reserved

Topic 1   Matter, Energy and Changes

Compounds
Different Atoms Chemically Bonded. Fixed Composition. Chemically Separated.

Compounds are pure substances composed of two or more different elements that are *chemically* combined in a fixed ratio. The properties and composition of a compound are definite or the same in all samples of the compound. Compounds can be decomposed or broken down into simpler substances by *chemical methods* only. Properties of a compound are different from those of the elements found in the compound. Calcium bromide ($CaBr_2$), water (H_2O), and ammonia (NH_3) are examples of compounds.

The **Law of definite proportions** states that elements in a compound are combined in a *fixed ratio* by mass. *For example:*
The composition in every sample of water, H_2O, is always 89% oxygen to 11% hydrogen.
That means any 10-gram sample of water contains 8.9 grams of oxygen and 1.1 grams of hydrogen.

Examples of Compounds
$H_2O(l)$ (water) $CO_2(g)$ (carbon dioxide)
$NH_3(g)$ (ammonia) $NaCl(s)$ (sodium chloride)

Compounds are similar to elements in that:
- Both are pure substances.
- Both always have homogeneous properties.
- Both have fixed and definite composition in all samples.

Compounds are different from elements in that:
- Compounds can be chemically separated or decomposed into simpler substances.
- Elements cannot be chemically or physically separated.

Practice 5
Which list consists only of substances that can be chemically decomposed?
1) $K(s)$ and $KCl(aq)$
2) $CO(aq)$ and $CO_2(g)$
3) $Co(s)$ and $CaCl_2(s)$
4) $LiBr(s)$ and $CCl_4(l)$

Practice 6
Which change must occur for HF to form from its elements?
1) A physical change.
2) A chemical change.
3) A phase change.
4) A nuclear change.

Practice 7
MgO is different from Mg in that MgO
1) is a pure substance
2) has the same unique properties
3) can be chemically separated
4) can be physically separated

Mixtures
Different Substances Physically Combined. Variable Composition. Physically Separated.

Mixtures are types of matter that are composed of two or more different substances that are *physically* combined. The proportion of the substances in a mixture may vary or can change from one sample to another. A mixture retains the properties of the individual substances.
A mixture can be separated into its components only by *physical methods*.
A mixture can be classified as homogeneous or heterogeneous.

Examples of Mixtures
NaCl*(aq)*   (salt water)   HCl*(aq)* (hydrochloric acid solution)
$C_6H_{12}O_6$*(aq)* (sugar solution)   Concrete and air are also mixtures

Homogeneous mixtures
A mixture is classified as homogeneous if:
- The components of the mixture are *uniformly and evenly* mixed throughout.

- The mixture has one phase, and the individual substances can't be seen.

- Samples taken within the same mixture have the *same* composition.

Heterogeneous mixtures
A mixture is classified as heterogeneous if:
- The components of the mixture are *not uniformly* mixed throughout.

- The mixture is in many phases, and the individual substances can be seen.

- Samples taken within the same mixture have *different* compositions.

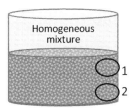
Samples 1 and 2 have the same composition.

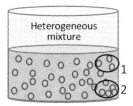
Samples 1 and 2 have different compositions.

Aqueous solutions are homogeneous mixtures made with water. A scoop of salt in a glass of water makes an aqueous solution. *(aq)* symbol next to a chemical formula indicates that the substance is an aqueous solution or a homogeneous mixture. Examples: NaCl*(aq)* and CO_2*(aq)*.

Mixtures are similar to compounds in that:
- Both are composed or made up of two or more different substances.
- Both can be separated into their components.

Mixtures are different from compounds in that:
- Components of mixtures are *physically* combined, and the composition can be changed or varied.
  In compounds, they are *chemically* combined, and the composition is definite (fixed).

- Components of mixtures can be separated by *physical methods*.
  In compounds, they can be separated by *chemical methods*.

- Mixtures can be classified as homogenous or heterogeneous.
  Compounds are always homogeneous

Practice 8
Which is a mixture of substances?
1) Cl_2*(g)*   3) $MgCl_2$*(s)*
2) H_2O*(l)*   4) KNO_3*(aq)*

Practice 9
Which is true of a KCl solution?
1) It is composed of substances that are chemically combined.
2) It is composed of substances that are physically combined.
3) It is composed of substances with the same atomic number.
4) It is a pure substance.

                    ©2017 E3 Scholastic Publishing. All Rights Reserved

Separation of Mixtures
Through Physical Methods. Depends on Difference in Physical Properties.

A mixture can be separated using one or more *physical methods.* The separation method or technique depends on the type of mixture and differences in the physical properties of the substances in the mixture.

Separation of Homogeneous Mixtures

Evaporation: *boiling point difference*
The process of heating a soluble salt solution to boil off the solvent and leave behind the solute.

Distillation: *boiling point difference*
The process of boiling off and collecting each liquid of a mixture from the lowest to the highest boiling point.

Crystallization: *solubility difference*
The process of recovering the solid of an aqueous mixture by evaporating off the water or cooling the solution.

Chromatography: *polarity difference*
The process of separating and analyzing the components of an ink or a pigment by how far they travel with the solvent.

Separation of Heterogeneous Mixtures

Filtration: *particle size or solubility difference*
The process of separating a solid from a liquid through a filter setup.

Decantation/Funnel Separation: *density difference*
The process of removing layers of liquids that do not dissolve well in each other.

Paper Chromatography

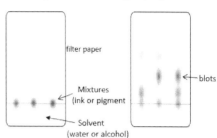

filter paper

Mixtures (ink or pigment

blots

Solvent (water or alcohol)

Filtration Apparatus

Ring stand
Iron ring
Filter paper
Glass funnel
Beaker

Classification of Matter: Summary Diagram

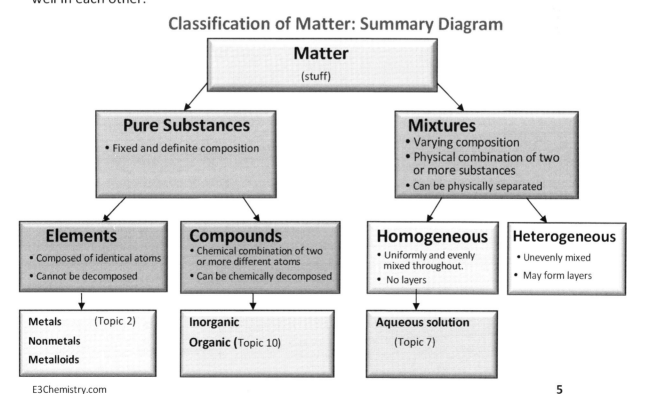

Matter (stuff)

Pure Substances
• Fixed and definite composition

Mixtures
• Varying composition
• Physical combination of two or more substances
• Can be physically separated

Elements
• Composed of identical atoms
• Cannot be decomposed

Compounds
• Chemical combination of two or more different atoms
• Can be chemically decomposed

Homogeneous
• Uniformly and evenly mixed throughout.
• No layers

Heterogeneous
• Unevenly mixed
• May form layers

Metals   (Topic 2)
Nonmetals
Metalloids

Inorganic
Organic (Topic 10)

Aqueous solution
(Topic 7)

Types of Matter: Practice Questions

Practice 10
Which type of matter can be separated only by physical methods?
1) a mixture   3) a pure substance
2) an element   4) a compound

Practice 11
Which two types of matter are chemical pure substances?
1) elements and compounds
2) solutions and compounds
3) elements and mixtures
4) solutions and mixtures

Practice 12
Which type of matter is composed of two or more different atoms chemically combined in a definite ratio?
1) a homogeneous mixture   3) an element
2) a heterogeneous mixture   4) a compound

Practice 13
The formula $N_2(g)$ is best classified as a(n)
1) compound   3) element
2) mixture   4) solution

Practice 14
When $NaNO_3(s)$ is dissolved in water, the resulting solution is classified as a
1) heterogeneous compound
2) homogeneous compound
3) heterogeneous mixture
4) homogeneous mixture

Practice 15
One similarity between all mixtures and compounds is that both
1) are heterogeneous
2) are homogeneous
3) combine in definite ratio
4) consist of two or more substances

Practice 16
Bronze contains 90 to 95 percent copper and 5 to 10 percent tin. Because these percentages can vary, bronze is classified as a(n)
1) compound   2) substance   3) element   4) mixture

Practice 17
When sample X is passed through a filter a white residue, Y, remains on the filter paper and a clear liquid, Z, passes through. When liquid Z is vaporized, another white residue remains. Sample X is best classified as
1) a heterogeneous mixture   3) an element
2) a homogeneous mixture   4) a compound

Practice 18
A mixture of crystals of salt and sugar is added to water and stirred until all solids have dissolved. Which statement best describes the resulting mixture?
1) The mixture is homogeneous and can be separated by filtration.
2) The mixture is homogeneous and cannot be separated by filtration.
3) The mixture is heterogeneous and can be separated by filtration.
4) The mixture is heterogeneous and cannot be separated by filtration.

Base your answers to questions 19 through 21 on the information below and on your knowledge of chemistry.

A student prepares two 141-gram mixtures, *A* and *B*. Each mixture consists of NH_4Cl, sand, and H_2O at 15°C. Both mixtures are thoroughly stirred and allowed to stand. The mass of each component used to make the mixtures is listed in the data table below.

Mass of the Components in Each Mixture

Component	Mixture A (g)	Mixture B (g)
NH_4Cl	40.	10.
sand	1	31
H_2O	100.	100.

19. Describe *one* property of sand that would enable the student to separate the sand from the other components in mixture *B*.

20. Which type of mixture is mixture *B*?

21. State evidence from the table indicating that the proportion of the components in a mixture can vary.

                    ©2017 E3 Scholastic Publishing. All Rights Reserved

Particle Diagrams of Matter

A particle diagram is used to show the composition of an element, a compound or mixture. Examples of particle diagrams are given below.

Concept Task: Be able to recognize or draw a particle diagram for an element, a compound or mixture.

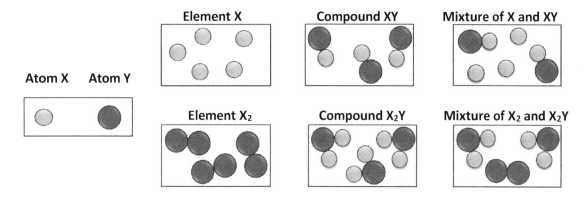

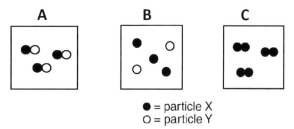

Base your answers to practice questions 22 through 24 on the particle diagrams below.

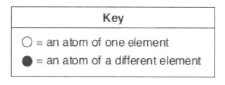

Practice 22
Which diagram or diagrams represents a compound of X and Y?
1) A and B   3) A only
2) A and C   4) B only

Practice 23
Which diagrams represent chemical pure substances?
1) A and B   3) A and C
2) B and C   4) A, B and C

Practice 24
Which best describes diagram B?
1) It is a mixture composed of physically combined substances.

2) It is a mixture composed of chemically combined substances.

3) It is a compound composed of physically combined substances.

4) It is a compound composed of chemically combined substances

Practice 25

Which particle diagram represents a mixture of three substances?

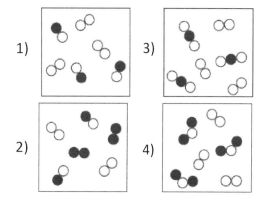

Lesson 2: Phases of Matter

Matter can exist in one of three main states or phases; *solid, liquid,* or *gas.* The nature of a substance determines the phase of the substance under normal conditions. Most substances can change from one phase to another. The nature of a substance also determines conditions necessary for the substance to change from one phase to another.

In this lesson, you will learn about the three phases of matter. You will also learn about phase changes of matter and the relationship to temperature and energy.

particle arrangement

Solid: *Definite Shape and Volume. Rigid. Crystalline Geometric Structure.*
A substance in the solid phase is relatively rigid, and has a definite volume and shape. Particles (atoms, molecules, or ions) of a substance in the solid state are orderly arranged in a *crystalline geometric structure.* Very strong attractive forces hold the particles close together and keep them in fixed positions. The particles vibrate but will not flow pass each other. *(s)* is used to indicate that a substance is in the solid state. Most substances are solids at standard conditions of temperature and pressure, STP. Aluminum (Al), gold (Au), and salt (NaCl) are solids at STP.

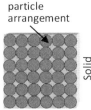

$H_2O(s)$

Liquid: *Definite Volume. No Definite Shape. Free Flowing.*
A substance in the liquid phase has a definite volume but not a definite shape. Particles are still close together, but they move more freely than those in the solid state. It is this free movement of particles that allows a contained liquid to take the shape of its container. (l) is used to indicate that a substance is in the liquid state. At STP, bromine (Br_2), water, (H_2O), and ammonia (NH_3) are liquids.

$H_2O(l)$

Gas: *No Definite Shape nor Volume. Fast Moving. Weak Forces.*
A substance in the gas phase has no definite volume nor shape. Particles move very freely because the attractive forces between them are very weak. If a gas is not contained, the particles will move indefinitely. If a gas is contained, the particles will move about to take the shape and volume of the container.
At STP, oxygen (O_2), helium (He), and carbon dioxide (CO_2) are gases.

$H_2O(g)$

Phases of Matter: Practice Questions.

Practice 26
In which phase does a substance has a definite volume but no definite shape?
1) aqueous   3) liquid
2) solid   4) gas

Practice 27
Substance X is a gas and substance Y is a liquid. One similarity between substance X and substance Y is that
1) both have definite shape
2) both have definite volume
3) both are compressible
4) both take the shapes of their containers

Practice 28
Which of the following substances have particles that are arranged in regular geometric pattern?
1) Al*(s)*   3) $CCl_4(l)$
2) Ar*(g)*   4) $NH_3(aq)$

Practice 29
Which substance takes the space and shape of its container?
1) gold   3) water
2) iron   4) hydrogen

                    ©2017 E3 Scholastic Publishing. All Rights Reserved

Phase Change
A Physical Change. No Change in Composition.

A **phase change** is a physical change. During a phase change, a substance changes its form (or state) without changing its chemical composition. Any substance can change from one phase to another given the right conditions of temperature and/or pressure. Most substances require a large change in temperature to go through one phase change. Water is one of a few chemical substances that can change through all three phases within a narrow range of temperature change. The six phase changes and their examples are given below.

Melting is a change from *solid* to *liquid.*	$H_2O\textit{(s)} \rightarrow H_2O\textit{(l)}$
Freezing is a change from liquid to *solid*	$H_2O\textit{(l)} \rightarrow H_2O\textit{(s)}$
Evaporation is a change from *liquid* to *gas*	$C_2H_5OH\textit{(l)} \rightarrow C_2H_5OH\textit{(g)}$
Condensation is a change from *gas* to *liquid*	$C_2H_5OH\textit{(g)} \rightarrow C_2H_5OH\textit{(l)}$
Deposition is a change from *gas* to *solid*	$CO_2\textit{(g)} \rightarrow CO_2\textit{(s)}$
Sublimation is a change from *solid* to *gas*	$CO_2\textit{(s)} \rightarrow CO_2\textit{(g)}$

$I_2\textit{(s)}$ (Iodine) and $CO_2\textit{(s)}$ (dry ice) are two substances that readily sublime at normal conditions. Most solids do not sublime.

Phase Changes and Energy
A substance changes phase when it has absorbed or released enough heat energy to rearrange its particles (atoms, molecules, or ions) from one form to another. Some phase changes require a release of heat by the substance, while others require heat to be absorbed.

Endothermic describes a process that absorbs heat energy.
Melting, *evaporation* and *sublimation* are endothermic phase changes.

Exothermic describes a process that releases heat energy.
Freezing, condensation and *deposition* are exothermic phase changes.

The diagram below summarizes phase changes and the relationship to energy.

Summary diagram of phase changes and energy is shown below.

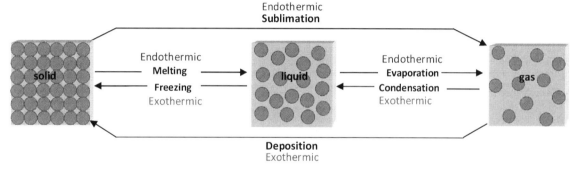

Phase Change and Energy: Practice Questions

Practice 30
Which phase change is exothermic?
1) $N_2(l) \rightarrow N_2(g)$ 3) $CH_4(g) \rightarrow CH_4(\ell)$
2) $Hg(s) \rightarrow Hg(l)$ 4) $I_2(s) \rightarrow I_2(g)$

Practice 31
Which equation is showing the sublimation of iodine?
1) $I_2(g) \rightarrow I_2(s)$ 3) $I_2(s) \rightarrow I_2(l)$
2) $I_2(s) \rightarrow I_2(g)$ 4) $I_2(g) \rightarrow I_2(l)$

Practice 32
   $NH_3(g) \rightarrow NH_3(s)$
The change represented above is
1) sublimation   3) condensation
2) evaporation   4) deposition

Practice 33
Heat is absorbed by a substance when it changes from
1) solid to gas   3) gas to solid
2) liquid to solid   4) gas to liquid

Practice 34
Which is true of ethanol as it changes from the liquid state to the gas state?
1) It absorbs heat as it condenses.
2) It absorbs heat as it evaporates.
3) It releases heat as it condenses.
4) It releases heat as it evaporates.

Temperature
A Measure of the Average Kinetic Energy.

A phase change of a substance occurs at a specific temperature. Every substance has its own melting point and boiling point.

Temperature is a measure of the average kinetic energy of particles in matter.

Kinetic energy is the energy due to the movement of particles in matter.
• The higher the temperature of a substance, the greater its kinetic energy.
• As temperature increases, the average kinetic energy also increases.

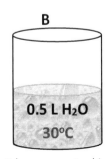

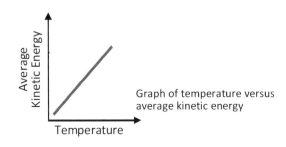
Graph of temperature versus average kinetic energy

Molecules of water in container B have a greater kinetic energy than those in container A because B is at a higher temperature.

Temperature of a substance is measured with a **thermometer**.
Degree Celsius (°C) and Kelvin (K) are the two most common units for measuring temperature. The mathematical relationship between Celsius and Kelvin is given by Reference *Table T* equation below.

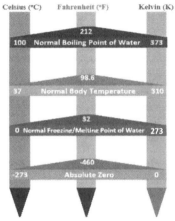
Temperature Scales

Table T $K = °C + 273$

According to this equation, the Kevin temperature value is always 273 units higher than the same temperature in Celsius.

Creating a thermometer scale of any unit requires two fixed reference points. *The freezing point (0°C, 273 K)* and the *boiling point (100°C, 373 K)* of water are typically used as the two reference points in creating a thermometer scale. Once the two reference points are marked on a thermometer, equal units are scaled and marked between the two points.

                                    ©2017 E3 Scholastic Publishing. All Rights Reserved

Temperature Conversion: Practice Questions

Concept Task: Be able to convert temperatures between Celsius and Kelvin units.

$$K = °C + 273$$

Practice 35
Which Celsius temperature is equivalent to +20 K?
1) -253   3) +253
2) -293   4) +293

Practice 36
The temperature of -30 °C is the same as
1) 30 K   3) 243 K
2) 303 K   4) 70 K

Practice 37
What is the equivalent of 546 K on a Celsius scale?
1) 273 °C   3) -273 °C
2) 818 °C   4) 546 °C

Practice 38
A liquid's freezing point is -38°C and its boiling point is 357°C. What is the number of Kelvin degrees between the boiling and the freezing point of the liquid?
1) 319   3) 592
2) 668   4) 395

Practice 39
Heat is being added to a given sample. Compared to the Celsius temperature of the sample, the Kelvin temperature will
1) always be 273° lower
2) always be 273° greater
3) have the same reading at 273°C
4) have the same reading at 0°C

Temperature and Kinetic Energy: Practice Questions

Concept Task: Be able to determine which temperature has the highest or lowest kinetic energy.

The higher the temperature, the higher the kinetic energy.

Practice 40
Which substance contains particles with the highest average kinetic energy?
1) NO(g) at 40°C   2) NO_2(g) at 45°C   3) N_2O(g) at 30°C   4) N_2O_3(g) at 35°C

Practice 41
Which water sample has molecules with the lowest average kinetic energy?

40°C   50°C   300 K   320 K
1)   2)   3)   4)

Practice 42
Which change in temperature is accompanied by the greatest increase in the average kinetic energy of a substance?
1) -20°C to 15°C   2) 15°C to -20 °C   3) -25°C to 30°C   4) 30°C to -25°C

Practice 43: *Base your answer on the pictures below:*

A   B   C

Explain how the average kinetic energy of sample *B* can be equal to the average kinetic energy of sample *C*.

Phase Change Diagrams

A **phase change diagram** shows the relationship between temperature and phase changes of a substance over time as the substance is heating or cooling.

A **heating curve** shows a change of a substance starting with the substance as a solid. Changes represented on a heating curve are endothermic because heat is being absorbed by the substance.

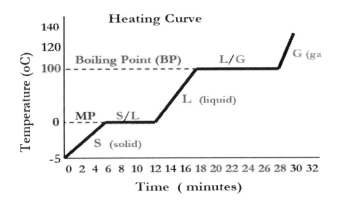

During segment S, L, or G: *Temperature is changing*
- One phase is present.
- Temperature increases.
- Kinetic energy increases.
- Potential energy stays the same.

During segment S/L or L/G: *Phase is changing*
- Two phases are present.
- Temperature stays the same.
- Kinetic energy stays the same.
- Potential energy increases.

The substance represented by this curve is likely water.

A **cooling curve** shows a change of a substance starting with the substance as a gas. Changes represented on a cooling curve are exothermic because heat is being released by the substance.

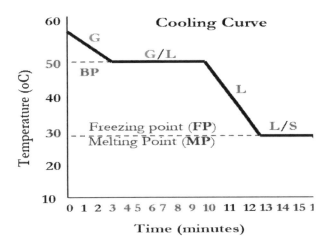

During segment G, L or S: *Temperature is changing*
- One phase is present.
- Temperature decreases.
- Kinetic energy decreases.
- Potential energy stays the same.

During segment G/L or L/S: *Phase is changing*
- Two phases are present.
- Temperature stays the same.
- Kinetic energy stays the same.
- Potential energy decreases.

The substance represented by this curve is not water.

©2017 E3 Scholastic Publishing. All Rights Reserved

44. The graph below represents the relationship between time and temperature as heat is added at constant rate to a sample of a substance.

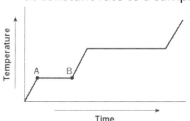

During interval AB which energy change occurs for the particles in this sample?
1) The potential energy of the particles increases.
2) The potential energy of the particles decreases.
3) The average kinetic energy of the particles increases.
4) The average kinetic energy of the particles decreases.

45. The graph below represents the uniform cooling of a substance, starting with the substance as a gas above its boiling point.

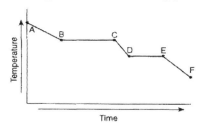

During which interval is the substance completely in the liquid phase?

1) AB   2) BC   3) CD   4) DE

46. The table below shows the data collected by a student as heat was applied at a constant rate to a solid below its freezing point.

Time (min)	Temperature (°C)	Time (min)	Temperature (°C)
0	20	18	44
2	24	20	47
4	28	22	51
6	32	24	54
8	32	26	54
10	32	28	54
12	35	30	54
14	38	32	58
16	41	34	62

What is the boiling point of this substance?

1) 32°C   2) 54°C   3) 62°C   4) 100°C

Base your answers to questions 47 through 49 on the information below.

Starting as a gas at 206°C, a sample of a substance is allowed to cool for 16 minutes. This process is represented by the cooling curve below.

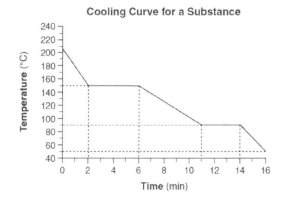

47. At what time do the particles of this sample have the highest average kinetic energy?

48. What is the boiling point of this substance?

49. Using the key below, draw two particle diagrams to represent the two phases of the sample at minute 12. Your response must include at least six particles for each diagram.

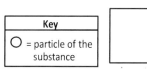

one phase at minute 12   another phase at minute 12.

Lesson 3 – Heat (Thermal) Energy and Heat Calculations

Thermal Energy is the energy produced by the random motion of particles (atoms, molecules, or ions) in a sample of matter. Thermal energy, therefore, is a type of kinetic energy.

Heat is the flow or transfer of thermal energy between two objects or areas. The direction of heat flow depends on the temperature difference. Heat always flows from an area or object of high temperature (metal at 65°C) to an area or object of low temperature (water at 25°C) until an equilibrium temperature is reached. The equilibrium temperature in the above diagram is 45°C (the sum of 65°C and 25°C divided by 2).

Heat
The Flow of Thermal Energy from High to Low Temperature.

During a chemical or physical change, heat is either absorbed or released.

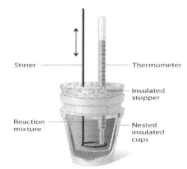

Exothermic describes a process that releases or loses heat.
As an object or a substance releases heat, its temperature decreases.

Endothermic describes a process that absorbs or takes in heat.
As an object or a substance absorbs heat, its temperature increases.

A **calorimeter** is a device that is used for measuring the amount of heat energy absorbed or released during a physical or chemical change.

Styrofoam Calorimeter
A calorimeter should be closed and well insulated when being used to measure heat during a reaction.

Joules and **calories** are units for measuring thermal energy.

J	joule	energy, work, quantity of heat	**Table D**

Heat Flow and Temperature: Practice Questions

Concept Task: Be able to determine or describe the direction of heat flow.

Practice 50
Object A and object B are placed next to each other. If object B is at 12°C, heat will flow from object A to object B when the temperature of object A is at
1) 6°C   2) 10°C   3) 12°C   4) 15°C

Practice 51
A solid material X is place in liquid Y. Heat will flow from Y to X when the temperature of
1) Y is 20°C and X is 30°C   3) Y is 15°C and X 10°C
2) Y is 10°C and X is 20°C   4) Y is 30°C and X is 40°C

Practice 52
Given the diagrams

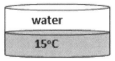

Which correctly describes the energy transfer when the metal object is dropped into the water?
1) Thermal energy will flow from the metal to water, and the water temperature will decrease.
2) Thermal energy will flow from the metal to water, and the water temperature will increase.
3) Chemical energy will flow from the metal to water, and the water temperature will decrease.
4) Chemical energy will flow from the metal to water, and the water temperature will increase.

 ©2017 E3 Scholastic Publishing. All Rights Reserved

Heat Calculations

The amount of heat energy absorbed or released by a substance can be calculated using one of the three heat equations given on *Reference Table T*. For a heat problem involving water, one of the heat constants on *Reference Table B* will also be needed to solve the problem.

Reference Table B
Heat Constants for Water

Specific Heat Capacity (**C**) of $H_2O(\ell)$	4.18 J/g°K
Heat of fusion (**H_f**)	334 J/g
Heat of Vaporization (**H_v**)	2260 J/g

Reference Table T
Heat Equations

$q = m \bullet C \bullet \Delta T$	*q is heat*
$q = m \bullet H_f$	*m is mass*
$q = m \bullet H_v$	

The notes below explain more about heat constants and equations.

Specific Heat Capacity
Heat absorbed to warm up or released to cool down.

The **specific heat capacity** of a substance is the amount of heat needed to change the temperature of a one-gram sample of the substance by just one Kelvin. The specific heat capacity is different for each substance.

The specific heat capacity (C) of water is 4.18 J/g•K **(See Table B).** In other words, a one-gram sample of water will absorb 4.18 Joules of heat to increase its temperature by one Kelvin, or release 4.18 Joules of heat to decrease its temperature by one Kelvin.

When the mass and specific heat capacity of a substance are known, the amount of heat (q) absorbed or released by that substance to change between any two temperatures can be calculated using Table T equation **q = mCΔT.**

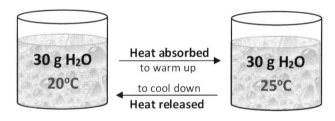

Heat (q) = mCΔT

m = mass of substance *(g)*
C = specific heat capacity *(J/g •K)*
ΔT = difference in temp *(K or °C)*
ΔT = high temp - low temp

Example 1: *Heat Calculation During Temp Change*
How much heat is released by a 30-gram sample of water to change its temperature from 20°C to 25°C?

q = (m)(C)(ΔT)

q = (30)(4.18)(5)   *numerical setup*

q **= 627 J**   *calculated result*

Practice 53
How much heat is released by a 15-gram sample of water when it is cooled from 40.°C to 30.°C?
1) 630 J   3) 63 J
2) 42 J   4) 130 J

Practice 54
What is the total amount of heat energy needed to change the temperature of a 65-gram sample of water from 25°C to 40.°C?
1) 6.3 x 10⁻² kJ   3) 1.1 x10⁻¹ kJ
2) 4.1 x 10⁰ kJ   4) 6.8 x 10¹ kJ

Practice 55 *Show a numerical setup and the result.*
What is the temperature change of a 5-gram sample of water that had absorbed 200 Joules of heat?

Heat of Fusion
Energy absorbed to melt or released to freeze.

The **heat of fusion** of a substance is the amount of heat needed to melt a one-gram sample of the substance at its melting point.

The heat of fusion of water is 334 J/g **(See Table B)**. In other words, a one-gram sample of water will absorb 334 joules of heat to melt, or release 334 joules of heat to freeze.

When the mass and heat of fusion of a substance are known, the amount of heat absorbed or released by the substance to change between the solid and liquid states can be calculated using the Table T equation **$q = mH_f$.**

Heat of Vaporization
Energy absorbed to evaporate or released to condensed.

The **heat of vaporization** of a substance is the amount of heat needed to vaporize a one-gram sample of the substance at its boiling point.

The heat of vaporization of water is 2260 J/g. In other words, a one-gram sample of water will absorb 2260 joules of heat to vaporize, or release 2260 joules of heat to condense.

When the mass and heat of vaporization of a substance are known, the amount of heat absorbed or released by the substance to change between the liquid and gas states can be calculated using the Table T equation **$q = mH_v$.**

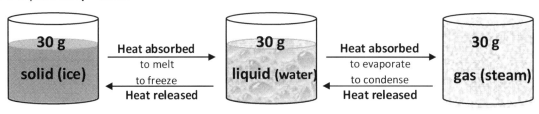

Heat (q) = mH_f   **Heat (q) = mH_v**

Example 2: *Heat Calculation During Melting*
How much heat is absorbed by a 30-g sample of ice to melt to liquid at its melting point?

     Heat = (m)(H_f)
     Heat = (30)(334)   *numerical setup*
     Heat = **10,040 J**   *calculated result*

Practice 56
The heat of fusion for an unknown substance is 220 J/g. How much heat is required to melt a 35-g sample of this substance at its melting point?
1) 255 J   3) 11690 J
2) 73480 J   4) 7700 J

Practice 57 *Show a numerical setup and the result.*
1200 Joules is removed from a sample of water to change it to ice at 0°C. What is the mass of the water?

Example 3: *Heat Calculation During Condensation*
Calculate the amount of heat that is released when a 30-g sample of steam changes to water at 100°C.

     Heat = (m)(H_v)
     Heat = (30)(2260)   *numerical setup*
     Heat = **67,800 J**   *calculated result*

Practice 58
How much heat must be added to 11 grams of water to change it to steam at its boiling point?
1) 2.3 kJ   3) 25 kJ
2) 0.21 kJ   4) 2486 kJ

Practice 59 *Show a numerical setup and the result.*
A 23-g sample of an unknown liquid substance absorbed 34 kJ of heat to change to gas at its boiling point. What is the heat of vaporization of the unknown liquid?

 ©2017 E3 Scholastic Publishing. All Rights Reserved

Practice 60
The heat of fusion of ice is 334 Joules per gram. Adding 334 Joules to one gram of ice at STP will cause the ice to
1) increase in temperature
2) decrease in temperature
3) change to water at a higher temperature
4) change to water at the same temperature

Practice 61
A beaker with water and the surrounding air are all at 24°C. After ice cubes are placed in the water, heat is transferred from
1) the water to the ice cubes
2) the water to the beaker
3) the ice cubes to the air
4) the beaker to the air

Base your answers to practice questions 62 through 64 on the information below.

A student investigated heat transfer using a bottle of water. The student placed the bottle in a room at 20.5°C. The student measured the temperature of the water in the bottle at 7 a.m. and again at 3 p.m. The data from the investigation are shown in the table below.

Water Bottle Investigation Data

7 a.m.		3 p.m.	
Mass of Water (g)	Temperature (°C)	Mass of Water (g)	Temperature (°C)
800.	12.5	800.	20.5

62. Compare the average kinetic energy of the water molecules in the bottle at 7 a.m. to the average kinetic energy of the water molecules in the bottle at 3 p.m.

63. State the direction of heat transfer between the surroundings and the water in the bottle from 7 a.m. to 3 p.m.

64. Show a numerical setup for calculating the change in the thermal energy of the water in the bottle from 7 a.m. to 3 p.m.

Base your answers to practice questions 65 through 67 on the information below.

Heat is added to a 200.-gram sample of $H_2O(s)$ to melt the sample at 0°C. Then the resulting $H_2O(\ell)$ is heated to a final temperature of 65°C.

65. Compare the amount of heat required to vaporize a 200.-gram sample of $H_2O(\ell)$ at its boiling point to the amount of heat required to melt a 200.-gram sample of $H_2O(s)$ at its melting point.

66. In the space below, show a numerical setup for calculating the total amount of heat required to raise the temperature of the $H_2O(\ell)$ from 0°C to its final temperature.

67. Determine the total amount of heat required to completely melt the sample.

Other Types of Energy
Although thermal energy is the only type of energy discussed in this topic, there are many other types and forms of energy. Some of them are discussed in different topics of this book. Examples of other types of energy are given below:

Potential (stored) energy: Chemical, nuclear, gravitational, and elastic energy.

Kinetic (motion) energy: Thermal, sound, electromagnetic, and electric energy.

Both potential and kinetic: Mechanical energy

Lesson 4 – Characteristics of Gases

Gas behavior is influenced by three key factors; volume (space of container), pressure and temperature. The relationships between these three factors are the basis for gas laws and gas theories. These laws and theories attempt to explain how gases behave.
In this lesson, you will learn about gas theories, gas laws and gas law calculations.

Kinetic Molecular Theory
Describes ideal gas behavior.

The **kinetic molecular theory** of an ideal gas is a model that is often used to explain the behavior of gases. This theory is summarized below.

• Gases are composed of individual particles.
• Distances between gas particles are far apart.
• Gas particles are in continuous, random, straight-line motion.
• When two particles of a gas collide, energy is transferred from one particle to another.
• Particles of a gas have no attraction to each other.
• Individual gas particles have no volume. Volume is negligible or insignificant.

An **ideal gas** is a theoretical gas that has all the properties summarized above.

A **real gas** is a gas that does exist. Examples of real gases are *oxygen, carbon dioxide, and helium.*

Since the kinetic molecular theory (summarized above) applies mainly to an ideal gas, the model cannot be used to predict an exact behavior of real gases. Therefore, real gases *deviate* from or do not behave exactly as an ideal gas for the following two reasons.

• Real gas particles do attract each other.
   Ideal gas particles are assumed to have no attraction to each other.

• Real gas particles do have volume.
   Ideal gas particles are assumed to have no volume.

Real gases with small molecular masses behave the most like an ideal gas.
Hydrogen (H) and helium (He), the two smallest real gases by mass, behave the most like an ideal gas in comparison to all other real gases.

Real gases behave more like an ideal gas under conditions of **high temperature** and **low pressure.**

For example: Hydrogen, a real gas, will deviate less from an ideal gas at
        300 K and 0.5 atm (in container A) than at 273 K and 1 atm (in container B).

A

0.5 atm

300 K

The hydrogen molecules in Container A will behave more like an ideal gas because it is at a lower pressure and a higher temperature than the hydrogen gas in Container B.

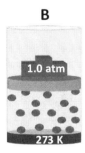

B

1.0 atm

273 K

          ©2017 E3 Scholastic Publishing. All Rights Reserved

Kinetic Molecular Theory and Deviation: Practice Questions

Practice 68
An ideal gas is made up of gas particles that
1) have volume
2) attract each other
3) can be liquefied
4) are in random motion

Practice 69
Real gases differ from an ideal gas because the molecules of real gases have
1) some volume and no attraction for each other
2) some volume and some attraction for each other
3) no volume and no attraction for each other
4) no volume and some attraction for each other

Practice 70
Under which two conditions do real gases behave least like an ideal gas?
1) High pressure and low temperature.
2) Low pressure and high temperature.
3) High pressure and high temperature.
4) Low pressure and low temperature.

Practice 71
The kinetic molecular theory assumes that the particles of an ideal gas
1) are in random, constant, straight line-motion
2) are arranged in regular geometric pattern
3) have strong attractive forces between them
4) have collision that result in the system losing energy

Practice 72
At STP, which will behave most like an ideal gas?
1) Fluorine   3) Oxygen
2) Nitrogen   4) Chlorine

Practice 73
According to the Periodic Table, which of the following gases will behave least like an ideal gas?
1) Ar   3) Xe
2) Ne   4) Kr

Practice 74
Under which conditions of temperature and pressure would oxygen behave most like an ideal gas?
1) 25°C and 100 kPa
2) 35°C and 100 kPa
3) 25°C and 80 kPa
4) 35°C and 80 kPa

Practice 75
A real gas will behave least like an ideal gas under which conditions of temperature and pressure?
1) 50°C and 0.5 atm
2) 50°C and 0.8 atm
3) 300 K and 0.5 atm
4) 300 K and 0.8 atm

Pressure, Volume, and Temperature of a Gas

Behavior of a gas is influenced by the volume, pressure, and temperature of the gas. The relationship between them are the basis for many gas laws and theories.

Volume
The volume of a confined gas is the amount of space in the container in which it is placed.

  Units: milliliters (mL) or liters (L)   1 L = 1000 mL

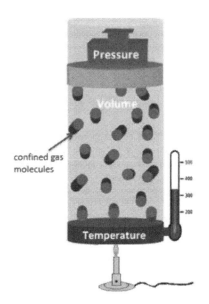

Pressure
The pressure of a gas is the amount of force the gas particles exert on the walls of the container. This pressure is equal, but opposite in magnitude, to the external pressure exerted on the gas.

  Units: atmosphere (atm) or Kilopascal (kPa)   1 atm = 101.3 kPa

Temperature
The temperature of a gas is a measure of the average kinetic energy of the gas particles. As temperature increases, the gas particles move faster, and their average kinetic energy increases.

  Units: degree Celsius (°C) or Kelvin (K)   K = °C + 273

STP	Standard Temperature: 273 K or 0°C	Table A
	Standard Pressure: 1 atm or 101.3 kPa	

Example 4: *Liters to Milliliters Conversion*

Express 2.35 L in milliliters.

Proportion setup

$$\frac{1\ L}{1000\ mL} = \frac{2.35\ L}{X}$$

$$X \quad = \quad (2.35)\,(1000\ mL)$$

$$X \quad = \quad \textbf{2350 mL}$$

Practice 76
Express 0.267 liters of O_2 in milliliters.

Practice 77
What is the equivalent of 3487.2 milliliters of helium in liters?

Example 5: *Kilopascals to Atmospheres Conversion*
The pressure on a gas 75 kPa. What is the pressure in atm?

Factor-label setup

$$75\ kPa \ \times \ \frac{1\ atm}{101.3\ kPa} \ = \ \textbf{0.74 atm}$$

Practice 78
What pressure, in kPa, is equivalent to 1.7 atm?

Practice 79
What is the pressure of 65 kPa in atm?

                         ©2017 E3 Scholastic Publishing. All Rights Reserved

Gas Laws: Relating Volume, Temperature and Pressure

Boyle's Law: At constant temperature, the volume of a set mass of a confined gas is inversely proportional to the pressure of the gas.
- As pressure increases, volume of the gas decreases.
  Doubling pressure cuts the volume in half.
  Reducing pressure in half doubles the volume.

Charles' Law: At constant pressure, the volume of a set mass of a confined gas is directly proportional to the Kelvin temperature.
- As temperature increases, volume of the gas increases.
  Doubling temperature doubles the volume of the gas.
  Reducing temperature in half cuts the volume in half.

Gay-Lussac's Law: At constant volume, the pressure of a set mass of a confined gas is directly proportional to the Kelvin temperature.
- As temperature increases, pressure of the gas increases.
  Doubling temperature doubles the pressure on the gas.
  Reducing temperature in half cuts the pressure in half.

Combined Gas Law

There are several gas law calculations that relate volume, pressure and temperature. Most of these calculations include other factors such as moles of the gas and a gas constant. Gas law calculations in this book focus on the **combined gas law**, which relates volume, pressure, and temperature, only. The combined gas law equation is the combination of the three laws described above. In all gas law problems, the *total number of moles (number of particles) of the gas sample stays the same*. The combined gas law equation can be found on *Reference Table T*.

TABLE T: Table of Equations and Formulas

Combined Gas Law	$\dfrac{P_1 V_1}{T_1} = \dfrac{P_2 V_2}{T_2}$	P = pressure V = volume T = temperature

V_1 = Initial volume (mL or L)
V_1 = New volume (mL or L)
P_1 = Initial pressure (atm or kPa)
P_2 = New pressure (atm or kPa)
T_1 = Initial Kelvin temperature (K)
T_2 = New Kelvin temperature (K)

Example 6: *Combined Gas Law Problem*

Hydrogen gas has a volume of 100 mL at STP. If temperature and pressure are changed to 546 K and 0.5 atm respectively, what will be the new volume of the gas?

$V_1 = 100$ mL $V_2 = $?

STP $\begin{cases} P_1 = 1 \text{ atm} \\ T_1 = 273 \text{ K} \end{cases}$ $P_2 = 0.5$ atm
                        $T_2 = 546$ K

$$\frac{P_1 \ V_1}{T_1} \qquad \frac{P_2 \ V_2}{T_2}$$

numerical setup $\begin{cases} \dfrac{(1)(100)}{273} \qquad \dfrac{(0.5)(V_2)}{546} \\[2mm] 54600 \quad = \quad (136.5)V_2 \end{cases}$

calculated result   **400 mL** = V_2

Practice 80

A gas sample has a volume of 1.4 L at a temperature of 20.K and a pressure of 1.0 atm. What will be the new volume when the temperature is changed to 40.K and the pressure is changed to 0.50 atm?

When one of the factors in a gas law problem is held constant, eliminating the constant from the combined gas law equation will yield the equation needed to set up and solve the problem. Three example problems with a constant are given and solved below.

Example 7: *Constant Temperature Problem*
At constant temperature, what is the new volume of a 3.0-L sample of oxygen gas if the pressure is changed from 0.50 atm to 0.25 atm?

V_1 = 3.0 L V_2 = ? (unknown)
P_1 = 0.50 atm P_2 = 0.25 atm

Eliminate T, the constant, from the combined gas law equation, set up, and solve.

$$P_1 V_1 = P_2 V_2$$

numerical setup

$$(0.50)(3.0) = (0.25)(V_2)$$

$$\frac{1.5}{0.25} = V_2$$

calculated result

$$6.0\ L = V_2$$

Practice 81 *Show a setup the calculated result.*
A 0.8-L sample of gas at STP had its volume changed to 2.0 liters. What is the pressure of the gas at this new volume?

Example 8: *Constant Pressure Problem*
The volume of a gas is 25 mL at 280 K. If the pressure is held constant, what will be the temperature of the gas when the volume is 75 mL?

V_1 = 25 mL V_2 = 75 mL
T_1 = 280 K T_2 = ?

Eliminate P, the constant, from the combined gas law equation, set up, and solve.

$$\frac{V_1}{T_1} = \frac{V_2}{T_2}$$

numerical setup

$$\frac{25}{280} = \frac{75}{T_2}$$

calculated result

$$T_2 = 840\ K$$

Practice 82
A sample of oxygen gas has a volume of 150. mL at 300. K. If the pressure is held constant and the temperature is raised to 600. K, calculate the new volume of the gas.

Example 9: *Constant Volume Problem*
At constant volume, the pressure on a gas changes from 20 kPa to 50 kPa when the temperature of the gas is changed to 303K. What was the initial temperature of the gas?

P_1 = 20 kPa P_2 = 50 kPa
T_1 = ? T_2 = 303 K

Eliminate V, the constant, from the combined gas law equation, set up, and solve.

$$\frac{P_1}{T_1} = \frac{P_2}{T_2}$$

numerical setup

$$\frac{20}{T_1} = \frac{50}{303}$$

calculated result

$$T_1 = 121\ K$$

Practice 83
A gas sample at 546 K has a pressure of 0.4 atm. If the volume of the gas sample is unchanged, what will be the new pressure of the gas if its temperature is changed to 136.5 K?

©2017 E3 Scholastic Publishing. All Rights Reserved

Practice 84

Which graph best illustrates the relationship between the Kelvin temperature of a gas and its volume when the pressure on the gas is held constant?

 1)   2)   3)   4)

Practice 85

A sample of gas is held at constant volume. Increasing the kelvin temperature of this gas sample causes the average kinetic energy of its molecules to
1) decrease and the pressure of the gas sample to decrease
2) decrease and the pressure of the gas sample to increase
3) increase and the pressure of the gas sample to decrease
4) increase and the pressure of the gas sample to increase

Practice 86

A cylinder with a movable piston contains a sample of gas having a volume of 6.0 liters at 293 K and 1.0 atmosphere. What is the volume of the sample after the gas is heated to 303 K, while the pressure is held at 1.0 atmosphere?
1) 9.0 L   2) 6.2 L   3) 5.8 L   4) 4.0 L

Base your answers to practice questions 87 through 89 on the information below.

A sample of helium gas is in a closed system with a movable piston. The volume of the gas sample is changed when both the temperature and the pressure of the sample are increased. The table below shows the initial temperature, pressure, and volume of the gas sample, as well as the final temperature and pressure of the sample.

Helium Gas in a Closed System

Condition	Temperature (K)	Pressure (atm)	Volume (mL)
Initial	200.	2.0	500.
final	300.	7.0	?

87. Convert the final pressure of the helium gas sample to kilopascal.

88. Compare the total number of gas particles in the sample under the initial conditions to the total number of gas particles in the sample under the final conditions.

89. In the space below show a correct numerical setup for calculating the final volume of the helium gas sample.

Base your answers to practice questions 90 through 92 on the information below

A gas sample is held at constant temperature in a closed system. The volume of the gas is changed, which causes the pressure of the gas to change. Volume and pressure data are shown in the table below.

Volume and Pressure of a Gas Sample

Volume (mL)	Pressure (atm)
1200	0.5
600	1.0
300	2.0
150	4.0
100	6.0

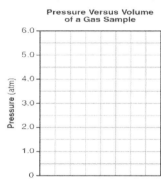

90. On the grid, mark an appropriate scale on the axis labeled "Volume (mL)."

91. On the same grid, plot the data from the table. Circle and connect the points.

92. Based on your graph, what is the pressure of the gas when the volume of the gas is 200. milliliters?

Avogadro's Law

Gases of Equal Volume, Temperature, and Pressure Have Equal Number of Gas Molecules

Avogadro's Law states that under the same temperature and pressure, gases of equal volume contain **equal number of molecules or particles.**

In the diagram to the right, container A contains oxygen gas and container B contains hydrogen gas.
Both gases have the same volume, temperature and pressure.
The number of molecules of O_2 in A is the same as the number of molecules of H_2 in B.

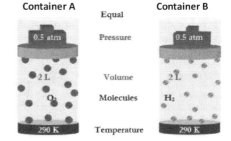

Practice 93

At STP, a 1.0 L sample of $H_2(g)$ would have the same number of gas molecules as
1) 0.5 L of He
2) 1.0 L of CO
3) 2.0 L of Ne
4) 3.0 L of N_2

Practice 94

Under which conditions would a 0.2 L sample of O_2 has the same number of molecules as a 0.2 L sample of N_2 that is at STP?
1) 0 K and 1 atm
2) 0 K and 2 atm
3) 273 K and 1 atm
4) 273 K and 2 atm

Practice 95

The table below gives the temperature and pressure of four different gas samples, each in a 1.5 L container:

Gas sample	Temperature (K)	Pressure (atm)
SO_2	200	1.5
Ar	300	3.0
N_2	200	1.5
O_2	300	1.5

Which two gas samples contain the same number of molecules?
1) Ar and O_2
2) SO_2 and Ar
3) Ar and N_2
4) SO_2 and N_2

Practice 96

A sample of oxygen gas is sealed in container X. A sample of hydrogen gas is sealed in container Z. Both samples have the same volume, temperature, and pressure. Which statement is true?
1) Container X contains more gas molecules than container Z.
2) Container X contains fewer gas molecules than container Z.
3) Containers X and Z both contain the same number of gas molecules.
4) Containers X and Z both contain the same mass of gas.

     ©2017 E3 Scholastic Publishing. All Rights Reserved

Lesson 5 – Physical and Chemical Properties and Changes

Properties are characteristics of a substance that can be used to identify and classify that substance. Two types of properties of matter are physical and chemical properties.

Physical Properties
Phase Change, Solubility, Density, Boiling Point, Melting Point.

A **physical property** is a characteristic of a substance that can be observed or measured without changing the chemical composition of the substance. Some physical properties of a substance depend on the sample size or amount, while others do not.

Extensive properties depend on the sample size or amount present.
Mass, weight and volume are examples of *extensive physical properties.*

Intensive properties do not depend on the sample size or amount.
Melting, freezing and boiling points, density, solubility, color, odor, conductivity, luster, and hardness are *intensive physical properties.*

• The difference in physical properties of substances make it possible to separate one substance from the others in a mixture.

Physical Change
No Change in Chemical Composition.

A **physical change** is the change of a substance from one form to another without altering its chemical composition. Examples of physical changes are listed below.

Phase Change   Size Change   Dissolving (forming a solution)

$H_2O(s) \rightarrow H_2O(l)$ $NaCl(s) \rightarrow Na^+(aq) + Cl^-(aq)$

Chemical Properties
It Burns, Reacts, Forms, Combines With, Decomposes Into.

A **chemical property** is a characteristic of a substance that is observed or measured through interaction with other substances. *Examples:*
It burns, it combusts, it decomposes, it reacts with, it forms, it combines with, or it rusts are some of the phrases that can be used to describe the chemical property of a substance.

Chemical Change
A Change in Chemical Composition

A chemical change is the change in composition and properties of one substance to those of other substances. A **chemical reaction** is the way a chemical change occurs. Compounds are formed or broken down through chemical reactions.
Compounds (NH_3, H_2O, $KClO_3$, etc.) are made or broken down through chemical reactions.

Types of reactions include *synthesis, decomposition, single replacement, double replacement, and combustion.* These reactions and others are discussed in Topics 5, 8, 9, 10 and 11.

Particle Diagrams After Physical and Chemical Changes

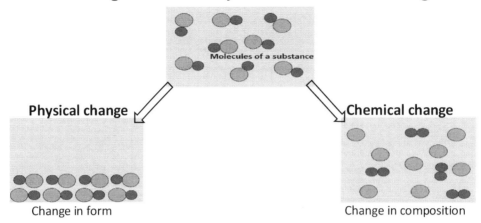

Physical change — Change in form

Molecules of a substance

Chemical change — Change in composition

Practice 97
Which best describes a chemical property of sodium?
1) It is a shiny metal.
2) It is smooth.
3) It reacts vigorously with water.
4) It is a hard solid.

Practice 98
A large sample of a solid calcium sulfate is crushed into smaller pieces. Which two physical properties are the same for both the large sample and one of the smaller pieces?
1) Mass and density.
2) Mass and volume.
3) Solubility and density.
4) Solubility and volume.

Practice 99
An example of a physical property of an element is the element's ability to
1) form a compound
2) react with oxygen
3) react with an acid
4) form an aqueous solution

Practice 100
During a chemical change, a substance changes its
1) density   3) solubility
2) composition   4) phase

Base your answers to questions 101 and 102 on the information below and on your knowledge of chemistry.

Some properties of the element sodium are listed below.
• is a soft, silver-colored metal
• melts at a temperature of 371 K
• oxidizes easily in the presence of air
• forms compounds with nonmetallic elements
• forms sodium chloride in the presence of chlorine gas

101. Convert the melting point of sodium to degrees Celsius.

102. Identify *one* chemical property and one physical property of sodium from this list.

Base your answer to the following question on the information below.

The reaction between aluminum and an aqueous solution of copper(II) sulfate is represented by the unbalanced equation below.

$$Al(s) + CuSO_4(aq) \rightarrow Al_2(SO_4)_3(aq) + Cu(s)$$

103. Explain why the equation represents a chemical change.

Vocabulary

Lesson 1: Classification of Matter

Pure substance
Element
Compound
Law of definite proportion

Mixture
Homogeneous mixture
Heterogeneous mixture
Aqueous solution

Chromatography
Distillation
Crystallization
Filtration
Decantation

Lesson 2: Phases of Matter and Temperature

Solid
Liquid
Gas
Condensation
Evaporation

Sublimation
Deposition
Exothermic
Endothermic
Temperature

Thermometer
Kinetic energy
Potential energy
Phase change diagram
Absolute Zero

Lesson 3: Heat and Heat Calculations

Thermal energy
Heat
Joules

Specific heat capacity
Heat of fusion
Heat of vaporization

Calorimeter

Lesson 4: Gas Laws and Calculations

Ideal gas
Kinetic molecular theory
Avogadro's law

Boyle's law
Charles' law
Gay-Lussac's law

Combined gas law
Dalton's law of partial pressure

Lesson 5: Physical and Chemical Properties

Physical property
Chemical property
Physical change
Chemical change

1. 2	4. **3**	7. 3	10. 1	13. 3	16. 4	18. 2
2. **3**	5. 4	8. 4	11. 1	14. 2	17. 1	
3. 2	6. 2	9. 2	12. 3	15. 2		

19. Sand has a larger particle size and higher density than water.   20. Heterogeneous
Sand is insoluble in H_2O.

21. A and B contain different grams or amounts of sand and H_2O.

22. 3	25. 2	28. 1	31. 2	34. 2	37. 1	40. 2
23. 3	26. 3	29. 4	32. 4	35. 1	38. 4	41. 2
24. 1	27. 2	30. 3	33. 1	36. 3	39. 2	42. 3

43. Average KE of B can be equal to the average KE of C if B has the same temperature as C.

44. 1   47. 0 minute   49.
45. 3   48. 150°C
46. 2

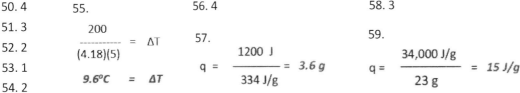

one phase at minute 12   another phase at minute 12

50. 4   55.   56. 4   58. 3
51. 3
52. 2 $\frac{200}{(4.18)(5)} = \Delta T$ 57.   59.
53. 1
54. 2 $9.6°C = \Delta T$ $q = \frac{1200\ J}{334\ J/g} = 3.6\ g$ $q = \frac{34,000\ J/g}{23\ g} = 15\ J/g$

60. 4
61. 1   65. More heat is required to boil than to melt
62. Average KE is higher in the bottle at 3 pm   66. q(heat) = (200)(4.18)(65)
63. From surroundings to the water in the bottle   (200 g)(4.18 J/g C)(65°C)
64. q = mCΔT
    q = (800)(4.18)(8.0) = **26,752 J**   67. 66,800 Joules

84. 3   90.
85. 4   91.

68. 4   80. $\frac{(1.4)(1)}{20} = \frac{(50)V_2}{40}$ 86. 2
69. 2   87. 709.1 kPa
70. 1 $V_2 = 0.56\ L$ 88. The number of gas particles
71. 1   is the same in both samples.
72. 1   81. $(101.3\ kPa)(0.8\ L) = (25.5\ kPa)V_2$ 89.
73. 3 $3.18\ L = V_2$ $\frac{(2.0)(500.)}{200.} = \frac{(7.0)X}{300.}$ 92. 0.3 atm ± 0.3 grid space
74. 4
75. 4   82. $\frac{150}{300} = \frac{V_2}{600}$
76. 267 mL
77. 3.4872 L $V_2 = 300\ mL$ 93. 2   97. 3   101. **98°C**
78. 172.38 kPa   94. 3   98. 3   102. physical: Any of the first 2 on the list.
79. 0.64 atm   95. 4   99. 4   chemical: Any of the last 3 on the list.
    83. $\frac{0.4}{546} = \frac{P_2}{136.5}$ 96. 3   100. 2   103. There is a change in composition.
                                      Reactants and products have different
        $V_2 = 0.1\ atm$ compositions.

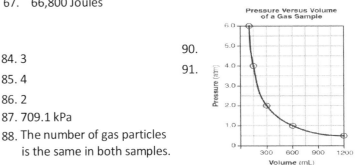

Pressure Versus Volume of a Gas Sample

Topic 2
The Periodic Table

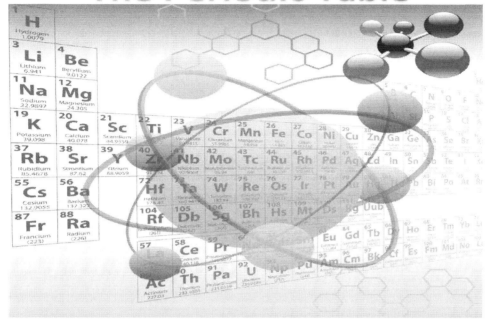

Lesson 1: Arrangement of the Elements

Lesson 2: Types of Elements and Properties

Lesson 3: Periodic Trends

Lesson 1 – Arrangement of the Elements

There are more than 100 known elements. Most of the elements are naturally occurring, while a few are artificially produced. The modern Periodic Table lists all known elements. The elements are *arranged on the Periodic Table in order of increasing atomic number.* Important information about an element can be found in the box of the element on the Periodic Table.

In this lesson, you will learn about the arrangement of the elements on the Periodic Table.

The Modern Periodic Table

Elements Arranged by Increasing Atomic Number

The modern Periodic Table, which is based on the work of Dmitri Mendeleev, has the following properties:

• The elements are arranged in the order of increasing atomic number.

• The three types of elements found on the Periodic Table are metals, nonmetals, and metalloids.

• More than two thirds (majority) of the elements are metals.

• The Periodic Table contains elements that are in all three phases (solid, liquid, and gas) at STP.

• Of more than 100 known elements at STP:
    Two (bromine and mercury) are liquids.
    Eleven are gases.
    The rest are solids.

• An element's symbol can be one (O), two (Au), or three (Uub) letters.
  The first letter of a symbol is always a capital letter.
  The second and third letters, if present, are lowercase.

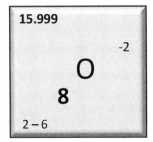

Atomic mass

Selected oxidation states (charges)

Element symbol

Atomic number

Electron configuration

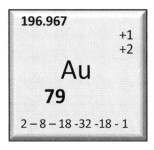

Information listed in the box of each element reveals a lot about the atomic structure of the element. Atomic structure is discussed in Topic 3.

The elements on the periodic table are placed in groups and periods. Every element has a group number and a period number. For an example: Phosphorus (P) is in Group 15, Period 3.

Groups
Vertical Columns. Same Valence Electrons. Similar Chemical Properties

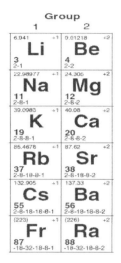

Groups are the vertical arrangements of the elements.
- Elements in the same group have the same number of valence electrons, therefore, similar chemical properties
- There are eighteen groups on the Periodic Table of the Elements

Group names are listed below.

Group 1 :   Alkali metals

Group 2 :   Alkaline earth metals

Group 3 – 12:   Transition metals

Group 17:   Halogens

Group 18:   Noble gases

Periods
Horizontal Rows. Same Number of Electron Shells (Energy Levels)

Periods are the horizontal rows of the Periodic Table.
- Elements in the same period have the same number of occupied electron shells.
- There are seven (7) periods of elements on the Periodic Table.

The **periodic law** states that the properties of the elements are a periodic function of their atomic numbers. In other words, by arranging the elements in order of increasing atomic number, a new period of elements is formed so that elements with similar chemical properties fall in the same group. The periodic law was proposed by Dmitri Mendeleev in 1869.

Practice 1
Which of the following information cannot be found in the box of an element on the periodic table?
1) Oxidation state   3) Atomic number
2) Phase   4) Atomic mass

Practice 2
The Periodic Table of the Elements contains elements that are
1) solids only
2) solids and liquids only
3) liquids and gases only
4) solids, liquids and gases

Practice 3
The observed regularities in the properties of the elements are periodic functions of their
1) atomic numbers   3) atomic mass
2) oxidation state   4) reactivity

Practice 4
The similarities in chemical properties of elements within the same group is due to similarity in
1) number of electron shells
2) valence electrons
3) oxidation state
4) chemical properties

Practice 5
Majority of the elements on the Periodic Table are
1) metals   3) metalloids
2) nonmetals   4) noble gases

Practice 6
Which of these elements has similar chemical properties as iodine?
1) Xe   2) Te   3) Br   4) S

Practice 7
Which list contains elements with greatest variation in chemical properties?
1) O, S and Se   3) N, P and As
2) Be, N, O   4) Ba, Sr and Ca

Practice 8
Which two elements have the same number of occupied electron shells
1) Mg and Be   3) Mg and O
2) Mg and Al   4) Mg and Ca

Practice 9
Element oxygen and sulfur can both form a bond with sodium with similar chemical formula. The similarity in their formula is due to
1) oxygen and sulfur having the same number of kernel electrons
2) oxygen and sulfur having the same number of valence electrons
3) oxygen and sulfur having the same number of protons
4) oxygen and sulfur having the same molecular structure

Base your answers to practice questions 10 through 12 on the information below.

Before atomic numbers were known, Mendeleev developed a classification system for the 63 elements known in 1872, using oxide formulas and atomic masses. He used an R in the oxide formulas to represent any element in each group. The atomic mass was listed in parentheses after the symbol of each element. A modified version of Mendeleev's classification system is shown in the table below.

Modified Version of Mendeleev's Table

Group →	I	II	III	IV	V	VI	VII
Oxide formulas	R_2O	RO	R_2O_3	RO_2	R_2O_5	RO_3	R_2O_7
1	H(1)						
2	Li(7)	Be(9.4)	B(11)	C(12)	N(14)	O(16)	F(19)
3	Na(23)	Mg(24)	Al(27.3)	Si(28)	P(31)	S(32)	Cl(35.5)
4	K(39)	Ca(40)		Ti(48)	V(51)	Cr(52)	Mn(55)
5	Cu(63)	Zn(65)			As(75)	Se(78)	Br(80)
6	Rb(85)	Sr(87)	Yt(88)	Zr(90)	Nb(94)	Mo(96)	
7	Ag(108)	Cd(112)	In(113)	Sn(118)	Sb(122)	Te(125)	I(127)
8	Cs(133)	Ba(137)	Di(138)	Ce(140)			

(Series)

10. Identify two elements on Mendeleev's table that combines with oxygen in the same ratio as magnesium.

11. Identify *one* characteristic used by Mendeleev to develop his classification system of the elements.

12. State one difference between Mendeleev's Table and the Modern Periodic Table.

E3 Scholastic Publishing. ©2017 All Rights Reserved

Lesson 2 – Types of Elements and their Properties

There are three general categories of elements: metals, nonmetals and metalloids. Elements in each category have a set of physical and chemical properties that can be used to distinguish them from elements in other categories.

In this lesson, you will learn about different types of elements, their locations in the Periodic Table, and their properties.

Physical Properties of Elements

There are several physical properties that are used to describe or identify the elements. Below are terms and definitions of these properties.

Malleable describes a solid that is easily hammered into a thin sheet. *ex. aluminum (Al)*

Ductile describes a solid that is easily drawn into a thin wire. *ex. copper (Cu)*

Brittle describes a solid that is easily broken into pieces when struck. *ex. sulfur (S)*

Luster describes the shininess of a substance. *ex. silver (Ag) or gold (Au)*

Conductivity describes how well heat or electricity can flow through the material.

Ionization energy is the energy needed to remove the most loosely bound valence electrons from an atom.

Electronegativity describes an atom's ability to attract electrons from another atom during bonding.

Melting point is the temperature at which a solid becomes a liquid.

Boiling point is the temperature at which a liquid becomes a gas (vapor).

Density describes the mass per volume ratio of an element.

Atomic radius describes the size of the atom of an element.

Use Reference Table S to find and compare values for these six properties of the elements.

Ionic radius describes the size of an atom after losing or gaining an electron to form an ion.

Types of Elements

Location of metals, metalloids, and nonmetals

Metals
Luster, Ductile, Malleable, Conductors, Low Electronegativity and Low Ionization Energy

Metal elements are located on the left side of the Periodic Table.
All elements in Groups 1 through 12 (except for hydrogen) are classified as a metal.
The rest of the metal elements are found near the bottom of Groups 13, 14 and 15.
The majority (about 75%) of the elements are metals.

General properties of metals are listed below.
- All metals (except Hg) exist as a solid at STP. Mercury (Hg) is the only liquid metal.
- Metallic solids are malleable, ductile, and have luster.
- Metals have high thermal (heat) conductivity and high electrical conductivity. Electrical conductivity is due to mobile or free moving electrons in metal atoms.
- Metals have low electronegativity values; they do not easily attract electrons.
- Metals have low ionization energy values; they lose electrons easily.
- Metals lose electrons and form a positive ion during chemical bonding.

Nonmetals
Brittle, Dull, No Conductivity, High Electronegativity and Ionization Energy

Nonmetal elements are located to the right of the Periodic Table.
All elements in Groups 17 and 18 (except astatine, At) are classified as nonmetals. The rest of the nonmetals are found near the top of Groups 14, 15, and 16. Hydrogen is also a nonmetal.

General properties of nonmetals are listed below.
- Nonmetals are found in all three phases: solid, liquid, and gas.
- Most nonmetals are either a gas or solid at STP. Bromine is the only liquid nonmetal.
- Solid nonmetals are generally brittle and dull (lack luster, not shiny).
- Nonmetals have low heat (thermal) and low electrical conductivity.
- Nonmetals have high electronegativity values; they attract electrons easily.
- Nonmetals have high ionization energy values; they do not lose electrons easily.
- Nonmetals generally gain electrons and form a negative ion during bonding.

Metalloids
Metallic and Nonmetallic Properties

Metalloids are the elements located between the metals and nonmetals along the thick zigzag line of the Periodic Table.

General properties of metalloids are listed below.
- Metalloids tend to have properties of both the metals and nonmetals.
- Their properties are more like those of metals and less like nonmetals.
- Metalloids exist only as solids at STP.

Types of Elements: **Summary of Properties**

	Phases at STP	Physical properties	Conductivity	Electrone-gativity	Ionization energy	Electrons In bonding	Common ion	Ionic size (radius)
Metals	solid liquid	malleable luster ductile	high	low	low	lose electrons	+ (positive)	smaller than atom
Nonmetals	solid liquid gas	brittle dull	low	high	high	gain electrons	- (negative)	bigger than atom
Metalloids	solid only	properties of metals and nonmetals	low	varies	varies	lose electrons	+ (positive)	smaller than atom

Types of Elements: Practice Questions

Practice 13
Elements that can be hammered into thin sheets are
1) ductile   2) luster   3) malleable   4) brittle

Practice 14
The tendency for an atom to give away its electrons during bonding is measured by its
1) atomic radius value   3) electronegativity value
2) density value   4) ionization energy value

Practice 15
Nonmetal elements on the Periodic Table can be found in which phase or phases at STP?
1) solid only   3) solid or liquid only
2) liquid only   4) solid, liquid and gas

Practice 16
Which two characteristics are associated with nonmetals?
1) Low first ionization energy and low electronegativity.
2) Low first ionization energy and high electronegativity.
3) High first ionization energy and low electronegativity.
4) High first ionization energy and high electronegativity.

Practice 17
Metalloids tend to have properties resembling
1) nonmetals only
2) metals only
3) both metals and nonmetals
4) neither a metal nor a nonmetal

Practice 18
Which is a property of most metals?
1) They tend to gain electrons easily when bonding.
2) They tend to lose electrons easily when bonding.
3) They are poor conductors of heat.
4) They are poor conductors of electricity.

Practice 19
Which of these elements is a metalloid?
1) Gallium   3) Phosphorus
2) Germanium   4) Tin

Practice 20
Which list consists of a metal, nonmetal, and metalloid respectively?
1) Al, B, Si   3) Ni, Si, P
2) Cr, C, Sb   4) C, Si, Ge

Practice 21
Which element is brittle and non-conducting solid?
1) S   2) Ne   3) Ni   4) Hg

Practice 22
Which of these elements has high thermal and electrical conductivity?
1) Iodine   3) Carbon
2) Phosphorus   4) Iron

Practice 23
Which properties best describes mercury?
1) It has luster.
2) It is brittle.
3) It has a high electronegativity value.
4) It is a poor electrical conductor.

Practice 24
Which is true of the element carbon?
1) It is malleable.
2) It has luster.
3) It has low electrical conductivity.
4) It is a gas at STP.

Group 1: Alkali Metals
One Valence Electron, +1 Charge, Very Reactive

Group 1
Alkali Metals

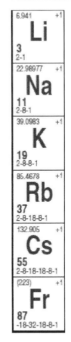

Alkali metals are the elements in Group 1 of the periodic table.

They include lithium, sodium, potassium, rubidium, cesium and francium.

Hydrogen is *not* an alkali metal even though it is placed in Group 1.

Properties or characteristics of alkali metals are listed below.
- One valence (outer shell) electron.
- Form a positive one (+1) ion by losing their one valence electron during bonding.
- Very low electronegativity and very low ionization energy values.
- Found in nature in compounds, not in free or atomic state, due to high reactivity.
- Are obtained from electrolytic reduction of fused salt compounds (**Na**Cl, **K**Br, etc.).
- If **X** represents a **Group 1** atom:

  XY is the general formula of a Group 1 atom bonding with a **Group 17** halogen (**Y**).

  X$_2$O is the general formula of a Group 1 atom bonding with **O** to form an oxide.
- Francium (Fr), a radioactive element, is the most reactive of all metals.
- All alkali metals are solids at room temperature.

Group 2: Alkaline Earth Metals
Two Valence Electrons, +2 Charge

Group 2
Alkaline Earth

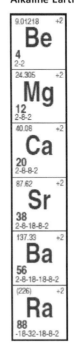

Alkaline earth metals are the elements in Group 2 of the periodic table.

They include beryllium, magnesium, calcium, strontium, barium, and radium.

Properties of alkaline earth metals are listed below.
- Two valence (outer shell) electrons.
- Form positive two (+2) ion by losing all two valence electrons during bonding.
- Found in nature as compounds, not in free or atomic state, due to high reactivity.
- Are obtained from fused salt compounds (MgCl$_2$, CaBr$_2$, etc.).
- If **M** represents a **Group 2** atom:

  MY$_2$ is the general formula of a Group 2 atom bonding with a **Group 17** halogen (**Y**).

  MO is the general formula of a Group 2 atom bonding with **O** to form an oxide.
- Radium (Ra), a radioactive element, is the most reactive metal in this group.
- All alkaline earth metals are solids at room temperature.

Groups 3 – 12: Transition Metals
Multiple Positive Charges, Form Colored Compounds

Transition metals are the elements in Groups 3 through 12 of the periodic table. Properties of these elements vary widely, however, some unique properties can be observed among them.

Properties of transition metals are listed below.
- They tend to form multiple positive oxidation numbers.
- Most can lose electrons in two or more different sublevels of their atoms.
- Their ions usually form colorful compounds.
   $CuCl_2$ is a bluish color compound.
   $FeCl_2$ is an orange color compound

Groups 3-12 Transition Metals

3	4	5	6	7	8	9	10	11	12
Sc 21	Ti 22	V 23	Cr 24	Mn 25	Fe 26	Co 27	Ni 28	Cu 29	Zn 30
Y 39	Zr 40	Nb 41	Mo 42	Tc 43	Ru 44	Rh 45	Pd 46	Ag 47	Cd 48
La 57	Hf 72	Ta 73	W 74	Re 75	Os 76	Ir 77	Pt 78	Au 79	Hg 80
Ac 89	Rf 104	Db 105	Sg 106	Bh 107	Hs 108	Mt 109	Ds 110	Rg 111	Cn 112

Group 17: Halogens
Seven Valence Electrons, -1 Charge, Highly Reactive

Halogens are the elements in Group 17 of the periodic table. They include fluorine, chlorine, bromine, and iodine.

Properties of halogens are listed below.
- They exist as diatomic (two-atom) elements; F_2, Cl_2, Br_2, I_2.
- Seven valence (outer-shell) electrons.
- High electronegativity and high ionization energy values.
- Form negative one (-1) ion by gaining one electron to fill their valence shells.
- If **Y** represents a **Group 17 halogen:**
   XY is the general formula of a Group 17 halogen bonding with a **Group 1** atom (**X**).
   MY₂ is the general formula of a Group 17 atom bonding with a **Group 2** atom (**M**).
- The only group containing elements in all three phases at STP.
   Gases (fluorine and chlorine)   Liquid (bromine)   Solid (iodine)
- Fluorine is the most reactive of the group, and the most reactive nonmetal overall.
- Astatine (At) in this group is a metalloid, not a halogen.

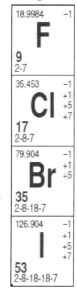

Group 17 Halogens

Group 18: Noble Gases

Full Valence Shells with Two or Eight Electrons. Non-reactive.

Noble gases are the elements in Group 18 of the periodic table.

They include helium, neon, argon, krypton, xenon, and radon.

Properties of noble gases are listed below.

- They exist as monatomic (one-atom) molecule; He, Ne, Ar.
- All are gases at STP.
- They all have full and stable valence shells with eight electrons.
  Helium (He) is full and stable with its two electrons.
- They neither gain, lose nor share electrons because their valence shells are full.
- Noble gases are non-reactive, so they do not form many compounds.
- Argon (Ar) and Xenon (Xe) have been found to produce a few stable compounds with fluorine.

Group 18
Noble gases

Group Properties: **Summary Table**

Group Number	Group Name	Types of Elements in the Group	Phases (at STP)	Number of Valence Electrons (in bonding)	Common Oxidation Number (charge)	Ionic Compound General Formula
1	Alkali metals	Metal	Solid (all)	1 (lose)	+1	XY with halogens (halide) X_2O with oxygen (oxide)
2	Alkaline earth	Metal	Solid (all)	2 (lose)	+2	MY_2 with halogens MO with oxygen
3-12	Transition metals	Metal	Liquid (Hg) Solid (the rest)	varies (lose)	Multiple +charges	varies (form colorful compounds)
13	-	Metalloid Metal	Solid (all)	3 (lose)	+3	LY_3 with halogens L_2O_3 with oxygen
14	-	Nonmetal Metalloid Metal	Solid (all)	4 (lose or share)	varies	varies
15	-	Nonmetal Metalloid Metal	Gas (N) Solid (the rest)	5 (gain or share)	-3	varies
16	Oxygen group	Nonmetal Metalloid	Gas (O) Solid (the rest)	6 (gain or share)	-2	X_2O with alkali metals MO with alkaline earth
17	Halogens (Diatomic)	Nonmetal	Gas (F and Cl) Liquid (Br) Solid (I)	7 (gain or share)	-1	XY with alkali metals MY with alkaline earths
18	Noble gases (Monatomic)	Nonmetal	Gas (all)	Full (2 or 8) (neither gain lose, nor share)	0	Form very few compounds. XeF_4 is the most common.

E3 Scholastic Publishing. ©2017 All Rights Reserved

Group Properties: Practice Questions

Practice 25
Which element is a noble gas?
1) Neon   3) Fluorine
2) Oxygen   4) Nitrogen

Practice 26
Iron is best classified as a(n)
1) transition nonmetal
2) transition metal
3) alkali metal
4) alkaline earth metal

Practice 27
The element in Group 17 Period 4 is a(n)
1) transition metal   3) alkali metal
2) halogen   4) noble gas

Practice 28
Which set contains elements that are never found in nature in their atomic state?
1) K and Na   3) Na and Ne
2) K and S   4) Na and C

Practice 29
Element X is a solid that is brittle, lack luster, and has six valence electrons. In which group on the Periodic Table would element X be found?
1) 1   3) 15
2) 2   4) 16

Practice 30
Element Z is in Period 3 of the Periodic Table. Which element is Z if it forms an oxide with a formula of Z_2O_3?
1) Na   3) Mg
2) Al   4) Cl

Practice 31
Which of these oxides will likely form a colored solution when dissolved in water?
1) Na_2O 3) CaO
2) SO_2 4) Mn_2O

Base your answers to practice questions 32 and 33 on the information below.

There are six elements in Group 14 on the Periodic Table. One of these elements has the symbol Uuq, which is a temporary, systematic symbol. This element is now known as flerovium.

32. State the expected number of valence electrons in an atom of the element flerovium in the ground state.

33. Identify an element in Group 14 that is classified as a metalloid.

Allotropes
Same Element, Different Structural Forms, Different Properties

Allotropes are different molecular or crystalline forms of the same element in the same state.

Differences in molecular structures give allotropes of the same element different physical properties (color, hardness, density, melting point, etc.) and different chemical properties and reactivities.

Majority of the elements do not have allotropic forms.
Three common allotropes are listed below.

Oxygen allotropes
Oxygen gas (O_2) and ozone (O_3) are different molecular forms of oxygen.
They have different chemical and different physical properties.

Carbon allotropes
Diamond, graphite, and fullerene are different molecular forms of carbon.
They have different chemical and different physical properties.

Two molecular structures of oxygen.

Phosphorus allotropes
White, red, and black are different molecular forms of phosphorus.
They have different chemical and different physical properties.

Allotropes: Practice Questions

Practice 34

Two forms of solid carbon, diamond and graphite, differ in their physical properties due to the difference in their

1) atomic numbers
2) crystal structures
3) isotopic abundance
4) percent composition

Practice 35

Which statement describes oxygen gas, $O_2(g)$, and ozone gas, $O_3(g)$?

1) They have different molecular structures, only.
2) They have different properties, only.
3) They have different molecular structures and different properties.
4) They have the same molecular structure and the same properties.

Lesson 3. Periodic Trends

Periodic trends are specific patterns in properties of the elements that exist on the Periodic Table. Certain properties of the elements change orderly within a group or period as the elements are considered one after the other. The trend in atomic number is an example of a periodic trend found on the Periodic Table.

As elements are considered one after the other from:

Left to **Right** across a Period: Atomic number of the elements increases.

Top to **Bottom** down a Group: Atomic number of the elements increases.

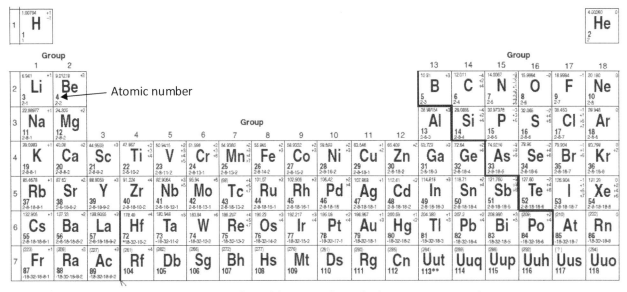

Many other trends exist on the periodic table even though they are not as obvious.

In this lesson you will learn of the following trends:

      Trends in atomic radius (size).

      Trends in metallic and nonmetallic properties.

      Trends in electronegativity and ionization energy.

Trends in Atomic Size (Atomic Radius)
Increase Top to Bottom and Right to Left.

Atomic radius is defined as half the distance between two nuclei of the same atom when they are joined together. Atomic radius gives a good approximation of the size of an atom.
The atomic radii of the elements can be found on **Reference Table S.**
The trend in atomic radius is as follows:

Top to **Bottom** down a **Group**: Atomic size (radius) increases *due* to an increase in the number of *electron shells.*

Left to **Right** across a **Period**: Atomic (size) radius decreases *due* to an increase in nuclear charge.

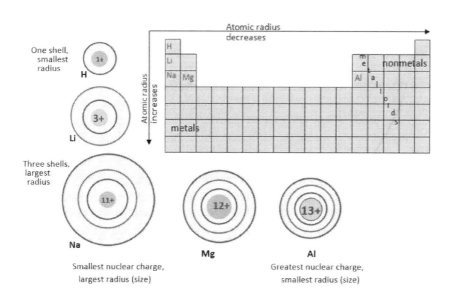

Use **Reference *Table S*** to identify and compare atomic radii (sizes) for any given set of elements.

Atomic Number	Symbol	Name	Atomic Radius (pm)
1	H	hydrogen	32
2	He	helium	37
3	Li	lithium	130.
4	Be	beryllium	99
5	B	boron	84
6	C	carbon	75
7	N	nitrogen	71
8	O	oxygen	64
9	F	fluorine	60.
10	Ne	neon	62
11	Na	sodium	160
12	Mg	magnesium	140
13	Al	aluminum	124
14	Si	silicon	114

Concept Task: Be able to determine the element with the largest or smallest radius (size).
*Use **Table S** to identify and compare.*

Practice 36
Which of the following elements has the largest atomic radius?
1) K   2) Ca   3) Al   4) Na

Practice 37
Which list of elements is arranged in order of increasing atomic radii?
1) Li, Be, B, C   3) Sc, Ti, V, Cr
2) Sr, Ca, Mg, Be   4) F, Cl, Br, I

Practice 38
The atom of which element is bigger than the atom of calcium?
1) Sr   2) Sc   3) Mg   4) Be

Practice 39
Which atom has a bigger atomic radius than the atom of sulfur?
1) Oxygen, because it has more electron shells.
2) Oxygen, because it has a smaller nuclear charge.
3) Phosphorus, because it has more electron shells.
4) Phosphorus, because it has a smaller nuclear charge.

Trends in Electronegativity and Ionization Energy
Increase Bottom to Top. Decrease Left to Right

Electronegativity: *Tendency to Attract or Gain Electrons*
Electronegativity defines an atom's tendency to attract (or gain) electrons from another atom during chemical bonding. The electronegativity value assigned to each element is relative to one another. The higher the electronegativity value, the more likely it is for the atom to attract electrons during bonding.

Fluorine (F) is assigned the highest electronegativity value of 4.0.
Fluorine has the greatest ability or tendency to attract electrons during bonding.

Francium (Fr) is assigned the lowest electronegativity value of 0.7.
Francium has the least ability or tendency to attract electrons during bonding.

Ionization Energy: *Energy to Remove or Tendency to Lose Electrons.*
Ionization energy is the amount of energy needed to remove an electron from an atom. The *first ionization energy* is the energy to remove the most loosely bound electron from an atom. Ionization energy measures the tendency of an atom to lose electrons and form a positive ion. The lower the first ionization energy of an atom, the easier or the more likely it is for that atom to lose its most loosely bound valence electron and form a positive ion.

Metals lose electrons because of their low ionization energies.
The *alkali metals* in Group 1 generally have the lowest ionization energies, which is why they readily lose electrons and react very easily.

Nonmetals have a low tendency to lose electrons because of their high ionization energies.
The *noble gases* in Group 18 tend to have the highest ionization energy values. Since these elements already have a full valence shell of electrons, a high amount of energy is required to remove any electron from their atoms.

Top to **Bottom** down a **Group**:   Electronegativity (tendency to gain or attract electrons) decreases.
                         Ionization energy (tendency to lose electrons) decreases

Left to **Right** across a **Period**:   Electronegativity increases
                         Ionization energy increases

Electronegativity and ionization energy values for the elements are given on **Reference Table S.**

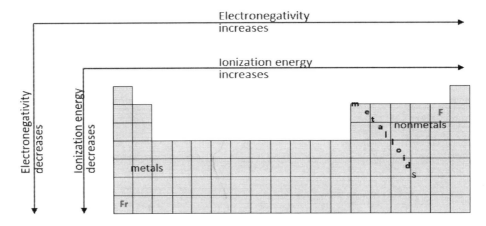

Topic 2

The Periodic Table

Trends in Electronegativity and Ionization Energy: **Practice Problems**

Concept Task: Be able to determine which element has the greatest or least tendency to attract electrons.

Greatest Attraction for Electrons *(most likely to gain):*
• Element with the HIGHEST electronegativity value.
  ex. **Si** has a greater tendency to attract electrons than **Al**.

Least Attraction for Electrons *(least likely to gain):*
• Element with the LOWEST electronegativity value.

Concept Task: Be able to determine which element has the greatest or least tendency to lose electrons.

Greatest Tendency to Lose Electrons:
• Element with the LOWEST ionization energy value
  ex. **Al** has a greater tendency to lose electrons than **Si**.

Least Tendency to Lose Electrons
• Element with the HIGHEST ionization energy value.

Use Reference ***Table S*** to locate and compare electronegativity and ionization energy values.

Atomic Number	Symbol	Name	First Ionization Energy (kJ/mol)	Electro-negativity
1	H	hydrogen	1312	2.2
2	He	helium	2372	—
3	Li	lithium	520.	1.0
4	Be	beryllium	900.	1.6
5	B	boron	801	2.0
6	C	carbon	1086	2.6
7	N	nitrogen	1402	3.0
8	O	oxygen	1314	3.4
9	F	fluorine	1681	4.0
10	Ne	neon	2081	—
11	Na	sodium	496	0.9
12	Mg	magnesium	738	1.3
13	Al	aluminum	578	1.6
14	Si	silicon	787	1.9
15	P	phosphorus (white)	1012	2.2

Practice 40
As the elements of Group 1 on the Periodic Table are considered in order of increasing atomic radius, the ionization energy of each successive element generally
1) decreases
2) increases
3) remains the same

Practice 41
Which of these elements is most likely to attract electrons from another atom during chemical bonding?
1) Fe   2) C   3) Al   4) Cs

Practice 42
Which of these elements has a greater tendency to attract electron than phosphorus?
1) Silicon   3) Boron
2) Arsenic   4) Sulfur

Practice 43
Which of the following elements has the greatest tendency to lose its valence electrons?
1) Be   2) S   3) Ne   4) Ca

Practice 44
Aluminum will lose its most loosely bound electron less readily than
1) Calcium   3) Indium
2) Nitrogen   4) Scandium

Practice 45
Which sequence of elements is arranged in order of decrease tendency to attract electrons during chemical bonding?
1) Al, Si, P   3) Cs, Na, Li
2) I, Br, Cl   4) C, B, Be

Trends in Metallic and Nonmetallic Properties

Trends in metallic and nonmetallic properties vary. For metals, the most reactive metals are on the bottom left corner of the table. *Francium* is the most reactive of all metals. For nonmetals, the most reactive nonmetals are on the top right corner of the table. *Fluorine* is the most reactive of all nonmetals. Trends in metallic and nonmetallic properties are summarized below:

Top to **Bottom** down a **Group**:
Metallic properties and reactivity increase *(ex. K is more reactive than Na)*
Nonmetallic properties and reactivity decrease *(ex. Br is less reactive than Cl)*

LEFT to **Right** across a **Period**:
Metallic properties and reactivity decrease. *(ex. Mg is less reactive than Na)*
Nonmetallic properties and reactivity increase. *(ex. Cl is more reactive than S)*

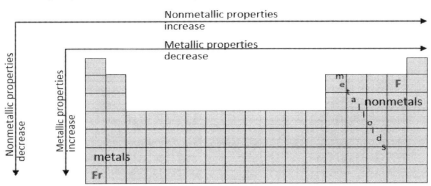

Concept Task: Be able to determine which element has the most (or least) metallic or nonmetallic properties.

The element **farthest left** and **lowest down**: Strongest metallic / Least nonmetallic characteristics.

The element **farthest right** and **highest up**: Least metallic / Strongest nonmetallic characteristics.

Practice 46
Which of the following element has the most pronounced metallic characteristics?
1) C   2) Co   3) Al   4) Rb

Practice 47
Which of these elements has greatest nonmetallic properties?
1) Se   2) Te   3) Br   4) I

Practice 48
Which of these halogens is the least reactive on the Period Table?
1) I   2) Br   3) Cl   4) F

Practice 49
Which of these elements has stronger metallic characteristics than aluminum?
1) He   2) Mg   3) Ga   4) Si

Practice 50
Which of these elements has stronger nonmetallic properties than chlorine?
1) sulfur   3) fluorine
2) selenium   4) bromine

Practice 51
Which part of the Periodic Table contains elements with the strongest nonmetallic properties?
1) Upper right   3) Upper left
2) Lower right   4) Lower left

E3 Scholastic Publishing. ©2017 All Rights Reserved

Other Properties of the Elements

Reference Table S contains other physical properties of the elements. These properties are *melting point, boiling point, and density.*

Periodic trends are observable for some of these properties within groups 1,2, 17 and 18.
For example:
Melting and boiling points of the elements in groups 1 and 2 tend to decrease from top to bottom.
Density of the elements in groups 17 and 18 tend to increase from top to bottom.
These trends are not consistent across a period because each period contains varieties of elements.
Comparison questions for these properties can be answered by using Reference Table S to locate and compare the values for the given elements.

Reference Table S

Atomic Number	Symbol	Name	Melting Point (K)	Boiling* Point (K)	Density** (g/cm³)
1	H	hydrogen	14	20.	0.000082
2	He	helium	—	4	0.000164
3	Li	lithium	454	1615	0.534
4	Be	beryllium	1560.	2744	1.85
5	B	boron	2348	4273	2.34
6	C	carbon	—	—	—
7	N	nitrogen	63	77	0.001145
8	O	oxygen	54	90.	0.001308
9	F	fluorine	53	85	0.001553
10	Ne	neon	24	27	0.000825
11	Na	sodium	371	1156	0.97
12	Mg	magnesium	923	1363	1.74
13	Al	aluminum	933	2792	2.70
14	Si	silicon	1687	3538	2.3296

Melting point is the temperature at which a solid turns to a liquid. Solid lithium will melt to a liquid at 454 K (181°C).

Boiling point is the temperature at which a liquid turns to a gas. Liquid nitrogen will boil to a gas at only 77 K (-196°C).

Density of a substance measures how much mass is within a given volume (space) of the substance. Density, the mass per volume ratio, for any substance can be calculated using the **Table T** equation:

Density	$d = \dfrac{m}{V}$	d = density m = mass V = volume

Since the density values of the elements at STP are listed on this table, students are often asked to setup and calculate either the volume or mass of a given sample of an element.

Example 1
Calculate the volume of an aluminum block that has a mass of 43.5 grams at STP.

$$\text{Volume} = \frac{\text{mass}}{\text{density}} = \frac{43.5\text{ g}}{2.70\text{ g/cm}^3} = \boxed{\textbf{16.1 cm}^3}$$

numerical setup   *calculated result*

Practice 52
Which element has the highest melting point?
1) tantalum   3) osmium
2) rhenium   4) hafnium

Practice 53
What is the density of N_2 at STP?
1) .000825 g/cm³
2) .001650 g/cm³
3) .00115 g/cm³
4) .00130 g/cm³

Practice 54
Which element has the greatest density at STP?
1) scandium   3) silicon
2) selenium   4) sodium

Practice 55
At STP, a 7.49-gram sample of an element has a volume of 1.65 cubic centimeters. The sample is most likely
1) Ta   3) Te
2) Tc   4) Ti

Practice 56   *show a setup and the result*
Calculate the volume of a 31.03-gram piece of zinc at STP.

Practice 57   *Show a setup and the result*
What is the mass of a 6.00-cm³ block of gold at STP?

Base your answers to practice questions 58 through 61 on the information below.

The atomic number and corresponding atomic radius of the Period 3 elements are shown in the data table below.

Data Table

Atomic Number	Atomic Radius (pm)
11	160.
12	140.
13	124
14	114
15	109
16	104
17	100.
18	101

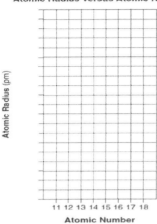

Atomic Radius Versus Atomic Number

58. On the grid, mark an appropriate scale on the axis labeled "Atomic Radius (pm)."

59. On the grid, plot the data from the data table. Circle and connect the points.

60. Explain, in terms of electrons, the change in radius when a sodium atom becomes a sodium ion.

61. State the general relationship between the atomic number and the atomic radius for the Period 3 elements.

Base your answers to practice questions 62 and 63 on the information below.

Three elements, represented by *D*, *E*, and *Q*, are located in Period 3. Some properties of these elements are listed in the table below.

Properties of Samples of Three Elements at Room Temperature and Standard Pressure

Element	Phase	Mass (g)	Density (g/cm³)	Oxide Formula
D	solid	50.0	0.97	D_2O
E	solid	50.0	1.74	EO
Q	solid	50.0	2.00	QO_2 or QO_3

62. Identify the group on the Periodic Table to which element *D* belongs.

63. Using Table S, identify element Q.

Base your answers to practice questions 64 and 65 on the information below.

The table below lists physical and chemical properties of six elements at standard pressure that correspond to known elements on the Periodic Table. The elements are identified by the code letters, D, E, G, J, L, and Q.

Properties of Six Elements at Standard Pressure

Element D	Element E	Element G
Density 0.00018 g/cm³	Density 1.82 g/cm³	Density 0.53 g/cm³
Melting point −272°C	Melting point 44°C	Melting point 181°C
Boiling point −269°C	Boiling point 280°C	Boiling point 1347°C
Oxide formula (none)	Oxide formula E_2O_5	Oxide formula G_2O

Element J	Element L	Element Q
Density 0.0013 g/cm³	Density 0.86 g/cm³	Density 0.97 g/cm³
Melting point −210°C	Melting point 64°C	Melting point 98°C
Boiling point −196°C	Boiling point 774°C	Boiling point 883°C
Oxide formula J_2O_5	Oxide formula L_2O	Oxide formula Q_2O

65. Letter Z corresponds to an element on the Periodic Table other than the six listed elements. Elements G, Q, L, and Z are in the same group, as shown in the diagram below.

G

Q

L

Z

Based on the trend in the melting points for elements G, Q, and L listed in the "Properties of Six Elements at Standard Pressure" table, estimate the melting point of element Z, in degrees Celsius.

64. Identify, by code letter, the element that is a noble gas in the "Properties of Six Elements at Standard Pressure" table.

Vocabulary

Lesson 1: Arrangement of the Elements

Periodic Law
Group
Period

Lesson 2: Types of Elements and Properties

Malleable	Metal
Luster	Nonmetal
Brittleness	Metalloid
Ductile	Alkali metal
Ionization energy	Alkaline earth metal
Electronegativity	Transition metal
Density	Halogen
Atomic radius	Noble gas
	Allotrope

Lesson 3: Periodic Trends

Periodic trend

1. 2

2. 4

3. 1

4. 2

5. 1

6. 3

7. 2

8. 2

9. 2

10. Be, Ca, Zn, Sr, Cd, Ba

11. Oxide formula, atomic mass

12. Mendeleev's table is arranged by atomic mass.

The modern periodic table is arranged by atomic number.

13. 3

14. 3

15. 4

16. 4

17. 3

18. 2

19. 2

20. 2

21. 1

22. 4

23. 1

24. 3

25. 1

26. 2

27. 2

28. 1

29. 4

30. 2

31. 4

32. 4

33. Si

34. 2

35. 3

36. 1

37. 4

38. 1

39. 4

40. 1

41. 2

42. 4

43. 4

44. 3

45. 4

46. 4

47. 3

48. 1

49. 2

50. 3

51. 1

52. 2

53. 3

54. 2

55. 4

56. $\dfrac{31.03 \text{ g}}{7.134 \text{ g/cm}^3} = \textbf{4.350 cm}^3$

57. $(6.00 \text{ cm}^3)(19.3 \text{ g.cm}^3) = \textbf{115.8 g}$

58
and
59

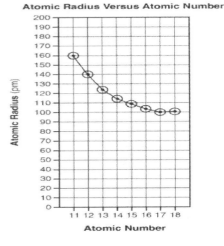

Atomic Radius Versus Atomic Number

60. As atomic number increases, atomic radius decreases.

61. Element 13 has a smaller nuclear charge than element 15

62. Group 1

63. Sulfur, S

64. D

65. A temperature below 64°C.

E3 Scholastic Publishing. ©2017 All Rights Reserved

Topic 3
Atomic Structure

Lesson 1: Models of the Atom

Lesson 2: Structure of an Atom

Lesson 3: Arrangement of Electrons

Lesson 4: Neutral Atoms and Ions

Lesson 1 – History of the Atomic Model

The **atom** is the basic unit of matter. Since an atom is very small and cannot be seen with the most sophisticated equipment, many scientists for hundreds of years have proposed different models of the atom to help explain the nature and behavior of matter.

In this lesson you will learn about these historical scientists, their experiments and proposed models of the atom.

Atomic Theories and Models of Atoms

Some of the atomic theories and models proposed by scientists over the years are briefly described below. On the next page the work of two of these scientists is further explained.

John Dalton: Hard-sphere (Cannonball) Model
- All matter is composed of atoms.
- Atoms are indivisible and indestructible building blocks of matter.
- Atoms of the same element are the same. Atoms of different elements are different.
- Atoms have no internal structures.

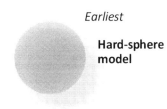

Earliest

Hard-sphere model

J.J. Thomson: Plum-pudding Model
- An atom is composed of negative electrons.
- The electrons are surrounded by positive charges to balance out.

Plum-pudding model

Ernest Rutherford: Empty-space Model
- An atom has a small, positive, high-mass center, the nucleus.
- Most of an atom is empty space.

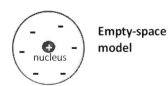

Empty-space model

Niels Bohr: Electron-shell (Planetary) Model
- Electrons in atoms go around the nucleus in orbit.
- Electrons have fixed energy in specific orbits.
- Electrons can gain or lose energy only by jumping from one orbit to another.
- Atoms absorb and release energy as an electron changes level.

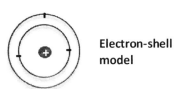

Electron-shell model

Many Scientists: Wave Mechanical (Electron-cloud) Model
- Atom has a small, dense, positive nucleus.
- Protons and neutrons are in the nucleus.
- Electrons are in *orbitals* outside the nucleus.

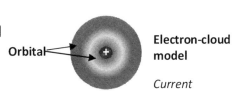

Orbital

Electron-cloud model

Current

The *wave-mechanical* model is the currently accepted model of the atom. In the wave-mechanical model, electrons are found outside the nucleus in regions called orbitals.

Orbitals are the most probable location of finding an electron with a certain amount of energy in an atom. The wave-mechanical model brought together the work and discoveries of many scientists that span hundreds of years.

Cathode Ray Experiment

J.J. Thomson conducted the cathode ray experiment that further supports the existence of negatively charged particles in atoms.

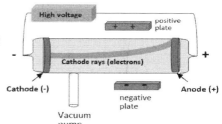

The setup
A tube with a metal disk at each end was set up to trace a beam from an electrical source. The metals were connected to the electrical source.
 Anode: The metal disk that is positive (+).
 Cathode: The metal disk that is negative (−).

Results
A beam of light (ray) traveled from the cathode end to the anode end of the tube. When electrically charged positive and negative plates were brought near the tube, the beam was deflected toward or attracted the positive plate. The beam was repelled by the negative plate.

Conclusions
The beam was composed of negatively charged particles.
The term "electron" was later used to describe the negative particles of an atom.

Gold-Foil Experiment

Ernest Rutherford conducted the gold-foil experiment that led to his proposed empty-space theory of an atom.

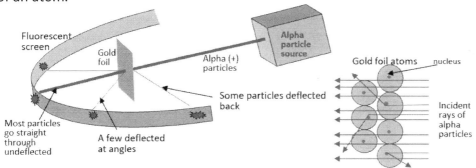

The setup
Equipment was set up to fire alpha particles at a gold foil.
 • Alpha particles are positive, and similar to helium nuclei.

A fluorescent screen was set up around the foil
 • The screen will detect paths of particles after hitting the gold foil.

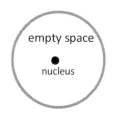

An atom is mostly
an empty space

Result 1
Most of the alpha particles went straight through the gold foil undeflected.

Conclusion 1
 An atom is mostly an empty space (Empty-space Theory).

Result 2
A few of the particles were deflected back or hit the screen at angles.

Conclusion 2
The center of an atom, the nucleus, is dense, positive, and very small.

History of Atomic Models: Practice Questions

Practice 1
The modern model of an atom shows that electrons are
1) orbiting the nucleus in fixed path
2) found in regions called orbital
3) combined with neutrons in the nucleus
4) located in a solid sphere covering the nucleus

Practice 2
In the wave-mechanical model, the orbital is a region in space of an atom where there is a
1) high probability of finding an electron
2) high probability of finding a neutron
3) circular path in which electrons are found
4) circular path in which neutrons are found

Practice 3
The modern model of the atom is based on the work of
1) one scientist over a short period of time
2) one scientist over a long period of time
3) many scientists over a short period of time
4) many scientists over a long period of time

Practice 4
Which group of atomic models is listed in order from the earliest to the most recent?
1) Hard-sphere model, wave-mechanical model, electron-shell model
2) Hard-sphere model, electron-shell model, wave mechanical model
3) Electron-shell model, wave-mechanical model, hard-sphere model
4) Electron-shell model, hard-sphere model, wave-mechanical model

Practice 5
Which order of diagrams correctly shows the historical models of the atom from the earliest to the most modern?

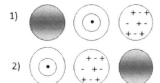

Base your answers to practice questions 6 through 9 on the information below and on your knowledge of chemistry.

A student compares some models of the atom. These models are listed in the table below in order of development from top to bottom.

Models of the Atom

Model	Observation	Conclusion
Dalton model	Matter is conserved during a chemical reaction.	Atoms are hard, indivisible spheres of different sizes.
Thomson model	Cathode rays are deflected by magnetic/electric fields.	Atoms have small, negatively charged particles as part of their internal structure.
Rutherford model	Most alpha particles pass straight through gold foil but a few are deflected.	An atom is mostly empty space with a small, dense, positively charged nucleus.
Bohr model	Unique spectral lines are emitted by excited gaseous elements.	Packets of energy are absorbed or emitted by atoms when an electron changes shells.

6. State *one* conclusion about the internal structure of the atom that resulted from the gold foil experiment.

7. State *one* way in which the Bohr model agrees with the Thomson model.

8. Using the conclusion from the Rutherford model, identify the charged subatomic particle that is located in the nucleus.

9. State the model that first included electrons as subatomic particles.

Lesson 2 – Structure of an Atom

Although the atom is described as the smallest unit of matter, it is also composed of much smaller particles called **subatomic particles**. The three subatomic particles are protons, electrons, and neutrons.

In this lesson, you will learn more about the modern atom and the subatomic particles. You will also learn the relationships between the subatomic particles, atomic number, and mass number of an atom.

Atom
Smallest Unit of Matter

The **atom** is the basic unit of matter. It is composed of three subatomic particles: Protons, electrons and neutrons. The only atom without a neutron is a hydrogen atom with a mass of 1, hydrogen - 1.

- An atom is mostly empty space.
- An atom has a small dense positive core, the nucleus, with negative electron-cloud surrounding the nucleus.
- Elements are composed of atoms with the same atomic number.
- Atoms of the same element are similar.
- Atoms of different elements are different.

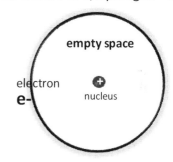

Nucleus
Center of an Atom. Contains Protons and Neutrons.

The **nucleus** is the center or core of an atom.
- The nucleus contains protons and neutrons.
- The overall charge of the nucleus is positive due to the protons.
- The nucleus is much smaller and denser in comparison to the rest of the atom.
- Most of an atom's mass , (over 99%) is found within the nucleus.

A lithium atom nucleus

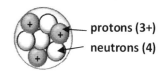

Protons
Positive Charge, 1 Atomic Mass Unit, Found in Nucleus

Protons are positively charged subatomic particles found in the nucleus of an atom.

- A proton has a mass of one atomic mass unit (1 u) and a +1 charge.
- A proton is about 1836 times more massive (heavier) than an electron.
- All atoms of the same element have the same number of protons.
- The number of protons is equal to the atomic number of an element.
- *Nuclear charge* is the total charge of all the protons in the nucleus.
  For example, lithium, atomic number 3, has a nuclear charge of +3.

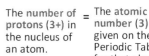
The number of protons (3+) in the nucleus of an atom. = The atomic number (3) given on the Periodic Table for that element.

Electrons
Negative Charge, Zero Mass. Found in Orbitals.

Electrons are negatively charged subatomic particles found in orbitals outside the nucleus of an atom.

- An electron has insignificant mass (zero) and a -1 charge.
- An electron has a mass that is $^{1}/_{1836}$th that of a proton or neutron.
- The arrangement of electrons in an atom determines the chemical properties of the element.
- The number of electrons is the same as the number of protons in a neutral atom.

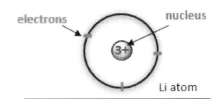

In a neutral Li atom, the number of electrons (3 e-) is the same as the number of protons (3+).

In all neutral atoms, there are equal numbers of electrons to protons.

Neutrons
Zero Charge, 1 Atomic Mass Unit. Found in the Nucleus

Neutrons have no charge, and are located inside the nucleus.

- A neutron has a mass of 1 atomic mass unit (1 u) and zero charge.
- A neutron has approximately the same mass as a proton.
- Atoms of the same element have different numbers of neutrons.

Two Different Lithium Nuclei

3 protons 3
4 neutrons 5

Different atoms of the same element have the same number of protons but different numbers of neutrons

Protons, electrons and neutrons differ in mass, charge, and location in an atom. The table below summarizes information about all three particles.

NOTE: Some information on this Table can be found on **Reference Table O.**

Subatomic particle	Symbol	Mass	Charge	Location
Proton	$^{\text{mass } 1}_{\text{charge }+1}p$	1 amu	+1	Nucleus
Neutron	$^{1}_{0}n$	1 amu	0	Nucleus
Electron	$^{0}_{-1}e$	0 amu	-1	Orbital (outside the nucleus)

Atomic Structure

Atomic Number
Number of Protons

Atomic number identifies each element.

- Atomic number of an element is *equal* to the number of protons.
- All atoms of the same element have the same atomic number because they have the same number of protons.
- Atomic numbers can be found on the periodic table.
- Elements on the periodic table are arranged in the order of increasing atomic number.

Periodic Table

Li nucleus

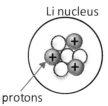

protons

The atomic number of Li (3) is equal to the number of protons (3) in the nucleus of all lithium atoms.

Nucleons
Protons and Neutrons

Nucleons are particles in the nucleus of an atom.
- Nucleons account for the total mass of an atom.
- The total number of nucleons in an atom is equal to the sum of protons *plus* neutrons.

Two Different Lithium Nuclei

 3p 4n

 3p 5n

The total number of nucleons for this Li atom is **7** (3p + 4n = **7**)	The total number of nucleons for this Li atom is **8** (3p + 5n = **8**)

Mass Number
Mass of Protons and Neutrons

Mass number identifies an isotope of a given element.
- Atoms of the same element differ in mass numbers due to *different numbers of neutrons*.
- The mass number is equal to the mass of protons *plus* neutrons.

The mass number for this Li atom is **7** atomic mass unit (**u**) (3 u + 4 u = **7 u**)	The mass number for this Li atom is **8 u.** (3 u + 5 u = **8 u**)

Concept Task: Be able to determine and compare number of subatomic particles.

Summary of Relationships Between Atomic Particles in Neutral Atoms

protons = atomic # = nuclear charge = electrons = mass # - neutrons = nucleons - neutrons

electrons = atomic # = nuclear charge = protons = mass # - neutrons = nucleons - neutrons

neutrons = mass # - protons = mass # - atomic number = Mass # - electrons = nucleons - protons

mass # = nucleons = protons + neutrons = nuclear charge + neutrons = atomic # + neutrons

Relating one Particle to another in Neutral Atoms. Practice Questions

Practice 10
Which particles are found in the nucleus of an atom?
1) Electron, only.
2) Neutrons, only.
3) Protons and electrons.
4) Protons and neutrons.

Practice 11
Compare to the entire atom, the nucleus of an atom is
1) smaller and contains most of atom's mass
2) larger and contains most of atom's mass
3) smaller and contains little of atom's mass
4) larger and contains little of atom's mass

Practice 12
Which is true of protons and neutrons?
1) They have approximately the same mass and the same charge.
2) They have approximately the same mass but different charge.
3) The have different mass and different charge.
4) They have different mass but the same charge.

Practice 13
An electron has a charge of
1) -1 and the same mass as a proton
2) -1 and a smaller mass than a proton
3) +1 and the same mass a proton
4) +1 and a smaller mass than a proton

Practice 14
The mass of a proton is approximately
1) 1/2000 times the mass of a neutron and a unit positive charge
2) 1/2000 times the mass of a neutron and a unit negative charge
3) 2000 times the mass of an electron and a unit positive charge
4) 2000 times the mass of an electron and a unit negative charge

Practice 15
The mass number of an element is always equal to the number of
1) protons plus electrons
2) protons plus positrons
3) neutrons plus positrons
4) neutrons plus protons

Practice 16
The number of neutrons in the nucleus of an atom can be determined by
1) adding the mass number to the atomic number of the atom
2) adding the mass number to the number of electrons of the atom
3) subtracting the atomic number from the mass number of the atom
4) subtracting the mass number from the atomic number of the atom

Practice 17
A neutral atom contains 12 neutrons and 11 electrons. The number of protons in this atom is
1) 1 2) 11 3) 12 4) 23

Practice 18
What is the number of electrons in a neutral atom of fluorine?
1) 9 2) 19 3) 10 4) 28

Practice 19
The number of neutrons in a neutral atom with a mass number of 86 and 37 electrons is
1) 86 2) 37 3) 123 4) 49

Practice 20
What is the atomic number of a neutral element whose atoms contain 60 neutrons and 47 electrons?
1) 13 2) 47 3) 60 4) 107

Practice 21
What is the mass number of an atom that contains 19 protons, 18 electrons, and 20 neutrons?
1) 19 2) 38 3) 39 4) 58

Practice 22
How many nucleons are there in an atom with a nuclear charge of +20 and 23 neutrons?
1) 58 2) 20 3) 3 4) 43

Practice 23
What is the nuclear charge of an atom with 16 protons, 18 electrons, and 17 neutrons?
1) +16   3) +18
2) +17   4) +33

E3 Scholastic Publishing. ©2017 All Rights Reserved

Isotopes
Same Element. Same Protons. Different Neutrons. Different Mass.

Isotopes are different atoms of the same element. They have the same number of protons but different numbers of neutrons.

For example: There are a few different atoms of the element lithium. The nucleus of all atoms of lithium contains the same number of protons. The difference between these atoms is the number of neutrons in the nucleus. Since all lithium atoms have the same number of protons (3), they all have the same atomic number of 3. Since they have different numbers of neutrons, they have different mass numbers.

These different atoms of lithium are referred to as isotopes of lithium.

Isotopes of the same element must have:

- *Different* mass numbers
- *Different* amounts of nucleons

- *Same* atomic number
- *Same* number of protons
- *Same* number of electrons
- *Same* chemical reactivity

- *Different* amounts of neutrons

7   mass number   8

$^{7}_{3}Li$ $^{8}_{3}Li$

3   atomic number   3

4 (mass number – atomic number) 5

Isotope Symbols

Isotopes of an element have different mass numbers. The mass number of an atom is written next to the element's name or symbol to distinguish that atom from the others.
Lithium–7 and Lithium–8 are names to two lithium isotopes. The 7 and 8 are the mass numbers of these two isotopes.

There are other notations that are used to represent isotopes of elements.

*Element – **mass number** (nuclide name)*	*Lithium – 7*	*Lithium – 8*
Symbol – **mass number** notation	*Li – 7*	*Li – 8*
Common isotope notation	$^{7}_{3}Li$	$^{8}_{3}Li$
Nuclear diagram notation	4 n / 3 p	5 n / 3 p

Isotope Symbols: Practice Questions

Concept Task: Be able recognize symbols that are isotopes of the same element.

Practice 24
Which two notations represent isotopes of the same element?

1) $^{40}_{19}K$ and $^{40}_{20}Ca$ 3) $^{23}_{11}Na$ and $^{24}_{12}Na$

2) $^{20}_{10}Ne$ and $^{22}_{10}Ne$ 4) $^{16}_{8}O$ and $^{17}_{8}N$

Practice 25
Which pair are isotopes of the same element?

1) $^{226}_{91}X$ and $^{226}_{91}X$ 3) $^{226}_{91}X$ and $^{227}_{91}X$

2) $^{227}_{91}X$ and $^{227}_{90}X$ 4) $^{226}_{90}X$ and $^{227}_{91}X$

Practice 26
Which two nucleus diagrams are from atoms of the same element?

1) (10 p / 10 n) (11 p / 11 n)   3) (18 p / 20 n) (18 p / 22 n)

2) (10 p / 11 n) (10 p / 11 n)   4) (18 p / 20 n) (20 p / 10 n)

Practice 27
Which isotope notation is correct for magnesium -26?

1) $^{26}_{26}Mg$ 3) $^{26}_{12}Mg$

2) $^{12}_{26}Mg$ 4) $^{14}_{12}Mg$

Practice 28
Which diagram correctly represents the nucleus for the isotope symbol $^{59}_{28}X$?

1) (59 p / 28 n)   3) (28 p / 59 n)

2) (31 p / 28 n)   4) (28 p / 31 n)

Practice 29
Each diagram below represents the nucleus of a different atom.

(1p)   (1p / 1n)   (1p / 2n)   (2p / 2n)
  D   E   Q   R

Which diagrams represent nuclei of the same element?

1) D and E, only   3) Q and R, only
2) D, E, and Q   4) Q, R, and E

The element boron, a trace element in Earth's crust, is found in foods produced from plants. Boron has only two naturally occurring stable isotopes, boron-10 and boron-11.

30. Write an isotopic notation of the heavier isotope of the element boron. Your response must include the atomic number, the mass number, and the symbol of this isotope.

31. State, in terms of subatomic particles, *one* difference between the nucleus of a carbon-11 atom and the nucleus of a boron-11 atom.

Two isotopes of potassium are K-37 and K-42.

32. Explain, in terms of subatomic particles, why K-37 and K-42 are isotopes of potassium.

33. How many valence electrons are in an atom of K-42 in the ground state?

Determining and Comparing Particles in Atoms

Example comparisons are given for the two atoms below.

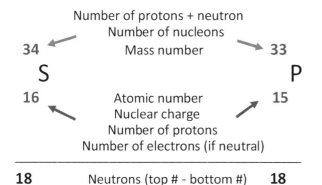

34	Number of protons + neutron Number of nucleons Mass number	33
S		P
16	Atomic number Nuclear charge Number of protons Number of electrons (if neutral)	15

___

18   Neutrons (top # - bottom #)   **18**

The following comparisons can be made of the two atoms to the left:

^{34}S has **more nucleons** than ^{33}P.

^{33}P has one **fewer proton** than ^{34}S.

^{34}S has a **greater nuclear charge** than ^{33}P.

P-33 has the **same** number of **neutrons** as **S-34**.

Determining and Comparing Particles in Atoms: Practice Questions

Concept Tasks: Be able to determine and compare number of subatomic particles from any given isotope notation. *Be sure to utilize the periodic table.*

Practice 34
What is the total number of protons and neutrons in the nuclide, ^{127}I ?
1) 53   2) 127   3) 74   4) 180

Practice 35
The nucleus of the atom, $^{107}_{47}$Ag,   contains

1) 60 neutrons, and has a nuclear charge of +47
2) 60 electrons, and has a nuclear charge of +47
3) 47 neutrons, and has a nuclear charge of +107
4) 47 electrons, and has a nuclear charge of +107

Practice 36
What is the structure of krypton - 85?
 1) 49 electrons, 49 protons, and 85 neutrons
 2) 49 electrons, 49 protons, and 49 neutrons
 3) 36 electrons, 36 protons, and 85 neutrons
 4) 36 electrons, 36 protons, and 49 neutrons

Practice 37
The nucleus of chlorine – 35 has
 1) 17 protons, and the atom has a mass number of 35
 2) 17 electrons, and the atom has a mass number of 35
 3) 35 protons, and the atom has a mass number of 17
 4) 35 electrons, and the atom has a mass number of 17

Practice 38
An atom of K- 37 and an atom of K – 42 differ in their total number of
1) electrons   3) neutrons
2) protons   4) positron

Practice 39
Compare to the atom of $^{40}_{20}$Ca, the atom of $^{38}_{18}$Ar has

 1) a greater nuclear charge
 2) the same number of nuclear charge
 3) greater number of neutrons
 4) the same number of neutrons

Practice 40
Which nuclide contains the greatest number of neutrons?
1) ^{207}Pb   2) ^{203}Hg   3) ^{207}Ti   4) ^{208}Bi

Practice 41
Which symbol has the smallest nuclear charge?
1) Cu – 65   3) Zn – 64
2) Ga – 69   4) Ge - 72

Practice 42
In which nucleus is the ratio of protons to neutrons 1 : 1?
1) B – 12   3) C – 13
2) N – 14   4) O – 15

Atomic Mass Unit (u)
Based on Carbon-12

An **atomic mass unit (amu** or **u)** is the unit for measuring the mass of an atom or a particle by comparing it to the mass of carbon – 12.

$$1 \text{ u} = \frac{1}{12}\text{th the mass of } {}^{12}C$$

Interpretations:

Hydrogen – **1** (1 u) has a mass that is $1/12$th the mass of ${}^{12}C$.

Lithium – **6 (**6 u) has a mass that is $6/12$th, half, the mass of ${}^{12}C$.

Magnesium – **24** (24 u) has a mass that is $24/12$th, 2 times, the mass of ${}^{12}C$

Practice 43

Which could have an atom with a mass that is approximately three times that is of C-12?

1) O   3) Li

2) Cl   4) Kr

Atomic Mass
Average Mass of all Naturally Stable Isotopes of an Atom. Based on Mass and Relative Abundance.

The **atomic mass** of an element is the weighted average mass of all the naturally occurring stable isotopes of that element. Natural samples of an element consist of a mix of two or more isotopes (different atoms). Usually, there is a lot of one isotope and very little of the others. The atomic mass of an element given on the Periodic Table is calculated from both the *masses* and the *relative abundances* (percentages) of the *individual naturally occurring isotopes* of that element.

For example:
A natural sample of chlorine consists mainly of two isotopes; Chlorine atoms with a mass of 35 **(Cl-35)** and chlorine atoms with a mass of 37 **(Cl-37).** The relative (percent) abundances of these isotopes are approximately 75% of Cl-35 and 25% of Cl-37. That means three of every four chlorine atoms in a natural sample of chlorine will have a mass of 35 amu as shown below.

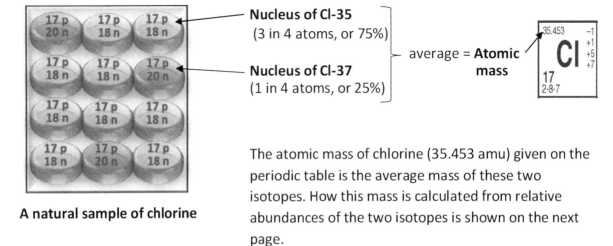

A natural sample of chlorine

The atomic mass of chlorine (35.453 amu) given on the periodic table is the average mass of these two isotopes. How this mass is calculated from relative abundances of the two isotopes is shown on the next page.

Concept Task: Be able to calculate the average weighted atomic mass of an element given the naturally occurring isotopes and their percent abundances.

Example 1

A natural sample of chlorine contains 75.76% of ^{35}Cl (atomic mass = 34.97 u) and 24.24% of ^{37}Cl (atomic mass = 36.97 u). Calculate the atomic mass of chlorine. Show a setup.

	^{35}Cl	^{37}Cl	*isotopes given*
Step 1:	.7576	.2424	*change % given to decimal*
Step 2:	x 34.97 u	x 36.97 u	*multiply by atomic mass of the isotope*

Step 3: (.7576 x 34.97 u) + (.2424 x 36.97 u) *numerical setup (add both products)*

26.493 + 8.961 = **35.454 u** *result (atomic mass of Cl)*

Example 2

The data table to the right shows three isotopes of neon. Calculate the atomic mass of neon.

Isotope	Atomic Mass (atomic mass units)	Percent Natural Abundance
^{20}Ne	19.99	90.9%
^{21}Ne	20.99	0.3%
^{22}Ne	21.99	8.8%

	Ne-20	Ne-21	Ne-22
Step 1:	.909	.003	.088
Step 2:	x 19.99 u	x 20.99 u	x 21.99 u

Step 3: (.909 x 19.99 u) + (.003 x 20.99 u) + (.088 x 21.99 u) *numerical setup*

18.171 u + .063 u + 1.935 u = **20.169 u** *result (atomic mass'*

Practice 44

Which statement best explains why most atomic masses on the Periodic Table are decimal numbers?
1) Atomic masses are determined relative to an H−1 standard.
2) Atomic masses are determined relative to an O−16 standard.
3) Atomic masses are a weighted average of the naturally occurring isotopes.
4) Atomic masses are an estimated average of the artificially produced isotopes.

Practice 45

Two isotopes of element X have average atomic mass of 54 amu. What are the relative percentages of these two isotopes of element X?
1) 80% of ^{50}X and 20% of ^{55}X
2) 20% of ^{50}X and 80% of ^{55}X
3) 50% of ^{50}X and 50% of ^{55}X
4) 75% of ^{50}X and 25% of ^{55}X

Practice 46

A sample of naturally occurring boron contains 19.78% of boron-10 (atomic mass = 10.01 u) and 80.22% of boron-11 (atomic mass = 11.01 u). Which numerical setup can be used to determine the atomic mass of naturally occurring boron?
1) (0.1978)(10.01) + (0.8022)(11.01)
2) (0.8022)(10.01) + (0.1978)(11.01)
3) (0.1978)(10.01)/(0.8022)(11.01)
4) (0.8022)(10.01)/(0.1978)(11.01)

Practice 47

Show a numerical setup and the calculated atomic mass of silicon given the following three natural isotopes.

92.23% of ^{28}Si (atomic mass = 27.98 u)

4.67% of ^{29}Si (atomic mass = 28.98 u)

3.10% of ^{30}Si (atomic mass = 29.97 u)

Lesson 3 – Location and Arrangements of Electrons

According to the wave-mechanical model of atoms, electrons are found in orbitals outside the nucleus. An **orbital** describes the most probable or likely region outside the nucleus where an electron can be found. The orbital of valence electron depends on the energy of the electron. While one electron of an atom may have enough energy to occupy an orbital far from the nucleus, another electron of that same atom may have just enough energy to occupy a region closer to the nucleus. The result is the formation of energy levels or electron shells around the nucleus of the atom. The arrangement of electrons in atoms is complex. In this lesson, you will learn the basic and simplified arrangement of electrons in electron shells. You will also learn of electron transition or movement from one shell to another, and the production of bright-line spectra of colors.

Electron Shells and Electron Configurations

Electron shells refer to the orbits of electrons around the nucleus of an atom.
• The first electron shell is the closest to the nucleus, and contains electrons with the least amount of energy.
• The electron shell farthest from the nucleus contains electrons with the most amount of energy.
• On the Periodic Table, the period or horizontal row number of an element indicates the total number of electron shells in the atom of that element.

Electron configuration shows the arrangement of electrons in an atom.
The electron configuration of an atom can be found in the box of the element on the Periodic Table.

Bohr or shell diagram can be drawn to show electrons in the electron shells of an atom.

Periodic Table for Phosphorus

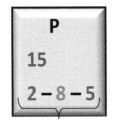

Electron Configuration

1st shell: **2** electrons

2nd shell: **8** electrons

3rd shell: **5** electrons

Bohr's (Shell) Diagram for P

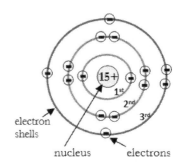

Valence Electrons
Electrons in the Outer (Last) Shell

Valence electrons are the electrons in the outermost electron shell of an atom. The valence shell of an atom is the outermost shell that contains electrons. The number of valence electrons in an atom is always the last number in the configuration.
• Elements in the same group or vertical column of the Periodic Table have the *same number of valence electrons*, therefore, *similar chemical reactivity*.

Phosphorus has **5 valence** electrons. Its valence shell is the 3rd shell.

Interpreting Electron Configurations

Concept Task: Be able to interpret electron configurations

Study the electron configuration below.

$$2 - 8 - 8 - 1$$

1st   2nd   3rd   4th

E L E C T R O N   S H E L L

4 electron shells (the atom is in the 4th Period)
1st shell is the shell containing electrons with lowest energy
4th shell is the shell containing electrons with greatest energy
4th shell is the valence (outermost) shell
1 is the number of valence electrons
19 is the total number of electrons (2 + 8 + 8 + 1 = 19)

The configuration is of a neutral K atom in the ground state.

Practice 48
How many electron shells containing electrons are found in an atom of strontium?
1) 2   2) 5   3) 18   4) 38

Practice 49
Which of these atoms in the ground state has the most number of electron shells containing electrons?
1) Cs–132   3) Xe–134
2) I–127   4) Na–23

Practice 50
In the electron configuration 2 – 8 – 3 – 1, which shell contains electrons with the greatest energy?
1) 1st   2) 2nd   3) 3rd   4) 4th

Practice 51
In a bromine atom in the ground state, the electrons that has the least amount of energy are located in the
1) first electron shell   3) third electron shell
2) second electron shell   4) fourth electron shell

Practice 52
How do the energy and the most probable location of an electron in the third shell of an atom compare to the energy and the most probable location of an electron in the first shell of the same atom?
1) In the third shell, an electron has more energy and is closer to the nucleus.
2) In the third shell, an electron has more energy and is farther from the nucleus.
3) In the third shell, an electron has less energy and is closer to the nucleus.
4) In the third shell, an electron has less energy and is farther from the nucleus.

Practice 53
Which element has a total of 5 valence electrons present in the fifth shell?
1) Sb   2) Bi   3) I   4) Br

Practice 54
Which set of symbols represents atoms with valence electrons in the same electron shell?
1) Ba, Br, Bi   3) O, S, Te
2) Sr, Sn, I   4) Mn, Hg, Cu

Base your answers to questions 55 and 56 on the information below and on your knowledge of chemistry.

The Bohr model of the atom was developed in the early part of the twentieth century. A diagram of the Bohr model for one atom, in the ground state, of a specific element, is shown below. The nucleus of this atom contains 4 protons and 5 neutrons.

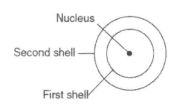

Bohr Model

Nucleus

Second shell

First shell

55. State the number of electrons in *each* shell in this atom in the ground state.
Number of electrons in first shell:

Number of electrons in second shell:

56 State the atomic number and the mass number of this element.
Atomic number:

Mass number:

Ground State, Excited State, and Spectral Lines

An atom is most stable when its electrons occupy the lowest available electron shells. When this is the case, the atom is said to be in the ground state. When one or more electrons of an atom occupy a higher energy level than they should, the atom is said to be in the excited state. Facts related to ground and excited state atoms are summarized below.

Ground State Atom: *Low Energy, Normal Configuration*

When an atom is in the ground state:

- The electron configuration is the same as given on the periodic table.
- Electrons are filled in order from the lowest to highest energy shell.
- Energy of the atom is at its lowest, and the atom is stable.
- A ground state electron must *absorb* energy to go from a low shell to a higher shell. Ex. from 2nd to 3rd.

14.0067

N

7
2-5

◄—— **Ground state** configuration for nitrogen.

Same as on the Periodic Table

Excited State Atom: *High Energy State*

When an atom is in the excited state:

- The electron configuration is different from that on the periodic table
- The energy of the atom is at its highest, and the atom is unstable
- An excited state must *release* energy to return from a high shell to a lower level. Ex. From 3rd to 2nd.
- A *spectrum of colors* is produced when an excited electron releases energy and returns to the ground state.

N

7

1 − 6

2 − 4 − 1

Two possible **excited state** configurations for nitrogen.

These configurations are different from that on the periodic table for nitrogen, *but* the **total number of electrons is still 7.**

Excited and Ground State Configurations: Practice Questions

Concept Task: Be able to determine if an electron configuration is in the ground or excited state. Be sure to utilize the Periodic Table.

Practice 57
Which is the ground state configuration for a chlorine atom?
1) 2 − 8 − 7   3) 2 − 8 − 8 − 7
2) 2 − 8 − 8   4) 2 − 8 − 6 − 1

Practice 58
Which electron configuration is possible for a strontium atom in the excited state?
1) 2 − 8 − 18 − 10   3) 2 − 8 − 18 − 8 − 1
2) 2 − 8 − 18 − 7 − 3   4) 2 − 8 − 18 − 8 − 2

Practice 59
Which is an excited state electron configuration for a neutral atom with 16 protons and 18 neutrons?
1) 2 − 8 − 5 − 1   3) 2 − 8 − 6 − 2
2) 2 − 8 − 8   4) 2 − 8 − 6

Practice 60
The electron configuration 2 − 8 − 2 is of a
1) sodium atom in the ground state
2) magnesium atom in the ground state
3) sodium atom in the excited state
4) magnesium atom in the excited state

Practice 61
The electron configuration 2−8−18−5−1 could be of
1) an arsenic atom in the ground state
2) an arsenic atom in the excited state
3) a selenium atom in the ground state
4) a selenium atom in the excited state

Bright-line Spectrum

Energy Released by an Excited Electron Returning to the Ground State

A **bright-line spectrum** is produced when an electron in an excited state releases or emits energy as it returns to the ground state. When viewed through a *spectroscope,* the light energy released by the electrons separates into bright, colored lines. Just like a *"fingerprint,"* each element produces a unique pattern of lines. Each colored line corresponds to a specific wavelength in the visible light part of the spectrum.

Spectral lines (bright-line spectra)

The chart below shows the bright-line spectra for hydrogen, lithium, sodium and potassium. A bright-line spectrum of an unknown mixture is compared to those of H, Li, Na and K. The elements in the unknown mixture can be identified by matching the lines in the unknown to those for H, Li, Na and K.

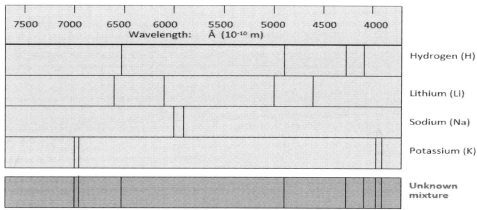

The unknown mixture contains **potassium** and **hydrogen.**
Lines in the spectrum of the unknown match all the lines
in the spectra for potassium and hydrogen.

Flame Test

For Identification of Metallic Ions

A **flame test** is a lab procedure in which compounds of metallic ions are heated over a Bunsen burner to produce different flame colors.
• The flame color that is produced is the light energy released by an excited electron returning to the ground or low state of the atom.
The color of the flame that is observed can be used to identify the metal ion that's in the substance. However, since two or more metallic ions can produce similar colors, flame test results are not very reliable for identification.
A **spectroscope** is a device that is used to separate light into color patterns or spectra at different wavelengths. When a flame color produced during a flame test procedure is viewed through a spectroscope, it is separated into bright-line spectra. Each flame color will produce a unique bright-line spectrum, which provides a more reliable result for identification of the metal ion in each compound

Electron Transition: Practice Questions

Concept Task: Be able to determine which electron transition will produce spectral lines.

Low to higher shell
Ex. 5th shell to 6th shell
• Energy is absorbed or gained by the electron

High to Lower shell
Ex. 6th shell to 5th shell
• Energy is released or emitted by the electron
• Bright-line spectra is produced

Practice 62
As an electron moves from the 3rd electron shell to the 4th electron shell, the energy of the atom
1) increases as the electron absorbs energy
2) increases as the electron releases energy
3) decreases as the electron absorbs energy
4) decreases as the electron releases energy

Practice 63
Electron transition between which two electron shells will produce bright-line spectrum of colors?
1) 2nd to 3rd   3) 1st to 4th
2) 3rd to 4th   4) 2nd to 1st

Practice 64
As an electron in an atom moves between electron shells, which transition would cause the electron to absorb the most energy?
1) 1st to 2nd   3) 2nd to 4th
2) 2nd to 1st   4) 4th to 2nd

Base your answers to practice questions 65 through 67 on the information below.

The bright-line spectra for three elements and a mixture of elements are shown below.

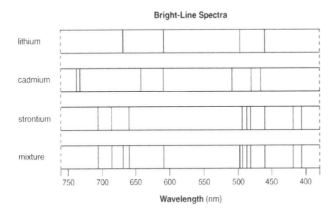

Bright-Line Spectra

65. State the total number of valence electrons in a cadmium atom in the ground state.

66. Identify all the elements in the mixture.

67. Explain, in terms of both electrons and energy, how the bright-line spectrum of an element is produced.

Base your answer to the practice question 68 on the information below.

An atom in an excited state has an electron configuration of 2-7-2.

68. Write the electron configuration of this atom in the ground state.

E3 Scholastic Publishing. ©2017 All Rights Reserved

Lesson 4 – Neutral Atoms and Ions

Other than the noble gases in group 18, elements have incomplete valence or outermost electron shells. For this reason, most elements need to lose, gain or share electrons when bonding to get a full valence shell and become more stable. A neutral atom may lose all its valence electrons to form a new valence shell that is filled. A neutral atom may also gain or share electrons to fill its valence shell. An ion is formed when a neutral atom loses or gains electrons.

Neutral Atoms: *Equal Numbers of Electrons and Protons*
A neutral atom has an equal number of protons and electrons. The electron configuration given on the Periodic Table for each element is for the neutral atom in the ground state.

Ions: *Unequal Numbers of Electrons and Protons*
An ion is a charged atom with unequal numbers of electrons and protons.
An ion is formed when a neutral atom loses or gains electrons.
An ion has a different chemical property and reactivity from the neutral atom.

A **positive ion** is a charged atom with **fewer electrons (-)** than protons (+).
- A positive ion is formed when a neutral atom loses one or more electrons.
- Metals and metalloids tend to lose electrons and form positive ions.
- Ionic radius or size of a positive ion is always smaller than the atomic radius because the ion has one *fewer electron shell.*

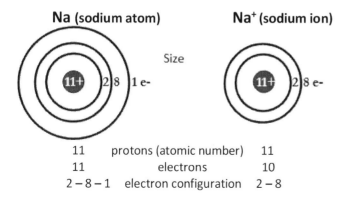

11	protons (atomic number)	11
11	electrons	10
2 – 8 – 1	electron configuration	2 – 8

A **negative ion** is a charged atom with **more electrons (-)** than protons (+).
- A negative ion is formed when a neutral atom gains one or more electrons.
- Nonmetals tend to gain electrons and form negative ions.
- The ionic radius or size of a negative ion is always larger than the atomic radius because the ion has *more electrons*.

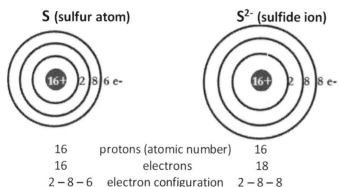

16	protons (atomic number)	16
16	electrons	18
2 – 8 – 6	electron configuration	2 – 8 – 8

Charge of ion = atomic number – electrons
(number of protons)

Example 3
What is the charge of a manganese ion with 21 electrons?

Charge = atomic number – electrons
Charge = 24 – 21 = **+3**

Particles in Ions: Practice Questions

Practice 69
Which changes occur as an atom becomes a positively charge ion?
1) The atom gains electrons, and the number of protons increases.
2) The atom gains electrons, and the number of protons remains the same.
3) The atom loses electrons, and the number of protons decreases.
4) The atom loses electrons, and the number of protons remains the same.

Practice 70
A neutral oxygen atom (O) differs from an ion of oxygen (O^{2-}) in that the atom has
1) more protons   3) fewer protons
2) more electrons   4) fewer electrons

Practice 71
How does the size of N^{3-} ion compares to the size of N atom?
1) N^{3-} is bigger than N because the N^{3-} has 3 more electrons.
2) N^{3-} is bigger than N because the N^{3-} has 3 fewer electrons.
3) N^{3-} is smaller than N because the N^{3-} has 3 more electrons.
4) N^{3-} is smaller than N because the N^{3-} has 3 fewer electrons.

Practice 72
An ion of which element has a larger radius than an atom of the same element?
1) aluminum   2) chlorine   3) magnesium   4) lithium

Practice 73
The total number of electrons in a Br $^-$ ion is
1) 36   2) 35   3) 34   4) 54

Practice 74
What is the total number of electrons in a Cr^{3+} ion?
1) 3   2) 21   3) 24   4) 27

Practice 75
An atom has a nuclear charge of +50 and 46 electrons. The net ionic charge of this atom is
1) +46   2) -46   3) -4   4) +4

Practice 76
The electron configuration for As^{3-} is
1) $2-8-18-5$ 3) $2-8-17-6$
2) $2-8-18-8$ 4) $2-8-18-5-3$

Base your answers to questions 77 through 79 on the information below.

The atomic radius and the ionic radius for some Group 1 and some Group 17 elements are given in the tables below.

Atomic and Ionic Radii of Some Elements

Group 1

Particle	Radius (pm)
Li atom	130.
Li+ ion	78
Na atom	160.
Na+ ion	98
K atom	200.
K+ ion	133
Rb atom	215
Rb+ ion	148

Group 17

Particle	Radius (pm)
F atom	60.
F- ion	133
Cl atom	100.
Cl- ion	181
Br atom	117
Br- ion	?
I atom	136
I- ion	220.

77. Write both the name and the charge of the particle that is gained by an F atom when the atom becomes an F⁻ ion.

78. Explain, in terms of electron shells, why the radius of a K^+ ion is greater than the radius of an Na^+ ion.

79. Estimate the radius of a Br ⁻ ion.

                                         ©2017 E3 Scholastic Publishing. All Rights Reserved

Vocabulary

Lesson 1: Models of the Atom

Hard Sphere model	Empty Space model	Wave-mechanical model
Plum-pudding model	Bohr's model	Orbital

Lesson 2: Structure of an Atom

Atom	Electron	Mass number
Nucleus	Nucleon	Atomic mass
Neutron	Isotope	Atomic mass unit
Proton	Atomic number	

Lesson 3: Arrangement of Electrons

Electron shell	Bright-line spectrum	Valence electron
Ground state	Spectroscope	Lewis electron-dot diagram
Excited state	Flame test	
Quanta		

Lesson 4: Neutral Atoms and Ions

Neutral atom
Ion
Positive ion
Negative ion

1. 2
2. 1
3. 4
4. 2
5. 3

6. An atom is mostly empty space.
   Nucleus has a small, dense, positive charge
7. Both include a negative charged particle as one of the atomic particles.
8. protons
9. Thomson model

10. 4	14. 3	18. 1	22. 4	26. 3
11. 1	15. 4	19. 4	23. 1	27. 4
12. 2	16. 3	20. 2	24. 2	28. 4
13. 2	17. 2	21. 3	25. 3	29. 2

30. $_{5}^{11}B$

31. Carbon-11 has more protons.   Carbon 11 has fewer neutrons.
    Boron -11 has fewer protons.   B-11 has more neutrons.

32. They both contain the same number of protons, but different numbers of neutrons.
33. one (1) valence electron.

34. 2	37. 1	40. 3	43. 2	46. 1
35. 1	38. 3	41. 1	44. 3	
36. 4	39. 4	42. 2	45. 2	

47. (.9223 x 27.98) + (.0467 x 28.98) + (0.0310 x 29.97) = **28.09 u**

48. 2	50. 4	52. 2	54. 2
49. 1	51. 1	53. 1	

55. Number of electrons in first shell: **2**
    Number of electrons in second shell: **2**

56. Atomic number: **4**
    Mass number: **9 u**

57. 1	60. 2	63. 4	65. 2
58. 2	61. 4	64. 3	
59. 1	62. 1		

66. Lithium and strontium, Li and Sr

67. Bright-line spectrum is produced when excited electrons release energy as they returned to the ground state

68. 2-8-1

69. 4
70. 4
71. 1
72. 2
73. 1
74. 2
75. 4
76. 2

77. electron, -1

78. A K^+ ion has more electron shells than an Na^+ ion.
    Na^+ ion has two electron shells, K^+ ion has three electron shells.

79. Any value between 190 pm to 210 pm is reasonable.

Topic 4
Chemical Bonding

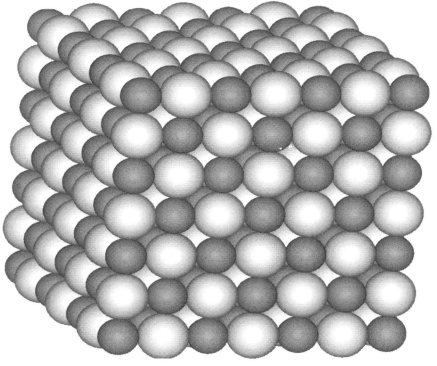

Lesson 1: Stability and Energy in Bonding

Lesson 2: Types of Chemical Bonds and Substances

Lesson 3: Molecular Polarity and Intermolecular Forces

Lesson 4: Lewis Electron-dot Diagrams in Bonding

Lesson 1: Chemical Bonding and Atom Stability

Chemical bonding is the simultaneous attraction of two positive nuclei to negative electrons. Chemical bonding is the "glue" that holds particles (atoms, ions, or molecules) together in matter. Since most atoms do not have full valence shells, they must bond with other atoms. When atoms bond, energy of the atoms decreases as they become more stable.

In this lesson, you will learn about stability and energy in bonding.

Bonding and Stability

A Bonded Atom is Similar to its Nearest Noble Gas, and is More Stable.

Atoms bond so they can attain full valence shells and become stable.

The **octet rule** states that a stable valence shell configuration must have eight electrons.

• An atom can get a full and stable valence shell configuration by

       transferring or **accepting electrons** (during ionic bonding)

       or

       sharing electrons (during covalent bonding)

• Each atom in a bond has an electron configuration that is similar to its *nearest noble gas* atom.

For example:

In a bond between sodium and chlorine in the compound NaCl:

Na (atomic number 11) resembles Ne (atomic number 10). Cl (atomic number 17) resembles Ar (atomic number 18).

In **NaCl**, **Na** is the **Na$^+$** ion (10 electrons). The configuration of Na$^+$ is 2–8, which is the same as that of Ne, 2–8.

 In a bond, Na resembles Ne.

In NaCl, **Cl** is the **Cl$^-$** ion (18 electrons). The configuration of Cl$^-$ is 2–8–8, which is the same as that of Ar, 2–8–8.

 In a bond, Cl resembles Ar.

Practice 1
When a sulfur atom bonds with sodium atoms to form the compound Na$_2$O, the configuration of oxygen in the compound is similar to
1) Na   3) Ne
2) O   4) Ar

Practice 2
The electron configuration of Sr and H ions in the formula SrH$_2$ are similar to those of elements
1) Kr and He   3) Ar and Ne
2) Rb and He   4) Ca and Li

Practice 3
Atom X and atom Y bond to form a compound. The electron configuration of X in the bond is 2 – 8 – 8. The electron configuration of Y in the compound is 2 – 8. Which two atoms could be X and Y?
1) X could be magnesium and Y could be sulfur
2) X could be calcium and Y could be sulfur
3) X could be magnesium and Y could be nitrogen
4) X could be calcium and Y could be nitrogen

Base your answers to practice questions 4 and 5 on the information below.

Ozone, O$_3$(g), is produced from oxygen, O$_2$(g), by electrical discharge during thunderstorms. The unbalanced equation below represents the reaction that forms ozone.

$$O_2(g) \xrightarrow{\text{electricity}} O_3(g)$$

4. Explain, in terms of electron configuration, why an oxygen molecule is more stable than an oxygen atom.

5. Explain why the equation represents a chemical change.

 ©2017 E3 Scholastic Publishing. All Rights Reserved

Chemical Bonding and Energy

All chemical substances contain some potential energy.

Potential energy is *stored in the bonds* holding particles of substances together.

The amount of potential energy of a substance depends on the *composition and structure* of the substance.

Bond formation between two atoms is exothermic.
Exothermic processes release heat energy.

$$H \ + \ Cl \ \rightarrow \ H-Cl \ + \ \textbf{Energy}$$

As energy is released when two atoms form a bond:
- Potential energy of the atoms decreases.
- Stability of the atoms increases.
- Stability of the chemical system increases.

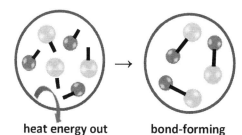

heat energy out   bond-forming

Bond breakage is endothermic.
Endothermic processes absorb heat energy.

$$H-Cl \ + \ \textbf{Energy} \ \rightarrow \ H \ + \ Cl$$

As energy is absorbed during the breaking of a bond
- Potential energy of the atoms increases.
- Stability of the atoms decreases.
- Stability of the chemical system decreases.

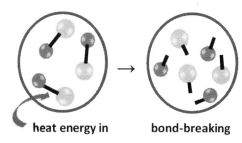

heat energy in   bond-breaking

Chemical Bonding and Energy: Practice Questions

Concept Task: Be able to relate energy to bonding.

Practice 6
When two atoms form a bond to produce a chemical substance, the stability of the chemical system
1) decreases as energy is absorbed
2) increases as energy is absorbed
3) decreases as energy is released
4) increases as energy is released

Practice 7
Given the balanced equation:

$$I_2 \ + \ energy \ \rightarrow \ I \ + \ I$$

Which statement describes the process represented by this equation?
1) A bond is formed, and energy is absorbed.
2) A bond is formed, and energy is released.
3) A bond is broken, and energy is absorbed.
4) A bond is broken, and energy is released.

Practice 8
Given the equation

$$H_2 \ + \ O_2 \ \rightarrow \ H_2O$$

Which statement best describes the process taking place as bonds are broken and formed?

1) The breaking of O–O bond releases energy.
2) The breaking of H–H bond releases energy.
3) The forming of H–O bond absorbs energy.
4) The forming of H–O bond releases energy.

Practice 9
When two fluorine atoms combined to form a molecule of fluorine, energy is
1) always absorbed
2) always released
3) sometimes absorbed
4) sometimes released

Lesson 2 – Types of Chemical Bonds and Substances
Ionic, covalent, and metallic

Intramolecular forces are bonds that hold atoms together to create molecules and compounds. *Ionic, covalent,* and *metallic* are types of bonding between the atoms of a substance. Bonding between atoms is a result of atoms competing for electrons to fill their valence shells.
In this lesson, you will learn about the types of bonding between atoms, and types of substances and their properties.

Ionic Bonds
Transfer of Electrons from a Metal to a Nonmetal

Ionic bonds are forces holding charged particles together in ionic compounds. Ionic bonds are formed by the transfer of one or more electrons from a metal to a nonmetal.

- The metal atom always loses or transfers electrons and becomes a positively charged ion.

- The nonmetal atom always gains or accepts electrons and becomes a negatively charged ion.

- An ionic bond is formed by the electrostatic attraction between the positive metal ions and the negative nonmetal ions.

- The electronegativity difference between the nonmetal and metal atoms in an ionic bond is usually 1.7 or greater.

Ionic compounds are formed by positively and negatively charged particles. There are two categories of ionic compounds.

Ionic Compounds with Only Ionic Bonds: *Composed of Two Elements*
These compounds are composed of two different atoms. They are *binary* ionic compounds composed of positively charged metal and negatively charged nonmetal atoms.
Example compounds in this category are given below.

NaCl	**K$_2$O**	**LiBr**
sodium chloride	*potassium oxide*	*lithium bromide*

Ionic Compounds with Both Ionic and Covalent Bonds: *Composed of Three or more Elements*
These compounds usually have three or more different atoms because they contain a polyatomic ion. Polyatomic ions (**See Table E**) are ions usually containing two or more nonmetal atoms with an excess charge. Bonding within most polyatomic ions is *covalent*. Compounds of this category are generally formed by the electrostatic attraction (*ionic bond*) between a positive metal (or NH_4^+) and a negative polyatomic ion.
Example compounds in this category are given below.

NaNO$_3$	**CaSO$_4$**	**(NH$_4$)$_2$O**
sodium nitrate	*calcium sulfate*	*ammonium oxide*

Physical Properties of Ionic Substances
- Hard, brittle, crystalline *solids* at STP
- High melting points • Soluble in water
- Electrolytes; good electrical conductivity as *liquids* or in *aqueous* solutions. Conductivity is due to *mobile (free moving) ions* in liquid and aqueous forms.

---

metal   nonmetal

22.98977	+1
Na	
11	
2-8-1	

35.453	−1
Cl	+1 +5 +7
17	
2-8-7	

loses ↓   gains ↓
e-   e-

Na$^+$ Cl$^-$

Na$^+$ Cl$^-$

Ionic bond
Electrostatic attraction between the positive and negative ions.

Opposites attract.

Table E: Polyatomic Ions

Formula	Name	Formula	Name
H$_3$O$^+$	hydronium	CrO$_4^{2-}$	chromate
Hg$_2^{2+}$	mercury(I)	Cr$_2$O$_7^{2-}$	dichromate
NH$_4^+$	ammonium	MnO$_4^-$	permanganate
C$_2$H$_3$O$_2^-$ CH$_3$COO$^-$	acetate	NO$_2^-$	nitrite
		NO$_3^-$	nitrate

Metal ion   Polyatomic ion

Na$^+$ N O$_3^-$

Na$^+$ N O$_3^-$

Ionic bond   Covalent bond
(forms compound)   (forms Polyatomic ion)

Covalent Bonds
Sharing of Electrons by Two Nonmetals

Covalent bonds are forces holding atoms of nonmetals together in covalent and molecular substances. Covalent bonding occurs when two nonmetal atoms share their valence electrons.
- The electronegativity difference between the two nonmetals in a covalent bond is usually less than 1.7.
- A single or multiple (double or triple) covalent bond can form between two nonmetal atoms depending on the number of electrons they share.
- Sharing in covalent bonds could be *equal* or *unequal*.

Polar Covalent: *Unequal Sharing by Two Different Nonmetals*
Polar covalent bonds are formed by unequal sharing of electrons between two different nonmetal atoms. A polar covalent bond is the most common type of bond between atoms of molecular substances. *Examples:* HCl and CO.

Nonpolar Covalent: *Equal Sharing by the Same Nonmetal*
Nonpolar covalent bonds are formed by equal sharing of electrons between two of the same nonmetal atoms. Nonpolar bonds are commonly found in diatomic (two-atom) elements. *Examples:* fluorine, F_2, and nitrogen, N_2.

Molecular substances are substances containing molecules. A **molecule** is a group of covalently bonded atoms. A molecular substance is classified as polar or nonpolar depending on the symmetry of its molecules.

Polar Substances: *Asymmetrical Molecules. Uneven Charge Distribution.*
Polar molecular substances contain molecules that have asymmetrical structures. A molecule is asymmetrically shaped when charges are *unevenly distributed* within the molecule. Uneven charge distribution means that the molecule has positive and negative ends. A polar molecule is only formed by polar covalently bonded atoms, as in HBr and NH_3.

Nonpolar Substances: *Symmetrical Molecules. Even Charge Distribution.*
Nonpolar molecular substances contain molecules that have symmetrical structures. A molecule is symmetrically shaped when charges are *evenly distributed* within the molecule. Even charge distribution means that the molecule does not have positive and negative ends. Nonpolar means no poles. A nonpolar molecule can be formed by nonpolar covalently bonded atoms (as in O_2) or by polar covalently bonded atoms (as in CH_4).

Physical Properties of Molecular Substances
- Could be a *solid, liquid* or *gas* • Low melting points
- Low solubility in water • Nonelectrolytes (except for acids).

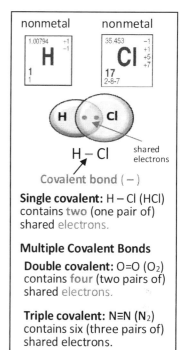

nonmetal   **nonmetal**

Single covalent: H – Cl (HCl) contains two (one pair of) shared electrons.

Multiple Covalent Bonds

Double covalent: O=O (O_2) contains four (two pairs of) shared electrons.

Triple covalent: N≡N (N_2) contains six (three pairs of) shared electrons.

Polar covalent bond *(different atoms)*

H – Cl   C = O

Nonpolar covalent bond *(same atom)*

F – F   N ≡ N

Polar substances *(asymmetrical)*

hydrogen bromide (HBr)

H – Br

ammonia (NH_3)

H – N – H
  |
  H

Nonpolar substances *(symmetrical)*

oxygen (O_2)

O = O   with nonpolar bonds

methane (CH_4)

H
  |
H – C – H   with polar bonds
  |
  H

Other Types of Covalent Bonds

Coordinate Covalent Bonds: *Found in Polyatomic Ions*
A coordinate covalent bond is formed when both shared electrons are provided by only one of the atoms in the bond.
• The bond is formed when H^+ (hydrogen ion, proton), which does not have an electron, bonds with a molecule such as NH_3 (ammonia) or H_2O (water)

• NH_3 and H_2O molecules have lone pairs of electrons that they can share with an H^+ (hydrogen ion, proton) that has no electron. Two polyatomic ions containing coordinate covalent bonds are given below. These ions are listed on **Reference Table E – Selected Polyatomic Ions**

H_3O^+ (hydronium ion) *forms from* H_2O (water) and H^+ (hydrogen ion).

NH_4^+ (ammonium ion*) forms from* NH_3 (ammonia) and H^+ (hydrogen ion).

Network Covalent Bonds: *No Discrete Particles*
A network covalent bond holds the nonmetal atoms of a network solid compound together. Compounds formed by network covalent bonding cannot exist as discrete individual molecules. Below are three network solid compounds.

SiO_2	SiC	C
(Silicon dioxide)	*(Silicon carbide)*	*(Diamond)*

Physical Properties of Network Solids
• Very hard *solids* at STP   • Extremely high melting points.
• Insoluble in water.   • No electrical conductivity

Metallic Bonds and Substances
Positive Metal Ions in Sea of Electrons

A metallic bond is the force that holds metal atoms together in metallic substances. Metallic bonding is described as "positive metal ions immersed in a sea of mobile valence electrons." Substances containing metallic bonds are metallic elements.

Ca (calcium)   **Au** (Gold)   **Fe** (iron) *(see Periodic Table)*

Physical Properties of Metallic Substances
• Hard *solids* at STP (except for mercury, Hg, a *liquid*)
• High melting points   • Insoluble in water
• Electrical conductivity due to *mobile (free moving) electrons.*

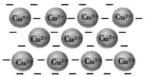

Metallic bonding in copper.
Positive Cu^{2+} ions in a sea of mobile valence electrons (−).

Type of Substance	Phase at Room Temp.	Physical Properties (Characteristics)		
		Melting Point	Conductivity	Solubility (in water)
Metallic	Solid (except Hg liquid)	Very High	Good (High) as solids and liquids	No (insoluble)
Ionic	Solid only	High	Good (High) as liquids and aqueous	Yes (soluble)
Molecular	Solid, liquid, gas	Low	Poor (low) in all phases	Yes (slightly soluble)
Network solid	solid only	Extremely high	Very poor in all phases	No (insoluble)

                                             ©2017 E3 Scholastic Publishing. All Rights Reserved

Types of Chemical Bonds: Summary Table

Bond Type	Type of Elements Involve in Bonding	Bond Description	Electronegativity Difference	Type of Substances Containing the Bond
Metallic	metal atoms of the same element	positive ions in sea of electrons	-------------	metallic substances (Ag, K, Cu)
Ionic	metal - nonmetal	transfer (losing and gaining) of electrons	1.7 or greater	ionic substances (NaCl, K2O, LiBr)
Covalent	nonmetals only	sharing of electrons	less than 1.7	molecular substances (H_2O, NH_3, CH_4, O_2,)
Polar covalent	two different nonmetals	unequal sharing of electrons	greater than 0 but less than 1.7	polar substances (H_2O, NH_3) nonpolar substances (CH_4, CO_2)
Nonpolar covalent	nonmetal atoms with the same electronegativity	equal sharing of electrons	zero (0)	diatomic molecules (H_2, O_2)
Coordinate Covalent	two different nonmetals	one atom provides both shared electrons	------------------	polyatomic ions (NH_3^+, H_3O^+)
Network solid covalent	nonmetals only	no discrete particles	------------------	network solids (C, SiC, SiO_2)

Types of Chemical Bonds: Practice Questions

Concept Task: Be able to facts relating to the different bond types.

Practice 10
Which type of bond is formed when electrons are shared between two atoms?
1) Covalent   3) Ionic
2) Metallic   4) Hydrogen

Practice 11
The transfer of electrons from a metal to a nonmetal will result in the formation of
1) hydrogen bond   3) ionic bond
2) covalent bond   4) metallic bond

Practice 12
Two atoms share electrons equally, the bond formed is mostly
1) polar and covalent
2) ionic and covalent
3) metallic and covalent
4) nonpolar and covalent

Practice 13
Two atoms with an electronegativity difference of 0.4 form a bond that is
1) ionic, because electrons are shared
2) ionic, because electrons are transferred
3) covalent, because electrons are shared
4) covalent, because electrons are transferred

Practice 14
When one atom loses one or more electrons to another, the bond formed between the two atoms is best described as
1) ionic with electronegativity difference greater than 1.7
2) ionic with electronegativity difference less than 1.7
3) covalent with electronegativity difference greater than 1.7
4) covalent with electronegativity difference less than 1.7

Practice 15
Atom X bonds with another atom X to form X_2 molecule. The bond in this molecule is
1) polar because electrons are shared equally
2) nonpolar because electrons are shared equally
3) polar because electrons are shared unequally
4) nonpolar because electrons are shared unequally

Practice 16
When a nonmetal atom forms ionic bond with a metal, the nonmetal becomes a
1) positive ion, because it had gained electrons
2) positive ion, because it had gained protons
3) negative ion, because it had gained electrons.
4) negative ion, because it had gained protons.

Concept Task: Be able to relate formulas to bond types.

Practice 17
Which formula contains ionic bonds?
1) ClO_2 2) SO_2 3) Li_2O 4) HI

Practice 18
In which compound would the atoms form a bond by sharing their electrons?
1) CS_2 2) CaS   3) AgI   4) Hg

Practice 19
Which two atoms are held together by a polar covalent bond?
1) H – H   3) Al – H
2) H – O   4) Al – O

Practice 20
In which substance do the atoms share electrons equally to form a bond?
1) SiC   2) Ag   3) NH_3 4) Br_2

Practice 21
Metallic bonding will form between the atoms of which substance?
1) Nickel   3) Carbon
2) Sodium chloride   4) Hydrogen

Practice 22
Which compound contains both ionic and covalent bonds?
1) Mg_3N_2 3) H_2O_2
2) $NaClO_3$ 4) O_2

Practice 23
Element X combines with rubidium to form an ionic bond. In which Group of the Periodic Table could element X be found?
1) Group 1   3) Group 2
2) Group 13   4) Group 16

Practice 24
Which element would most likely form a covalent bond with a chlorine atom?
1) Iron   3) Phosphorus
2) Beryllium   4) Potassium

Practice 25
Which pair of electron configurations belong to atoms that will share electrons when they bond with each other?
1) $2 - 8 - 2$ and $2 - 8 - 1$
2) $2 - 8 - 6$ and $2 - 8 - 18 - 7$
3) $2 - 8 - 18 - 8$ and $2 - 8 - 13 - 1$
4) $2 - 8 - 5$ and $2 - 8 - 18 - 8 - 1$

Practice 26
The structure of which molecule is nonpolar with polar covalent bonds?

1)   H – S
         |
         H

                       Cl
                       |
3) Cl – C – Cl
                        |
                        Cl

2) O = O   4) Na – F

Practice 27
Which substance is nonpolar with nonpolar covalent bonds?
1) I_2 3) $NaNO_3$
2) SO_2 4) CF_4

Practice 28
Which structural formula represents a polar molecule?
1) H – H   3) Na – H
2) H – Br   4) Cl – Cl

Practice 29
Which type of molecule is CF_4?
1) Polar, with a symmetrical distribution of charge.
2) Polar, with an asymmetrical distribution of charge.
3) Nonpolar, with a symmetrical distribution of charge.
4) Nonpolar, with an asymmetrical distribution of charge.

 ©2017 E3 Scholastic Publishing. All Rights Reserved

Types of Substances and Properties: Practice Questions

Practice 30
The compound $C_{12}H_{22}O_{11}$ is best described as
1) a molecular solid with low melting point and low electrical conductivity as aqueous
2) a molecular solid with high melting point and high electrical conductivity as aqueous
3) an ionic solid with low melting point and low electrical conductivity as aqueous
4) an ionic solid with high melting point and high electrical conductivity as aqueous

Practice 31
Which is a metallic substance?
1) C   3) Sn
2) H_2 4) F

Practice 32
Which substance at STP conducts electricity because the substance contains mobile electrons?
1) NaCl   3) Mg
2) S   4) HBr

Practice 33
Which is binary ionic compound?
1) CaS   3) CO_2
2) $CaSO_4$ 4) CH_4

Practice 34
Which compound contains both ionic and covalent bonds?
1) $AlCl_3$ 3) C_2H_6
2) NO_3 4) KNO_3

Practice 35
A solid substance was tested in the laboratory. The test results are listed below.
• Dissolves in water
• Is an electrolyte
• Melts at a high temperature
Based on these results, the solid substance could be
1) Cu   3) $CuBr_2$
2) C   4) $C_6H_{12}O_6$

Practice 36
Which is a molecular compound?
1) K_2O 3) Li_2SO_4
2) CH_4 4) Hg

Practice 37
Which two substances are covalent compounds?
1) $C_6H_{12}O_6(s)$ and $KI(s)$
2) $C_6H_{12}O_6(s)$ and $HCl(g)$
3) $KI(s)$ and $NaCl(s)$
4) $NaCl(s)$ and $HCl(g)$

Base your answers to practice questions 38 through 40 on the information below.

In 1864, the Solvay process was developed to make soda ash. One step in the process is represented by the balanced equation below.

$$NaCl + NH_3 + CO_2 + H_2O \rightarrow NaHCO_3 + NH_4Cl$$

38. Write the chemical formula for one compound in the equation that contains both ionic bonds and covalent bonds.

39. Explain, in terms of valence electrons, why the bonding in NaCl is ionic.

40. Write the chemical formula for one compound with bonding similar to NH_3.

Base your answers to practice questions 41 and 42 on the information below.

A student tested the conductivity of three magnesium substances and noted the following observations.

       Magnesium strip, Mg(s) .... Conducts electrical current
       Magnesium nitrate solid, $Mg(NO_3)_2(s)$............ No electrical conductivity
       Magnesium nitrate solution, $Mg(NO_3)_2(aq)$ .... Conducts electrical current

41. Explain, in terms of atomic particles, why the magnesium strip conducts electrical current.

42. Explain why the solution of magnesium nitrate conducts electrical current but the solid magnesium nitrate did not. Include both the solid and solution in your answer.

Lesson 3: Molecular Polarity and Intermolecular Forces

Bond polarity in a substance refers to the extent of the positive and negative electrical charges on two bonded atoms.
• Polarity of a bond depends largely on the *electronegativity difference (ED)* between the two atoms.
• The bigger the difference in electronegativity, the greater the ionic and polar characteristics of the bond.
• The smaller the difference in electronegativity, the greater the covalent characteristics of the bond.

Degree of Polarity
Depends on the Electronegativity Difference

Comparing degree of polarity between two or more substances can be done by determining and comparing the electronegativity difference (ED) of the bonded atoms.

To calculate electronegativity difference between two atoms in a bond:
Step 1 : **Use Table S** to get electronegativity values for the two atoms in each formula
Step 2: Determine ED = High electronegativity value – Low electronegativity value

To determine which formula is most or least ionic or polar, use the information below.
The formula with the **highest ED** is the **most ionic, most polar,** and **least covalent.**

The formula with the **lowest ED** is the **least ionic, least polar,** and **most covalent.**

Use the ED scale below to determine most and least characteristics of a bond.

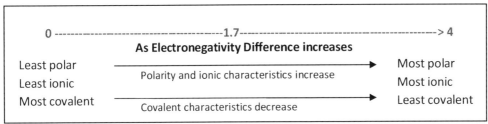

Concept Task: Be able to determine which formula is most or least ionic, covalent or polar.

The note below shows how to calculate electronegativity difference (ED) and compare degree of polarity for MgCl₂, LiCl, and KCl.

Table S

Atomic Number	Symbol	Electro-negativity
3	Li	1.0
12	Mg	1.3
17	Cl	3.2
19	K	0.8

MgCl₂	**LiCl**	**KCl**
Cl = 3.2	Cl = 3.2	Cl = 3.2
Mg = <u>1.3</u>	Li = <u>1.0</u>	K = <u>0.8</u>
ED 1.9	**2.2**	**2.4**
(Lowest ED)		*(Highest ED)*

MgCl₂ is
least ionic
least polar
most covalent

KCl is
most ionic
most polar
least covalent

Practice 43
Which bond is the least ionic?
1) Al – O   3) Li – O
2) N – O   4) S – O

Practice 44
The bonding in which compound has the greatest degree of ionic character?
1) KBr   3) HF
2) BeO   4) PCl₃

Practice 45
Which chemical bond has the greatest degree of covalent characteristics?
1) C – O   3) H – O
2) F – O   4) N – O

Practice 46
Which molecule is the most polar?
1) H – Br   3) H – Cl
2) H – F   4) H – I

©2017 E3 Scholastic Publishing. All Rights Reserved

Intermolecular Forces (IMFs)

Intermolecular forces are forces that exist between molecules in molecular substances. Intermolecular forces hold molecules of molecular substances together in liquid and solid states. These forces exist in molecular substances because of unequal charge distribution within molecules. Intermolecular forces are generally weaker than the intramolecular forces (bonding between atoms) of the substance. Three types of intermolecular forces are discussed below.

Dipole-dipole Interaction
Found in Polar Substances such as HCl, HBr, H_2O.

Polar substances are *dipole* because their molecules have two poles; positive and negative poles or ends. In a polar substance, the force of attraction between the molecules of the substance is called *dipole-dipole* interaction. This force of attraction exists between the positive end of one molecule and the negative end of another molecule. The more polar the substance, the stronger the dipole-dipole attraction between the molecules, and the higher the boiling point of the substance.

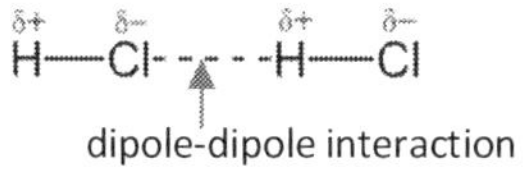

$$H\text{—}Cl \cdots H\text{—}Cl$$

dipole-dipole interaction

Hydrogen Bonding
Exists in H_2O, NH_3 and HF. Account for their High Boiling Points.

Hydrogen bonding is a strong dipole-dipole intermolecular force that exists in highly polar substances such as **H_2O** (water), **NH_3** (ammonia) and **HF** (hydrogen fluoride). Hydrogen bonding is the reason that water has a much higher boiling and melting points and lower vapor pressure than similar substances such as H_2S and H_2Te. The same is true for NH_3 and HF. The melting and boiling points of NH_3 and HF are much higher than those of similar substances, PH_3 and HCl respectively, because of the hydrogen bonding in NH_3 and HF. Hydrogen bonding exists in these three substances (H_2O, NH_3 and HF) but not in similar substances because the hydrogen atom in each substance is bonded to an atom (O, N, or F) that has a *small radius* and high *electronegativity.* The combination of small radius and high electronegativity allows molecules of H_2O, NH_3 and HF to be highly polar in comparison to similar substances. Hydrogen Bonding in water is shown below.

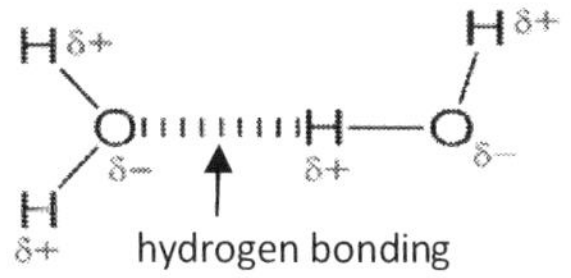

hydrogen bonding

London-dispersion (Van der Waals) Forces
Found in Nonpolar Substances

London-dispersion forces are weak intermolecular force that hold molecules of nonpolar substances together in the liquid and gas states. When electrons momentarily shift in nonpolar molecules, partial positive and negative charges occur on the molecules. A weak attraction bonds the positive end of one molecule to the negative end of another molecule. London-dispersion forces make it possible for a nonpolar substance like CO_2 gas (carbon dioxide) to be changed to CO_2 solid (dry ice). Because the molecules are held weakly together, nonpolar solids such $CO_2(s)$ and $I_2(s)$ sublime or change to gas easily at room temperature.

Bonding in Water

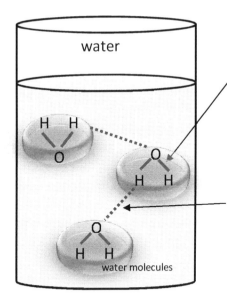

In a molecular substance, such as water, there are two forces holding particles of the substance together in the liquid or solid state.

Intramolecular (Polar Covalent Bonding)
- Holds O and H atoms together to make water molecules.
- Chemical properties or reactions of water require the breaking of this bond.
- A stronger bond than the intermolecular force.

Intermolecular (Hydrogen Bonding)
- Holds water molecules together in the solid and liquid states.
- Physical properties such as vapor pressure, boiling and melting points, depend on the strength of these forces.
- A weaker force than the intramolecular forces.

Hydrogen Bonding in Water
The O end of one molecule *attracts* the H end of another molecule.

Relating Intermolecular Forces to Melting Point, Boiling Point, and Vapor Pressure

Many physical properties of a substance depend on the strength of the intermolecular forces (IMFs) holding particles of the substance together. These properties include melting point, boiling point, and vapor pressure. Melting point and boiling point are the temperature that a substance melts and boils, respectively. Vapor pressure is the pressure that evaporated molecules of a liquid exert on the surface of the liquid.

When any of these properties for several substances are compared:

*The substance with the **highest melting point, highest boiling point** or **lowest vapor pressure** has the **strongest intermolecular forces.***

*The substance with the **lowest melting point, lowest boiling point** or **highest vapor pressure** has the **weakest intermolecular forces.***

Comparing Intermolecular Forces Among Similar Substances

Similar molecular substances have different strength of intermolecular forces holding their molecules together. The wide difference in the boiling points and vapor pressures among similar substances are due to the difference in the strength of intermolecular forces. Three aspects of molecular substances that determine the strength of intermolecular forces are explained on the next page.

 ©2017 E3 Scholastic Publishing. All Rights Reserved

1. Polarity of the Molecules: *Most Polar, Highest Boiling and Melting Points*

Polar substances generally have stronger intermolecular forces than nonpolar substances. Therefore, polar substances tend to have higher boiling points, higher melting points, and lower vapor pressures when compared to nonpolar substances. An example comparison is shown below.

Molecular Substance	Relative Strength of Intermolecular Forces (IMFs)	Relative Boiling Point
CH_4 (nonpolar)	Weaker (London-dispersion)	Lower (-161°C)
CH_3Cl (polar)	Stronger (dipole-dipole)	Higher (-22.4°C)

2. Size of Molecules: *Biggest Size, Highest Boiling and Melting Points*

The strength of intermolecular forces among similar nonpolar substances varies depending on the size of their molecules. In general, intermolecular forces (IMF) are stronger in a nonpolar substance with a large molecular mass when compared to a similar substance of a smaller molecular mass. The relative comparison of molecular size, IMF strength, and boiling point for three groups of nonpolar substances are shown below.

Halogens	Noble Gases	Hydrocarbons	Relative Size of Molecule	Relative Strength of IMFs	Relative Boiling Point
F_2	He	CH_4	Smallest	Weakest	Lowest
Cl_2	Ne	C_2H_6			
Br_2	Ar	C_3H_8	Biggest	Strongest	Highest

Note: As the size of the molecules increases among similar nonpolar substances, the strength of intermolecular forces (London-dispersion), as well as boiling and melting points also increase.

3. Phase of a Substance/Distance Between the Molecules

The strength of intermolecular forces of a substance varies depending on the phase of the substance. In general, intermolecular forces are stronger between molecules of a substance in the solid phase. The force is weaker when the substance is in the gas phase. This is best observed among the Group 17 halogens.

Halogen	Phase at STP	Relative Strength of intermolecular forces
F_2 and Cl_2	Gas	Weaker
Br_2	Liquid	A little stronger
I_2	Solid	Strongest

> At STP, Iodine is a solid, and fluorine and chlorine are gases because iodine has stronger intermolecular forces when compared to fluorine or chlorine.

Intermolecular Forces: Practice Questions

Practice 47
The degree of polarity of a chemical bond in a molecule of a compound can be predicted by determining the difference in the
1) melting points of the elements in the compound
2) densities of the elements in the compound
3) electronegativities of the bonded atoms in a molecule of the compound
4) atomic masses of the bonded atoms in a molecule of the compound

Practice 48
Which set of properties are due to the strength of intermolecular forces between molecules?
1) Vapor pressure and boiling point.   3) Molar mass and vapor pressure.
2) Boiling point and molar density.   4) Vapor pressure and molar density.

Practice 49
Which kind of bonds are found in a sample of $H_2O(l)$?
1) Covalent bonds, only   3) Both covalent and hydrogen bonds
2) Hydrogen bonds, only   4) Both ionic and hydrogen bonds

Practice 50
In which substance would the force of attraction between the molecules be considered hydrogen bonding?
1) $O_2(g)$ 2) $NH_3(l)$ 3) $NaCl(s)$ 4) $CO_2(g)$

Practice 51
Which of the following has the lowest boiling point?
1) He   2) Xe   3) Ne   4) Kr

Practice 52
Which of the following substances has the highest normal boiling point?
1) C_2H_4 2) C_3H_6 3) C_4H_8 4) C_5H_{10}

Practice 53
The abnormally high boiling point of HF as compared to HCl is primarily due to intermolecular forces of attraction called
1) network bonds   3) electrovalent forces
2) Van der Waals forces   4) hydrogen bonding

Practice 54
At 298 K, the vapor pressure of H_2O is less than the vapor pressure of CH_3OH because H_2O has
1) larger molecules   3) stronger intermolecular forces
2) smaller molecules   4) weaker intermolecular forces

Base your answers to practice questions 55 through 57 on the table below.

Physical Properties of Four Gasses

Name of Gas	hydrogen	hydrogen chloride	hydrogen bromide	hydrogen iodide
Molecular Structure	H-H	H-Cl	H-Br	H-I
Boiling Point (K) at 1 Atm	20.	188	207	237
Density (g/L) at STP	0.0899	1.64	?	5.66

55. Explain, in terms of intermolecular forces, why hydrogen has a *lower* boiling point than hydrogen bromide.

56. Explain, in terms of electronegativity difference, why the bond in H − Cl is more polar than the bond in H − I.

57. Identify the bonding in H − H.

 ©2017 E3 Scholastic Publishing. All Rights Reserved

Lesson 4 – Lewis Electron-dot Diagrams

Valence electrons are the electrons in the outermost electron shell of an atom. Valence electrons are directly involved in all chemical bonding. During ionic bonding, valence electrons are lost by a metal to form a positive ion, and are gained by a nonmetal to form a negative ion. During covalent bonding, nonmetal atoms share their valence electrons.

In this lesson you will learn how to show different bond types using Lewis electron-dot diagrams.

Lewis Electron–dot Diagrams for Neutral Atoms and Ions

A **Lewis electron- dot diagram** is a notation that shows the symbol of an atom and dots to represent valence electrons of the atom. Lewis electron-dot diagrams can be drawn for neutral atoms, ions and compounds.

Concept Task: Be able to draw Lewis electron-dot diagrams.

Practice 58
Draw the electron-dot diagrams for the following atoms.

Neutral atoms
A Lewis electron-dot diagram for a neutral atom is the symbol of the atom surrounded by dots equal to the number of its valence electrons.

	e- configuration	*valence electrons*	*dot diagram*
Sodium atom (Na)	$2-8-1$	*1*	**Na ·**
Phosphorus atom (P)	$2-8-5$	*5*	**·P:**

Magnesium

Silicon

Positive ions
A Lewis dot-diagram for a positive ion is just the symbol of the ion, which can be determined from the periodic table.

	e- configuration	*valence electrons*	*dot diagram*
Sodium ion (Na⁺)	$2-8$	8	**Na⁺**
Beryllium ion (Be²⁺)	2	2	**Be²⁺**

Argon

Practice 59
Draw the electron-dot diagrams for the following ions.

Calcium ion

Potassium ion

Negative ions
A Lewis electron-dot diagram for a negative ion is the symbol of the ion in brackets, and 8 dots around the atom.
A negative hydrogen ion (H⁻) is the only exception with just 2 dots. Hydrogen has only one electron shell (the 1st), which has enough orbitals for just two electrons.

	e- configuration	*valence electrons*	*dot diagram*
Phosphide ion (P³⁻)	$2-8-8$	8	$[:\!P\!:]^{3-}$
Hydride ion (H⁻)	2	2	$[H:]^{-}$

Oxide ion

Bromide ion

Note: Use the periodic table to get the correct charge of an ion.

Lewis Electron-dot for Ionic Compounds

Ionic compounds are composed of positive(+) and negative(-) ions. The positive ion is formed by a metal atom transferring or losing its valence electrons to a nonmetal. The nonmetal accepts or gains the electrons to become a negative ion. Lewis electron-dot diagram for an ionic compound must show the Lewis electron-dot symbols for both the positive and negative ions of the substance.

A *correct* Lewis electron-dot diagram for any given ionic compound must show the following:
  The *correct* symbol and charge of the positive and negative ions in the formula.
  The *correct* number of each ion in the formula.
  The *correct* number of dots around the negative ion.
  A bracket should surround the dot diagram of the negative ion.

Lewis electron-dot diagrams for four ionic compounds are given below.

Substance Name	Formula	Lewis Electron-dot Diagram
Sodium chloride	NaCl	$Na^+ \left[:\ddot{Cl}: \right]^-$
Calcium bromide	$CaBr_2$	$Ca^{2+}\ 2\left[:\ddot{Br}: \right]^-$
Potassium oxide	K_2O	$2K^+ \left[:\ddot{O}: \right]^{2-}$
Magnesium hydride	MgH_2	$^-\left[H\ddot{}\, \right] Mg^{2+} \left[H\ddot{}\, \right]^-$

Note: o represents valence electrons transferred from the metal element.

The Importance of Having the Correct Number of Each Ion.

Compounds are neutral; the sum of charges in a compound must equal zero.

In calcium bromide, 2 bromide ions (each with -1 charge) are needed to equalize the charge of 1 calcium ion (a +2 charge).

In potassium oxide, 2 potassium ions (each with +1 charge) are needed to equalize the charge of 1 oxide ion (a -2 charge).

Concept Task: Be able to draw Lewis electron-dot diagrams for ionic compounds.

Practice 60
Draw the Lewis electron-dot diagram for each substance.

Lithium Iodide

Magnesium chloride

Potassium hydride

Aluminum fluoride

Aluminum oxide

Strontium oxide

Barium sulfide

Calcium hydride

©2017 E3 Scholastic Publishing. All Rights Reserved

Lewis electron-dot Diagrams for Molecular Substances

Molecular substances are composed of nonmetal atoms that share their valence electrons. Each pair of electrons (2 electrons) shared between two atoms forms a single covalent bond. The Lewis electron-dot diagram for a molecular substance must show the sharing of electrons by the nonmetal atoms.

A *correct* Lewis electron-dot diagram for any given molecular substance must show the following:
  The *correct* symbol and number of each nonmetal atom.
  The *correct* number of shared valence electrons between the atoms.
  The *correct* number of unshared valence electrons around the atoms.

In the examples below, Lewis electron-dot diagrams are drawn for some common polar and nonpolar substances. Two different but correct Lewis structures are drawn for each substance.

Polar Substances (These diagrams have asymmetrical shapes.)

Substance Name	Formula	Lewis Electron-dot Diagram
Hydrogen chloride	HCl	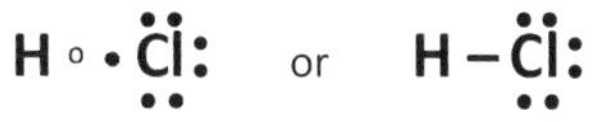
Water	H_2O	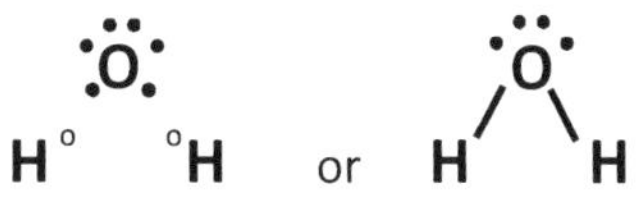
Ammonia	NH_3	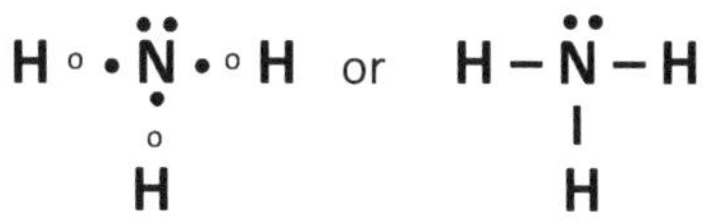

Concept Task: Can draw Lewis electron-dot diagrams for molecular substances.

Practice 61

Draw Lewis electron-dot diagrams for the following.

Hydrogen fluoride

Hydrogen sulfide

Hydrogen

Bromine

Carbon tetrafluoride

Nonpolar Substances (These diagrams have symmetrical shapes.)

Substance name	formula	Lewis electron-dot diagram
Chlorine	Cl_2	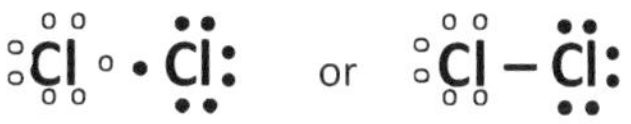
Carbon dioxide	CO_2	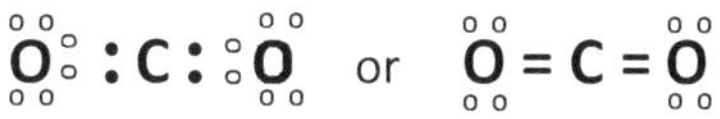
Methane	CH_4	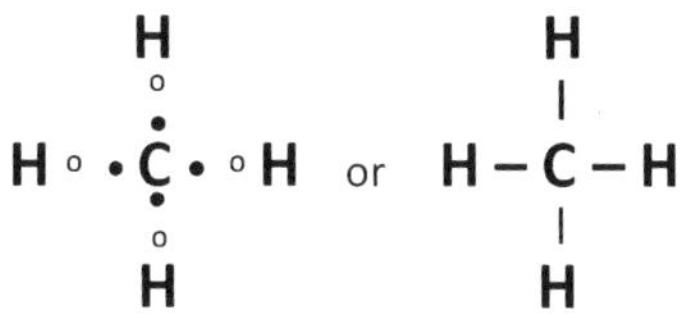
Carbon tetrachloride	CCl_4	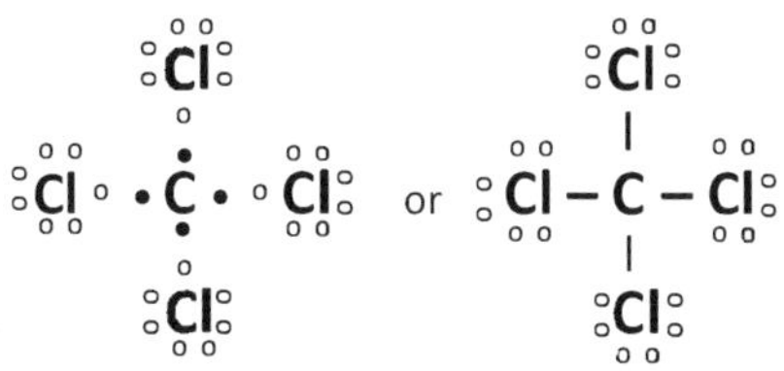

Lewis Electron-dot Diagrams: Practice Questions

Practice 62

In the Lewis electron-dot diagram $H\!:\!\ddot{C}l\!:$ the dots represent
1) valence electrons of H only
2) valence electrons for both the H and C atom
3) valence electrons of Cl only
4) all the electrons found in H and C atoms

Practice 63

Which electron-dot symbol is correctly drawn for the atom it represents?

1) $:\!\ddot{N}$ 2) $:\!\ddot{\ddot{F}}\!:$ 3) $:\!\ddot{\ddot{O}}\!:$ 4) $:\!\ddot{\ddot{Ne}}\!:$

Practice 64

Which Lewis electron-dot diagram represents a fluoride ion?

1) $\left[:\!\ddot{\ddot{F}}\!:\right]^{-}$ 2) $\left[:\!\dot{\ddot{F}}\!:\right]^{-}$ 3) $:\!\ddot{\ddot{F}}\!:$ 4) $:\!\ddot{\ddot{F}}\!:$

Practice 65

Which electron-dot formula represents ionic bonding between two atoms?

1) $_{x}^{x}\!Br\,_{xx}^{\times}\!\ddot{Br}\!:$ 2) $H\stackrel{\times}{:}\ddot{Br}:$ 3) $Na^{+}\left[\stackrel{\times\times}{\times}F\stackrel{\times}{\times}\right]^{-}$ 4) $H\stackrel{\times}{:}\stackrel{\times\times}{\underset{\times\times}{F}}\stackrel{\times}{\times}$

Practice 66

Which Lewis electron-dot diagram represents calcium oxide?

1) $Ca\!:\!\ddot{\ddot{O}}\!:$ 2) $\!:\!Ca\!:\!\ddot{\ddot{O}}\!:$ 3) $\left[:\!\overset{\bullet\times}{Ca}\!\overset{\times}{\bullet\bullet}\right]^{2+}\!O^{2-}$ 4) $Ca^{2+}\left[:\!\overset{\bullet\bullet}{\underset{\times\times}{O}}\!:\right]^{2-}$

Base your answers to practice questions 67 through 69 on the information below.

The Lewis electron-dot diagrams for three substances are shown below.

$K^{+}\left[:\!\ddot{\ddot{Br}}\!:\right]^{-}$ $H\!:\!\overset{\bullet\bullet}{\underset{H}{N}}\!:\!H$ $H\!:\!\overset{\overset{H}{\bullet\bullet}}{\underset{\underset{H}{\bullet\bullet}}{C}}\!:\!H$

   Diagram 1   Diagram 2   Diagram 3

67. Determine the total number of electrons in the bonds between the nitrogen atom and the three hydrogen atoms represented in diagram 2.

68. Explain, in terms of distribution of charge, why a molecule of the substance represented in diagram 3 is nonpolar.

69. Identify the noble gas that has atoms with the same electron configuration as the positive ion represented in diagram 1, when both the atoms and the ion are in the ground state.

         ©2017 E3 Scholastic Publishing. All Rights Reserved

Vocabulary

Lesson 1: Stability and Energy in Bonding
Chemical bond
Octet rule
Exothermic
Endothermic

Lesson 2: Types of Bonds and Substances
Intramolecular force
Ionic bond
Covalent bond
Polar covalent bond
Nonpolar covalent bond
Molecule

Polar substance
Nonpolar substance
Coordinate covalent bond
Network solid
Metallic bond

Lesson 3: Molecular Polarity and Intermolecular Forces
Intermolecular forces
Hydrogen bond

Lesson 4: Valence Electrons and Lewis Electron-dot Diagrams
Valence electron
Lewis electron-dot diagram

1. 3

2. 1

3. 4

4. In the oxygen molecule, the oxygen atoms have a complete valence shell.

5. The composition of the product is different from the composition of the reactant.
   There's a change in composition.

6. 4	11. 3	16. 3	21. 1	26. 3	31. 3	36. 2
7. 3	12. 4	17. 3	22. 2	27. 1	32. 3	37. 2
8. 4	13. 3	18. 1	23. 4	28. 2	33. 1	
9. 2	14. 1	19. 2	24. 3	29. 3	34. 4	
10. 1	15. 2	20. 4	25. 2	30. 1	35. 3	

38. $NaHCO_3$

39. Electrons are transferred from Na to Cl.   Electrons are lost and gained.

40. CO_2 or H_2O

41. The magnesium strip conducts electrical current because its valence electrons are mobile.

42. The solution conducts electrical current because it contains mobile ions.
    The ions in the solid are not moving freely, but in the solution, they are.

43. 2	46. 2	49. 3	52. 4
44. 1	47. 3	50. 2	53. 4
45. 4	48. 1	51. 1	54. 3

55. Hydrogen has weaker intermolecular forces than hydrogen bromide.

56. The electronegativity difference in H-Cl is greater than the difference in H-I.

57. nonpolar covalent

58. 59. 60. 61.

62. 2

63. 4

64. 1

65. 3

66. 4

67. six, 6

68. Charge is evenly distributed in the molecule.
    Charge distribution is symmetrical in diagram 3.

69. Argon, Ar.

©2017 E3 Scholastic Publishing. All Rights Reserved

Topic 5
Chemical Formulas and Equations

Lesson 1: Types of Chemical Formulas

Lesson 2: Chemical Nomenclature

Lesson 3: Types of Chemical Reactions and Balancing Equations

Lesson 1 – Chemical Formulas

Chemical formulas are used to represent the composition of pure substances; elements and compounds. A chemical formula expresses the *qualitative* and *quantitative* compositions of a substance. **Qualitative** information in a formula shows the types of atoms or ions that make up the substance. **Quantitative** information in a formula shows how many of each atom or ion is in the substance. The number of each atom in a formula is shown with a subscript. A **subscript** in a chemical formula is the whole number written to the bottom right of each atom in a formula.

Examples of chemical formulas:

NaCl (sodium chloride)   **CO$_2$** (carbon dioxide)   **H$_2$O** (water)   **H$_2$** (hydrogen)

Each of these formulas shows both the qualitative and quantitative composition of the substance.

The composition of a substance can be determined by counting the number of atoms or ions in the formula of the substance.

Counting Atoms in Formulas

	Example Formula	*Number of Each Atom*	*Total Number of Atoms*
Simple formula	H_2SO_4	2 **H** atoms 1 **S** atom 4 **O** atoms	**Three** different atoms. **7** total atoms
Formula with parentheses	$(NH_4)_2O$	2 **N** atoms (1 x 2) 8 **H** atoms (4 x 2) 1 **O** atom	**Three** different atoms. **11** total atoms
Formula of a hydrate	$CuSO_4 \cdot 5H_2O$	1 **Cu** atom 1 **S** atom 9 **O** atoms (4 + 5) 10 **H** atoms (5 x 2)	**Four** different atoms. **21** total atoms

Ratio of Ions in Formulas

Ionic compounds are composed of positive and negative ions. The composition of ionic compounds can also be expressed by the number or ratio of the ions in the formula.
Below, the ratio of ions are determined for three ionic compounds.

Type of Compound	*Example Formula*	*Ions in Formula*		*Ratio of Ions*
Binary Ionic Compound	$CaCl_2$ calcium chloride	Ca^{2+} calcium ion	Cl^- chloride ion	**1** Ca^{2+}: **2** Cl^-
Polyatomic Ion Compound (with parentheses)	$Al_2(SO_4)_3$ aluminum sulfate	Al^{3+} aluminum ion	SO_4^{2-} sulfate ion	**2** Al^{3+} : **3** SO_4^{2-}
Polyatomic Ion Compound (without parentheses)	KNO_3 potassium nitrate	K^+ potassium ion	NO_3^- nitrate ion	**1** K^+ : **1** NO_3^-

Use Reference *Table E* to confirm the symbol and name of a polyatomic ion.
Use the *Periodic Table* to confirm the charge and symbol of an element.

©2017 E3 Scholastic Publishing. All Rights Reserved

Counting Atoms and Ions: Practice Questions

Concept Task: Be able to determine the number of an atom or the total number of atoms in a substance.

Practice 1
What is the total number of sulfur atoms in 1 mole of $Fe_2(SO_4)_3$?
1) 1   2) 12   3) 3   4) 4

Practice 2
How many hydrogen atoms are in the hydrate $(NH_4)_3PO_4 \bullet 5H_2O$?
1) 12   2) 19   3) 22   4) 14

Practice 3
What is the total number of atoms in the formula $Ca(ClO_3)_2$?
1) 3   2) 10   3) 2   4) 9

Practice 4
What is the total number of atoms in one formula unit of $MgSO_4 \bullet 7H_2O$?
1) 27   2) 13   3) 16   4) 20

Practice 5
How many <u>different kinds</u> of atoms are present in NH_4ClO_3?
1) 5   2) 7   3) 3   4) 4

Concept Task: Be able to determine the ratio of ions in an ionic compound.

Practice 6
In the compound Al_2S_3, the mole ratio of aluminum ion to sulfur ion is
1) 2 : 3   2) 3 : 2   3) 13 : 16   4) 27 : 16

Practice 7
What is the ratio of sodium ion to phosphate ion in the formula Na_3PO_4?
1) 4 : 3   2) 3 : 4   3) 1 : 3   4) 3 : 1

Practice 8
In a sample of solid $Ba(NO_3)_2$, the ratio of barium ions to nitrate ions is
1) 1 : 1   2) 1 : 2   3) 1 : 3   4) 1 : 6

Practice 9
What is the ratio of ammonium ion to sulfate ion in the formula $(NH_4)_2SO_4$?
1) 2 : 1   2) 1 : 2   3) 8 : 4   4) 4 : 1

Chemical Formulas and Equations

Topic 5

Types of Chemical Formulas
Molecular, Structural, Empirical

There are three types of chemical formulas that can be used to show the composition of a substance.

A **molecular formula** shows the true composition of a known substance.

A **structural formula** shows how the atoms in a substance are bonded together.

An **empirical formula** shows the simplest or smallest whole-number ratio in which the atoms of a substance are combined.

Examples of the three formulas are shown below:

	water	ethane	glucose
Molecular	H_2O	C_2H_6	$C_6H_{12}O_6$
Structural	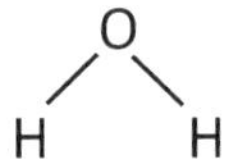	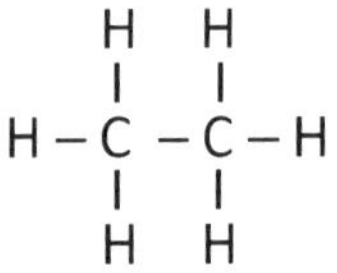	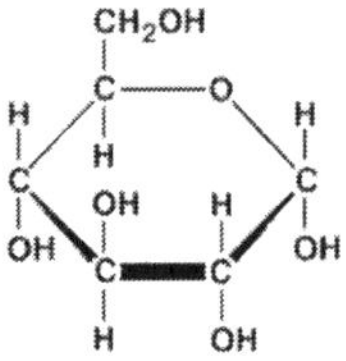
Empirical	H_2O	CH_3	CH_2O

H_2O is a molecular formula, as well as an empirical formula. Subscripts in H_2O can't be reduced to a simpler form.

C_2H_6 is reduced to CH_3 by dividing each subscript of the formula by **2** (the Greatest Common Factor).

$C_6H_{12}O_6$ is reduced to CH_2O by dividing each subscript of the formula by **6** (the Greatest Common Factor).

Concept Task: Be able to recognize empirical formulas

Practice 10
Which is an empirical formula?
1) C_2H_4 3) Ca_3P_2
2) $C_6H_{12}O_6$ 4) C_4H_6

Practice 11
Which compound has the same empirical and molecular formula?
1) C_2H_6 3) $C_6H_{12}O_6$
2) H_2O_2 4) N_2O

Practice 12
An example of an empirical formula is
1) C_4H_{10} 3) $C_6H_{12}O_6$
2) CH_2O 4) $HC_2H_3O_2$

Concept Task: Be able to reduce a molecular formula to the empirical formula.

Practice 13
Which molecular formula is correctly paired with its empirical formula?
1) C_2H_2 and C_2H_4 3) HO and H_2O
2) CH_2 and C_2H 4) NO_2 and N_2O_4

Practice 14
What is the empirical formula for a compound with the molecular formula of $C_6H_{12}Cl_2O_2$?
1) C_3H_6ClO 3) $CHClO$
2) CH_2ClO 4) $C_6H_{12}Cl_2O_2$

Practice 15
What is the empirical formula for the structure shown below?

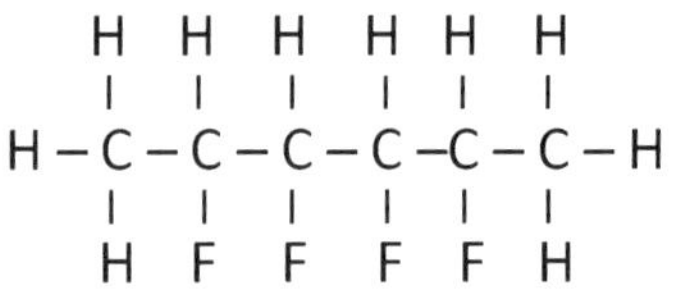

1) $C_6H_{10}F_4$ 3) $C_3H_2F_2$
2) $C_3H_5F_2$ 4) CHF

Practice 16
The reaction between 1-butene, C_4H_8, and bromine, Br_2, forms the compound 1,2-dibromobutane, $C_4H_8Br_2$.
Write the empirical formula for the product.

©2017 E3 Scholastic Publishing. All Rights Reserved

Lesson 2 – Chemical Nomenclature

There are millions of known chemical substances, with many more being discovered yearly. **Chemical nomenclature** refers to the systematic rules for naming and writing formulas of chemical substances. The International Union of Pure and Applied Chemistry (IUPAC) is the organization that makes recommendations as to how chemical substances are named.

In this lesson, you will learn how to apply IUPAC rules to writing formulas and names for compounds in different classes of *inorganic* compounds.

Writing Chemical Formulas
Sum of Charges Must Equal Zero

A chemical formula is correctly written for a known substance when both the qualitative and quantitative information of the formula are correct. This means:
• Element or ion symbols in a formula must be correct for the substance.
• Subscripts of the elements or ions in a formula must be in the correct ratio so that the sum of the charges is equal to zero.
  All compounds are electrically neutral. Examples are given below.

Name: Lithium bromide   Strontium fluoride   Chromium(III) phosphate   Ammonium carbonate

Formula:	**LiBr**	**SrF$_2$**	**CrPO$_4$**	**(NH$_4$)$_2$CO$_3$**
Explanations:	One -1 Br ion cancels out one +1 Li ion.	Two -1 F ions cancel out one +2 Sr ion.	One -3 PO$_4$ ion cancels out one +3 Cr ion.	Two +1 NH$_4$ ions cancel out one -2 CO$_3$ ion.

Writing Chemical Formulas Using the Criss-cross Method
Chemical formulas can also be written by following the criss-cross method steps below. Examples on the next page follow these steps.

Step 1:   **Write** the correct ion symbols for the chemical name.
Use the Periodic Table to get the correct ion symbol for an element.
Use Table E to get the correct polyatomic ion symbol.
Always put parentheses around polyatomic ion like so, $(SO_4)^{2-}$.

Step 2: **Criss-cross** charge values so each becomes the subscript for the other atom.

Step 3: **Clean up** formula after criss-crossing by:
Reducing subscripts that are reducible to empirical form.
Do not change subscripts of the polyatomic ion.

Remove parentheses if subscript outside parentheses is a 1.

Keep parentheses if subscript outside parentheses is greater than 1.

Steps shown above and on the next pages are to ensure that your final (correct) formula has the correct element symbols and correct subscripts for the compound name that is given.

Chemical Formulas and Equations　　　　　　　Topic 5

Writing Formulas Ionic Compounds

Binary ionic compounds have formulas that are composed of two different elements: A metal and a nonmetal. IUPAC names of binary compounds always end with –ide.

Examples: Calcium brom<u>ide</u>, Aluminum sulf<u>ide</u>, and Zinc ox<u>ide</u>

Concept Task: Be able to write the correct chemical formula to a given binary ionic compound.

Examples
Steps listed on the previous page are followed to write the correct formulas to the three binary ionic compounds below.

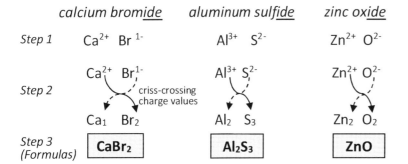

Ionic compounds containing a polyatomic ion (Table E)
Polyatomic ions are composed of two or more atoms with an excess charge. Most polyatomic ions have negative charges. *Reference Table E* lists some common polyatomic ions. IUPAC names of polyatomic ions typically end with -*ate* or –*ite*. Examples of compounds containing a polyatomic ion are: sodium *nitrate,* calcium *sulfite,* and *ammonium* oxide.

Concept Task: Be able to write the correct chemical formula to a given ionic compound containing a polyatomic ion.

Examples
Steps listed on the previous page are followed to write the correct formulas to three ionic compounds containing a polyatomic ion.

	sodium nitrate	calcium sulfite	ammonium oxide
Step 1	$Na^{1+}\ (NO_3)^{1-}$	$Ca^{2+}\ (SO_3)^{2-}$	$(NH_4)^{1+}\ O^{2-}$
Step 2	$Na^{1+}\ (NO_3)^{1-}$	$Ca^{2+}\ (SO_3)^{2-}$	$(NH_4)^{1+}\ O^{2-}$
Step 3 (formulas)	$Na_1\ (NO_3)_1$	$Ca_2\ (SO_3)_2$	$(NH_4)_2\ O_1$
	$\boxed{NaNO_3}$	$\boxed{CaSO_3}$	$\boxed{(NH_4)_2\,O}$

Practice 17
What is the correct chemical formula for cesium oxide?
1) CsO_2 3) Cs_2O_3
2) CsO 4) Cs_2O

Practice 18
Which formula is correct for magnesium sulfide?
1) MgS 3) Mg_2S_2
2) MnS 4) Mn_2S_2

Practice 19
Which is the formula for calcium nitride?
1) CaN 3) Ca_2N_3
2) Ca_3N_2 4) Ca_3N_3

Practice 20
Write the correct formulas for:

Aluminum nitride

Strontium fluoride

Silver iodide

Practice 21
Which formula is correct for magnesium phosphate?
1) Mg_2PO_7 3) $MgPO_4$
2) $Mg_2(PO_4)_3$ 4) $Mg_3(PO_4)_2$

Practice 22
Which is the correct formula for ammonium sulfate?
1) NH_4SO_4 3) $NH_4(SO_4)_2$
2) $(NH_4)_2(SO_4)_2$ 4) $(NH_4)_2SO_4$

Practice 23
Which is the correct formula for zinc carbonate?
1) $ZnCO_3$ 3) $Zn_2(CO_3)_2$
2) $ZnCO_6$ 4) $ZnCO$

Practice 24
Write the correct formulas for:

Lithium hydrogen carbonate

Cadmium nitrite

Calcium thiosulfate

　　　　　　　©2017 E3 Scholastic Publishing. All Rights Reserved

Writing Formulas for Compounds Containing an Atom with Multiple Oxidation States

The **stock system** nomenclature uses Roman numerals in parentheses to distinguish names of compounds produced by different positive oxidation states of an atom. A compound made with one positive oxidation charge of an element has a different formula from a compound made with another positive oxidation charge of that same element. Examples of stock system names are given below.

Iron(**II**) chloride   (**II**) indicates that iron with a charge of **+2** formed this compound with chlorine.

Iron(**III**) chloride   (**III**) indicates that iron with a charge of **+3** formed this compound with chlorine.

Nitrogen(**IV**) oxide   (**IV**) indicates that nitrogen with a charge of **+4** formed this compound with oxygen.

Concept Task: Be able to recognize or write the correct chemical formula to a compound with Stock system nomenclature.

Examples

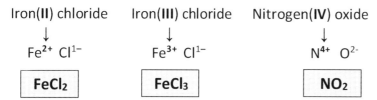

Practice 25
The formula for lead(II) oxide is
1) PbO   3) PbO_2
2) Pb_2O 4) Pb_2O_3

Practice 26
The correct formula for manganese(IV) sulfide is
1) Mn_4S 3) MnS_2
2) Mn_4S_2 4) Mn_4S_4

Practice 27
Which formula is correct for copper(II) chlorate?
1) Cu_2Cl 3) $CuCl_2$
2) $Cu(ClO_3)_2$ 4) Cu_2ClO_3

Practice 28
Which formula correctly represents lead(IV) thiosulfate?
1) $Pb_2S_2O_3$ 3) $Pb(S_2O_3)_2$
2) PbS_2O_3 4) $PbSO_3$

Practice 29.
Write the chemical formulas for:
Chromium(III) oxide

Titanium(IV) sulfate

Iron(II) dichromate

Phosphorus(V) sulfide

Naming Ionic Compounds
IUPAC name is correctly written for a given ionic compound when:
- Atoms and/or ions in the formula are correctly named
- Name ending, if necessary, is correctly applied
- Roman numeral, if necessary, is correctly used

When a chemical formula for an ionic compound is given, the following steps may be useful in determining or writing the correct IUPAC name for the compound.

Step 1: **Write** names of elements and/or polyatomic ions in the formula

Step 2: **Change** the ending of a nonmetal element to –ide
     Do not make any change to the name of a metal or polyatomic ion.

Step 3: For a metal with multiple positive(+) oxidation numbers, determine its charge value and use it in parentheses to name the compound.

Naming Ionic Compounds

Concept Task: Be able to name different types of compounds. The steps listed on the previous page are followed to write correct IUPAC names to the compounds given below.

Binary ionic compounds contain just two elements: a metal and nonmetal. *Examples* are $ZnCl_2$, CaO and Li_3N. Naming a binary compound involves changing the nonmetal ending to *-ide*.

$ZnCl_2$ | CaO | Li_3N

Zinc chloride | **Calcium oxide** | **Lithium nitride**

Compounds containing a polyatomic ion generally has three or more elements. Examples are $Mg_3(PO_4)_2$, NH_4NO_3 and NH_4Cl. When naming compounds containing a polyatomic ion, no change should be made to the name of the polyatomic ion or the metal element. Polyatomic ions are listed on Reference Table E.

$Mg_3(PO_4)_2$ | NH_4NO_3 | NH_4Cl

Magnesium phosphate | **Ammonium nitrate** | **Ammonium chloride**

Compounds containing an element with multiple oxidation numbers must be named using the Stock system. In each of the formulas below, the first element has multiple positive oxidation numbers as seen on the Periodic Table. The Stock system naming uses a Roman numeral inside a parenthesis to identify which positive oxidation number of the element formed the compound.

SnF_4 | N_2O | $Fe_3(PO_4)_2$

Tin(IV) fluoride | **Nitrogen(I) oxide** | **Iron(II) phosphate**

In some formulas like the three above, the *subscript* of the second symbol is used as the Roman numeral (or the +charge) value in parentheses. In some formulas like the two below, the *+charge value* of the metal is determined mathematically by following steps given in the box below.

	CrN_2	$MnSO_4$
Assign −charge value.	Cr N_2^{3-}	Mn $(SO_4)_1^{2-}$
Multiply −charge by **subscript** to get total negative in formula.	2 x 3- = -6	1 x 2- = -2
Determine **total positive** needed to make charges = 0	+6	+2
Use the **+charge** as the **Roman numeral** in parentheses to name the formula.	**Chromium(VI) nitride**	**Manganese(II) sulfate**

Practice 30
What is the correct IUPAC name for the formula Na_2S?
1) Sodium(III) sulfide
2) Sodium sulfide
3) Sodium(III) sulfate
4) Sodium sulfate

Practice 31
Write the correct names for:
FrO

Ag_2S

ZrI_4

Practice 32
What is the correct name for the compound with the formula $AlPO_4$?
1) Aluminum(IV) phosphate
2) Aluminum(III) phosphide
3) Aluminum phosphate
4) Aluminum phosphide

Practice 33
Write the correct names for:
$Ca(MnO_4)_2$

$Al_2(SO_3)_3$

Practice 34
What is the correct name for the compound $CrPO_4$?
1) Chromium(III) phosphate
2) Chromium(III) phosphide
3) Chromium(II) phosphate
4) Chromium(II) phosphide

Practice 35
The correct IUPAC name for PbO_2 is
1) Lead(I) oxide
2) Lead(II) oxide
3) Lead(III) oxide
4) Lead(IV) oxide

Practice 36
Write the correct IUPAC names for the following compounds:
VBr_2

$Co(HSO_4)_3$

$Mn(CrO_4)_2$

Topic 5 _____ Chemical Formulas and Equations
Writing and Naming Covalent and Molecular Substances

Covalent and molecular compounds are composed only of nonmetal atoms. Binary compounds, which contain two different nonmetals, are commonly named with IUPAC recommended prefixes. A **prefix** in a chemical name indicates how many of the nonmetal atom is in the given compound.

The table below lists prefixes for naming covalent compounds.

Number of Atom	Prefix	Number of Atom	Prefix
1	mono-	6	hexa-
2	di-	7	hepta-
3	tri-	8	octa-
4	tetra-	9	nona-
5	penta-	10	deca-

Writing Formulas: Use these three simple rules.

• Prefixes are interpreted into subscripts for the elements.
• Absence of a prefix on the first nonmetal means that there is just one of that atom.
• No criss-crossing or reducing of formulas into an empirical form.

Examples

Molecular name	Carbon **mono**xide	**di**nitrogen **tetro**xide
Interpretation	**1** C **1** O	**2** N 4 O
Formula	CO	N_2O_4

Naming Formulas: Use these three simple rules.

• Change subscript to the corresponding prefix.
• Do not use a prefix for the first nonmetal atom if there is only one of the atom (see PCl_3).
• The "a" or "o" of a prefix is dropped if the addition of the prefix resulted in a name having two vowels next to each other. In N_2O_5, the **a** in pent**ao**xide is dropped, and the formula is correctly named dinitrogen pent**o**xide.
• Change the name ending for the second nonmetal atom to -ide.

Examples

PCl_3	N_2O_5	H_2S
1 Phosphorus **3** Chlorine	**2** nitrogen **5** oxygen	**2** hydrogen **1** sulfur
Phosphorus **trichloride**	**di**nitrogen **pent**oxide	**di**hydrogen **mono**sulfide

Practice 37

Write the correct chemical formulas for the following compounds:

Dibismuth trichloride
Bi_2Cl_3

Silicon tetrafluoride
SiF_4

Ditatanium trioxide
Ti_2O_3

Tetraphosphorus hexoxide
P_4O_6

Carbon disulfide
CS_2

Boron triiodide
BI_3

Practice 38
Write the correct IUPAC name for each of the following formulas:

H_2S
Dihydrogen Sulfide

OF_2
Oxygen difluoride

Hg_2Cl_2
Dimercury dichloride

XeF_6
xenon hexafluoride

V_2H
divanadium hydride

PF_5
Phosphorus Pentafluoride

Lesson 3 – Chemical Reactions and Equations

An **equation** shows the changes that are taking place in one or more substances. There are three major types of changes, and each can be represented with an equation.

Chemical change equations show changes in chemical compositions of one or more substances.

Example $2H_2(g) + O_2(g) \rightarrow 2H_2O(l)$

Physical change equations show the change in state or phase of a substance. In physical changes, the chemical composition of the substance does not change.

Example $H_2O(s) \rightarrow H_2O(l)$

Nuclear equations show changes in the nucleus contents of one or more atoms to that of other atoms.

Example $^{220}_{87}Fr \rightarrow \, ^{4}_{2}He + \, ^{216}_{85}At$

In this lesson of topic 5, only chemical changes and equations are discussed.
In topic 1 - Matter and Energy**:** Phase changes, which are physical changes, were discussed.
In topic 12 - Nuclear Chemistry: Nuclear changes and equations will be discussed.

Chemical Equations

A chemical equation uses symbols to show changes in the chemical compositions of one or more substances during a chemical reaction. A chemical reaction is the process that leads to a chemical change.

Reactants are the starting substances that are present before a chemical reaction.
Reactants are shown to the *left* of the arrow in an equation.

Products are the substances that remain at the end of a chemical reaction.
Products are shown to the *right* of the arrow in an equation.

A **coefficient** is a whole number in front of a substance to show the number of moles or how many of that substance is taking part in the reaction.

An example of a chemical equation and its components is shown below.

Reactants	yield or produce	**Products**
$Zn(s) + $ **2**$HCl(aq)$	$\longrightarrow$	$ZnCl_2(aq) + H_2(g)$
$\downarrow$		$\downarrow$

Coefficient of 2 indicates that there are 2 moles of HCl.	**Coefficient of 1** indicates that there is 1 mole of $ZnCl_2$.
A coefficient of 2 or more is always written in front of the substance.	A coefficient of 1 is never written in front of the substance.

(s), (ℓ), (g), and *(aq)* are sometimes written to show the phase of each substance taking part in the reaction.

©2017 E3 Scholastic Publishing. All Rights Reserved

Types of Reactions
Synthesis, Decomposition, Replacements, Combustion

There are many types of chemical reactions. Five of them are defined and explained below. Diagrams and example equations representing each type of reaction are given to the right of each reaction. Many other types of chemical reactions are discussed in topics 8 through 11 of this book.

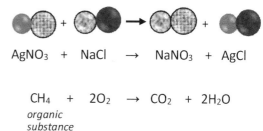

reactants   yield   products

Synthesis reactions always involve two or more substances as reactants. During a synthesis reaction, the reactants combine to form one compound product.

$$2H_2 \ + \ O_2 \ \rightarrow \ 2H_2O$$

Decomposition reactions always involve one single substance as a reactant. During a decomposition reaction, the reactant breaks down or decomposes into two or more products.

$$2H_2O \ \rightarrow \ 2H_2 \ + \ O_2$$

Single replacement reactions typically involve a compound and a free element as reactants. During a single replacement reaction, the free element replaces one of the elements in the compound. This reaction only occurs when the free element reactant is more reactive than the element in the compound it is replacing.

$$Zn \ + \ 2HCl \ \rightarrow \ ZnCl_2 \ + \ H_2$$

Double replacement reactions usually involve two compounds in aqueous phase. During a double replacement reaction, the ions of the compounds switch partners. This reaction is also called metathesis.

$$AgNO_3 \ + \ NaCl \ \rightarrow \ NaNO_3 \ + \ AgCl$$

Combustion reactions typically involve the burning of an organic substance in the presence of oxygen. Water and carbon dioxide are produced in combustion reactions.

$$\underset{\text{organic substance}}{CH_4} \ + \ 2O_2 \ \rightarrow \ CO_2 \ + \ 2H_2O$$

Concept Task: Be able to identify types of reactions.

Practice 39
Which equation represents a single replacement reaction?
1) $H^+ \ + \ OH^- \rightarrow H_2O$
2) $2Cu \ + \ O_2 \ \rightarrow \ 2CuO$
3) $CuCO_3 \ \rightarrow \ CuO \ + \ CO_2$
4) $Ag \ + \ 2CuNO_3 \ \rightarrow \ Ag(NO_3)_2 \ + \ 2Cu$

Practice 40
Which of the following equations is showing a decomposition reaction?
1) $(NH_4)_2CO_3 \ \rightarrow \ 2NH_3 \ + \ CO_2 \ + \ H_2O$
2) $4NH_3 + \ 5O_2 \ \rightarrow \ 4NO \ + \ 6H_2O$
3) $NH_3 \ + \ H_2O \ \rightarrow \ NH_4OH$
4) $N_2 \ + \ 3H_2 \ \rightarrow \ 2NH_3$

Practice 41
The reaction
$$3CaO \ + \ P_2O_5 \ \rightarrow \ Ca_3(PO_4)_2$$
is best described as
1) synthesis
2) decomposition
3) single replacement
4) double replacement

Practice 42
Given the equation:
$$CuSO_4 \ + \ Pb(NO_3)_2 \ \rightarrow \ PbSO_4 + Cu(NO_3)_2$$
What type of reaction is represented by the equation?
1) Decomposition
2) Single replacement
3) Synthesis
4) Double replacement

Balanced Equations
Conservation of Atoms, Mass, Charge and Energy

Law of Conservation states that during a chemical reaction atoms, mass, charges and energy are neither created nor destroyed. This means that during a chemical reaction, atoms, mass, charges, and energy are conserved so that the amount of each before and after the reaction is the same. A **balanced chemical** equation is a way of showing conservation in a chemical reaction.

Conservation of Atoms

In the balanced equation below, atoms on the reactant and product sides are equal.

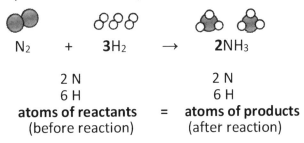

$$N_2 \quad + \quad 3H_2 \quad \rightarrow \quad 2NH_3$$

2 N	2 N
6 H	6 H
atoms of reactants =	**atoms of products**
(before reaction)	(after reaction)

The equation above is balanced because it has the correct ratio of smallest *whole-number coefficients* needed to make the number of atoms on both sides equal. In other words, the substances in the reaction are represented in the correct *mole* proportions.

Note: When counting atoms in a formula, always multiply the coefficient by the subscript.

Example: **2NH$_3$**

coefficient (**2**) x subscript (**3**) = 6 H atoms

Practice 43
Which of the following equations is correctly balanced?
1) $CO \quad + \quad O_2 \rightarrow 2CO_2$
2) $2SO_2 \quad + \quad O_2 \rightarrow SO_3$
3) $CO \quad + \quad 2O_2 \rightarrow CO_2$
4) $2SO_2 \quad + \quad O_2 \rightarrow 2SO_3$

Practice 44
Which of these equations shows conservation of atoms?
1) $KBr \quad \rightarrow \quad K \quad + \quad Br_2$
2) $CuCO_3 \rightarrow CuO \quad + \quad CO_2$
3) $2KClO_3 \rightarrow 2KCl \quad + \quad 2O_2$
4) $CaCO_3 \rightarrow CO_2 \quad + \quad 2CaO$

Practice 45
If equation is balanced properly, both sides of the equation must have the same number of
1) atoms
2) molecules
3) coefficients
4) moles of molecules

Practice 46
What is conserved during chemical reactions?
1) Energy, only
2) Both matter and energy
3) Matter, only
4) Neither matter nor energy

How to Balance Equations
An equation is balanced when it contains the correct ratio of *smallest whole-number coefficients.* This allows the number of each atom on both sides of the equation to be the same or conserved.

Rules to Balancing Equations:
• Change only the coefficients of substances. Don't ever change the subscripts of a formula
• Coefficients in the balanced equation must be in the smallest whole-number ratio

Suggestions for Balancing Equations
• List and count each atom on both sides of the equation.
• Make a table to keep track of the number of atoms as coefficients are changed.
• Try balancing one atom at a time.
• Every time a coefficient is changed, RECOUNT and note the number of each atom affected by the change. Be sure to count atoms correctly.
• Always change coefficients of free elements (ex. Na, Cl$_2$) last.
• Always put parentheses around polyatomic ions and count them as one unit.
• Make sure that the final coefficients are in the smallest whole-number ratio.

　　　　　　©2017 E3 Scholastic Publishing. All Rights Reserved

Balancing Equations
Only Coefficients (Moles) Should Be Changed

When a balancing equation problem is given as a multiple choice question, you could be asked to:

Determine the coefficient in front of one of the substances.

The sum of all the coefficients.

The mole ratio of two substances.

To correctly answer any of these questions, the unbalanced equation must first be correctly balanced.

Examples of Unbalanced and Balanced Equations

Unbalanced $Li_3N \rightarrow Li + N_2$

Balanced $2Li_3N \rightarrow 6Li + N_2$

Sum of Coefficients = 2   + 6   + 1 = **9**

Unbalanced $Ca(OH)_2 + H_3PO_4 \rightarrow Ca_3(PO_4)_2 + H_2O$

Balanced $3Ca(OH)_2 + 2H_3PO_4 \rightarrow Ca_3(PO_4)_2 + 6H_2O$

Sum of Coefficients = 3   + 2   + 1   + 6   = **12**

Unbalanced $C_3H_4 + O_2 \rightarrow CO_2 + H_2O$

Balanced $C_3H_4 + 4O_2 \rightarrow 3CO_2 + 2H_2O$

Sum of Coefficients = 1   + 4   + 3   + 2   = **10**

Practice 47
When the equation ___ Na + ___ H_2O → ___ H_2 + ___ $NaOH$
is correctly balanced using the smallest whole number coefficients, what is the coefficient of H_2O?
1) 1   2) 2   3) 3   4) 4

Practice 48
Given the unbalanced equation ___ H_2O_2 → ___ H_2O + ___ O_2
What is the sum of all coefficients when the equation is balanced using the smallest whole-number coefficients?
1) 5   2) 9   3) 3   4) 4

Practice 49. *Balance each of the following equations using the smallest whole-number coefficients.*

___ $Al(s)$ + ___ $CuSO_4(aq)$ → ___ $Al_2(SO_4)_3(aq)$ + ___ $Cu(s)$

___ $Ca(OH)_2$ + ___ $(NH_4)_2SO_4$ → ___ $CaSO_4$ + ___ NH_3 + ___ H_2O

___ C_5H_{12} + ___ O_2 → ___ CO_2 + ___ H_2O

Chemical Formulas and Equations   Topic 5

Completing Equations

Some balancing equation problems involve determining the substance that is missing in the incomplete equation. The missing substance that is determined must make for a balance equation.

Concept Task: Be able to predict the missing substance in an incomplete equation.

Example 1

Given the incomplete equation below
$$X \rightarrow MgCl_2 + 3O_2.$$ Substance X is

1) $MgClO$ 2) $Mg(ClO)_2$ 3) $Mg(ClO_2)_2$ 4) $Mg(ClO_3)_2$

Count the atoms on the product side
   1 Mg   2 Cl   6 O
Substance X must have the exact same atoms to make the equation balance.

Choose Choice 4 $Mg(ClO_3)_2$ because it contains
   1 Mg   2 Cl   6 O

Check: $Mg(ClO_3)_2 \rightarrow MgCl_2 + 3O_2$ is balanced

Example 2

Given the incomplete equation:
$$4Fe + 3O_2 \rightarrow 2X$$ Which compound is represented by X?

1) FeO 2) Fe_2O_3 3) Fe_3O_2 4) Fe_3O_4

Count the atoms on the reactant side:
   4 Fe   6 O

The coefficient of X is 2. Substance X must have half the atoms counted above:
   2 Fe and 3 O.

Choose: Choice 2, Fe_2O_3

Check: $4Fe + 3O_2 \rightarrow 2Fe_2O_3$ is balanced

Practice 50
Given the balanced equation:
$$2Na + 2H_2O \rightarrow 2X + H_2$$
What is the correct formula for the product represented by the letter X?

1) NaO   3) Na_2O
2) NaOH   4) Na_2OH

Practice 51
Given the incomplete equation:
$$2N_2O_5 \rightarrow$$

Which set of products completes and balances the incomplete equation?

1) $2N_2 + 3O_2$ 3) $2N_2 + 2O_2$
2) $4NO_2 + O_2$ 4) $2NO + 2O_2$

Practice 52
Given the incomplete equation below:
$$3Ca(OH)_2 + 2H_3PO_4 \rightarrow Ca_3(PO_4)_2 + X$$

Which correctly represents X?

1) $3H_2$ 3) $3H_2O$
2) $6H_2$ 4) $6H_2O$

Practice 53
In the equation
$$X + 7O_2 \rightarrow 4CO_2 + 6H_2O$$

Which correctly represents X?

1) $2C_4H_6$ 3) $2C_2H_6$
2) C_2H_6 4) C_4H_6

104   ©2017 E3 Scholastic Publishing. All Rights Reserved

Topic 5   Chemical Formulas and Equations

Conservation of Mass in Reactions

The Law of Conservation of Mass states that during a chemical reaction, mass is neither created nor destroyed. In a closed chemical reaction system, mass is conserved so that the total mass of the products is equal to the total mass of the reactants as shown below.

$$3Fe \quad + \quad 2O_2 \quad \rightarrow \quad Fe_3O_4$$

$$20.9 \text{ g} \quad + \quad 8.0 \text{ g} \quad = \quad 28.9 \text{ g}$$

Total mass before reaction = *Total mass after reaction*

(28.9 g)   *(28.9 g)*

Practice 54

Given the balanced equation representing a reaction:

$$2H_2 \quad + \quad O_2 \quad \rightarrow \quad 2H_2O$$

What is the total mass of oxygen that must react with 8 grams of hydrogen to form 72 grams of water?

1) 8 g   3) 64 g
2) 36 g   4) 80 g

Practice 55

Given the balanced equation for the reaction:

$$2NaCl(l) \quad \rightarrow \quad 2Na(s) \ + \ Cl_2(g)$$

A 1170.-gram sample of NaCl(l) completely reacts, producing 460. grams of Na(s). What is the total mass of $Cl_2(g)$ produced?

1) 355 g   3) 1420. g
2) 710. g   4) 1630. g

Base your answers to practice questions 56 and 57 on the information below.

A tablet of one antacid contains citric acid, $H_3C_6H_5O_7$, and sodium hydrogen carbonate, $NaHCO_3$. When the tablet dissolves in water, bubbles of CO_2 are produced. This reaction is represented by the incomplete equation below.

$$H_3C_6H_5O_7(aq) \ + \ 3NaHCO_3(aq) \ \rightarrow \ Na_3C_6H_5O_7(aq) \ + \ 3CO_2(g) \ + \ 3 \underline{\quad H_2O \quad} (l)$$

56. Write the formula of the missing product.

57. Write the formula of the negative ion in the aqueous sodium hydrogen carbonate.

Base your answers to practice questions 58 and 59 on the information below.

In an experiment, 2.54 grams of copper completely reacts with sulfur, producing 3.18 grams of copper(I) sulfide.

58. Write the chemical formula of the compound produced.

59. Determine the total mass of sulfur consumed.

Base your answers to practice questions 60 and 61 on the information below.

The Solvay process is a multistep industrial process used to produce washing soda, $Na_2CO_3(s)$. In the last step of the Solvay process, $NaHCO_3(s)$ is heated to 300°C, producing washing soda, water, and carbon dioxide. This reaction is represented by the balanced equation below.

$$2NaHCO_3(s) \ + \ \text{heat} \ \rightarrow \ Na_2CO_3(s) \ + \ H_2O(g) \ + \ CO_2(g)$$

60. Write the IUPAC name for washing soda.

61. Identify the type of chemical reaction represented by the equation.

Vocabulary

Lesson 1: Chemical Formulas

Chemical formula
Qualitative
Quantitative
Subscript

Molecular formula
Empirical formula
Structural formula

Lesson 2: Chemical Nomenclature

Chemical nomenclature
Binary compound
Stock system

Lesson 3: Chemical Equations

Reactant
Product
Coefficient
Synthesis
Decomposition

Single replacement
Double replacement
Combustion
Law of conservation

©2017 E3 Scholastic Publishing. All Rights Reserved

1. 3   5. 4   9. 1   13. 4
2. 3   6. 1   10. 3   14. 1
3. 4   7. 4   11. 4   15. 2
4. 1   8. 2   12. 2   16. C_2H_4Br

17. 4   20. AlN   21. 4   24. $LiHCO_3$
18. 1 SrF_2 22. 4 Cd_3N_2
19. 2   AgI   23. 1 CaS_2O_3

26. 3   29. Cr_2O_3 30. 2   32. 4
27. 2 $Ti(SO_4)_2$ 31. francium oxide   33. calcium permanganate
28. 3 $FeCr_2O_7$ silver sulfide   aluminum sulfite
                  P_2S_5 zirconium iodide

34. 1   36. Vanadium(II) bromide   37. Bi_2Cl_3 P_4O_6
35. 4   cobalt(III) hydrogen sulfate SiF_4 CS_2
                  manganese(IV) chromate Ti_2O_3 BI_3

38.   dihydrogen monosulfide   xenon hexafluoride
       oxygen difluoride   divanadium monohydride
       dimercury dichloride   phosphorous pentafluoride

39. 4   42. 4   45. 1   48. 1
40, 1   43. 4   46. 2
41. 1   44. 2   47. 2

49.

   $\underline{2}$ Al(s)   + $\underline{3}$ $CuSO_4$(aq) $\rightarrow$ __$Al_2(SO_4)_3$(aq)   + $\underline{3}$Cu(s)

   __$Ca(OH)_2$ +   __ $(NH_4)_2SO_4$ $\rightarrow$ __$CaSO_4$ + $\underline{2}$ NH_3 + $\underline{2}H_2O$

   __C_5H_{12} + $\underline{8}O_2$ $\rightarrow$ $\underline{5}CO_2$ + $\underline{6}$ H_2O'

50. 2   56. H_2O
51. 2.   57. HCO_3^-
52. 4   58. Cu_2S
53. 3   59. 0.64 grams
54. 3   60. sodium carbonate
55. 2   61. decomposition

©2017 E3 Scholastic Publishing. All Rights Reserved

Topic 6
The Mole Concept and Calculations

Lesson 1: Mole Concept and Calculations in Formulas

Lesson 2: Mole Concept and Calculations in Equations

Lesson 1: Mole Concept and Calculations in Formulas

A **mole** is a unit that describes the quantity of 6.02×10^{23}. A mole is, therefore, a unit of quantity in the same sense that a dozen refers to the quantity of 12.

The following are all units of quantities:

1 dozen eggs   = **12** eggs

1 gross of apples = **144** apples

1 mole of atoms   = **602000000000000000000000** atoms

A mole contains a very large quantity of material, and is only used when referring to the number of particles (atoms, molecules, ions, or electrons, etc.) in chemical substances.
The number, **602000000000000000000000**, is called **Avogadro's number**. It is always written in its scientific notation form: 6.02×10^{23}.

Stoichiometry is the study and calculations of relative quantities of substances in chemical formulas (composition stoichiometry) and chemical equations (reaction stoichiometry).

In this lesson you will learn to interpret and calculate molar quantities in chemical formulas.

Interpretations of Moles in Chemistry Questions

The term "mole" is used often in chemistry questions that involve formulas and equations.
How "mole" is interpreted in the question depends on what is asked for in the question.

Below are example questions in which "mole" is used.

How many *moles* of hydrogen atoms are in *1 mole* of H_3PO_4?

What is the mass of *one mole* of H_3PO_4?

What is the *mole ratio* of H_2 to O_2 in the equation: $2H_2$ + O_2 $\rightarrow$ $2H_2O$

Your ability to correctly answer these questions depends on your understanding of mole concepts and its many interpretations.

©2017 E3 Scholastic Publishing. All Rights Reserved

Moles of Atoms in Formulas

The number of moles of an atom in a given formula can be determined by counting how many of that atom are in the formula and then multiplying that by the number of moles of the substance.

Concept Task: Be able to determine the number of moles of atoms in any given moles of a substance.

moles of atom A = given moles of substance x number of atom A in the formula

Example 1 *equation setup*
How many moles of sulfur atoms are in 1 mole of $Al_2(SO_4)_3$?

moles of S   = 1 mole x 3 S atoms = **3 moles of S atoms**

Example 2 *factor-label setup*
How many moles of sulfur atoms are in 2 moles of $Al_2(SO_4)_3$?

$$2\ moles\ Al_2(SO_4)_3 \ \times \ \frac{3\ moles\ S\ atom}{1\ mole\ Al_2(SO_4)_3} = \textbf{6 moles of S atoms}$$

Example 3 *equation setup*
How many moles of oxygen atoms are in 1 mole of $CaCO_3 \cdot 2H_2O$?

moles of O = 1 mole x   5 O atoms   =   **5 moles O of atom**

Example 4 *factor-label setup*
How many moles of oxygen atoms are in 0.5 moles of $CaCO_3 \cdot 2H_2O$?

$$0.5\ moles\ \ CaCO_3 \cdot 2H_2O \ \times \ \frac{5\ moles\ O}{1\ mole\ CaCO_3 \cdot 2H_2O} = \textbf{2.5 moles of O atom}$$

Practice 1
What is the total number of moles of hydrogen in 1 mole of $(NH_4)_2HPO_4$?
1) 5   2) 7   3) 8   4) 9

Practice 2
How many moles of oxygen atoms are present in one mole of $CaSO_4 \cdot 3H_2O$?
1) 7   2) 4   3) 3   4) 5

Practice 3
What is the total number of moles of atoms in one mole of $Mg(ClO_4)_2$?
1) 13   2) 11   3) 8   4) 3

Practice 4
The total moles of atoms in one mole of $BaCl_2 \cdot 2H_2O$ is
1) 6   2) 7   3) 8   4) 9

Practice 5
What is the total number of moles of hydrogen atoms in 2 moles of $(NH_4)_2SO_4$?
1) 8   2) 4   3) 16   4) 2

Practice 6
The total number of oxygen atoms in 0.5 mole of $CaCO_3 \cdot 7H_2O$ is
1) 10   2) 2   3) 5   4) 4

Practice 7
What is the total number of moles of atoms in 2 moles of H_2SO_4?
1) 14   2) 7   3) 12   4) 6

Practice 8
How many moles of water are in 2.5 moles of $(NH_4)_2CO_3 \cdot 5H_2O$?
1) 5   2) 2.5   3) 12.5   4) 18

Molar Mass

The **molar mass** of a substance is the mass, in grams, of 1 mole of that substance. One mole of a substance contains 6.02×10^{23} particles (atoms, molecules, or ions) found in that substance.
For example, water is composed of water molecules:
One mole of water contains 6.02×10^{23} (602000000000000000000000) molecules of water.
The molar mass of water, which is 18 g, is the mass of 6.02×10^{23} molecules of water.
Below are the different variations of molar mass.

Atomic mass specifically refers to the mass of 1 mole of an element.
Molecular mass is commonly used when referring to the mass of 1 mole of a molecular substance.
Formula mass is commonly used when referring to the mass of 1 mole of any substance.

Regardless of the substance given in a question, the mass of one mole of a substance is *the sum of the mass of all atoms* in the formula. You are shown how to calculate molar mass in the set below.

Formula Mass Calculations

Gram-atomic mass is the mass, in grams, of 1 mole of an element.
Gram-atomic mass is found on the Periodic Table of the Elements.

> **Gram-atomic mass** = mass of 1 mole of atoms = **Atomic mass** of the element on the Periodic Table

Gram-formula mass is the mass of 1 mole of a substance.
Gram-formula mass is the *sum* of all the atomic masses in a formula.

> **Gram-formula mass** = Mass of 1 mole of a substance = **Sum of atomic masses** in a formula

There a few different methods to set up and calculate the formula (or molecular) mass of a substance. Regardless of the method, the following three steps will be involved.

Step 1: Determine how many of each element is in the formula. *Count correctly.*

Step 2: Multiply the number of each element by their atomic mass from Periodic Table.
Round off the atomic mass as in examples 5 and 6 if its allowed.

Step 3: Add up the total mass of all the elements in the formula to get the formula mass.

Example 5: *Calculation of Formula Mass.*
What is the gram-formula mass of H_2O?

$$2\,H \;+\; 1\,O \quad \text{rounded atomic mass from the Periodic Table}$$
$$2(1) \;+\; 1(16)$$
$$2 \;+\; 16 \quad \text{numerical setup}$$

Formula mass = **18 g/mol**   *calculated result*

Example 6: *Calculation of Formula Mass.*
What is the formula mass of $(NH_4)_2SO_4$?

$$2\,N \;+\; 8\,H \;+\; 1\,S \;+\; 4\,O$$
$$2(14) \;+\; 8(1) \;+\; 1(32) \;+\; 4(16)$$
$$28 \;+\; 8 \;+\; 32 \;+\; 64 \quad \text{numerical setup}$$

Formula mass = **132 g/mol**   *calculated result*

Example 7: *Calculation of Formula Mass.*

What is the gram-formula mass of $NaNO_3 \bullet 4H_2O$?

Atoms	Atomic Mass	x How Many	= Total Mass
Na	23.989 g	1	23.989 g
N	14.007 g	1	14.007 g
H	1.008 g	8	8.064 g
O	15.999 g	7	111.993 g

Formula mass = **158.053 g/mol**

Molar Mass Calculations: **Practice Questions**

Practice 9
What is the gram-atomic mass of gold?
1) 11 g/mol   2) 79 g/mol   3) 197 g/mol   4) 80 g/mol

Practice 10
What is the mass in grams of 1 mole of Co?
1) 27   2) 28   3) 12   4) 59

Practice 11
Which of these elements has the greatest gram-atomic mass?
1) Br   2) Ge   3) Fe   4) Ca

Practice 12
What is the mass of 1 mole of H_3PO_4?
1) 82   2) 98   3) 24   4) 30

Practice 13
The gram formula mass of $(NH_4)_3PO_4$ is
1) 149 g   2) 120 g   3) 404 g   4) 300 g

Practice 14
What is the molecular mass of $C_3H_5(OH)_3$?
1) 48 g/mole   2) 58 g /mole   3) 74 g/mole   4) 92 g/mole

Practice 15
What is the gram formula mass of $CuSO_4 \cdot 3H_2O$?
1) 214 g   2) 250 g   3) 294 g   4) 178 g

Practice 16
Which of these substances has the smallest gram-molecular mass?
1) CO_2 2) HNO_3 3) HCl 4) H_2O_2

Practice 17   *Show a numerical setup and the calculated result.*
Calculate the formula mass of $Al_2(SO_4)_3$.

Practice 18   *Show a numerical setup and the calculated result.*
Calculate the molecular mass of $CH_3(CH_2)_2COOH$.

Practice 19   *Show a numerical setup and the calculated result.*
Calculate the molar mass of the hydrate $Ba(OH)_2 \cdot 8H_2O$.

Moles and Mass Calculations in Formulas

The mass of one mole of a substance is the gram-formula mass of that substance. In other words, 6.02×10^{23} particles or one mole of a given substance has a mass equal to the calculated gram-formula mass. What if there are more than one mole (more than 6.02×10^{23} particles of that substance)? It makes sense to think that a sample containing more than one mole of a substance (more than 6.02×10^{23} particles) will have a mass that is greater than the calculated gram-formula mass. Likewise, a sample containing less than one mole of a substance (fewer than 6.02×10^{23} particles) will have a mass that is less than the calculated gram-formula mass. The mathematical relationship between moles and mass is given by the **Table T** equation.

 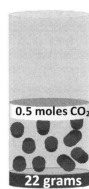

1 mol CO_2

0.5 moles CO_2

44 grams **22 grams**
formula mass

$$\text{number of moles} = \frac{\text{given mass}}{\text{gram-formula mass}}$$

Example 8: *Moles from Mass Calculation. Table T Equation Setup*
How many moles of H_2O are in 100. grams of the substance?

$$\textbf{Number of moles} = \frac{100.\text{ g}}{18.0 \text{ g/mol}} = \textbf{5.60 mol } H_2O$$

Example 9: *Moles from Mass Calculation. Factor-label Setup.*
What is the number of moles of ammonium sulfate, $(NH_4)_2SO_4$, in 50 grams of the substance?

$$50 \text{ g } (NH_4)_2SO_4 \times \frac{1 \text{ mol } (NH_4)_2SO_4}{132 \text{ g } (NH_4)_2SO_4} = \textbf{0.38 mol } (NH_4)_2SO_4$$

Example 10: *Mass from Moles Calculation. Table T Equation Setup.*
What is the mass of 3.0 moles of water, H_2O?

Mass = given moles x gram-formula-mass

Mass =   3.0   x   18   = **54 g** H_2O

Example 11: *Mass from Moles Calculation. Factor-label Setup.*
What is the mass of 0.2 moles of ammonium sulfate?

$$0.2 \text{ mol } (NH_4)_2SO_4 \times \frac{132 \text{ g } (NH_4)_2SO_4}{1 \text{ mol } (NH_4)_2SO_4} = \textbf{26.4 g } (NH_4)_2SO_4$$

The gram-formula mass of H_2O and $(NH_4)_2SO_4$ were calculated on page 110.
Italicized units in factor-label setups cancel out.

Moles and Mass Calculations in Formulas: Practice Problems

Concept Task: Be able to set up and calculate moles of a substance from a given mass.

Practice 20
What is the total number of moles represented by 46 grams of Na?
1) 23 moles
2) 0.5 moles
3) 2.0 moles
4) 1.0 moles

Practice 21
A student measured 56 grams of Fe_2O_3 for a laboratory experiment. How many moles of Fe_2O_3 is this mass represents?
1) 1.00
2) 0.35
3) 0.50
4) 2.00

Practice 22
Which setup is correct for calculating the number of moles in 576 g of $Al(ClO_3)_3 \bullet 6H_2O$?

1) 576 x 384

2) $\dfrac{576}{384}$

3) 6 x 576

4) $\dfrac{384}{576}$

Practice 23 *Show a setup and the calculated result.*
Calculate the number of moles in a 184-g sample of $C_3H_5(OH)_3$.

Practice 24 *Show a setup and the calculated result.*
What is the number of moles represented in 100 grams of $Na_2CO_3 \bullet 10H_2O$?

Concept Task: Be able to set up and calculate mass of a substance from a given number of moles.

Practice 25
What is the total mass of 2 moles of Ar?
1) 18 g
2) 36 g
3) 40 g
4) 80 g

Practice 26
The total mass of 0.25 mole of H_2 gas is
1) 2 g
2) 0.5 g
3) 8 g
4) 4 g

Practice 27
What is the total mass in grams of 3 moles of $Al_2(CrO_4)_3$?
1) 134
2) 402
3) 1206
4) 1530

Practice 28
Which set up is correct for calculating the mass of 0.6 mole of $Ca(OH)_2$?

1) $\dfrac{74}{0.6}$

2) 0.6 x 74

3) $\dfrac{58}{0.6}$

4) 0.3 x 58

Practice 29 *Show a setup and the calculated result.*
Calculate the mass of grams of 0.1 mole of $C_6H_{12}O_6$?

Practice 30 *Show a setup and the calculated result.*
What is the mass of 2.3 moles of $CuSO_4 \bullet 5H_2O$?

Base your answer to question 31 on the information below and on your knowledge of chemistry.

Paintball is a popular recreational activity that uses a metal tank of compressed carbon dioxide or nitrogen to launch small capsules of paint. A typical tank has a volume of 508 cubic centimeters. A 340.-gram sample of carbon dioxide is added to the tank before it is used for paintball. At 20.°C, this tank contains both $CO_2(g)$ and $CO_2(l)$. After a paintball game, the tank contains only $CO_2(g)$.

31. Determine the total number of moles of CO_2 added to the tank before it is used for paintball.

Mole and Volume Calculations

Molar volume is the volume or space occupied by one mole (6.02×10^{23} particles) of a gas at STP. The molar volume of any gas at STP is 22.4 liters.

If there are more than one mole (more than 6.02×10^{23} particles) of a gas at STP, the volume of the gas will be greater than 22.4 liters. Likewise, a gas sample that occupies a smaller volume than 22.4 liters at STP is less than one mole (contains fewer than 6.02×10^{23} particles) of the gas. The mathematical equations to set up and solve moles and volume problems at STP are given below.

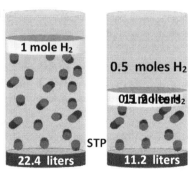

1 mole H_2

0.5 moles H_2

STP

22.4 liters　　　11.2 liters

1 mole = 22.4 Liters

Volume = given moles x 22.4 L

$$\textbf{Moles} = \frac{\text{given volume}}{22.4 \text{ L}}$$

Example 12　*equation setup*

How much volume is occupied by 5 moles of O_2 gas at STP?

1) 2 L　　2) 4.5 L　　3) 10 L　　4) 112 L

Volume　=　5　x　22.4　　*numerical setup*

Volume = 112 L　　　　*calculated result*

Choice 4

Example 13　*factor-label setup*

At STP, a sample of H_2 gas has a volume of 15 liters. How many moles of H_2 is in the sample?

Given volume　x　mole/liters ratio at STP

$$15 \text{ liters } O_2 \text{ x } \frac{1 \text{ mole } O_2}{22.4 \text{ liters } O_2}$$ *numerical setup*

0.67 moles O_2　　　　*calculated result*

Practice 32
What is the volume of 1.50 moles of an ideal gas at STP?
1) 11.2 L　　　　　3) 33.6 L
2) 22.4 L　　　　　4) 14.9 L

Practice 33
What is the volume of 0.1 mole of O_2 gas at STP?
1) 2.24 L　　　　　3) 44.8 L
2) 4.48 L　　　　　4) 224 L

Practice 34
Which substance will occupy a volume of 67.2 L at STP?
1) 1.0 mole of He　　3) 67.2 mole of Ne
2) 3.0 mole of H_2　　4) 1509 mole of N_2

Practice 35　*Show a setup and the result.*
A closed cylinder at STP contains 3.50 moles of CO_2. Calculate the volume of the gas.

Practice 36　*Show a setup and the result.*
A sample of helium gas is in a 10.0-liter closed container at STP. What is the number of moles of the sample?

　　　　©2017 E3 Scholastic Publishing. All Rights Reserved

Mole and Avogadro's Number Calculations

Avogadro's number describes the number of particles in one mole of a substance. One mole of any substance contains 6.02×10^{23} particles (atoms, molecules, ions, or formula unit) of that substance. 6.02×10^{23} is called the Avogadro's number, named after the Italian scientist Amadeo Avogadro, who first proposed this number.

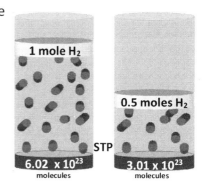

If there are more than one mole of a substance, then there is more than 6.02×10^{23} particles of that substance. Likewise, a substance containing fewer than 6.02×10^{23} particles is less than one mole. The mathematical equations to set up and solve moles and number of particle problems are given below.

$$1 \text{ mole } = 6.02 \times 10^{23}$$

Number of Particles $=$ given moles x (6.02×10^{23})	or **Moles** $= \dfrac{\text{given number of particles}}{6.02 \times 10^{23}}$

Concept Task: Be able to set up and calculate problems involving moles and the number of particles.

Example 14   *equation setup*
How many molecules of F_2 are in 2.50 moles of the substance?

1) 5.00   3) 2.41×10^{23}
2) 90.0   4) 1.51×10^{24}

Number of molecules $= 2.50 \times (6.02 \times 10^{23})$ *setup*

Number of molecules $= \mathbf{1.51 \times 10^{24}}$ *calculated result*

Choice 4

Example 15   *factor-label setup*
A sample of sodium contains 4.5×10^{23} atoms. How many moles of atoms do this represents?

Given particle   x   mole/particle ratio

4.5×10^{23} Na atoms   x $\dfrac{1 \text{ mole Na}}{6.02 \times 10^{23} \text{ Na atoms}}$ *setup*

0.75 moles Na   *calculated result*

Practice 37
What is the total number of molecules in 0.25 mole of NO_2?
1) 2.5×10^{23} 3) 24.08
2) 4.515×10^{23} 4) 1.5×10^{23}

Practice 38
What is the total number of atoms in 2.31 moles of sodium?
1) 1.39×10^{24} 3) 2.31×10^{24}
2) 2.606   4) 1.39×10^{23}

Practice 39
Which gas sample contains 9.03×10^{23} molecules of the gas?
1) 0.5 mole of N_2 3) 1.5 moles of NH_3
2) 1 mole of He   4) 2 moles of CH_4

Practice 40   *Show a setup and the result.*
A 5.0-moles of gold is used to electroplate a jewelry piece. Calculate the number of gold atoms that coated the jewelry piece.

Practice 41 *Show a setup and the result.*
A helium balloon is filled with 8.12×10^{25} molecules of helium. Calculate the number of moles of the gas in the balloon.

Mixed Problems

The **mole map** below may be useful in solving mole problems involving mixed quantities. The dot (•) end of an arrow indicates what is given, and the pointy (▲) end of an arrow points to what needs to be calculated. The conversion factor between moles and each quantity (mass, volume, or number of particles) is given between the arrows.

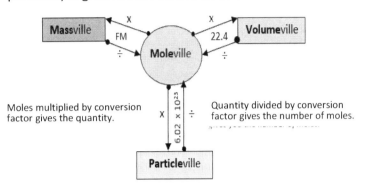

Moles multiplied by conversion factor gives the quantity.

Quantity divided by conversion factor gives the number of moles.

Example 16   *mole map two-step setup*

What is the number of liters in 50 grams of O_2 at STP?
1) 22.4 L   2) 44.8 L   3) 35.0 L   4) 1120 L

Step 1: Find moles = Given mass ÷ Formula mass of O_2
          moles =   50 *g* ÷ 32 *g/mol* = 1.6 mol

Step 2: Find Volume =   Moles x 22.4 L
          Volume = 1.6 *mol* x 22.4 L / *mol* = **35.0 L**
                                                    Choice 3

Example 17   *factor-label setup*

How many grams of carbon dioxide, CO_2, are in a 100 L sample of the gas at STP?

$$100 \ L \ CO_2 \ \ x \ \ \frac{1 \ mole \ CO_2}{22.4 \ L \ CO_2} \ x \ \frac{44 \ g \ CO_2}{1 \ mole \ CO_2} \quad setup$$

196.4 g CO_2   *calculated result*

Example 3   *factor- label setup.*

How many particles of NaCl are in a 10-gram sample of the salt?

$$10 \ g \ NaCl \ x \ \frac{1 \ mole \ NaCl}{58 \ g \ NaCl} \ x \ \frac{6.02 \ x \ 10^{23} \ NaCl \ particles}{1 \ mole \ NaCl}$$

1.04 x 10^{23} NaCl particles   *calculated result*

Practice 42

What is the total volume occupied by a 132-g sample of $CO_2(g)$ at STP?
1) 22.4 L   3) 44.8 L
2) 33.6 L   4) 67.2 L

Practice 43

How many molecules are contained in 127 grams of iodine (I_2)?
1) 1.50 x 10^{23} 3) 9.03 x 10^{23}
2) 3.01 x 10^{23} 4) 12.4 x 10^{23}

Practice 44

1.0 x 10^{24} molecules of water, H_2O, has a mass of
1) 18 g   3) 30 g
2) 1.67 g   4) 60 g

Practice 45 *Show a setup and the result.*

A closed cylinder contains 576 grams of SO_2 gas at STP. Calculate the volume of the gas?

Practice 46 *Show a setup and the result.*

A 2-gram sample of sodium, Na, reacted with water. How many atoms of sodium was in the sample?

Practice 47 *Show a setup the result.*

Calculate the mass of a 72.5 L sample of ammonia gas, NH_3, at STP.

                    ©2017 E3 Scholastic Publishing. All Rights Reserved

Percent Composition

Percent composition by mass indicates the portion of a mass of a substance that is due to the mass of individual elements in the substance.

Concept Task: Be able to calculate the percent composition of any element in a given substance. Use *Reference **Table T*** equation and steps below.

$$\text{Percent composition} = \frac{\text{Mass of the element in a formula (part)}}{\text{Formula mass of the given formula (whole)}} \times 100$$

To determine percent composition of any element in a formula

Step 1: *Determine* the total mass of each element in the formula

Step 2: *Add up* all the mass to get the formula mass

Step 3: *Divide* the mass of the element in question by the formula mass, then multiply by 100

Example 18
What is the percent composition of each element in $Mg(ClO_3)_2$?

Step 1: Determine mass of each element in $Mg(ClO_3)_2$

$$1\ Mg\ =\ 1(24\ g)\ \ \ =\ \ \ 24\ g\ Mg$$
$$2\ Cl\ \ =\ 2(35\ g)\ \ \ =\ \ \ 70\ g\ Cl$$
$$6\ O\ \ \ =\ 6(16\ g)\ \ \ =\ \ \ 96\ g\ O$$

Step 2: Formula mass $Mg(ClO_3)_2$ = 190 g $Mg(ClO_3)_2$

Step 3: Calculate percent composition of each element

$$\% \ Mg\ =\ \frac{24\ g}{190\ g} \times 100 \qquad setup$$

$$\mathbf{\% \ Mg}\ =\ \mathbf{12.6\ \%} \qquad calculated\ result$$

$$\% \ Cl\ =\ \frac{70\ g}{190\ g} \times 100 \qquad setup$$

$$\mathbf{\% \ Cl}\ =\ \mathbf{36.8\ \%} \qquad calculated\ result$$

$$\% \ O\ =\ \frac{96\ g}{190\ g} \times 100 \qquad setup$$

$$\mathbf{\% \ O}\ =\ \mathbf{50.5\ \%} \qquad result$$

Practice 48
In the formula $Mg(CN)_2$, what is the approximate percent by mass of carbon?
1) 16 %
2) 24 %
3) 32 %
4) 48 %

Practice 49
What is the approximate percent composition of $CaBr_2$?
1) 20 % calcium and 80 % bromine
2) 25 % calcium and 75 % bromine
3) 30 % calcium and 70 % bromine
4) 35 % calcium and 65 % bromine

Practice 50
Which compound has the greatest composition of sulfur by mass?
1) $Fe_2(SO_4)_3$
2) $Fe_2(SO_3)_3$
3) $FeSO_4$
4) $FeSO_3$

Practice 51
Which compound of gold will produce the least mass of gold?
1) Gold(I) oxide
2) Gold(III) oxide
3) Gold(I) sulfide
4) Gold(III) sulfide

Practice 52   *Show a setup and the result.*
Calculate the percent by mass of hydrogen in the formula $C_3H_5(OH)_3$?

Percent Composition of Hydrates

Hydrates are ionic compounds that contain water within their crystal structures.
Names and formulas of three common hydrates are given below:

$CaCl_2 \bullet 2H_2O$ Calcium chloride dihydrate   (**di**hydrate means **2**H_2O)

$MgSO_4 \bullet 7H_2O$ Magnesium sulfate heptahydrate (**hepta**hydrate means **7**H_2O)

$CuSO_4 \bullet 5H_2O$ Copper(II) sulfate pentahydrate (**penta**hydrate means **5**H_2O)

The formula mass or the mass of 1 mole of a hydrate is due in parts to the mass of the water.
The percent by mass of water in a hydrate can be calculated using the equation below.

Concept Task: Be able to calculate the percent by mass of water in a hydrate.

$$\text{Percent } H_2O \text{ in a Hydrate} = \frac{\text{Total mass of } H_2O \quad \text{(part)}}{\text{Formula mass of hydrate (whole)}} \times 100$$

To determine percent of water in a hydrate:

Step 1: Determine the total mass of water in the hydrate.

Step 2: Determine the formula mass of the hydrate.

Step 3: Divide the mass of water by the formula mass of the hydrate, then multiply by 100.

Example 19
What is the percent composition of water in the hydrate $MgSO_4 \bullet 7H_2O$

Step 1: Mass of water, 7H$_2$O

$$14 \text{ H} = 14(1) = 14 \text{ g}$$
$$7 \text{ O} = 7(16) = 112 \text{ g}$$
$$\overline{\qquad\qquad}$$
$$\text{Mass of } 7H_2O = 126 \text{ g } H_2O$$

Step 2: Formula Mass of the hydrate, MgSO$_4$ • 7H$_2$O

$$1 \text{ Mg} = 1(24) = 24 \text{ g}$$
$$1 \text{ S} = 1(32) = 32 \text{ g}$$
$$14 \text{ H} = 14(1) = 14 \text{ g}$$
$$11 \text{ O} = 11(16) = 176 \text{ g}$$
$$\overline{\qquad\qquad}$$
$$\text{Formula mass} = 246 \text{ g } MgSO_4 \bullet 7H_2O$$

Step 3: Calculate % H$_2$O in the hydrate

$$\text{\% } H_2O = \frac{126 \text{ g}}{246 \text{ g}} \times 100 \quad \textit{numerical setup}$$

$$\text{\% } H_2O = \mathbf{51.2 \text{ \%}} \qquad \textit{calculated result}$$

Practice 53
The percent composition of water in the hydrate $CoCl_2 \bullet 6H_2O$ is
1) 45.6%   3) 7.6%
2) 60.0%   4) 2.5%

Practice 54
The percent by mass of water in $BaCl_2 \bullet 2H_2O$ (formula mass = 243) is equal to

1) $\dfrac{18}{243} \times 100$ 3) $\dfrac{36}{243} \times 100$

2) $\dfrac{243}{18} \times 100$ 4) $\dfrac{243}{36} \times 100$

Practice 55
Which hydrate contains the greatest percent of water by mass?
1) $LiCl \bullet H_2O$ 3) $CuSO_4 \bullet 5H_2O$
2) $CaCl_2 \bullet 2H_2O$ 4) $FeBr_3 \bullet 6H_2O$

Practice 56 *Show a setup and the result.*
Calculate the percent composition of water in $Ca(NO_3)_2 \bullet 3H_2O$ (calcium nitrate trihydrate)

Percent Composition of Hydrates from Experiment Data

When a hydrate is heated, the water in its crystal structure will evaporate out. The substance that remained after all the water of hydration is driven off is the **anhydrous** solid. If the mass of a hydrate and of the anhydrous solid are known, the mass of water that was in the hydrate can be determined. From this mass, the percent of water in the hydrate can be calculated.

hydrate		water removed		anhydrous
+	heat	$\rightarrow$	+	
5.0 g		**1.5 g**		**3.5 g**

$$\textbf{\% Water} \; = \; \frac{\text{Mass of water}}{\text{Mass of hydrate}} \; \text{x } 100 \; = \; \frac{1.5 \text{ g}}{5.0 \text{ g}} \; \text{x } 100 \; = \; \textbf{30 \%}$$

Concept Task: Be able to set up and calculate the percent composition of water in a hydrate from lab data.

Step 1: If necessary, *determine* the mass of the anhydrous solid and the mass of the hydrate from the experimental information given.

Step 2: Determine the mass of water (Mass of hydrate - Mass of anhydrous)

Step 3: Divide the mass of water by the mass of the hydrate, then multiply by 100

Example 20
A 2.8-gram sample of a hydrate is heated until all the water of hydration is driven off. The substance remaining in the evaporation dish has a mass of 2.1 grams. What is the percent of water in the hydrate?

Mass of water = hydrate - anhydrous
Mass of water = 2.8 g   -   2.1 g =   0.7 g

% water   = $\dfrac{0.7 \text{ g}}{2.8 \text{ g}}$ x 100   *numerical setup*

% water   =   **25 %**   *calculated result*

Example 21
During a laboratory experiment to determine percent of water in a hydrate, a student collected the following data
  Mass of evaporated dish ....   32.1 g
  Mass of hydrate + dish ....   37.5 g
  Mass of anhydrous + dish ....   35.8 g
What is the percent of water in the hydrate?

Step 1: Mass of hydrate   = 37.5 g − 32.1 g = 5.4 g
       Mass of anhydrous = 35.8 g − 32.1 g = 3.7 g

Step 2: Mass of water   = 5.4 g − 3.7 g = 1.7 g

Step 3: Percent of water

  % water = $\dfrac{1.7 \text{ g}}{5.4 \text{ g}}$ x 100   *numerical setup*

  % water = **31.5 %**   *calculated result*

Practice 57
A student heated a 9.10-gram sample of an unknown hydrated salt to a constant mass of 5.41 grams. What percent by mass of water did the salt contain?
1) 3.69 %   3) 40.5 %
2) 16.8 %   4) 59.5 %

Practice 58
A 4.10-gram sample of a hydrate was heated to a constant mass. The anhydrous that remained has a mass of 3.70 grams. What is the percent by mass of water in the hydrate?
1) 9.8 %   3) 11%
2) 90 %   4) 0.40 %

Practice 59   *Show a setup and the result*
A hydrated salt was heated in a crucible until the anhydrous compound that remained has a constant mass. The following data were recorded.

Mass of crucible	17.2 g
Mass of hydrate + crucible	22.0 g
Mass of anhydrous + crucible	20.4 g

Calculate the percent composition of water in the hydrated compound?

Molecular Formula from Empirical Formula and Mass

A **molecular formula** shows the true composition of a substance. For an example, water has a molecular formula of H_2O. This formula shows the true composition of water.

The **molecular mass** or the mass of 1 mole of water, 18 grams, is calculated from this formula.

An **empirical formula** of shows the simplest ratio in which atoms of a substance are combined.

If the empirical formula and molecular mass of a substance are known, the molecular formula of the substance can be determined by following the steps below.

Concept Task: Be able to determine the molecular formula of a substance from a given molecular mass and empirical formula.

To determine molecular formula

Step 1: Determine the mass of the empirical formula
Step 2: Determine how many units of the empirical formula there are by dividing the given molecular mass by the calculated empirical mass from step 1
Step 3: Determine the molecular formula by multiplying each subscript of the empirical formula by step 2 answer

Example 22

A substance has a molecular mass of 116 g and an empirical formula of C_2H_5. What is the molecular formula of this substance?

Step 1: Mass of C_2H_5 = 2C + 5H = 2(12) + 5(1) = 29 g

Step 2: $\dfrac{\text{molecular mass}}{\text{empirical mass}} = \dfrac{116 \text{ g}}{29 \text{ g}} = \textbf{4}$

Step 3: Molecular formula = $\textbf{4}(C_2H_5)$ = $\textbf{C}_8\textbf{H}_{20}$

Practice 60

What is the molecular formula of a substance with a molecular mass 54 g and an empirical formula of C_2H_3?
1) C_2H_3 3) C_6H_9
2) C_4H_6 4) C_3H_2

Practice 61

A compound has a molecular mass of 284 g and an empirical formula of P_2O_5. What is the molecular formula of this compound?
1) P_4O_{10} 3) P_5O_2
2) P_2O_5 4) $P_{10}O_4$

Practice 62

A compound has an empirical formula of HCO_2 and a mass of 180 g/mole. What is the molecular formula of this compound?
1) HCO_2 3) $H_4C_4O_8$
2) $H_2C_2O_4$ 4) $H_6C_6O_{12}$

Base your answers to practice questions 63 through 65 on the information below.

Vitamin C, also known as ascorbic acid, is water soluble and cannot be produced by the human body. Each day, a person's diet should include a source of vitamin C, such as orange juice. Ascorbic acid has a molecular formula of $C_6H_8O_6$ and a gram-formula mass of 176 grams per mole.

63. Write the empirical formula for ascorbic acid.

$C_3H_4O_3$

64. Determine the number of moles of vitamin C in an orange that contains 0.071 gram of vitamin C.

65. Show a numerical setup for calculating the percent composition by mass of oxygen in ascorbic acid.

Base your answers to practice questions 66 through 68 on the information below.

Arsenic is often obtained by heating the ore arsenopyrite, FeAsS. The decomposition of FeAsS is represented by the balanced equation below.

$$FeAsS(s) \rightarrow FeS(s) + As(g)$$

In the solid phase, arsenic occurs in two forms. One form, yellow arsenic, has a density of 1.97 cm³/g at STP. The other form, gray arsenic, has a density of 5.78 cm³/g at STP. When arsenic is heated rapidly in air, arsenic(III) oxide is formed.

Although arsenic is toxic, it is needed by the human body in very small amounts. The body of a healthy human adult contains approximately 5 milligrams of arsenic.

66. Calculate the percent composition by mass of arsenic in arsenopyrite.
   Your response must include *both* a correct numerical setup and the calculated result.

67. Write the formula for the compound produced when arsenic is heated rapidly in air.

68. When heated, a 125.0-kilogram sample of arsenopyrite yields 67.5 kilograms of FeS.
   Determine the total mass of arsenic produced in this reaction.

Lesson 2– Mole Concept and Calculations in Equations

A chemical equation shows changes that are taking place in a chemical reaction. A balanced chemical equation is a recipe for changing one or more chemical substances to different substances.

Consider the balanced equation: N_2 + $3H_2$ → $2NH_3$

This balanced equation reads as a recipe in the following way:
1 mole of nitrogen (N_2) is combined or reacted with **3** moles of hydrogen (**$3H_2$**)
to yield or make **2** moles of ammonia (**$2NH_3$**).

A balanced chemical equation shows the mole proportions (ratios) of reactants and products of a reaction. From these mole ratios, any number of moles of a product can be made by combining more or less of the reactants in the same proportion as given in the equation.
In this lesson, you will learn how to interpret and solve problems that involve mole proportions in chemical equations.

Mole Ratio in Equations
Ratio of Coefficients

The **coefficients** in front of substances in a balanced equation indicate the **number of moles** of the substances. From these coefficients, mole ratios of substances can be determined as shown in the example below.

Concept Task: Be able to determine the mole ratio of substances in a balanced equation.

To determine mole ratio of substances in an equation:

Step 1: Identify the coefficients of the substances

Step 2: If the coefficients are reducible, reduce them by the *greatest common factor* (GCF).

Example 1

In the equation:

  $4NH_3$ + $5O_2$ → $4NO$ + $6H_2O$

Mole ratios of substances in the reaction are listed below.

Mole ratio of NH_3 to O_2 is **4 : 5**

Mole ratio of NH_3 to NO is **1 : 1**
          (reduced from 4 : 4 by GCF of 4)

Mole ratio of NO to H_2O is **2 : 3**
          (reduced from 4 : 6 by GCF of 2)

Practice 69
In the balanced equation below:

  $2KClO_3$ → $2KCl$ + $3O_2$

What is the mole ratio of $KClO_3$ decomposed to O_2 produced?
1) 2 : 2   3) 2 : 3
2) 1 : 3   4) 1 : 1

Practice 70
Given the balanced equation

  $2C_2H_6$ + $7O_2$ → $4CO_2$ + $6H_2O$

What is the mole ratio of C_2H_6 combusted to that of H_2O produced in the reaction?
1) 4 : 6   3) 3 : 1
2) 1 : 3   4) 1 : 1

Practice 71
Given the reaction:

$3Cu + 8HNO_3 → 3Cu(NO_3)_2 + 2NO + 4H_2O$

The number of moles of NO produced to that of HNO_3 reacted is
1) 1 : 4   3) 8 : 2
2) 4 : 1   4) 2 : 8

©2017 E3 Scholastic Publishing. All Rights Reserved

Mole to Mole Problems in Equations

When the number of moles of one substance in a reaction is given, the number of moles of any other substance in the reaction can be calculated using ratios in the balanced equation.
A mole to mole problem is given and solved in the example below.

Concept Task: Be able to set up and solve a mole-to-mole problem in a given equation.

Example 27:
Given the balanced equation below:

$$4NH_3 + 5O_2 \rightarrow 6H_2O + 4NO$$

What is the total number of moles of oxygen that will be consumed to produce 10 moles of water?

Two setups to solving the problem are given below.

Proportion Setup

numerical setup
$$\frac{5}{X} = \frac{6}{10}$$
$$6X = 50$$

calculated result $\quad$ **X = 8.33 mol O$_2$**

Factor-label Setup

moles given $\quad$ x $\quad$ mole ratio of O_2/H_2O
in the question $\qquad$ in the equation

$$10 \; mol \; H_2O \; \times \; \frac{5 \; mol \; O_2}{6 \; mol \; H_2O} = \textbf{8.33 mol O}_2$$

numerical setup $\qquad\qquad\qquad$ calculated result

Practice 72
Given the reaction below:
$$Mg + 2H_2O \rightarrow Mg(OH)_2 + H_2$$
The number of moles of water needed to react with 3 moles of magnesium is
1) 6 moles $\qquad$ 3) 3 moles
2) 0.50 moles $\qquad$ 4) 4 moles

Practice 73
Given the reaction
$$C_3H_8 + 5O_2 \rightarrow 3CO_2 + 2H_2O$$
How many of moles of CO_2 is produced from reacting 0.25 moles of C_3H_8?
1) 0.75 $\qquad$ 3) 5.0
2) 0.80 $\qquad$ 4) 11

Practice 74 *Show a numerical setup and the result.*
Given the reaction:
$$6CO_2 + 6H_2O \rightarrow C_6H_{12}O_6 + 6O_2$$
Calculate the number of moles of CO_2 that will react to produce 1.75 moles of $C_6H_{12}O_6$.

$$1.75 \times \frac{6}{1} = 10 \cdot 3$$

Practice 75 *Show a numerical setup and the result.*
Given a balanced chemical equation below:
$$3Cu(s) + 2H_3PO_4(aq) \rightarrow Cu_3(PO_4)_2(s) + 3H_2(g)$$
Calculate the number of moles of copper needed to react with 0.15 moles of phosphoric acid.

$$15 \times \frac{3}{2} = .225$$

Volume to Volume Problems in Equations

When the volume of one substance in a reaction is known, the volume of any other gaseous substance in the reaction can be calculated as shown in the example below.

Concept Task: Be able to set up and solve a volume-to-volume problem in a given equation.

Example 28:

Given the balanced equation below:

$$C_3H_8 \; + \; 5O_2 \; \rightarrow \; 3\,CO_2 \; + \; 4\,H_2O$$

How many liters of propane, C_3H_8, will react to produce 9 liters of CO_2?

Two setups to solving the above problem are given below.

Proportion setup

numerical setup
$$\frac{1}{X} = \frac{3}{9}$$
$$3X = 9$$

calculated result
$$X = \textbf{3 mol C}_3\textbf{H}_8$$

Factor-label setup

mole given   x   mole ratio of C_3H_8/CO_2
in question   in equation

$$9 \; mol \; CO_2 \; \times \; \frac{1 \; mol \; C_3H_8}{3 \; mol \; CO_2} \; = \; \textbf{3 mol C}_3\textbf{H}_8$$

numerical setup   calculated result

Practice 76

According to the reaction below:

$$2SO_2(g) \; + \; O_2(g) \; \rightarrow \; 2SO_3(g)$$

What is the total number of liters of $O_2(g)$ that will react completely with 89.6 liters of SO_2 at STP?

1) 1.0 L   3) 0.500 L
2) 22.4 L   4) 44.8 L

Practice 77

Given the reaction:

$$C_2H_4 \; + \; 3O_2 \; \rightarrow \; 2CO_2 \; + \; 2H_2O$$

At STP, how many liters of CO_2 are produced when 15 liters of O_2 are consumed?

1) 10 L   3) 15 L
2) 30 L   4) 45 L

Practice 78   *Show a setup and the result.*

Given the reaction:

$$2C_2H_6(g) \; + \; 7O_2(g) \rightarrow 4CO_2(g) \; + \; 6H_2O(g)$$

Calculate the total number of liters of $CO_2(g)$ produced by the complete combustion of 35 liters of $C_2H_6(g)$ at STP.

Practice 79   *Show a setup and the result.*

Given the balanced combustion reaction below:

$$C_3H_8 \; + \; 5O_2 \; \rightarrow \; 3CO_2 \; + \; 2H_2O$$

Calculate the volume of propane, C_3H_8, that will completely react with 22.4 liters of oxygen, O_2, at STP.

 ©2017 E3 Scholastic Publishing. All Rights Reserved

Mass to Mass Problems in Equations

When the mass of one substance in a reaction is known, the mass of any other substance in the reaction can be calculated as shown in the example below.

In the previous problem, volume to volume, proportions were setup with a mix of two units (mole/volume). This was done because at STP the volume of one mole of all gases is the same. In a mass to mass problem, mole/mass proportion cannot be used to setup and solve the problem because the mass of one mole of each substance is different.

Concept Task: Be able to set up and solve mass-to-mass problem in a given equation.

Example 29:
Given the balanced equation below:

$$2KClO_3 \rightarrow 2KCl + 3O_2$$

How many grams of KCl are produced by decomposing 100 g of $KClO_3$?

Proportion setup

$$\frac{\text{Mass of } 2KClO_3}{100 \text{ g}} = \frac{\text{Mass of } 2KCl}{X}$$

$$\frac{244 \text{ g}}{100 \text{ g}} = \frac{148 \text{ g}}{X}$$

$$244X = 14800$$

$$X = \boxed{60.7 \text{ g KCl}}$$

Factor-label setup

mass given in question x mol/FM of $KClO_3$ x mole ratio $KCl/KClO_3$ in equation x mass/FM of KCl

$$100 \text{ g } KClO_3 \times \frac{1 \text{ mol } KClO_3}{122 \text{ g } KClO_3} \times \frac{2 \text{ mol } KCl}{2 \text{ mol } KClO_3} \times \frac{74 \text{ g } KCl}{1 \text{ mol } KCl} = \boxed{60.7 \text{ g } KCl}$$

Formula mass of $KClO_3$	Mass of $2KClO_3$	Formula mass of KCl	Mass of 2KCl
1 K 1(39) = 39 g		1K 1(39) = 39 g	
1 Cl 1(35) = 35 g	2(122 g) = 244 g	1Cl 1(35) = 35 g	2(74 g) = 148 g
3 O 3(16) = 48 g		74 g	
122 g			
Use in factor-label setup	use in proportion setup	use in factor-label setup	use in Proportion setup

Practice 80
Given the reaction:

$$Mg + 2HCl \rightarrow MgCl_2 + H_2$$

What is the total number of grams of Mg consumed when 1 g of H_2 is produced?
1) 6.0 g   3) 3.0 g
2) 12 g   4) 24 g

Practice 81
Given the balanced equation below:

$$3Cu + 8HNO_3 \rightarrow 3Cu(NO_3)_2 + 2NO + 4H_2O$$

The total number of grams of Cu needed to produce 188 grams of $Cu(NO_3)_2$ is
1) 64   3) 32
2) 128   4) 124

Practice 82   *Show a setup and the result.*
According to the reaction:

$$2C_2H_2 + 5O_2 \rightarrow 4CO_2 + 2H_2O$$

Calculate the grams of CO_2 produced from combusting 80 grams of C_2H_2.

Practice 83   *Show a setup and the result.*
Given the reaction:

$$4Fe + 3O_2 \rightarrow 2Fe_2O_3$$

Calculate the mass of Fe_2O_3, iron(III) oxide, that will be produced from 20 grams of Fe.

Base your answers to practice questions 84 and 85 on the information below.

Given the balanced equation representing a reaction:
$$2C_2H_6 + 7O_2 \rightarrow 4CO_2 + 6H_2O$$

84. Determine the total number of moles of oxygen that react completely with 8 moles of C_2H_6
Show a numerical setup and the calculated result.

85. Determine the mass of 5.20 moles of C_2H_6 (gram-formula mass = 30.1 grams/mole).
Show a numerical setup and the calculated result.

Base your answers to practice questions 86 through 88 on the information below.

Rust on an automobile door contains $Fe_2O_3(s)$. The balanced equation representing one of the reactions between iron in the door of the automobile and oxygen in the atmosphere is given below.

$$4Fe(s) + 3O_2(g) \rightarrow 2Fe_2O_3(s)$$

86. What is the mole ratio of iron reacted to iron(III) oxide formed as rust on an automobile door?

87. Determine the gram-formula mass of the product of this reaction.

88. Identify the type of chemical reaction represented by this equation.

Base your answers to practice questions 89 through 91 on the information below.

Some dry chemicals can be used to put out forest fires. One of these chemicals is $NaHCO_3$. When $NaHCO_3(s)$ is heated, one of the products is $CO_2(g)$, as shown in the balanced equation below.

$$2NaHCO_3(s) + heat \rightarrow Na_2CO_3(s) + H_2O(g) + CO_2(g)$$

89. Identify the type of chemical reaction represented by this equation.

90. Determine the total number of moles of $CO_2(g)$ produced when 7.0 moles of $NaHCO_3(s)$ is completely reacted. Show a numerical setup and the calculated result.

91. Show a correct numerical setup for calculating the percent composition by mass of carbon in the product Na_2CO_3.

Vocabulary
Lesson 1: Mole Concept and Calculations in Formulas

Mole

Avogadro's number

Molar mass

Gram atomic mass

Gram-formula mass

Percent composition

Hydrate

Anhydrous

Lesson 2: Mole Concept and Calculations in Equations

The Mole Concept and Calculations Answers to Practice Questions Topic 6

1. 4
2. 1
3. 2

4. 4
5. 3
6. 3

7. 1
8. 3
9. 3

10. 4
11. 1
12. 2

13. 1
14. 4
15. 1
16. 4

17. 2(27) + 3(32) + 12(16) = **342 g/mol**

18. 4(12) + 2(16) + 8(1) = **88 g/mol**

19. 1(137) + 10(16) + 18(1) = **315 g/mol**

20. 1
21. 2
22. 2

23. moles = $\dfrac{184 \text{ g}}{92 \text{ g/mol}}$ = **2 mol**

24. moles = $\dfrac{100 \text{ g}}{286 \text{ g/mol}}$ = **0.35 mol**

25. 4
26. 2
27. 3
28. 2

29. mass = (0.1 mol) (180 g/mol) = **18 g**

30. mass = (2.3 mol) (250 g/mol) = **575 g**

31. moles = $\dfrac{349 \text{ g}}{44.0 \text{ g/mol}}$ = **7.93 mol**

32. 1
33. 1
34. 3

35. volume = (3.50 mol) (22.4 L/mol) = **78.4 L**

36. moles = $\dfrac{10.0 \text{ L}}{22.4 \text{ L/mol}}$ = **0.446 mol**

37. 4
38. 1
39. 3

40. (5.0 mol) (6.02×10^{23} atoms/mol)
    = **3.01×10^{24} atoms**

41. moles = $\dfrac{8.12 \times 10^{25}}{6.02 \times 10^{23}}$ = **135 mol**

42. 4
43. 2
44. 3

45. 576 g SO_2 x $\dfrac{1 \text{ mole } SO_2}{64 \text{ g } SO_2}$ x $\dfrac{22.4 \text{ L } SO_2}{1 \text{ mole } SO_2}$ = **201.6 L**

46. 2 g Na x $\dfrac{1 \text{ mole } Na}{23 \text{ g } Na}$ x $\dfrac{6.02 \times 10^{23} \text{ } Na}{1 \text{ mole } Na}$ = **5.23×10^{22}**

47. 72.5 L NH_3 x $\dfrac{1 \text{ mole } NH_3}{22.4 \text{ L } NH_3}$ x $\dfrac{17 \text{ g } NH_3}{1 \text{ mole } NH_3}$ = **55 g NH_3**

48. 3
49. 1
50. 2
51. 1

52. % H = $\dfrac{8 \text{ g}}{92 \text{ g}}$ x 100 = **8.7 % H**

53. 1
54. 3
55. 3

56. % H_2O = $\dfrac{54 \text{ g}}{218 \text{ g}}$ x 100 = 24.8 % H_2O

57. 3
58. 1

59. % H_2O = $\dfrac{1.6 \text{ g}}{4.8 \text{ g}}$ x 100 = **33.3 % H_2O**

60. 2
61. 1
62. 3

63. $C_3H_4O_2$

64. 4.03×10^{-4} moles or 0.000403 moles

65. % O = $\dfrac{96 \text{ g}}{176 \text{ g}}$ x 100 = 54.5 % O

66. % As = $\dfrac{75 \text{ g}}{163 \text{ g}}$ x 100 = **46 % As**

67. **As_2O_3**

68. **57.5 g As**

69. 3
70. 2
71. 1
72. 1
73. 1

74. $\dfrac{6}{x} = \dfrac{1}{1.75}$ x = (6)(1.75) = **10.5 mol**

75. 0.15 mol H_3PO_4 x $\dfrac{3 \text{ mol Cu}}{2 \text{ mol } H_3PO_4}$ = **0.225 mol Cu**

130

©2017 E3 Scholastic Publishing. All Rights Reserved

76. 4

77. 1

78. $\dfrac{2}{35} = \dfrac{4}{x}$ $x = \dfrac{(35)(4)}{2}$ = **70 L CO₂**

79. 22.4 L O₂ $\times \dfrac{1 \text{ mol } C_3H_8}{5 \text{ mol } O_2}$ = **4.48 L O₂**

80. 2

81. 1

82. $\dfrac{52 \text{ g}}{80 \text{ g}} = \dfrac{176 \text{ g}}{x}$ *x = 270.8 g CO₂*

83. 20 g Fe $\times \dfrac{1 \text{ mol Fe}}{56 \text{ g Fe}} \times \dfrac{2 \text{ mol Fe}_2O_3}{4 \text{ mol Fe}} \times \dfrac{160 \text{ g Fe}_2O_3}{1 \text{ mol Fe}_2O_3}$ = **28.6 g Fe₂O₃**

84. $\dfrac{2}{8} = \dfrac{7}{x}$ $x = \dfrac{(8)(7)}{2}$ = **28 mol O₂**

85. mass = (5.20 mol C₂H₆) (30.1 g/mol) = **157 g C₂H₆**

86. 2 : 1

87. 2(Fe) + 3(O₂) = 2(55.854 g) + 3(15.999) = **159.705 g/mol**

88. synthesis or metathesis

89. decomposition

90. $\dfrac{2}{7} = \dfrac{1}{x}$ $x = \dfrac{7}{2}$ = **3.5 mol CO₂**

91. % C = $\dfrac{\text{mass of C}}{\text{mass of Na}_2CO_3} \times 100$ = $\dfrac{12.011}{105.98} \times 100$ = **11.3 % Na₂CO₃**

©2017 E3 Scholastic Publishing. All Rights Reserved

Topic 7
Solutions

Lesson 1: Properties of Aqueous Solutions

Lesson 2: Solubility

Lesson 3: Descriptions of Solutions

Lesson 4: Expressions of Solution Concentration

Lesson 5: Boiling Point and Vapor Pressure

Lesson 4: Changes in Physical Properties of Solutions

Lesson 1 - Properties of Aqueous Solutions

Solutions are homogeneous mixtures. A homogeneous mixture is a type of mixture in which all components are evenly and uniformly mixed throughout the mixture. One good example of a solution is saltwater. Milk is also a homogeneous mixture. Although there are different types of solutions, the discussion in this topic will focus on aqueous solutions only.

In this lesson, you will learn about properties of aqueous solutions.

Components of Aqueous Solutions
Solute and Solvent

Aqueous solutions are solutions in which the solvent is water.
Aqueous solutions consist of two main components; solute and solvent.
Below are definitions and facts related to these components.

Solute

A solute is the substance being dissolved in a solution.
A solute is always present in a smaller amount than the solvent.
Solute can be a solid, liquid or gas.
Dissolving of a solute in water to make a solution is a physical change.

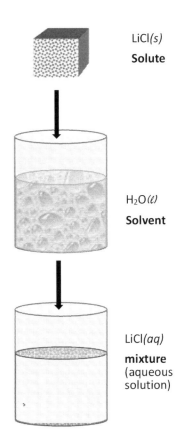

LiCl(*s*)
Solute

Solvent (Water)

A solvent is the substance in which the solute is dispersed.
A solvent is always present in a greater amount relative to the solute.
In aqueous solutions, the solvent is always water.
In all solutions, the solvent is usually a liquid.

H_2O(*ℓ*)
Solvent

Aqueous Solution (Mixture)

An aqueous solution is a mixture of a solvent (water) and solute.
The equation below shows the dissolving of lithium chloride (solute) in water.

LiCl(*aq*)
mixture
(aqueous solution)

$$LiCl(s) \quad + \quad H_2O(\ell) \xrightarrow{\text{dissolving}} LiCl(aq)$$

Solute   **solvent**   **mixture**

(s) solid   *(ℓ)* liquid   *(aq)* aqueous

 ©2017 E3 Scholastic Publishing. All Rights Reserved

Hydration of Ions in Solutions

Oxygen Attracts Positive Ion, Hydrogen Attracts Negative Ion

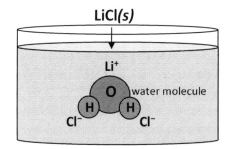

Dissolving of LiCl salt.

Molecule-ion attraction

When a salt (**LiCl**) is placed in water, the salt crystals interact with water molecules, H_2O, to dissolve.

In LiCl solution: LiCl*(aq)*

Li^+ (the positive ion of the salt) attracts
O (the negative end of a water molecule)

Cl^- (the negative ion of the salt) attracts
H (the positive ends of a water molecule)

Opposites attract.

Properties and Separation of Solutions

The following are some general characteristics of properly made solutions.
• Solutions are homogenous mixtures; the components are evenly mixed throughout.
• Solutions are generally clear.
• Solutions that are colorful likely contain an ion of a transition element.
• Solutions are transparent and do not disperse light.
• Particles in a solution will not settle to the bottom of the container or separate into layers.
• The solute and solvent of a solution can be separated by evaporation, distillation, or crystallization.

Evaporation is the process of heating a solution to boil off the solvent and leave behind the solute.

Distillation is the process of boiling off and collecting each liquid of a mixture from the lowest to the highest boiling point.

Crystallization is a process of recovering a solid solute from a mixture by *evaporating* off the water. When a solution is boiled, water will evaporate out of the mixture, leaving behind ions of the solute to re-crystallize. Crystallization can also be accomplished by slowly cooling the solution.

Filtration cannot be used to remove or separate the solute particles from the solvent of a true solution. Particles of both the solute and solvent are generally smaller than holes of a filter. As a result, both the solute and solvent will go through a filtering equipment.

Examples of Solutions

A chemical formula can only be used to represent pure substances such as elements and compounds. Aqueous solutions are represented by symbols, not chemical formulas. A symbol for an aqueous solution is not a chemical formula of that solution.
Below are examples of five aqueous solutions

Solution name	Solution (mixture) symbol	Solute	Solvent
Sodium chloride solution	NaCl*(aq)*	NaCl*(s)* or Na$^+$Cl$^-$	$H_2O(\ell)$
Potassium nitrate solution	KNO$_3$*(aq)*	KNO$_3$*(s)* or K$^+$NO$_3^-$	$H_2O(\ell)$
Sugar solution	C$_6$H$_{12}$O$_6$*(aq)*	C$_6$H$_{12}$O$_6$*(s)*	$H_2O(\ell)$
Carbon dioxide solution	CO$_2$*(aq)*	CO$_2$*(g)*	$H_2O(\ell)$
Ethanol (alcohol) solution	C$_2$H$_5$OH*(aq)*	C$_2$H$_5$OH*(ℓ)*	$H_2O(\ell)$

NOTE: The aqueous symbol, *(aq)*, next to a formula of a substance always indicates that the substance is dissolved in water.

Properties and Separation of Solutions: Practice Problems

Practice 1
All aqueous mixtures must contain
1) water   2) sodium chloride   3) oxygen   4) sand

Practice 2
The process of recovering a salt from a solution by evaporating the solvent is known as
1) decomposition   2) crystallization   3) reduction   4) filtration

Practice 3
In a true solution, the dissolved particles
1) are visible to the eyes
2) will settle out on standing
3) are always solids
4) cannot be removed by filtration

Practice 4
When sample X is passed through a filter paper a white residue, Y, remains on the paper and a clear liquid, Z, passes through. When Z is vaporized, another white residue remains. Sample X is best classified as
1) an element
2) a compound
3) a heterogeneous mixture
4) a homogeneous mixture

Practice 5
An aqueous solution of copper sulfate is poured into a filter paper cone. What passes through the filter paper?
1) Only the solvent.
2) Only the solute.
3) Both solvent and solute.
4) Neither the solvent nor solute.

Practice 6
A small amount of $LiNO_3$ is dissolved in H_2O to make a solution. In this solution
1) $LiNO_3$ is the solute
2) $LiNO_3$ is the solvent
3) H_2O is the solute
4) H_2O is the precipitate

Practice 7
What happens when KI(s) is dissolved in water?
1) I^- ions are attracted to the oxygen atoms of water.
2) K^+ ions are attracted to the oxygen atoms of water.
3) K^+ ions are attracted to the hydrogen atoms of water.
4) No attractions are involved; the crystal just falls apart.

Base your answer to practice question 8 on the information below.

A 2.0-liter aqueous solution contains a total of 3.0 moles of dissolved NH_4Br at 25°C and standard pressure.

8. Identify the *two* ions present in the solute. Include name and symbol for both ions.

Base your answer to practice question 9 on the information below.

Given the balanced equation for the dissolving of $NaNO_3(s)$ in water:

$$NaNO_3(s) \xrightarrow{H_2O} Na^+(aq) + NO^-(aq)$$

9. Using the key to the right, draw at least two water molecules near each ion in the box. Your drawing must show the correct orientation of each water molecule when it is near the Na^+ ion or NO_3^- ion in the solution.

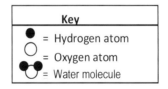

Key	
●	= Hydrogen atom
○	= Oxygen atom
●◌●	= Water molecule

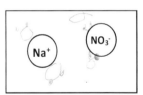

Lesson 2 – Solubility

Not every substance that is put in water will dissolve. Some substances dissolve very well, others very little, and some not at all. In addition, how well a given substance dissolves in water is affected by conditions such as temperature and/or pressure.

In this lesson, you'll learn about factors that affect how well substances dissolve in water. You will also learn how to determine which substance will dissolve and which will not dissolve in water.

Solubility: *How Well a Solid Dissolves*

Solubility describes the extent to which a substance will dissolve in water under a given set of conditions.

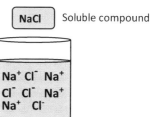

Soluble means that a substance has *high* solubility.
Soluble salts dissolve very well in water to produce a solution with a high concentration of ions.
Ex. NaCl (sodium chloride) is soluble in water.

Insoluble means that a substance has *low* solubility.
Insoluble salts dissolve very little in water to produce a solution with a low concentration of ions.
Ex. AgCl (silver chloride) is insoluble in water.

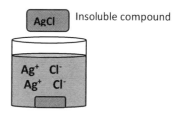

Miscibility: *How Well Liquids Mix*

Miscibility describes the extent to which two or more liquids will mix.

Miscible refers to two liquids with *high* miscibility.
Two miscible liquids will mix evenly and will not form layers.
Ex. Ethanol (alcohol) and water are miscible liquids.

Immiscible refers to two liquids with *low* miscibility.
Two immiscible liquids will not mix evenly and may separate into layers.
Ex. Oil and water are immiscible liquids.

Factors that Affect Solubility

The extent to which a solute will dissolve in water depends largely on the following three factors: Temperature, pressure, and nature of the solute.

Temperature: *Affects the Solubility of Solids, Liquids, and Gases.*

The effect of temperature on the solubility of a solute varies depending if the solute is a solid or gas. Table G (The Solubility Curves) shows the solubility of a few selected solutes at different water temperatures.

Solid solutes: ↑*Temperature* ↑*Solubility*
The solubility of many solids increases with increasing water temperature. KCl*(s)* and $C_6H_{12}O_6$*(s)* dissolve better in 45°C water than in 25°C water.

t 45°C.

Gaseous Solutes: ↓*Temperature* ↑*Solubility*
The solubility of a gas increases with decreasing water temperature. O_2*(g)* and CO_2*(g)* dissolve better in 25°C water than in 45°C water.

The 25°C water contains more dissolved O_2 gas.

Pressure: *Affects the Solubility of Gases only.*

For a given gaseous solute, the solubility of the solute changes with a change in pressure.

Gaseous solutes: ↑*Pressure* ↑*Solubility*
The solubility of a gas increases with increasing pressure. O_2*(g)* and CO_2*(g)* dissolve better in a high-pressure system than in a low-pressure system.

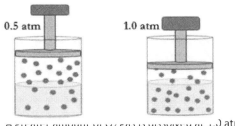

Solid solutes: *No Effect*
Pressure has no effect on the solubility of a solid. The amount of $NaNO_3$*(s)* or KCl*(s)* that dissolves in water will not be affected by a change in pressure.

A greater amount of O_2 gas is dissolved at 1.0 atm.

Nature of Solutes: *Like Dissolves Like*

"Like dissolves like" means that a solute dissolve better in solvents of the same polarity.

Ionic solutes: *Higher Solubility in Polar Solvents (Water)*
NaCl*(s)* and $LiNO_3$(s) dissolve well in water because they are *alike in terms of polarity.*
• Water is a polar substance with positive and negative ends.
• Ionic solids such as NaCl*(s)* and $LiNO_3$(s) are composed of positive and negative ions.

Nonpolar solutes: *Higher Solubility in Nonpolar Solvents*
I_2(s), iodine, which has no positive and no negative ends, has a low solubility in water.
• I_2(s) dissolves much better in a solvent like CCl_4*(l)*, carbon tetrachloride, because they are both nonpolar substances.

©2017 E3 Scholastic Publishing. All Rights Reserved

Solubility Factors: Practice Questions

Practice 10
The solubility of a salt in a given volume of water depends largely on the
1) surface area of the salt crystals
2) pressure on the surface of the water
3) rate at which the salt and water are stirred
4) temperature of the water

Practice 11
Which change will have the least effect on the solubility of a solid?
1) Increase in temperature
2) Increase in surface area
3) Decrease in temperature
4) Decrease in pressure

Practice 12
A change in pressure has the greatest effect on the solubility of a solution that contains a
1) solid in a liquid
2) gas in a liquid
3) liquid in a liquid
4) liquid in a solid

Practice 13
Which change will increase the solubility of a gas in water?
1) Increase in pressure and decrease in temperature.
2) Increase in pressure and increase in temperature.
3) Decrease in pressure and increase in temperature.
4) Decrease in pressure and decrease in temperature.

Concept Task: Be able to relate solubility of a substance to temperature and pressure

Practice 14
The solubility of which substance will not be affected by an increase in pressure?
1) $MgCl_2$
2) SO_3
3) CO_2
4) N_2

Practice 15
As the temperature of water increases, which substance will show a decrease in solubility?
1) $CaBr_2$
2) KNO_3
3) CO
4) KBr

Practice 16
As the pressure of a system is changed from 1 atm to 2 atm, the solubility of which substance will be most affected by this change?
1) $HCl(\ell)$
2) $HCl(g)$
3) LiCl(s)
4) $LiCl(\ell)$

Practice 17
At standard pressure, water at which temperature will contain the most dissolved NH_4Cl particles?
1) 5°C
2) 10°C
3) 15°
4) 20°C

Practice 18
At which temperature would 100 g $H_2O(\ell)$ contain the most dissolved oxygen?
1) 10°C
2) 20°C
3) 30°C
4) 40°C

Practice 19
Under which conditions would carbon dioxide be most soluble in water?
1) 10°C and 1 atm
2) 10°C and 2 atm
3) 20°C and 1 atm
4) 20°C and 2 atm

20. State the relationship between the solubility of $NH_3(g)$ in water and the temperature of the aqueous solution.

21. Explain, in terms of molecular polarity, why oxygen gas has a low solubility in water. Your response must include both oxygen and water.

Soluble and Insoluble Salts: Using the Solubility Guideline Table F.

Not every substance will dissolve in water.
A *soluble* substance dissolves well in water to produce a solution with high ion concentration.
An *insoluble* substances dissolves very little in water to produce a solution with low ion concentration.
The degree of solubility of an ionic solute depends on the nature of the ions it contains.
The *Solubility Guidelines Table F* is used for determining if a given ionic solute is soluble or insoluble.

Soluble Ions   **Table F**   **Insoluble Ions**

Ions That Form Soluble Compounds	Exceptions
Group 1 ions (Li$^+$, Na$^+$, etc.)	
ammonium (NH$_4^+$)	
nitrate (NO$_3^-$)	
acetate (C$_2$H$_3$O$_2^-$ or CH$_3$COO$^-$)	
hydrogen carbonate (HCO$_3^-$)	
chlorate (ClO$_3^-$)	
halides (Cl$^-$, Br$^-$, I$^-$)	when combined with Ag$^+$, Pb^{2+}, or Hg$_2^{2+}$
sulfates (SO$_4^{2-}$)	when combined with Ag$^+$, Ca^{2+}, Sr^{2+}, Ba^{2+}, or Pb^{2+}

Ions That Form Insoluble Compounds*	Exceptions
carbonate (CO$_3^{2-}$)	when combined with Group 1 ions or ammonium (NH$_4^+$)
chromate (CrO$_4^{2-}$)	when combined with Group 1 ions, Ca^{2+}, Mg^{2+}, or ammonium (NH$_4^+$)
phosphate (PO$_4^{3-}$)	when combined with Group 1 ions or ammonium (NH$_4^+$)
sulfide (S^{2-})	when combined with Group 1 ions or ammonium (NH$_4^+$)
hydroxide (OH$^-$)	when combined with Group 1 ions, Ca^{2+}, Ba^{2+}, Sr^{2+}, or ammonium (NH$_4^+$)

*compounds having very low solubility in H$_2$O

Concept Task: Be able to determine if a given ionic solute is soluble or insoluble.

Table F is used in explaining why each compound below is soluble or insoluble

LiCl   **lithium chloride**   *Soluble*
Li$^+$ ion (and all Group 1 ions) is listed on the soluble side.
Cl- ion, a halide ion, is also listed on the soluble side.
Neither ion is listed as an exception for the other.
Therefore, LiCl is a soluble compound.

Ag$_2$SO$_4$ **silver sulfate**   *Insoluble*
SO$_4^{2-}$ (sulfate ion) is listed on the soluble side with exceptions.
Ag$^+$ (silver ion) is listed as one of the exceptions for sulfates.
Therefore, Ag$_2$SO$_4$ is an insoluble compound.

Ba(OH)$_2$ **barium hydroxide**   *Soluble*
Hydroxide ion (OH$^-$) is listed on the insoluble side with exceptions.
Barium (Ba^{2+}) is listed as one of the exceptions for OH$^-$ ion.
Therefore, barium hydroxide is a soluble compound

MgSO$_4$ **magnesium sulfide**   *Insoluble*
Sulfide ion (S^{2-}) is listed on the insoluble side with exceptions.
Magnesium ion (Mg^{2+}) is not listed as an exception for S^{2-} ion.
Therefore, magnesium sulfide is an insoluble compound.

Practice 22
Based on Reference Table F, which substance is most soluble?
1) (NH$_4$)$_3$PO$_4$ 3) CaSO$_4$
2) PbCl$_2$ 4) AgI

Practice 23
Which of these saturated solutions has the lowest concentration of dissolved ions?
1) NaCl(aq)   3) NiCl$_2$(aq)
2) MgCl$_2$(aq)   4) AgCl(aq)

Practice 24
Which ion, when combined with chloride ions, Br—, forms an insoluble substance in water?
1) Fe^{2+} 3) Pb^{2+}
2) Mg^{2+} 4) Zn^{2+}

Practice 25
According to Table F, which chromate salt is soluble?
1) Calcium chromate
2) Zinc chromate
3) Cobalt(II) chromate
4) Iron(II) chromate

26. The dissolving of solid lithium bromide in water is represented by the balanced equation below:

LiBr*(s)* $\xrightarrow{\text{H}_2\text{O}}$ Li$^+$*(aq)* + Br$^-$*(aq)*

Based on Table *F*, identify *one* ion that reacts with Br$^-$ ions in an aqueous solution to form an insoluble compound.

Lesson 3 - Descriptions of Solutions and the Solubility Curves.

A solution can be described as saturated, unsaturated, supersaturated, dilute, or concentrated depending on four factors of the solution listed below.
Type of solute, amount of the solute, and amount and temperature of water.

The Solubility Curves Table G is used to determine the type of solution when the above information about the solution are known. In this lesson you will learn terms that are used to describe solutions. You will also learn how to use the Solubility Curves Table below to answer questions about a solution.

Solubility Curves Table G

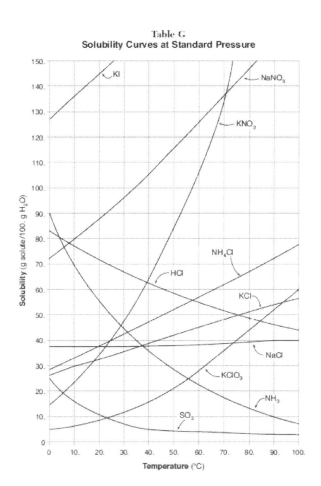

Table G
Solubility Curves at Standard Pressure

The curves on Table G show the change in the solubility of selected solids and gases in 100 grams of water at different temperatures.

Note the followings about the curves.

• *Solid solutes (ex. KCl)* have curves with positive slopes because the solubility of a solid increases as water temperature increases.

• *Gaseous solutes (ex. NH₃)* have curves with negative slopes because the solubility of a gas decreases as water temperature increases.

Table G is used to answer the following questions about a solution at a specified temperature.

• How many grams of a solute are needed to form a saturated solution?

• Is a solution saturated, unsaturated, or supersaturated?

• Which solute is most or least soluble?
Which solute is most or least dilute?
Which solute is most or least concentrated?

Descriptions of Solutions

Saturated solution: *Maximum Amount of Solute*
A solution containing the maximum amount of the solute that can be dissolved at a given water temperature. In a saturated solution, equilibrium exists between dissolved and undissolved particles. If additional solute is added, it will settle to the bottom as crystals.

Unsaturated solution: *Less Than the Maximum Amount of Solute*
A solution containing less than the maximum amount of the solute that can be dissolved at a given water temperature. An unsaturated solution can dissolve more solute.

Supersaturated solution: *More Than the Maximum Amount of Solute*
An unstable solution containing more than the maximum amount of the solute that can be dissolved at a given water temperature. A supersaturated solution is made by heating a saturated solution, adding more solute (which will dissolve at the new temperature) and then cooling down the solution.

Dilute solution: *Small Solute in Large Solvent*
A solution containing a smaller amount of dissolved solute relative to the amount of water (solvent).

Concentrated solution: *Large Solute in Little Solvent*
A solution containing a larger amount of dissolved solute relative to the amount of water (solvent).

Determining Type of Solution

To determine the type of solution from Table G

Step 1: Locate temp of the solution. Go up the temp line

Step 2: **Stop when you've gone up as** high as the grams of solute given in the question

Step 3: Note where you've stopped relative to the curve.

Above the Curve: Supersaturated

C is a supersaturated solution of NH_4Cl.

On the Curve: Saturated

B is saturated solution of NH_4Cl.

D is a saturated solution of $NaNO_3$.

Below Curve: Unsaturated

A is an unsaturated solution of NH_4Cl.

Solution A is dilute:

It contains small amount of solute (38 g) in a large amount of water (100 g).

Solutions C and D are concentrated:

Each contains a large amount of solute (68 g and 105 g) relative to the amount of water (100 g).

Very important before using Table G for Step 3.
If 100 g H_2O: Make no change to grams of solute
If 50 g H_2O: Double grams of solute first
If 200 g H_2O: Cut grams of solute in half first

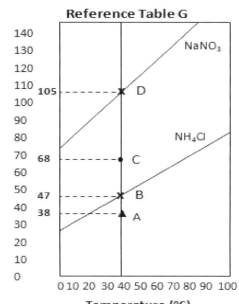

Reference Table G

Topic 7   Solutions

Descriptions of Solutions: Practice Problems

Practice 27
A solution containing 75 grams of KNO_3 in 100 grams of water at 50°C is considered to be
1) unsaturated   2) supersaturated   3) saturated

Practice 28
A solution containing 15 grams of NH_3 in 100 grams of water 90°C is best classified as
1) unsaturated   2) supersaturated   3) saturated

Practice 29
A solution of KCl contains 90 grams of the solute in 200 g of water at 60°C. This solution can be best classified as
1) unsaturated   2) supersaturated   3) saturated

Practice 30
If 70 grams of KI is dissolved in 50 grams of H_2O at 10°C, what will be the best description of this solution?
1) unsaturated   2) supersaturated   3) saturated

Practice 31
Based on Reference Table G, a solution of SO_2 that contains 15 g of the solute dissolved in 100 g of H_2O at 10°C is best described as
1) saturated and dilute   3) saturated and concentrated
2) unsaturated and concentrated   4) supersaturated and concentrated

Practice 32
A solution containing 100 grams of $NaNO_3$ in 100 grams at 40°C is best described as
1) unsaturated and dilute   3) saturated and concentrated
2) unsaturated and concentrated   4) supersaturated and concentrated

Practice 33
Based on Reference Table G, which of these substances is most soluble at 50°C?
1) $KClO_3$ 2) NaCl   3) NH_3 4) $NaNO_3$

Practice 34
Which of these saturated solution is the most dilute at 20°C?
1) $NH_4Cl(aq)$ 2) $KCl(aq)$ 3) $KClO_3(aq)$ 4) $NaNO_3(aq)$

Practice 35
According to Reference Table G, which solution at equilibrium contains 50 grams of solute per 100 grams of H_2O at 75°C?
1) An unsaturated solution of KCl.   3) A saturated solution of KCl.
2) An unsaturated solution of $KClO_3$.   4) A saturated solution of $KClO_3$.

Practice 36
A solution contains 100 grams of a nitrate salt dissolved in 100 grams of water at 50°C. The solution could be a
1) supersaturated solution of $NaNO_3$ 3) saturated solution of $NaNO_3$
2) supersaturated solution of KNO_3 4) saturated solution of KNO_3.

Amount of Solute to Make a Saturated Solution

A *saturated solution* contains the maximum amount of the solute that can be dissolved in the given amount of water at a specified temperature.

Concept Task: Be able to determine grams of solute to form a saturated solution using Table G.

Step 1: Locate the given temperature on the x-axis.

Step 2: Go up from the temperature point to intersect the curve for the given substance.

Step 3: Go left (from intersection point) to the y-axis and read the grams of solute.

Note that the grams of solute you determined on Table G is for 100 grams of H_2O.

You can adjust the ***saturated grams of solute*** if the amount of water in a question is different from 100 g.

If amount of water is 100 grams: The amount you determined in step 3 is the saturated amount.
72 g NH_4Cl

If amount of water is 200 grams: Double the amount you determined in step 3 to get the saturated amount.
144 g NH_4Cl

If amount of water is 50 grams: Cut the amount you determined in step 3 to get the saturated amount.
36 g NH_4Cl

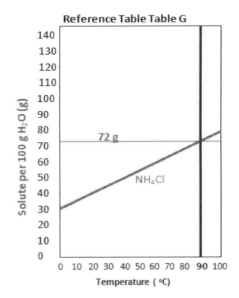

Reference Table Table G

Practice 37
How many grams of KCl must be dissolved in 100 g of H_2O at 60°C to make a saturated?
1) 30 g   2) 45 g   3) 56 g   4) 90 g

Practice 38
What is the approximate amount of $NaNO_3$ needed to saturate 50 grams of water that is at 10°C?
1) 80 g   2) 100 g   3) 40 g   4) 50 g

Practice 39
What is the maximum grams of ammonia, NH_3, that must be dissolved in 200 g of H_2O at 20°C to form a saturated ammonia solution?
1) 200 g   2) 110 g   3) 27.5 g   4) 55 g

Practice 40
According to Reference Table G, what is the approximate amount of potassium chlorate needed to form a saturated solution in 100 g of water at 10°C?
1) 10 g   2) 30 g   3) 15 g   4) 6 g

Practice 41
According to Reference Table G, which solution is a saturated solution at 30°C?
1) 12 grams of $KClO_3$ in 100 grams of water
2) 12 grams of $KClO_3$ in 200 grams of water
3) 30 grams of NaCl in 100 grams of water
4) 30 grams of NaCl in 200 grams of water

Practice 42
Which is a saturated solution?
1) 40 g NH_4Cl in 100 g of water at 50°C
2) 2 g SO_2 in 100 g water at 10°C
3) 52 g KCl in 100 g of water at 80°C
4) 120 g KI in 100 g water at 20°C

Practice 43
A solution contains 130 grams of KNO_3 dissolved in 100 grams of water. When 3 more grams of KNO_3 is added, none of it dissolves, nor do any additional crystals appear. Based on Reference Table G, the temperature of the solution is closest to
1) 65°C   2) 68°C   3) 70°C   4) 72°C

©2017 E3 Scholastic Publishing. All Rights Reserved

Adding More Solute to an Unsaturated Solution

A solution that is unsaturated can dissolve more solute. How many more grams of a solute that should be added to bring an unsaturated solution to saturation can be determined as shown below.

Grams of Solute to Add = Grams to Saturate − Grams of Solute in the Solution
                                     (use Table G)   *(given in question)*

Concept Task: Be able to determine the amount of solute that can be added to a solution to make it a saturated solution.

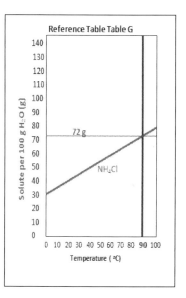

Reference Table Table G

Example 1
A solution of NH_4Cl contains 60 g of the solute in 100 g of water at 90°C. How many more grams of NH_4Cl must be added to make it a saturated solution at that temperature?

1) 90 g   2) 72 g   3) 40 g   4) 12 g

Grams of Solute to Add = Grams to saturate − Grams in solution
                                    (use Table G)   *(given in question)*

Grams of Solute to Add =   72 g   −   60 g   =   **12 g** NH_4Cl
                                                                        Choice 4

Practice 44
A solution contains 14 grams of KCl in 100 grams of water at 40°C. What is the maximum amount of KCl that must be added to make this a saturated solution?
1) 14 g   2) 20 g   3) 25 g   4) 54 g

Practice 45
An unsaturated solution of $NaNO_3$ contains 70 g of $NaNO_3$ dissolved in 100 g of water at 20°C. How many more grams of $NaNO_3$ are needed to make this a saturated solution?
1) 70 g   2) 95 g   3) 30 g   4) 18 g

Practice 46
How many more grams of HCl are needed in a solution containing 100 g of the solute in 200 grams of water at 20°C to make the solution saturated?
1) 44 g   2) 72 g   3) 144 g   4) 100 g

Practice 47
A student dissolved only 40 grams of NaCl in 80 grams of water that is at 90°C. To make this a saturated solution, the student must add to the solution
1) 10 g of NaCl   3) 10 g of H_2O
2) 20 g of NaCl   4) 20 g of H_2O

Amount of Solute Precipitate

When a salt solution that is saturated at one temperature is cooled to a lower temperature, a smaller amount of the solute will be soluble. As a result, the ions of the solute will re-crystallize and precipitate (settle out) from solution. A **precipitate** is a solid that forms out of a solution. The amount of the solute that precipitated at the lower temperature can be determined as shown below.

Example 2
According to Table G, how many grams of NH_4Cl will precipitate when a saturated solution made with 100 grams of water at 90°C is cooled to 60°C?

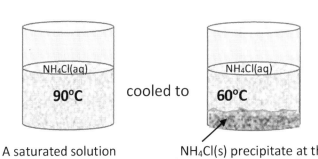

cooled to

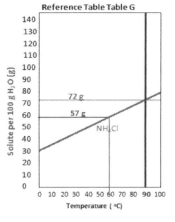

A saturated solution of NH_4Cl at 90°C

$NH_4Cl(s)$ precipitate at the lower temperature of 60°C.

Grams of Solid Precipitated = Saturated amount − Saturated amount
                              at the higher temp (90°C)   at the lower temp (60°C)

Grams of Solid Precipitated =   72 g   −   57 g   =   **15 g of NH_4Cl**

Practice 48
A saturated solution of KNO_3 is prepared with 100 grams of water at 70°C. What amount of KNO_3 will precipitate if the solution is cooled to 50°C?
1) 215 g   3) 135 g
2) 50 g   4) 20 g

Practice 49
When a saturated solution of $KClO_3$ that is made with 100 g of H_2O is cooled from 25°C to 10°C, some salt crystals reformed at the bottom of the beaker. How many grams of the $KClO_3$ salt is at the bottom of the beaker?
1) 5 g   3) 15 g
2) 10 g   4) 20 g

Practice 50
A test tube contains a saturated solution of KNO_3 that was prepared with 100 grams of H_2O at 60°C. If the test tube is cooled to 30°C, what will be found at the bottom of the test tube?
1) 30 g of KNO_3 3) 30 g of H_2O
2) 57 g of KNO_3 4) 57 g of H_2O

Base your answers to questions 51 through 54 on the information below.

A student uses 200 grams of water at 60°C to prepare a saturated solution of potassium chloride, KCl.

51. According to Reference Table G, how many grams of KCl must be used to create this saturated solution.

52. This solution is cooled to 10°C and the excess precipitate (settle) out. The resulting solution is saturated at 10°C. How many grams of KCl precipitated out of the original solution?

53. Identify the solute in this solution?

©2017 E3 Scholastic Publishing. All Rights Reserved

Lesson 4 – Expressions of Solution Concentration

Concentration of a solution indicates how much dissolved solute is in a given amount of the solution or solvent. In this lesson, you will learn two expressions of concentration; parts per million and molarity. Most questions dealing with concentration involve calculations. Equations for calculating the concentration of a solution can be found on **Reference Table T**.

Molarity Calculations: *moles per liter*

Molarity expresses the concentration of a solution in number of moles of solute per liter of the solution. The molarity concentration of a solution can be calculated using the equation below:

$$molarity = \frac{moles\ of\ solute}{liter\ of\ solution}$$

Table T

Example 3: *Calculating molarity*
What is the concentration of a solution that contains 1.4 moles of solute in 2.0 liters of the solution?

$$Molarity = \frac{1.4\ mol}{2.0\ L} \qquad numerical\ setup$$

Molarity = 0.7 M or 0.7 mol/L   *calculated result*

Example 4: *Calculating molarity from mass of solute*

A solution contains 80 grams of NaOH in 1000 mL of solution. What is the concentration of this solution? (formula mass of NaOH = 40 g)

$$Molarity = \frac{Given\ mass}{Formula\ mass\ \times\ Volume} = \frac{80}{40 \times 1} \qquad setup$$

Molarity = 2.0 M   *calculated result*

Example 5: *Calculating moles of solute*
How many moles of a solute are in 0.6 liters of a 1.5 molar solution?

moles = Molarity   ×   Volume
moles =   1.5   ×   0.6   *numerical setup*

moles = 0.9 moles   *calculated result*

Practice 54
A 0.25 liter of potassium chloride solution contains 0.75 moles of KCl. What is the concentration of this solution?
1) 0.33   3) 3.0 M
2) 0.75 M   4) 6.0 M

Practice 55
What is the concentration of a solution of KNO_3 (molecular mass = 101 g/mole) that contains 50.5 g of KNO_3 in 2.00 liters of the solution?
1) 25.25 M   3) 2.00 M
2) 0.500 M   4) 0.25 M

Practice 56
What is the total number of moles of solute in 2230 mL of 3.0 M NaOH solution?
1) 1.5 moles   3) 3.0 moles
2) 6.7 moles   4) 0.743 moles

Practice 57
How many milliliters of a .1 M KNO_3 solution would contain .02 moles of the solute?
1) 2000 mL   3) 5000 mL
2) 200 mL   4) 500 mL

Practice 58   *Show a setup and the result.*
What is the total number of moles in 500 mL of a 3.0 M KI solution?

Practice 59   *Show a setup and the result.*
What is the total volume of a 2.0 molar HCl solution that contains 45 grams of HCl?

Parts Per Million Calculations: *ppm*

Parts per million expresses the concentration of a solution in number of grams of the solute that is in every one-million part of the solution. Parts per million (ppm) concentration can be calculated using **Reference Table T** equation below:

$$\text{Parts per million (ppm)} = \frac{\text{mass of solute}}{\text{mass of solution}} \times 1\ 000\ 000$$

Example 6 *Calculating molarity from mass of solute*
A solution of carbon dioxide contains 0.5 grams of the solute in 500 grams of the solution. What is the concentration in parts per million?

$$\text{ppm} = \frac{0.5\ g}{500\ g} \times 1000000 \qquad \textit{numerical setup}$$

$$\text{ppm} = \textbf{1000 ppm} \qquad \textit{calculated result}$$

Example 7 *Calculating molarity from mass of solute and water*
A solution of sodium nitrate contains 50 grams of the solute in 1000 grams of water. What is the concentration of the solution in parts per million?

$$\text{ppm} = \frac{\text{Mass of solute}}{\text{Mass of solute} + \text{Mass of water}} \times 1000000$$

$$\text{ppm} = \frac{50\ g}{50\ g + 1000\ g} \times 1000000 \qquad \textit{setup}$$

$$\text{ppm} = \textbf{0.045 ppm} \qquad \textit{calculated result}$$

In example 2, the mass of the solute (50 g) is high relative to the mass of water (1000 g). The two masses must be added together to get the mass of the solution.

Example 8 *Calculating grams of solute*
How many grams of NH_4Cl is dissolved in 2000 grams solution to produce a concentration of 150 ppm?

$$\text{Grams of solute} = \frac{\text{ppm} \times \text{Grams of solution}}{1000000}$$

$$\text{Grams of solute} = \frac{150 \times 2000}{1000000} \qquad \textit{setup}$$

$$\text{Grams of solute} = \textbf{0.3 g } NH_4Cl \qquad \textit{calculated result}$$

Practice 60
What is the concentration of $O_2(g)$, in parts per million, in a solution that contains 0.008 grams of $O_2(g)$ dissolved in 1000 grams of $H_2O(\ell)$?
1) 0.8 ppm   3) 8 ppm
2) 80 ppm   4) 800 ppm

Practice 61
What is the concentration, in parts per million, of a solution containing 20 grams of $C_6H_{12}O_6$ in 80.0 grams of H_2O?
1) 2.50×10^5 ppm   3) 4.00×10^6 ppm
2) 2.00×10^5 ppm   4) 5.00×10^6 ppm

Practice 62
What is the concentration in parts per million of a solution containing 333 grams of $NaNO_3$ in 700 grams of H_2O?
1) 2.10×10^6 ppm   3) 4.75×10^5 ppm
2) 3.10×10^6 ppm   4) 3.22×10^5 ppm

Practice 63
How many grams of NaCl will dissolve in water to make 2000 grams of a 100 ppm solution?
1) 2 g   3) 0.2 g
2) 0.05 g   4) 0.5 g

Practice 64
A 500-gram $C_6H_{12}O_6$ solution has a concentration of 300 ppm. How many grams of $C_6H_{12}O_6(s)$ is in this solution?
1) 1.5×10^1 g   3) 4.5×10^1 g
2) 1.5×10^{-1} g   4) 4.5×10^{-1} g

Practice 65 *Show a setup and the result.*
A 3000-gram solution contains 1.5 grams of dissolved NaCl salt. What is the concentration of this solution in ppm?

Practice 66 *Show a setup and the result.*
How many grams of KNO_3 must be dissolved in water to make 100 grams of a 250-ppm solution?

         ©2017 E3 Scholastic Publishing. All Rights Reserved

Base your answers to practice questions 67 through 69 on the information below.

Scientists who study aquatic ecosystems are often interested in the concentration of dissolved oxygen in water. Oxygen, O_2, has a very low solubility in water, and therefore its solubility is usually expressed in units of milligrams per 1000. grams of water at 1.0 atmosphere pressure. The graph below shows a solubility curve of oxygen in water.

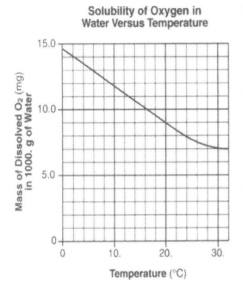

Solubility of Oxygen in Water Versus Temperature

67. A student determines that 8.2 milligrams of oxygen is dissolved in a 1000. gram sample of water at 15°C and 1.0 atmosphere of pressure. In terms of saturation, what type of solution is this sample?

68. A student prepared a solution of oxygen by dissolving 6.0 mg of oxygen in 1000 gram of water at 20°C. Determine how many more milligram of oxygen must be added to the solution to make it a saturated solution.

69. An aqueous solution has 0.007 gram of oxygen dissolved in 1000 grams of water. In the space to the right, calculate the dissolved oxygen concentration of this solution in parts per million. Your response should include both a correct numerical setup and calculated result.

Base your answers to questions 70 through 72 on the information below.

The compounds $NH_4Br(s)$ and $NH_3(g)$ are soluble in water. Solubility data for $NH_4Br(s)$ in water are listed in the table below.

Solubility of NH_4Br in H_2O

Temperature (°C)	Mass of NH_4Br per 100. g of H_2O (g)
0	60.
20.	75
40.	90.
60.	105
80.	120.
100.	135

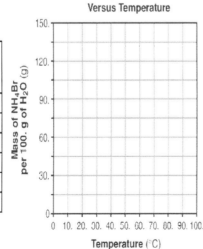

Solubility of NH_4Br in H_2O Versus Temperature

70. On the grid, plot the data from the data table. Circle and connect the points.

71. Compare the solubilities of $NH_4Br(s)$ and $NH_3(g)$, each in 100. grams of H_2O, as temperature increases at standard pressure. Your response must include *both* $NH_4Br(s)$ and $NH_3(g)$.

72. Determine the total mass of $NH_4Br(s)$ that must be dissolved in 200. grams of H_2O at 60.°C to produce a saturated solution.

Lesson 5 - Vapor Pressure and Changes to Properties of Water

Vapor is the gas form of a substance that is normally a liquid. For example, water is normally a liquid. Water vapor is the evaporated molecules of water in the gas phase.

Vapor pressure is the pressure exerted by the evaporated particles (vapor) of a liquid on the surface of the liquid.

Vapor pressure of a liquid depends only on the temperature of the liquid.

The higher the temperature of a liquid, the greater the vapor pressure. See *Reference Table H*.

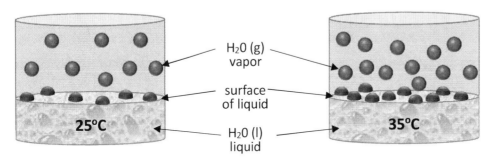

Boiling Point of a Liquid
When Vapor Pressure Equals Atmospheric Pressure

Boiling is the rapid phase change of a liquid to the vapor phase.

• *A liquid will boil when its vapor pressure is equal to the atmospheric pressure.*

Atmospheric pressure is the pressure exerted by the weight of air on the surface of an object.

Normal atmospheric pressure = Standard pressure = 101.3 kPa or 1 atm (Reference Table A)

The boiling point of a liquid is the temperature at which the vapor pressure of the liquid equals the atmospheric pressure.

For example: Water boils at 100°C at normal atmospheric pressure (101.3 kPa or 1 atm) because 100°C is the temperature of water that will produce a vapor pressure of 101.3 kPa or 1 atm. At different atmospheric pressures (higher or lower elevation), water boils at different temperatures.

Different substances have different boiling points because the strength of intermolecular forces varies among substances. Intermolecular forces are forces holding molecules of a substance together in the solid and liquid phases. Intermolecular forces must be broken for molecules of a liquid to vaporize. The stronger the intermolecular forces, the higher the temperature needed to break these forces. As a result, substances with strong intermolecular forces have higher boiling points than substances with weaker intermolecular forces.

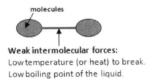

Weak intermolecular forces:
Low temperature (or heat) to break.
Low boiling point of the liquid.

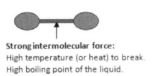

Strong intermolecular force:
High temperature (or heat) to break.
High boiling point of the liquid.

• Vapor pressure varies depending on the temperature of the liquid
• The higher the temperature of a liquid, the higher its vapor pressure
• Different substances have different vapor pressure at any given temperature
• Substance with strong intermolecular forces have low vapor pressures and high boiling points

 ©2017 E3 Scholastic Publishing. All Rights Reserved

Topic 7   Solutions

Reference Table H: Temperature vs. Vapor Pressure of Four Liquids

Table H below shows the relationship between temperature and vapor pressure of four liquids: propanone, ethanol, water, and ethanoic acids.

Table H can be used to determine the boiling point of any of the liquids at any atmospheric pressure.

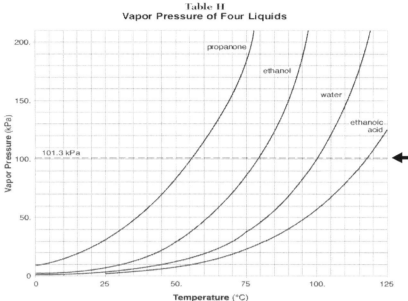

Table H
Vapor Pressure of Four Liquids

Reading Table H

At **75°C**, ethanol has a vapor pressure of **85 kPa.**

At an atmospheric pressure of **60 kPa**, water will boil at **87°C.**

Normal Pressure Line (101.3 kPa)

The normal boiling point (BP) of:
propanone = **56°C**
ethanoic acid = **118°C**

At Any Given Pressure:
Propanone (*lowest BP*) has the **weakest** intermolecular forces.

Ethanoic acid (**highest BP**) has the **strongest** intermolecular forces.

Practice 73
As water in a sealed container is cooled from 20°C to 10°C, its vapor pressure
1) decreases   2) increase   3) remains the same

Practice 74
When the vapor pressure of a liquid is equal to the atmospheric pressure, the liquid will
1) freeze   3) melt
2) boil   4) condense

practice 75
What is the vapor pressure of propanone at 45°C?
1) 70 kPa   3) 120 kPa
2) 101.3 kPa   4) 45 kPa

Practice 76
Which sample of water has the lowest vapor pressure?
1) 100 mL at 50°C   3) 300 mL at 40°C
2) 200 mL at 30°C   4) 400 mL at 20°C

Practice 77
The normal boiling point of ethanol is closest to
1) 80°C   3) 200°C
2) 100°C   4) 90°C

Practice 78
A liquid has a vapor pressure of 90 kPa at 75°C and a vapor pressure of 120 kPa at 90°C. At standard atmospheric pressure, the liquid will boil
1) at 75°C   3) above 75°C but below 90°C
2) at 90°C   4) above 90°C but below 100°C

Practice 79
Which liquid has the highest normal boiling point?
1) Propanone   3) Ethanol
2) Water   4) Ethanoic acid

Practice 80
Using your knowledge of chemistry and the information in Reference Table H, which statement concerning propanone and water at 50°C is true?
1) Propanone has a higher vapor pressure and stronger intermolecular forces than water.
2) Propanone has a higher vapor pressure and weaker intermolecular forces than water.
3) Propanone has a lower vapor pressure and stronger intermolecular forces than water.
4) Propanone has a lower vapor pressure and weaker intermolecular forces than water.

Changes in the Physical Properties of Water

When a solute is dissolved in water to make a solution, physical properties of the solution will be different from those of water. For example:

• ***A solution has a lower freezing point and a higher boiling point than pure water.***

Comparing Properties of a Solution to Pure Water

Pure water has the following physical properties:

- No dissolved particles.
- Boiling point at 100°C (at normal pressure)
- Freezing point at 0°C (at normal pressure)
- Vapor pressure of 101.3 kPa (at 100°C)
- No electrical conductivity

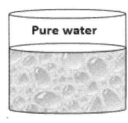

No dissolved particles

When a solute is dissolved in water to make a solution, these physical properties of water will change. These changes are listed below.

- **Number of dissolved particles** is increased. And as a result:

- **Boiling point** is increased or elevated.
  (The solution will boil at a temperature higher than 100°C)

- **Freezing point** is decreased or depressed.
  (The solution will freeze at a temperature lower than 0°C)

- **Vapor pressure** is decreased or lowered.
  (The solution will have a vapor pressure lower than that of pure water at any given temperature)

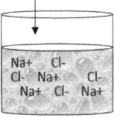

- **Electrical Conductivity** is increased.
  (The solution will conduct electrical current better than pure water)

How much higher the boiling point or lower freezing point of a solution in comparison to that of pure water depends on the following factors.
• The concentration of the particles in the solution
• The number of dissolved particles the solute produces in the water

These factors are discussed on the next page.

Practice 81
What occurs as a salt dissolves in water?
1) The number of ions in the solution increases, and the conductivity decreases.
2) The number of ions in the solution increases, and the conductivity increases.
3) The number of ions in the solution decreases, and the conductivity decreases.
4) The number of ions in the solution decreases, and the conductivity increases.

Practice 82
How do the boiling point and freezing point of a solution of water and calcium chloride at standard pressure compare to the boiling point and freezing point of water at standard pressure?
1) Both the freezing point and boiling point of the solution are higher.
2) Both the freezing point and boiling point of the solution are lower.
3) The freezing point of the solution is higher and the boiling point of the solution is lower.
4) The freezing point of the solution is lower and the boiling point of the solution is higher.

                                   ©2017 E3 Scholastic Publishing. All Rights Reserved

Effects of Concentration on Properties of a Solution

Effects of Concentration

Consider the following three solutions. The solutions contain the same solute (**KCl**), but their molarity concentrations are different.

Lowest concentration
Lowest boiling point
Highest freezing point

Highest concentration
Highest boiling point
Lowest freezing point

• **The solution with the highest concentration has the highest boiling point and the lowest freezing point.**

Effects of Number of Dissolved Particles

Consider the following three solutions. The solutions have different solutes (each producing different numbers of dissolved particles), but their molarity concentrations are the same (1 M).

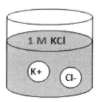
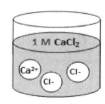

Molecular solute (CH₃OH)

1 dissolved particle

Lowest boiling point

Highest freezing point

Ionic solute (KCl)

2 dissolved particles

Ionic solute (CaCl₂)

3 dissolved particles

Highest boiling point

Lowest freezing point

• **The solution with the most dissolved particles (CaCl₂) always has the highest boiling point and the lowest freezing point.**

Ionic solutes will always produce more dissolved particles than molecular solutes because ionic substances are composed of two or more ions, and will dissolve into those ions in water.

Molecular solutes (except for acids) only disperse in water and do not ionize.

Properties of a Solutions: Practice Questions

Practice 83
As a solute is added to a solvent, what happens to the freezing point and the boiling point of the solution?
1) The freezing point decreases and the boiling point decreases.
2) The freezing point decreases and the boiling point increases.
3) The freezing point increases and the boiling point decreases.
4) The freezing point increases and the boiling point increases.

Practice 84
As water is added to a 0.10 M NaCl solution, the conductivity of the solution
1) decreases because the concentration of the ions decreases
2) decreases because the concentration of the ions remains the same
3) increases because the concentration of the ions decreases
4) increases because the concentration of the ions remains the same

Practice 85
Which 1 M solution will produce the greatest increase on the boiling point of water?
1) $CH_3OH(aq)$ 3) $CuCl_2(aq)$
2) $C_2H_4(OH)_2(aq)$ 4) $C_6H_{12}O_6(aq)$

Practice 86
Which 0.1 M solution has the highest boiling point?
1) $NaCl(aq)$ 3) $LiCl(aq)$
2) $CsCl(aq)$ 4) $MgCl_2(aq)$

Practice 87
Which 1 M solution has the lowest boiling point?
1) $KNO_3(aq)$ 3) $CaSO_4(aq)$
2) $K_2SO_4(aq)$ 4) $C_6H_{12}O_6(aq)$

Practice 88
Which concentration of NaOH has the highest freezing temperature?
1) 0.1 M   3) 1.5 M
2) 1.0 M   4) 2.0 M

Practice 89
Which solution will freeze at the lowest temperature?
1) 1 M Na_2SO_4 3) 1 M $NaNO_3$
2) 2 M Na_2SO_4 4) 2 M $NaNO_3$

Base your answer to the following question on the information below and on your knowledge of chemistry.

Rubbing alcohol is a product available at most pharmacies and supermarkets. One rubbing alcohol solution contains 2-propanol and water. The boiling point of 2-propanol is 82.3°C at standard pressure.

90. Determine the vapor pressure of water at a temperature equal to the boiling point of the 2-propanol.

Topic 7   Solutions

Base your answer to the following practice question on the information below.

Natural gas is a mixture that includes butane, ethane, methane, and propane. Differences in boiling points can be used to separate the components of natural gas. The boiling points at standard pressure for these components are listed in the table below.

Data Table

Component of Natural Gas	Boiling Point at Standard Pressure (°C)
butane	−0.5
ethane	−88.6
methane	−161.6
propane	−42.1

91. List the four components of natural gas in order of increasing strength of intermolecular forces.

_____   _____   _____   _____

Weakest intermolecular forces   *Strongest intermolecular forces*

Base your answers to practice questions 92 through 95 on the information below.

Molar Mass and Boiling Point of Four Substances

Substance	Molar Mass (g/mol)	Boiling Point at 1 atm (K)
methane	16	112
ethane	30.	185
propane	44	231
butane	58	273

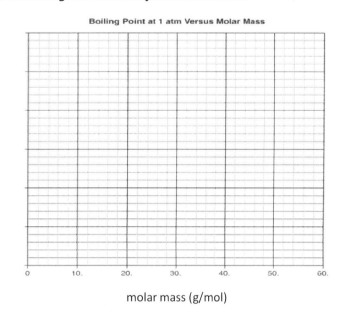

Boiling Point at 1 atm Versus Molar Mass

92. On the grid above, mark an appropriate scale on the axis labeled "Boiling Point (K)."

93. On the same grid, plot the data from the data table. Circle and connect the points.

94. Based on the data in the table, state the relationship between the boiling point at 1 atmosphere and molar mass for these four substances.

95. State, in terms of intermolecular forces, why the boiling point of propane at 1 atmosphere is lower than the boiling point of butane at 1 atmosphere.

Vocabulary

Lesson 1: Properties of Aqueous Solutions

Aqueous solution   Crystallization

Homogeneous mixture   Filtration

Solute   Hydration of ions

Solvent

Lesson 2: Solubility

Solubility   Miscibility

Soluble   Miscible

Insoluble   Immiscible

Lesson 3: Descriptions of Solutions

Saturated solution   Concentrated solution

Supersaturated solution   Dilute solution

Unsaturated solution

Lesson 4: Expression of Solution Concentration

Molarity

Parts per million

Lesson 5: Vapor Pressure and Changes to Properties of Water

Vapor

Vapor pressure

Boiling

©2017 E3 Scholastic Publishing. All Rights Reserved

1. 1
2. 2
3. 4
4. 4
5. 3
5. 1
7. 2

8. NH_4^+ (ammonium ion)
   Br^- (bromide ion)

9.

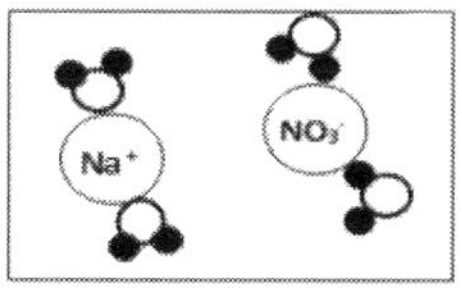

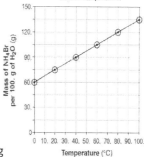

10. 4
11. 4
12. 2
13. 1
14. 1

15. 3
16. 2
17. 4
18. 1
19. 2

20. As temperature increases, the solubility of $NH_3(g)$ decreases.
    The solubility of $NH_3(g)$ is inversely related to the temperature of the solution.

21. Oxygen in nonpolar, and water is polar.
    Oxygen and water have different molecular polarities.

22. 1
23. 4

24. 3
25. 1

26. Ag^+, Pb^{2+}, or Hg_2^{2+}

27. 1
28. 2
29. 3
30. 2

31. 1
32. 2
33. 4
34. 3

35. 3
36. 2
37. 2
38. 3

39. 2
40. 4
41. 1
42. 3

43. 2
44. 3
45. 4
46. 1

47. 4
48. 2
49. 1
50. 2

51. 90 grams KCl

52. 30 grams KCl

53. KCl

54. 3
55. 4
56. 2
57. 2

58. moles = (3.0)(.500) = **1.5 moles**

59. volume = $\dfrac{45}{36 \times 20}$ = **0.63 L**

60. 3
61. 2
62. 4
63. 3
64. 1

65. ppm = $\dfrac{1.5}{3000}$ x 1000000 = **5.0 x 10^2 ppm**

66. grams of solute = $\dfrac{250 \times 100}{1000000}$ = **2.5 x 10^{-3} g**

67. unsaturated
68. 3 mg

69. ppm = $\dfrac{0.007}{1000}$ x 1000000 = **7 ppm**

70.

Example of a 1-credit response:

Solubility of NH_4Br in H_2O Versus Temperature

71. As temperature increases, the solubility of $NH_4Br(s)$ in H_2O
    increases and the solubility of $NH_3(g)$ in H_2O decreases.

    NH_4Br becomes more soluble and NH_3 becomes less soluble.

72. 210 g

73. 1
74. 2
75. 1
76. 4

77. 1
78. 3
79. 4
80. 2

81. 2
82. 4
83. 2
84. 1

85. 3
86. 4
87. 4
88. 1

89. 2
90. 50 kPa

91.

methane	ethane	propane	butane

Weakest intermolecular forces   *Strongest intermolecular forces*

92. and 93.

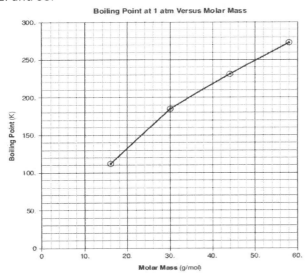

94. As molar mass increases, boiling point also increases.

95. Propane has weaker intermolecular forces than butane.
The intermolecular forces in butane are stronger than the intermolecular forces in propane.

©2017 E3 Scholastic Publishing. All Rights Reserved

Topic 8

Acids, Bases and Salts

Lesson 1: Definitions of Acids and Bases

Lesson 2: Acid-Base Reactions and Titration

Lesson 3: Salts and Electrolytes

Lesson 4: Formulas and Names of Acids

Acids, Bases and Salts

Topic 8

Properties of Acids and Bases: **Summary of General Characteristics**

Acids and bases have sets of properties that are used to identify them. Below is a summary of these properties. In the next few lessons, you will learn more about these characteristics of acids and bases.

Acids

Bases

S i m i l a r i t i e s

1) Are electrolytes
2) Change color of indicators
3) React with bases (in neutralization reactions to produce water and a salt

1) Are electrolytes
2) Change color of indicators
3) React with acids (in neutralization reaction) to produce water and a salt

D i f f e r e n c e s

4) Produce H^+ as the only positive ion in solutions
5) Contain more H^+ than OH^- in solutions
6) When added to water, increase H^+ concentration of the water
7) When added to water, decrease OH^- concentration of the water
8) When added to water, decrease pH
9) Have pH less than 7

10) Turn litmus red
11) Have no effect on phenolphthalein (stays colorless)

12) Taste sour

13) React with certain metals to produce salt and hydrogen gas

4) Produce OH^- as the only negative ion in solutions
5) Contain more OH^- than H^+ in solutions
6) When added to water, decrease H^+ ion concentration of the water
7) When added to water, increase OH^- ion concentration of the water
8) When added to water, increase pH
9) Have pH greater than 7

10) Turn litmus blue
11) Turn colorless phenolphthalein to pink

12) Taste bitter and feel slippery

Neutral Substances (at 25°C)

(1) Have pH of 7
(2) Have equal amounts of H^+ and OH^- ions

©2017 E3 Scholastic Publishing. All Rights Reserved

Lesson 1: Defining Acids and Bases

What is an acid? What is a base? These questions cannot be answered with just one simple definition. Acids and bases can be defined by different theories and properties.

In this lesson, you will learn how acids and bases are defined by theories and other characteristics. As you study this lesson, pay attention to similarities and differences between acids and bases.

Arrhenius Theory of Acids and Bases

Acids Yield H^+, Bases Yield OH^-

Arrhenius acids are substances that can produce H^+ (hydrogen ion or proton) as the only positive ion in solutions. Properties of acids are due to the properties of the H^+ ions they produce.
The H^+ ions produced by Arrhenius acids usually combine with H_2O to form H_3O^+ in solutions.
H^+ and H_3O^+ (hydronium ion) are synonymous with each other.
Acids are molecular substances.

Table K
Common Acids

Formula	Name
$HCl(aq)$	hydrochloric acid
$HNO_2(aq)$	nitrous acid
$HNO_3(aq)$	nitric acid
$H_2SO_3(aq)$	sulfurous acid
$H_2SO_4(aq)$	sulfuric acid
$H_3PO_4(aq)$	phosphoric acid
$H_2CO_3(aq)$ or $CO_2(aq)$	carbonic acid
$CH_3COOH(aq)$ or $HC_2H_3O_2(aq)$	ethanoic acid (acetic acid)

$$H^+ \quad + \quad H_2O \quad \rightarrow \quad H_3O^+$$

hydrogen ion   water   hydronium ion

Practice 1
According to Arrhenius theory, which list of compounds includes only acids?
1) HNO_3, H_2SO_4, and $C_6H_{12}O_6$ ✗
2) H_2PO_4, HCO_3, and NH_4Cl
3) $LiOH$, HNO_3, and CH_3OH
4) HF, H_2CO_3, and HNO_3

Practice 2
According to Arrhenius theory, which list of compounds includes only bases?
1) KOH, $Ca(OH)_2$, and CH_3OH
2) $LiOH$, $Ca(OH)_2$, and $C_2H_4(OH)_2$
3) $Mg(OH)_2$, $NaOH$, and $LiOH$
4) $NaOH$, $Ca(OH)_2$, and CH_3COOH

Arrhenius Bases are substances that can produce OH^- (hydroxide ion) as the only negative ion in solutions. Properties of bases are due to the properties of the OH^- ions they produced.
Most bases are ionic compounds.

Table L
Common Bases

Formula	Name
$NaOH(aq)$	sodium hydroxide
$KOH(aq)$	potassium hydroxide
$Ca(OH)_2(aq)$	calcium hydroxide
$NH_3(aq)$	aqueous ammonia

Practice 3
Aqueous solution of which of these substances contains hydroxide ions as the only negative ion?
1) C_2H_5OH 3) Na_2SO_4
2) $Ba(OH)_2$ 4) H_2SO_4

Practice 4
Which substance will dissolve in water to produce H_3O^+ (hydronium ion) as the only positive ion in the solution?
1) HF 3) $NaOH$
2) NH_4OH 4) KCl

Alternate Theory of Acids and Bases
Acids Donate H+, Bases Accept H+

The **Brönsted-Lowry theory** defines acids and bases by their ability to donate or accept a proton (H^+, hydrogen ion) in reactions.

Brönsted-Lowry acids are substances that ***donate a proton*** (H^+) in a reaction.

Brönsted-Lowry bases are substances that ***accept a proton*** (H^+) in a reaction.

$$H_2O \quad + \quad NH_3 \quad \leftrightarrow \quad NH_4^+ \quad + \quad OH^-$$
acid   *base*   *conjugate acid*   *conjugate base*

H_2O is an acid because it gives up H^+ and becomes **OH- (a base)**.
NH_3 is a base because it accepts the H^+ and becomes ***NH_4^+* (an acid)**.

When a Brönsted-Lowry acid and base react:

Two conjugate ***acid*** - **base** pairs can be determined:

Conjugate pair 1: ***H_2O*** and **OH^-**

Conjugate pair 2: ***NH_4^+*** and **NH_3**

> **Note:** Each conjugate acid-base pair contains similar species that differ only by one H atom. The acid in each pair contains one more H than the base.

Practice 5
In the reaction:

$$HBr + H_2O \rightarrow H_3O^+ + Br^-$$

Which two species are Bronsted-Lowry acids?

1) HBr and H_2O
2) HBr and H_3O^+
3) H_2O and Br^-
4) H_3O^+ and Br^-

Practice 6
Given the reaction:

$$H_2SO_4 + HPO_4^{2-} \rightarrow HSO_4^- + H_2PO_4^-$$

Which pair represents an acid and its conjugate base?

1) H_2SO_4 and HSO_4^-
2) H_2SO_4 and HPO_4^{2-}
3) HSO_4^- and $H_2PO_4^-$
4) HSO_4^- and HPO_4^{2-}

pH Values of Acids and Bases (at 25°C)

pH is a measure of the hydrogen ion (H^+) or hydronium ion (H_3O^+) concentration of a solution. A pH scale ranges in value from 0 - 14. Acids and bases can be defined by their pH values.

Acids are substances with pH values *less* than 7.

Neutral substances have pH values *equal* to 7.

Bases are substances with pH values *greater* than 7.

The strength of an acid or a base is determined by its pH value:
Strong acids have very low pH values.
Strong bases have very high pH values.

A typical ***pH scale*** is shown below. Some common substances are indicated below the scale to show their approximate pH values.

	Acid		Neutral		Base	
Strong		Weak		Weak		Strong
1---	---	---	---7---	---	---	---14
HCl		Acetic acid	H_2O	NH_3		NaOH

Practice 7
Which of these pH numbers indicates the highest level of acidity?
1) 7   2) 5   3) 10   4) 8

Practice 8
A compound whose water solution conducts electricity and have a pH of 9 could be
1) HCl   3) LiCl
2) NH_3 4) C_2H_5OH

Practice 9
Which aqueous solution would have a pH of 3?
1) $H_2O(\ell)$ 3) KOH(aq)
2) CH_3OH(aq)   4) HNO_3(aq)

Practice 10
Which solution could have a pH of 10?
1) NH_4OH 3) NaCl
2) $NaNO_3$ 4) Na_2SO_4

Practice 11
Substance X is dissolved in water to produce a solution with a pH of 2. Substance X is most likely
1) Lithium hydroxide   3) Ammonia
2) Methanol   4) Sulfuric acid

 ©2017 E3 Scholastic Publishing. All Rights Reserved

Topic 8

Acids, Bases and Salts

Acid-Base Indicators

Indicators are substances that change color in the presence of an acid or a base.

Acids and bases can be defined by the changes they cause on an indicator. Common indicators are listed on Reference Table M below.

Table M
Common Acid–Base Indicators

Indicator	Approximate pH Range for Color Change	Color Change
methyl orange	3.1–4.4	red to yellow
bromthymol blue	6.0–7.6	yellow to blue
phenolphthalein	8–9	colorless to pink
litmus	4.5–8.3	red to blue
bromcresol green	3.8–5.4	yellow to blue
thymol blue	8.0–9.6	yellow to blue

Reading Table M:

Methyl orange will be:
Red in pH below 3.1
Yellow in pH above 4.4

Thymol blue will be:
Yellow in pH below 8.0
Blue in pH above 9.6

Two common acid-base indicators are phenolphthalein and litmus paper

Phenolphthalein is a colorless indicator solution.

Acids have *no effect* on phenolphthalein
  • Phenolphthalein stays colorless in the presence of an acid.

Bases change colorless phenolphthalein to *pink*.
  • Phenolphthalein is a good indicator to test for the presence of a base.

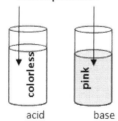

Phenolphthalein

colorless — acid

pink — base

Litmus papers come in a variety of colors. When wet with an acidic or a basic solution, a litmus paper will change color.

  • *Acids* are substances that will change litmus to *red*.

  • *Bases* are substances that will change litmus to *blue*.

Litmus papers

red — acid

blue — base

Practice 12
An indicator is used to test a water solution with a pH of 12. Which indicator color could be observed?
1) Colorless with litmus
2) Red with litmus
3) Colorless with phenolphthalein
4) Pink with phenolphthalein

Practice 13
In aqueous HNO_3 solution, phenolphthalein will be
1) pink, and litmus will be blue
2) pink, and litmus will be red
3) colorless, and litmus will be blue
4) colorless, and litmus will be red

Practice 14
Which substance would likely change bromcresol green from yellow to blue?
1) CH_3COOH 3) CH_3OH
2) NaOH   4) NaCl

Practice 15
In which solution will thymol blue indicator appear blue?
1) 0.1 M CH_3COOH 3) 0.1 M HCl
2) 0.1 M KOH   4) 0.1 M H_2SO_4

Practice 16
The following results were obtained when a solution was tested with methyl orange and litmus.

Methyl orange...... yellow
Litmus................... red

What is the pH of the solution?
1) 1   2) 3   3) 5   4) 10

Practice 17
Which indicator, when added to a solution, changes color from yellow to blue as the pH of the solution is changed from 5.5 to 8.0?
1) bromcresol green   3) methyl orange
2) bromthymol blue   4) litmus

Practice 18
Which indicator would best distinguish between a solution with a pH of 3.5 and a solution with a pH of 5.5?
1) thymol blue
2) litmus
3) bromthymol blue
4) bromcresol green

Relative Ions Concentration of Acids and Bases

Aqueous solutions contain both H^+ and OH^- ions. A solution can be defined as acidic, basic or neutral depending on the relative concentration of H^+ and OH^- ions in the solution.

Acidic solutions contain a higher concentration of H^+ ions than OH^- ions. The stronger the acid, the greater the H^+ ion concentration in comparison to the OH^- ion concentration.

Example: HCl(aq), hydrochloric acid solution, contains more H^+ ions than OH^- ions.

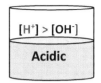

Neutral solutions and pure water contain equal amounts of H^+ and OH^- ions.

Example: NaCl(aq), a neutral salt solution, contains equal concentrations of H^+ and OH^- ions.

Basic solutions contain a higher concentration of OH^- ions than H^+ ions. The stronger the base, the greater the OH^- ion concentration in comparison to H^+ ion concentration.

Example: NaOH*(aq)*, sodium hydroxide solution, contains more OH^- ions than H^+ ions.

The mathematical relationship between H^+, OH^-, and pH is discussed on the next page.

Practice 19
The aqueous solution of CH_3COOH contains
1) equal molar of hydroxide and hydronium ions
2) more hydroxide than hydronium ions
3) more hydronium than hydroxide ions
4) neither hydronium nor hydroxide ions

Practice 20
Which are true of aqueous solution of $Mg(OH)_2$?
1) It contains more OH^- ion than H^+ ion, and is a nonelectrolyte.
2) It contains more OH^- ion that H^+ ion, and is an electrolyte.
3) It contains more H^+ than OH^-, and is a nonelectrolyte.
4) It contains more H^+ than OH^-, and is an electrolyte.

Practice 21
A solution with a pH of 7 contains
1) more H^+ than OH^-
2) more OH^- than H^+
3) equal number of H^+ and OH^-
4) neither H^+ nor OH^-

Practice 22
Which of these solutions contains higher concentration of OH^- ions than H_3O^+ ions?
1) HCl(aq)   3) $C_6H_{12}O_6$(aq)
2) KCl(aq)   4) $Ca(OH)_2$(aq)

Practice 23
Which substance will produce a solution with a higher concentration of hydrogen ions than hydroxide ions?
1) NH_3 3) KCl
2) H_2SO_4 4) CH_3COH

Practice 24
When tested, a solution turns red litmus to blue. This indicates that the solution contains more
1) H_3O^+ than OH^- ions, and has a pH above 7
2) H_3O^+ than OH^- ions, and has a pH below 7
3) OH^- than H_3O^+ ions, and has a pH above 7
4) OH^- than H_3O^+ ions, and has a pH below 7

Relating pH to H^+ Ion Concentration

The relationship between pH and H^+ ion concentration is shown below.

$$pH = -log\,[H^+]$$ or $$[H^+] = 10^-$$

When the $[H^+]$ or $[H_3O^+]$ of a solution is given as 1×10^{-x} M, the pH value = **x**

For example:

H_3O^+ Concentration	pH Value	Type of Solution
1.0×10^{-2} M	2	Acidic
1.0×10^{-8} M	8	Basic

If H^+ concentration *is not* in the form of 1×10^{-x}, a scientific calculator will be needed to calculate the pH. For example: What is the pH of a solution with $[H^+]$ of 5.4×10^{-8} M?

$$pH = -log\,[H^+] = -log\,(5.4 \times 10^{-8}) = \mathbf{7.26}$$

Comparing H^+ Ion Concentration of Two Solution

Based on the mathematical relationship of pH to $[H^+]$, a solution with a pH of 3 has a higher concentration of H^+ ions than a solution with a pH of 4.
- The lower the pH, the greater the H^+ ion concentration of the solution.
- As H^+ ion concentration of a solution increases, pH of the solution decreases.

Difference in $[H^+]$ of two solutions = $10^{(\text{difference in pH})}$
A solution of pH 3 has *10 times* more H^+ than a solution of pH 4.

1 value difference in pH = 10 times (fold) difference in $[H^+]$
As the solution changes from *pH 3* to *pH 5*, $[H^+]$ decreases *100 fold* because it is less acidic.

Practice 25
What is the pH of a solution with H_3O^+ concentration of 1.0×10^{-6} M?
1) 1   2) 10   3) 6   4) 8

Practice 26
What is the pH of a solution with H^+ concentration of 4.5×10^{-8} M?
1) 4.5   2) 8.0   3) 10.8   4) 7.3

Practice 27
A solution of which H^+ concentration has a pH of 2?
1) 1×10^{-12} M   3) 1×10^{-2} M
2) 1×10^{-10} M   4) 1×10^{-14} M

Practice 28
What is the hydronium ion concentration of a solution with a pH of 5.8
1) 1.0×10^{-5} M   3) 6.3×10^{-5} M
2) 1.6×10^{-6} M   4) 5.0×10^{-8} M

Practice 29
Compared to a solution with a pH of 5, a solution with a pH of 2 has
1) 1000 times more H^+, and is more acidic
2) 1000 times more H^+, and is more basic
3) 3 fold more H^+, and is more acidic
4) 3 fold more H^+, and is more basic

Practice 30
Liquid A has a neutral pH and liquid B has a pH of 9. The H^+ ion in B is
1) $1/10^{th}$ as great as that of A
2) $1/100^{th}$ as great as that of A
3) 10 fold as great as that of A
4) 100 fold as great as that of A

Practice 31
What is the pH of a solution that has a hydronium ion concentration 100 times greater than a solution with a pH of 6?
1) 4   3) 5
2) 3   4) 7

Base your answers to questions 32 through 34 on the information below.

Some carbonated beverages are made by forcing carbon dioxide gas into a beverage solution. When a bottle of one kind of carbonated beverage is first opened, the beverage has a pH value of 3.

32. State, in terms of the pH scale, why this beverage is classified as acidic.

33. Using Table M, identify one indicator that is yellow in a solution that has the same pH value as this beverage.

34. After the beverage bottle is left open for several hours, the hydronium ion concentration in the beverage solution decreases to 1/1000 of the original concentration. Determine the new pH of the beverage solution.

Base your answers to practice questions 35 through 38 on the graph below.

The graph shows the relationship between pH value and hydronium ion concentration for common aqueous solutions and mixtures.

pH Versus Hydronium Ion Concentration

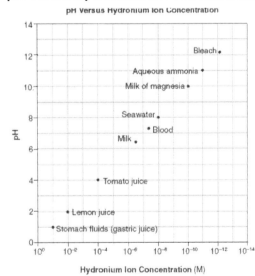

35. According to this graph, which mixture is approximately 100 times more acidic than milk of magnesia?

36. According to the graph, which mixture is approximately 10 times less acidic than aqueous ammonia?

37. What color is thymol blue when added to milk of magnesia?

38. What is the hydronium concentration of tomato juice?

               ©2017 E3 Scholastic Publishing. All Rights Reserved

Topic 8 Acids, Bases and Salts

Lesson 2: Reactions of Acids and Bases

Acids and bases undergo chemical reactions with other substances and with each other. In this lesson you will learn about reactions of acids and bases.

Acid - Metal Reactions
Produce Salt and Hydrogen

Acids react with certain metals to produce hydrogen gas and a salt. The reaction between an acid and a metal is a single replacement reaction. General equation and two example reactions are given below:

	Reactants			Products		
General equation:	Metal	+ Acid	→	Salt	+	Hydrogen gas
Example reaction 1:	Zn	+ 2HCl	→	$ZnCl_2$	+	H_2
Example reaction 2:	Mg	+ $2HNO_3$	→	$Mg(NO_3)_2$	+	H_2

Not every metal will react with acids to produce hydrogen gas and a salt. For a metal to react with an acid, the metal must be more reactive than hydrogen, H_2, on the Activity Series Table.

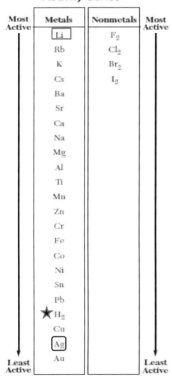

Reading Table J

Metals above H_2 (Li to Pb) *will* react spontaneously with an acid to produce H_2 gas.

Metals below H_2 (Cu to Au) *will not* react with any acid.

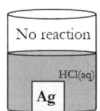

Practice 39
Which of the following metals is likely to react with nitric acid to produce hydrogen gas?
1) Silver
2) Gold
3) Chromium
4) Copper

Practice 40
Which reaction will not occur under standard conditions?
1) $Ag + H_2SO_4 → Ag_2SO_4 + H_2$
2) $Pb + H_2SO_4 → PbSO_4 + H_2$
3) $Zn + 2HCl → ZnCl_2 + H_2$
4) $Li + HCl → LiCl + H_2$

Practice 41
Which equation is showing a reaction that is likely to occur under STP?
1) $Au(s) + 2HBr(aq) → H_2(g) + AuBr_2(aq)$
2) $Cu(s) + 2HBr(aq) → H_2(g) + CuBr_2(aq)$
3) $Ag(s) + 2HBr(aq) → H_2(g) + AgBr_2(aq)$
4) $Sn(s) + 2HBr(aq) → H_2(g) + SnBr_2(aq)$

Neutralization Reaction
Acid and *Base* *Produce* *Salt* and *Water*

Neutralization is a chemical reaction between an acid and a base to produce a *salt* and *water.* A neutralization reaction is a double replacement reaction. During a neutralization reaction, equal moles of H^+ (of an acid) and OH^- (of a base) combine to neutralize each other.

General equation: acid   +   base $\rightarrow$ water   +   salt

Example reaction: HCl   +   NaOH $\rightarrow$ H_2O +   NaCl

                 hydrochloric acid   sodium hydroxide   water   sodium chloride

Net ionic equation: H^+ + OH^- $\rightarrow$ H_2O

The formula of the salt that is formed in a neutralization reaction can be determined by replacing the H of the acid with the metal of the base. In the reaction below:

$$H_2SO_4 \quad + \quad LiOH \quad \rightarrow \quad HOH \quad + \quad Li_2SO_4$$

       acid   base   water   salt

The **H** in H_2SO_4 is replaced by **Li** to form **Li_2SO_4** salt.

Concept Task: Be able to recognize neutralization reaction equations.

Practice 42
Which reaction represents a neutralization reaction?
1) Pb + $AgNO_3$ $\rightarrow$ Ag + $PbNO_3$
2) $LiOH$ + $HC_2H_3O_2$ $\rightarrow$ H_2O + $LiC_2H_3O_2$
3) NH_4Cl + $AgNO_3$ $\rightarrow$ NH_4NO_3 + $AgCl$
4) CH_4 + $2O_2$ $\rightarrow$ CO_2 + $2H_2O$

Practice 43
Which equation represents a neutralization reaction?
1) $Ca(OH)_2$ $\rightarrow$ Ca^{2+} + $2OH^-$
2) $CaCl_2$ $\rightarrow$ Ca^{2+} + $2Cl^-$
3) H^+ + OH^- $\rightarrow$ HOH
4) H^+ + F^- $\rightarrow$ HF

Practice 44
A neutralization reaction would likely occur between which two substances?
1) $H_2S(aq)$ and $Ca(ClO_4)_2(s)$
2) $H_2SO_3(aq)$ and $Ca(NO_3)_2(aq)$
3) $H_2SO_4(aq)$ and $Sr(OH)_2(aq)$
4) $SO_2(g)$ and $CaO(s)$

Concept Task: Be able to complete neutralization reaction equations.

water

$$HNO_3 \quad + \quad KOH \quad \rightarrow \quad KNO_3 + \quad H_2O$$

                 salt (the salt formula must be correctly written)

Practice 45
In the neutralization reaction
$3Ca(OH)_2$ + $2H_3PO_4$ $\rightarrow$ X + $6H_2O$, X is
1) $CaPO_4$ 3) CaH
2) $Ca_3(PO_4)_2$ 4) CaO

Practice 46
In the neutralization reaction:
   HF + NH_4OH $\rightarrow$ X + H_2O,
substance X is
1) NH_3 3) $(NH_4)_2O$
2) H_2 4) NH_4F

Practice 47
Complete the two neutralization reactions below.
   $2KOH$ + H_2SO_3 $\rightarrow$ _____   +   _____

   $2HC_2H_3O_2$ + $Mg(OH)_2$ $\rightarrow$ _____ + _____

Titration
Using a Solution of Known Concentration to Find Unknown Concentration

Titration is a lab process used for determining the unknown concentration of a solution by reacting it with another solution of a known concentration. During an acid – base titration lab, a base in a buret is slowly added to an acid solution in a flask. When the number of moles OH^- (from the base) is equal to the number of moles of H^+ (of the acid) in the flask, neutralization has occurred, and the *equivalence point* of the titration is reached. Phenolphthalein (a base indicator) is usually added to the acid beaker to indicate the endpoint. At the endpoint, the solution in the flask will turn a light-pink color indicating the acid is neutralized, and the solution is slightly basic. Titration is stopped at this point. When any three of the following are known about a titration problem, the unknown can be calculated using one of the two equations below.

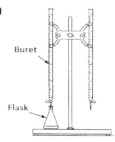

Buret

Flask

Acid – base titration set up

- **Volume** of the acid (V_A) in the flask
- **Concentration** of the acid (M_A)
- **Volume** of the base (V_B) dispense from buret
- **Concentration** of the base (M_B)

$(M_A) (V_A)$ $=$ $(M_B) (V_B)$ Table T Equation	Use this equation if the mole ratio of H^+ (of acid) to OH^- (of base) is 1 : 1. **For example:** A titration involving HCl and NaOH has **1**H^+ : **1**OH^- ratio.
$(M_A) (V_A) (\#H^+) = (M_B) (V_B) (\#OH^-)$	Use this equation if the mole ratio of H^+ to OH^- *is not* 1 : 1. **For example:** A titration involving H_2SO_4 and NaOH has **2**H^+ : **1**OH^- ratio. A titration involving HCl and $Ca(OH)_2$ has **1**H^+ : **2**OH^- ratio.

Example 1: *Problem with 1H⁺ to 1OH⁻ Ratio*

30 mL of 0.6 M HCl solution is neutralized with 90 mL NaOH solution. What is the concentration of the base?

$(M_A) (V_A)$ $=$ $(M_B)(V_B)$

$(0.6) (30)$ $=$ $(M_B)(90)$ ⎫

$\dfrac{(0.6) (30)}{90}$ $=$ M_B ⎬ *numerical setup*

⎭

0.2 M $=$ **M_B**   *calculated result*

Example 2: *Problem with 2H⁺ to 1OH⁻ Ratio*
How many milliliters of 1.5 M H_2SO_4 are needed to exactly neutralize 20. milliliters of a 1.5 M KOH solution?

$(M_A) (V_A) (\#H^+)$ $=$ $(M_B) (V_B) (\#OH^-)$

$(1.5) (V_A) (2)$ $=$ $(1.5) (20.) (1)$ ⎫

V_A $=$ $\dfrac{30}{3}$ ⎬ *numerical setup*

⎭

V_A $=$ **10 mL**   *calculated result*

Practice 48
If 100 mL of a 0.75 M HNO_3 is required to exactly neutralize 50 mL of NaOH, what is the concentration of the base?
1) 0.25 M   2) 0.75 M   3) 1.0 M   4) 1.5 M

Practice 49
How many milliliters of a 2.5 M LiOH solution are needed to completely neutralize 25 mL of a 1.0 M H_2SO_4 solution?
1) 10 mL   2) 50 mL   3) 20 mL   4) 8 mL

Practice 50 *Show a numerical setup and the result.*
How many mL of a 0.4 M nitric acid solution are required to neutralize 200 mL of a 0.16 M potassium hydroxide?

Practice 51 *Show a numerical setup and the result.*
20 mL of a 3.0 M HCl solution is titrated to the endpoint with 60 mL of $Mg(OH)_2$. What is the concentration of the base?

Base your answers to practice questions 52 through 54 on the information below.

In a titration, 3.00 M NaOH*(aq)* was added to an Erlenmeyer flask containing 25.00 milliliters of H_2SO_4*(aq)* and three drops of phenolphthalein until one drop of NaOH*(aq)* turned the solution a light-pink color. The following data were collected by a student performing this titration.

Initial NaOH*(aq)* buret reading: 14.45 milliliters
Final NaOH*(aq)* buret reading: 32.66 milliliters

52. Compare the number of moles of H^+(aq) ions to the number of moles of OH^-(aq) ions in the titration mixture when neutralization occurred.

53. Show a numerical setup and the calculated result for the concentration of the acid.

54. Write a balanced equation for the neutralization reaction that occurs.

Base your answers to practice questions 55 through 57 on the information below.

A student titrates 60.0 mL of HNO_3*(aq)* with 0.20 M NaOH*(aq)*. Phenolphthalein is used as the indicator. After adding 30.0 mL of NaOH*(aq)*, a color change remains for 25 seconds, and the student stops the titration.

55. What color change does phenolphthalein undergo during this titration?

56. What is the concentration of the HNO_3 that was titrated?

57. Complete the equation below for the reaction that occurs during the titration.

HNO_3*(aq)* + NaOH*(aq)* → _____   +   _____

Base your answers to questions 58 and 59 on the information below.

In one trial of an investigation, 50.0 milliliters of HCl(aq) of an unknown concentration is titrated with 0.10 M NaOH(aq). During the titration, the total volume of NaOH(aq) added and the corresponding pH value of the reaction mixture are measured and recorded in the table to the right.

Titration Data

Total Volume of NaOH(aq) Added (mL)	pH Value of Reaction Mixture
10.0	1.6
20.0	2.2
24.0	2.9
24.9	3.9
25.1	10.1
26.0	11.1
30.0	11.8

pH Value of Reaction Mixture Versus Total Volume of NaOH(aq) Added

Total Volume of NaOH(aq) Added (mL)

58. On the grid, plot the data from the table. Circle and connect the points.

59. In another trial, 40.0 milliliters of HCl(aq) is completely neutralized by 20.0 milliliters of this 0.10 M NaOH(aq). Calculate the molarity of the titrated acid in this trial. Your response must include both a numerical setup and the calculated result.

Lesson 3 – Salts and Electrolytes

One property that acids, bases and salts share is their ability to conduct electricity in aqueous solutions. Acids, bases and salts are electrolytes. In this lesson you will learn about substances that are electrolytes, and how electrolytes conduct electricity.

Salts
Crystalline Ionic Solids

Salts are ionic compounds composed of a positive ion (other than H^+) and a negative ion (other than OH^-).

• Salt is one of the **products of** an acid-base neutralization reaction.

• **Salts** are electrolytes; they conduct electricity when dissolved in water.

• Soluble salts are better electrolytes than insoluble salts.
  Table F can be used to determine soluble and insoluble salts.

Examples of salts are given below.

NaBr	CaSO₄	NH₄Cl
$NaBr$	$CaSO_4$	NH_4Cl
sodium bromide	calcium sulfate	ammonium chloride
metal -nonmetal	metal - polyatomic ion	NH_4 − nonmetal

Practice 60
Which compound is a salt?
1) $Ba(OH)_2$ 3) H_2SO_4
2) $BaCl_2$ 4) CH_3OH

Practice 61
Which list of compounds includes only salts?
1) HNO_3, $NaNO_3$, and $Ca(NO_3)_2$
2) C_2H_5OH, CH_3COOH, and $CaCl_2$
3) CH_3OH, $NaOH$, and $NaCl$
4) $Ca(NO_3)_2$, Na_2SO_4, and $MgCl_2$

Electrolytes
Conduct Electrical Current Because of Mobile Ions. Acids, Bases and Salts.

Electrolytes are substances that conduct electricity when dissolved in water.

• Electrolytes dissolve in water to produce a solution with positive (+) and negative (-) ions.

• Electrolytes conduct electricity because of the mobile ions in the solution.

• Acids (Table K), bases (Table L) and salts are electrolytes.

Nonelectrolytes are substances that do not produce ions when dissolved, therefore, they do not conduct electricity in solutions. Organic substances (other than organic acids) are typically nonelectrolytes. Organic substances are discussed in Topic 10.

Practice 62
Which 0.1 M solution contains electrolytes?
1) $C_6H_{12}O_6(aq)$ 3) $CH_3COOH(aq)$
2) $CH_3OH(aq)$ 4) $CH_3OCH_3(aq)$

Practice 63
Which two substances are electrolytes?
1) KCl and CH_3OH 3) C_2H_6 and $C_6H_{12}O_6$
2) $CaCl_2$ and $LiOH$ 4) HCl and CH_3OH

Practice 64
An example of a nonelectrolyte is
1) $C_2H_5CHO(aq)$ 3) $K_2SO_4(aq)$
2) $NH_4NO(aq)$ 4) $HF(aq)$

Practice 65
Which compound is a nonelectrolyte?
1) NH_3 3) CH_4
2) KBr 4) $CuCl_2$

Practice 66
Which salt will form a saturated solution with the highest electrical conductivity?
1) Potassium nitrate   3) Silver bromide
2) Lead sulfate   4) Zinc carbonate

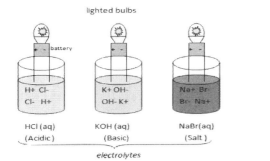

Electrolytes conduct electricity because of mobile ions in the solution.

Acid Formulas and Names

An acid can be classified as organic or inorganic. Inorganic acids can also be classified as binary or ternary acids. In this lesson you will learn about different types of acids and how they are named.

Chemical Formulas of Acids

Inorganic acids

Chemical formulas of inorganic acids generally start with H, followed by a nonmetal or a negative polyatomic ion.

Binary acid formulas are composed of just two different nonmetal atoms: A hydrogen atom and a different nonmetal atom.

Examples   HCl   hydrochloric acid
                H_2S hydrosulfuric acid

Ternary acid formulas are composed of three or more different atoms: A hydrogen atom and a polyatomic ion (Table E).

Examples HNO_3 nitric acid
                H_2SO_3 sulfurous acid

Organic acids
Chemical formulas of organic acids usually end with –COOH.

Examples: CH_3COOH ethanoic (acetic) acid
              $HCOOH$ methanoic acid

Practice 67
Write the correct formula for each of the following acids.

a) hydroiodic acid

b) chlorous acid

c) carbonic acid

Chemical Names of Inorganic Acids

Chemical names of acids vary depending if the acid is a binary, ternary, or an organic acid.

Binary acids have names that begin with **hydro-** and end with **–ic**.

Names of binary acids are formed by dropping the –gen of hydrogen and modifying the name ending of the nonmetal element to –ic.

	Examples	
	HCl	H_2S
Compound name:	Hydro*gen* chlor*ide*	Hydro*gen* sulf*ide*
Acid name:	Hydrochlor*ic* acid	Hydrosulfur*ic* acid

Ternary acids have names that reflect only the name of the polyatomic ion (See Table E).

If an acid contains a polyatomic ion ending with –ite, the name ending of the acid is **–ous.**

If an acid contains a polyatomic ion ending with –ate, the name ending of the acid is **–ic.**

Table E: Polyatomic Ions

SO_3^{2-}	sulfite
SO_4^{2-}	sulfate

Practice 68
Name the following acids

a) HClO

b) $HClO_4$

c) H_2Te

d) $H_2C_2O_4$

Examples	H_2SO_3	H_2SO_4
Polyatomic Ion name:	sulf**ite**	sulf**ate**
Acid name:	sulfur**ous** acid	sulfur**ic** acid

Base your answers to questions 69 through 74 on the information and diagrams below.

Four beakers each contain 100 milliliters of aqueous solution of equal concentration at 25°C.

KCl   CH₃OH   Ba(OH)₂   CH₃COOH

69. Which solutions contain electrolytes?

70. Which solution has the lowest pH?

71. Which solution is most likely to react with an Arrhenius acid to form a salt and water?

72. Which solution has the lowest freezing point?

73. What causes some aqueous solutions to have a low pH?

74. Explain how some aqueous solutions can conduct electrical current.

Base your answers to practice questions 75 and 76 on the information below.

Calcium reacts with water. This reaction is represented by the balanced equation below. The aqueous product of this reaction can be heated to evaporate the water, leaving a white solid, $Ca(OH)_2(s)$.

$$Ca(s) \ + \ H_2O(l) \ \rightarrow \ Ca(OH)_2(aq) \ + \ H_2(g)$$

75. Compare the electrical conductivity of the aqueous product in the reaction to the electrical conductivity of the white solid that remains after the water is evaporated from the solution.

76. Write the chemical name of the base produced in the reaction.

Vocabulary

Lesson 1: Properties of Acids and Bases

Arrhenius acid
Arrhenius base
Hydrogen ion
Hydronium ion
Hydroxide ion

Acidic
Basic
Indicator
pH

Lesson 2: Reactions of Acids and Bases

Neutralization
Titration.
 Endpoint

Lesson 3: Salts and Electrolytes

Salt
Electrolytes

                                    ©2017 E3 Scholastic Publishing. All Rights Reserved

1. 4	6. 1	11. 4	16. 2	21. 2	26. 4	31. 1
2. 3	7. 2	12. 4	17. 2	22. 4	27. 3	
3. 2	8. 2	13. 4	18. 4	23. 2	28. 2	
4. 3	9. 4	14. 1	19. 3	24. 3	29. 1	
5. 2	10. 1	15. 2	20. 2	25. 3	30. 2	

32. The pH of the beverage is below 7.   33. bromcresol green   34. pH of 6
    Its pH is between 0 and 7.

35. saltwater   36. bleach   37. blue   38. 1.0×10^{-4} M or 10^{-4}M

39. 3	43. 3
40. 1	44. 3
41. 4	45. 2
42. 2	46. 4

47.
$$2KOH + H_2SO_3 \rightarrow K_2SO_3 + 2H_2O$$
$$2HC_2H_3O_2 + Mg(OH)_2 \rightarrow Mg(C_2H_3O)_2 + 2H_2O$$

48. 4   50. $M_a(0.4) = (0.16)(200)$ **M_a = 80. mL**

49. 3   51. $(3.0)(20)(1) = M_b(60)(2)$ **M_b = 0.5 M**

52. The number of moles of H^+ ions is the same as the number of moles of OH- ions.

53. $M_a(25.00)(2) = (3.00)(18.21)(1)$ M_b = 1.09 M

54. $H_2SO_4 + 2NaOH \rightarrow Na_2SO_4 + 2H_2O$

55. Pink. Light pink.   56. 0.211 M

57. $HNO_3(aq) + NaOH(aq) \rightarrow \underline{NaNO_3(aq)} + \underline{H_2O(l)}$

58.

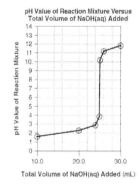

59. $M_a(40.0 \text{ mL}) = (0.10 \text{ M})(20.0 \text{ mL})$

    M_a = 0.050 M

60. 2	67 a. HI	68 a. hyperchlorus acid
61. 4	b. $HClO_2$	b. perchloric acid
62. 3	c. H_2CO_3	c. hydrotelluric acid
63. 2		d. oxalic acid
64. 1		
65. 3		
66. 1		

69. KCl   72. $Ba(OH)_2$

70. CH_3COOH 73. High H^+ or H_3O^+ ion concentration in the solution.

71. $Ba(OH)_2$ 74. Aqueous solutions contain mobile or free moving ions.

75. The electrical conductivity of the aqueous product is much greater than that of the white solid.
    The aqueous product has electrical conductivity, but the white solid has no electrical conductivity.

©2017 E3 Scholastic Publishing. All Rights Reserved

Topic 9
Kinetics and Equilibrium

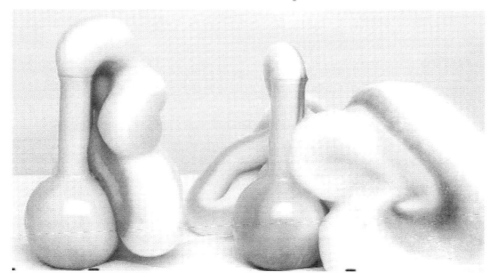

Lesson 1: Kinetics and Rate of Reactions

Lesson 2: Energy in Chemical Reactions

Lesson 3: Entropy

Lesson 4: Equilibrium

Lesson 1 – Kinetics

Kinetics is the study of rates and mechanisms of chemical reactions.

Rate is the speed at which a reaction is taking place.

A **mechanism** is a series of reactions that lead to the stable products of a reaction.

In this lesson you will learn mostly about rate of chemical reactions and factors that affect rate. You will also learn about energy associated with chemical reactions.

Rate of Reactions
Depends on Frequency of Effective Collisions

*The **rate of a reaction** is the speed at which a chemical or physical change occurs. Rate of a reaction can be measured in different ways.

For example, rate can be measured by:
•The number of moles of a reactant consumed or used up per unit time.
•The number of moles of a product produced per unit time.

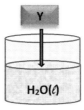

Equal amount of solid **X** and solid **Y** are simultaneously placed in separate beakers of water of equal temperature and volume.

X and Y are consumed as they react with water.

After 5 minutes, a smaller amount of X remained.
Therefore,
X reacted with (or is consumed in) water at a faster rate than Y.

Factors that Can Affect the Rate of a Reaction

Chemical and physical changes occur at different rates. Many factors affect the speed in which reactions occur. Changing one or more of these factors can increase or decrease the speed of a reaction. Some of these factors are listed below.

• **Nature or type** of reactants

• **Concentration or amount** of the reactants

• **Temperature** of reactants

• **Pressure or volume** of gaseous reactants

• **Addition of a catalyst**

 ©2017 E3 Scholastic Publishing. All Rights Reserved

Effective Collisions
Sufficient Kinetic Energy and *Proper Orientation*

Collision theory states that for a chemical reaction to occur between reactants, there must be *effective collisions* between the reacting particles.

Effective collisions occur when reacting particles collide with *sufficient or right amount of kinetic energy* and at the *proper orientation* or *angle.*
- Rate of a reaction depends on the frequency of (how often) effective collisions occur between particles.
- Any factor that can change the frequency of effective collisions between reacting particles will change the rate of that reaction.

The diagrams below show the difference between effective and ineffective collisions.

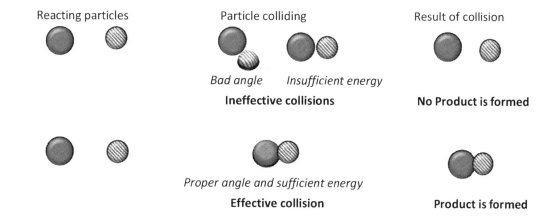

Activation Energy and Catalysts

Activation Energy: *Energy to Start a Reaction*
Activation energy is the energy needed to start a chemical reaction. All chemical reactions, both endothermic and exothermic, require some amount of activation energy. Any factor that can change the amount of activation energy for a reaction will change the rate of that reaction.

Catalysts: *Lower Activation Energy, Increase Rate*
A catalyst is any substance that increases the speed or rate of a reaction by lowering the activation energy. A catalyst in a reaction provides an *alternate lower activation energy pathway* so a reaction can occur faster.

Mg will burn in the presence of **O₂** to produce MgO as represented below.

$$2Mg + O_2 \rightarrow 2MgO$$

However, the magnesium strip must be lit with Bunsen burner flame before it can burn and react with O_2. The flame provides the **activation energy** needed to start the reaction.

Factors that Affect Rate of Reactions: **Summary Table**

In general:
A reaction rate is increased when effective collision between reacting particles is increased.

Factors that will increase effective collisions and reaction rate are summarized below.
Explanations of how each change will increase a reaction rate is also provided.

Increasing concentration of a reactant:

Increases the number of reacting particles.

Increases the frequency and effectiveness of collisions between reacting particles.

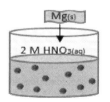
higher concentration, faster reaction

Increasing pressure on a gaseous reaction:
Increases the volume of gaseous reactants.
Increases the concentration of reactants.
Increases the frequency and effectiveness collisions.

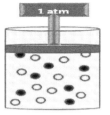 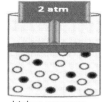
higher pressure, faster reaction

Increasing temperature of reactants:
Increases kinetic energy or speed of reacting particles.
Increases frequency of effective collisions.

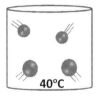
higher temperature faster reaction

Increasing surface area of a reacting solid:
Increases exposed area for a reaction.
Increases frequency of effective collisions.

Chunk of zinc
Pieces of zinc
Powder (grinded up) zinc

Least surface area. Slowest reaction.
Most surface area. Fastest reaction with acid.

Addition of a catalyst to a reaction:
Lowers activation energy.
Provides alternate pathway for a reaction to occur faster.

Nature of Reactants:
Reactions of ionic solutions are very fast (almost instantaneous) because no bond breaking is required.

Reactions of molecular substances are slow because reactions require the breaking of strong covalent bonds. High activation energy is usually required for reactions involving molecular substances.

Some metals, because of their atomic structure, react faster than others in solutions.

Reaction Rate: Practice Questions

Practice 1
In order for any chemical reaction to occur, there must always be
1) a bond that breaks in a reactant particle
2) a reacting particle with a high charge
3) effective collisions between reacting particles
4) a catalyst

Practice 2
Two particles collide with proper orientation. The collisions will be effective if the particles have
1) high activation energy
2) high electronegativity
3) sufficient potential energy
4) sufficient kinetic energy

Practice 3
Which conditions will increase the rate of a chemical reaction?
1) Decreased temperature and decreased concentration.
2) Decreased temperature and increased concentration.
3) Increased temperature and decreased concentration.
4) Increased temperature and increased concentration.

Practice 4
Increasing temperature speeds up a reaction by increasing
1) the effectiveness of collisions, only
2) the frequency of collisions, only
3) both the effectiveness and the frequency of the collisions
4) neither the effectiveness nor the frequency of the collisions

Practice 5
When a catalyst is added to a reaction, the reaction rate is increased because the catalyst
1) increases activation energy
2) decreases activation energy
3) increases potential energy of the reactants
4) decreases potential energy of the reactants

Practice 6
Given the reaction:
$$Mg(s) + 2HNO_3(aq) \rightarrow Mg(NO_3)_2(aq) + H_2(g)$$
At which temperature will the reaction occur at the greatest rate?
1) 10°C   2) 50°C   3) 30°C   4) 70°C

Practice 7
Given the reaction
$$CuSO_4(s) \rightarrow Cu^{2+}(aq) + SO_4^{2-}(aq)$$
The $CuSO_4(s)$ dissolves more rapidly when it is powdered because the increase in surface area allows for
1) increased exposure of solute to solvent
2) decreased exposure of solute to solvent
3) increased solute solubility
4) decreased solute solubility

Practice 8
Based on the nature of the reactants in each equation, which reaction at 25°C will occur at the fastest rate?
1) $KI(aq) + AgNO_3(aq) \rightarrow AgI(s) + KNO_3(aq)$
2) $C(s) + O_2(g) \rightarrow CO(g)$
3) $2SO_2(g) + O_2(g) \rightarrow 2SO_3(g)$
4) $NH_3(g) + HCl(g) \rightarrow NH_4Cl(s)$

Base your answers to practice questions 9 through 12 on the information below.

An investigation was conducted to study the effect of the concentration of a reactant on the total time needed to complete a chemical reaction. Four trials of the same reaction were performed. In each trial the initial concentration of the reactant was different. The time needed for the chemical reaction to be completed was measured. The data for each of the four trials are shown in the data table below.

Reactant Concentration and Reaction Time

Trial	Initial Concentration (M)	Reaction Time (s)
1	0.020	11
2	0.015	14
3	0.010	23
4	0.005	58

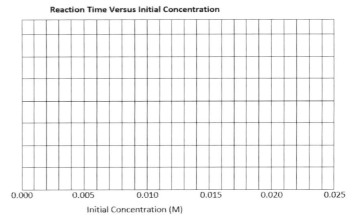

Reaction Time Versus Initial Concentration

9. On the grid, mark an appropriate scale on the axis labeled " Reaction Time*(s)*."
   An appropriate scale is one that allows a trend to be seen.

10. On the same grid, plot the data from the table. Circle and connect the points .

11. State the effect of the concentration of the reactant on the rate of the chemical reaction.

12. In a different experiment involving the same reaction, it was found that an increase in temperature increased the rate of the reaction. Explain this result in terms of collision theory.

Base your answers to practice questions 13 through 15 on the information below.

Given the reaction:

$$Zn(s) + 2HCl(aq) \longrightarrow H_2(g) + ZnCl_2(aq)$$

13. Describe the effect of increasing the concentration of HCl(aq) on the reaction rate and justify your response in terms of *collision theory.*

14. Identify one other variable that might affect the rate and should be held constant during this investigation.

15. Identify the independent variable in this investigation.

©2017 E3 Scholastic Publishing. All Rights Reserved

Lesson 2 - Energy in Chemical Reactions

During a chemical or physical change, substances absorb and release energy as bonds are broken and formed.
In this lesson you will learn about energy change in chemical and physical processes.

Energy in Reactions
Difference in Energy of Products and Reactants

Potential energy is the energy that is stored in the bonds of chemical substances. The amount of potential energy stored in a substance depends on its *structure* and *composition*.

Potential energy of reactants is the amount of energy stored in the bonds of the reactants. Reactants are the substances that are present at the start of a chemical reaction.

Potential energy of products is the amount of energy stored in the bonds of the products. Products are the substances that remain at the end of a chemical reaction.

Heat of reaction (ΔH) is the overall or net energy absorbed or released during a reaction. ΔH of a reaction is the difference between the potential energy of the products and of the reactants.

$$\Delta H \ = \ \text{Energy of products} \ - \ \text{Energy of reactants}$$

Heat of reaction, ΔH, can be negative or positive.

Negative heat of reaction ($-\Delta H$) means that:
• The products of a reaction have *less energy* than the reactants
• The reaction is exothermic because heat is released.

Positive heat of reaction ($+\Delta H$) means that:
• The products of a reaction *have more* energy than the reactants
• The reaction is endothermic because heat is absorbed.

Exothermic and Endothermic Reactions

Some chemical reactions absorb energy while others release energy.
Reactions that release energy are exothermic.
Reactions that absorb energy are endothermic.
Since most chemical and physical processes occur in some form of a liquid or aqueous environment, measuring the temperature of the liquid before and after a reaction is one way to tell if a reaction is exothermic or endothermic.
If heat is released during a reaction, the temperature of the liquid will be higher after the reaction.
If heat if absorbed during a reaction, the temperature of the liquid will be lower after the reaction.

Exothermic Reactions
Release Energy. Negative ΔH (−ΔH)

Exothermic reactions occur when the products that are formed in a reaction contain less energy than the reactants. Since the products have less energy than the reactants, the reactants had lost or released energy during the chemical change. When heat energy is released to the surrounding area where the reaction is occurring, the temperature of the surroundings goes up or increase as shown in the diagram to the right.

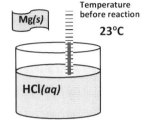

In exothermic reactions:
• Products have less potential energy than the reactants
• Energy is released or lost, and the temperature of the surroundings increases
• Heat of reaction, ΔH, is always negative (-ΔH)
• Equations for exothermic reactions always show the energy that is released to the *right* of the arrow as shown below:

$$Mg + 2HCl \rightarrow MgCl_2 + H_2 + \textbf{Energy}$$

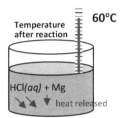

Endothermic Reactions
Absorb Energy. Positive ΔH (+ΔH)

Endothermic reactions occur when the products that are formed in a reaction contain more energy than the reactants. Since the products have more energy than the reactants, the reactants had gained or absorbed energy during the chemical change. When heat energy is absorbed from the surrounding area where the reaction is occurring, the temperature of the surroundings goes down (or decrease) as shown in the diagram to the right.

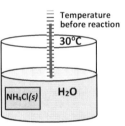

In endothermic reactions:
• Products have more potential energy than the reactants
• Energy is absorbed, and the temperature of the surroundings area decreases
• Heat of reaction, ΔH, is always positive (+ΔH)
• Equations for endothermic reactions always show the energy that is absorbed to the *left* of the arrow as shown below:

$$NH_4Cl(s) + \textbf{Energy} \rightarrow NH_4^+(aq) + Cl^-(aq)$$

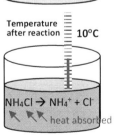

A summary of exothermic and endothermic reactions is given below. Use this table for quick study and comparison of the two reactions.

Reaction	Potential Energy of Reactants	Potential Energy of Products	Energy Change	Temperature of Surroundings	Heat of Reaction (ΔH)
Exothermic	Higher	Lower	Released	Increases	Negative (-ΔH)
Endothermic	Lower	Higher	Absorbed	Decreases	Positive (+ΔH)

      ©2017 E3 Scholastic Publishing. All Rights Reserved

Exothermic and Endothermic Reactions: **Practice Questions**

Practice 16
Solid X and solid Y were dissolved in separate 100 mL beakers of water. The water temperatures were recorded as shown in the table below.

	Salt X	Salt Y
Initial water temperature	40.3°C	40.3°C
Final water temperature	34.5°C	46.1°C

Which statement is the best conclusion from the above information?
1) The dissolving of only Salt X was exothermic.
2) The dissolving of only Salt Y was endothermic.
3) The dissolving of both Salt X and Salt Y was exothermic.
4) The dissolving of Salt X was endothermic and the dissolving of Salt Y was exothermic.

Practice 17
A thermometer is in a beaker of water. Which statement best explains why the thermometer reading initially increases when $LiBr(s)$ is dissolved in the water?
1) The dissolving of the $LiBr(s)$ is endothermic, so energy is gained by the water.
2) The dissolving of the $LiBr(s)$ is exothermic, so energy is gained by the water.
3) The dissolving of the $LiBr(s)$ is endothermic, so energy is lost by the water.
4) The dissolving of the $LiBr(s)$ is exothermic, so energy is lost by the water.

Practice 18
Given the reaction: XW + energy $\rightarrow$ W

Which is true of this reaction?
1) The reaction is exothermic with $-\Delta H$.
2) The reaction is exothermic with $+\Delta H$.
3) The reaction is endothermic with $-\Delta H$.
4) The reaction is endothermic with $+\Delta H$.

Practice 19
Given the reaction: A $\rightarrow$ B + energy

Which statement is true of the reaction below?
1) A has more energy than B, and ΔH is positive.
2) B has more energy than A, and ΔH is positive.
3) A has more energy than B, and ΔH is negative.
4) B has more energy than A, and ΔH is negative.

Practice 20
Given the reaction: $2HBr$ + 73 kJ $\rightarrow$ H_2 + Br_2
The heat of reaction, ΔH, is

1) +73, because energy is released
2) +73, because energy is absorbed.
3) -73, because energy is released.
4) -73, because energy is absorbed.

Base your answers to practice questions 21 and 22 on the equation below.

Given the reaction:

$$2H_2(g) + O_2(g) \rightarrow 2H_2O(l) + 571.6 \text{ kJ}$$

21. Identify the information in this equation that indicates the reaction is exothermic.

22. Compare the potential energy of the reactants to that of the products in the reaction.

Reference Table I - Heat of Reaction

Reference Table I below lists equations for selected physical and chemical changes and their heat of reaction, ΔH, values. Some equations have $-\Delta H$, and some have $+\Delta H$.

Everything that was previously disccussed about exothermic reactions in the previous pages applies to all reactions on this table with $-\Delta H$.

Everything was previously disccussed about endothermic reactions in the previous pages applies to all reactions on this table with $+\Delta H$.

Table I
Heats of Reaction at 101.3 kPa and 298 K

Reaction	ΔH (kJ)*
$CH_4(g) + 2O_2(g) \longrightarrow CO_2(g) + 2H_2O(\ell)$	-890.4
$C_3H_8(g) + 5O_2(g) \longrightarrow 3CO_2(g) + 4H_2O(\ell)$	-2219.2
$2C_8H_{18}(\ell) + 25O_2(g) \longrightarrow 16CO_2(g) + 18H_2O(\ell)$	-10943
$2CH_3OH(\ell) + 3O_2(g) \longrightarrow 2CO_2(g) + 4H_2O(\ell)$	-1452
$C_2H_5OH(\ell) + 3O_2(g) \longrightarrow 2CO_2(g) + 3H_2O(\ell)$	-1367
$C_6H_{12}O_6(s) + 6O_2(g) \longrightarrow 6CO_2(g) + 6H_2O(\ell)$	-2804
$2CO(g) + O_2(g) \longrightarrow 2CO_2(g)$	-566.0
$C(s) + O_2(g) \longrightarrow CO_2(g)$	-393.5
$4Al(s) + 3O_2(g) \longrightarrow 2Al_2O_3(s)$	-3351
$N_2(g) + O_2(g) \longrightarrow 2NO(g)$	+182.6
$N_2(g) + 2O_2(g) \longrightarrow 2NO_2(g)$	+66.4
$2H_2(g) + O_2(g) \longrightarrow 2H_2O(g)$	-483.6
$2H_2(g) + O_2(g) \longrightarrow 2H_2O(\ell)$	-571.6
$N_2(g) + 3H_2(g) \longrightarrow 2NH_3(g)$	-91.8
$2C(s) + 3H_2(g) \longrightarrow C_2H_6(g)$	-84.0
$2C(s) + 2H_2(g) \longrightarrow C_2H_4(g)$	+52.4
$2C(s) + H_2(g) \longrightarrow C_2H_2(g)$	+227.4
$H_2(g) + I_2(g) \longrightarrow 2HI(g)$	+53.0
$KNO_3(s) \xrightarrow{H_2O} K^+(aq) + NO_3^-(aq)$	+34.89
$NaOH(s) \xrightarrow{H_2O} Na^+(aq) + OH^-(aq)$	-44.51
$NH_4Cl(s) \xrightarrow{H_2O} NH_4^+(aq) + Cl^-(aq)$	+14.78
$NH_4NO_3(s) \xrightarrow{H_2O} NH_4^+(aq) + NO_3^-(aq)$	+25.69
$NaCl(s) \xrightarrow{H_2O} Na^+(aq) + Cl^-(aq)$	+3.88
$LiBr(s) \xrightarrow{H_2O} Li^+(aq) + Br^-(aq)$	-48.83
$H^+(aq) + OH^-(aq) \longrightarrow H_2O(\ell)$	-55.8

* The ΔH values are based on molar quantities represented in the equations.
A minus sign indicates an exothermic reaction.

Reading Table I

● **Equation with $-\Delta H$ (exothermic)**

$2C(s) + 3H_2(g) \rightarrow C_2H_6(g) \qquad \Delta H = -84$ kJ.

According to the equation and ΔH value:

• The formation of **1** mole of C_2H_6 (ethane) releases 84 kJ (kilojoules) of heat energy.

• The formation of **2** moles of C_2H_6 will release **2**(84 kJ) or 168 kJ of heat energy.

• The product of this reaction has less energy than the reactants.

✸ **Equation with $+\Delta H$ (endothermic)**

$NH_4Cl(s) \rightarrow NH_4^+(aq) + Cl^-(aq) \quad \Delta H = +14.78$ kJ

According to the equation and ΔH value:

• The dissolving of **1** mole of NH_4Cl (ammonium chloride) absorbs 14.78 kJ of heat energy.

• The dissolving of **0.5** moles of NH_4Cl will absorb **0.5** (14.78 kJ) or 7.39 kJ of heat energy.

• The products of this process have more energy than the reactant.

Reference Table I - Heat of Reaction: Practice Questions

Concept Task: Be able to determine which reaction absorbs or releases energy.

Practice 23
Which substance is formed through endothermic reaction?
1) $HI(g)$ 2) $H_2O(l)$ 3) $NH_3(g)$ 4) $H_2O(g)$

Practice 24
Based on Reference Table I, the formation of 1 mole of which substance releases the greatest amount of heat energy?
1) C_2H_2 2) NO 3) C_2H_6 4) NH_3

Practice 25
In which reaction, according to Reference Table I, do the products have lower energy content than the reactants?
1) $C(s) + O_2(g) \rightarrow CO_2(g)$ 3) $N_2(g) + O_2(g) \rightarrow 2NO(g)$
2) $2C(s) + H_2(g) \rightarrow C_2H_2(g)$ 4) $N_2(g) + 2O_2(g) \rightarrow 2NO_2(g)$

Concept Task: Be able to interpret a reaction based on its ΔH value.

Practice 26
Given the reaction: $CH_4(g) + 2O_2(g) \rightarrow 2H_2O(g) + CO_2(g)$

What is the overall result when $CH_4(g)$ burns according to this reaction?
1) Energy is absorbed and ΔH is negative.   3) Energy is released and ΔH is negative.
2) Energy is absorbed and ΔH is positive.   4) Energy is released and ΔH is positive.

Practice 27
Which is true for formation of 1 mole of NH_3 from its elements?
1) It releases 91.8 kJ of energy   3) It releases 45.9 kJ of energy
2) it absorbs 91.8 kJ of energy   4) It absorbs 45.9 kJ of energy

Practice 28
When 2 moles of $KNO_3(s)$ is dissolved in water, the water temperature
1) increases as 34.89 kJ of energy is released.   3) decreases as 34.89 kJ of energy is absorbed
2) increases as 69.78 kJ of energy is released.   4) decreases as 69.78 kJ of energy is absorbed

Practice 29
According Reference Table I, what is the heat of reaction for the formation of 2 moles of $H_2O(l)$ from hydrogen gas and oxygen gas at 1 atmosphere and 298 K?
1) -571.6 kJ   2) -483.6 kJ   3) -285.8 kJ   4) -241.8 kJ

Practice 30
Given the balanced equation:
$4Fe(s) + 3O_2(g) \rightarrow 2Fe_2O_3(s) + 1640$ kJ

Which phrase best describes this reaction?
1) endothermic with ΔH = +1640 kJ   3) exothermic with ΔH = +1640 kJ
2) endothermic with ΔH = −1640 KJ   4) exothermic with ΔH = −1640 kJ

Potential Energy Diagrams
Show Energy Measurements and Energy Change in a Reaction

A **potential energy diagram** shows changes in the heat energy of substances over the course of a reaction. To understand potential energy diagrams, it is important to review components of a chemical reaction. These components are represented on potential energy diagrams.

Consider this equation:

A + B$_2$ →   ABB   →   AB + B
reactants   *activated*   *products*
                        complex

Reactants (A and B$_2$) are substances that are present at the beginning of the reaction.

Products (AB and B) are substances formed at the end of the reaction.

The **activated complex** (ABB) is a high energy intermediate substance that is formed during the reaction. Because of its high energy, an activated complex is unstable and will always break down or rearrange to form more stable products. An activated complex is not usually shown in a reaction equation. However, for a potential energy diagram to be accurately drawn for any reaction, activated complex must be represented on the diagram.

Exothermic Reaction Diagram
(drawn for the reaction above)

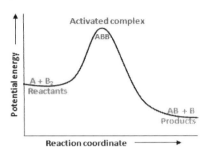

Endothermic Reaction Diagram
(drawn for the reverse of the reaction to the right)

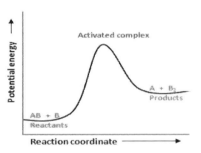

Practice 31
Which potential energy diagram best represents a reaction that has a positive heat of reaction?

1)

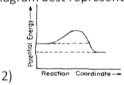
2)

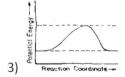
3)

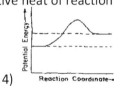
4)

Practice 32
Given the reaction, A   +   B →   C + 50 kJ

Which diagram below best represents the potential energy change for this reaction?

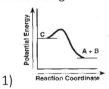
1)

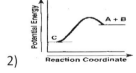
2)

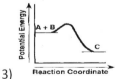
3)

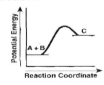
4)

Practice 33
The potential energy diagram below was drawn for a reaction that forms 2 moles of a substance.

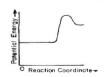

According to Reference Table I, which substance was formed from the reaction?

1) 2Al$_2$O$_3$(s)   2) 2HI(g)   3) 2H$_2$O(ℓ)   4) 2NH$_3$(g)

                    ©2017 E3 Scholastic Publishing. All Rights Reserved

Potential Energy Diagram Measurements

The potential energy diagrams below show the energy measurements of substances through a course of a reaction. The left diagram shows measurements for a reaction that is uncatalyzed. The right diagram shows energy measurements for the same reaction with a catalyst added. A catalyst speeds up a reaction by lowering the activation energy. In the diagram on the right, certain energy measurements for the reaction are lower with a catalyst.

NOTE the following about each diagram:
The y axis is potential energy. The x axis is the reaction coordinate or progress of the reaction. The curves represent potential energy of substances that are present at different times over the course of the reaction, starting with reactants and ending with products.

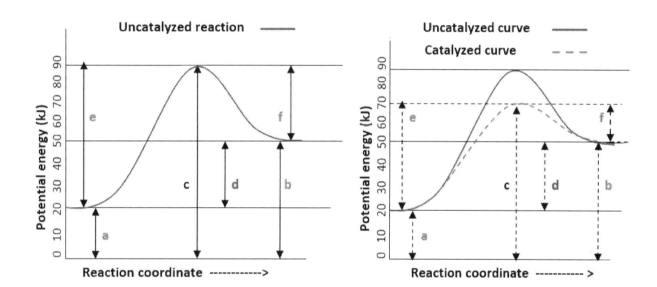

The potential energy measurements for three substances are shown with arrows a, b and c.
These arrows are always drawn from the bottom of the diagram:

(a) Potential Energy of the Reactants   (no change with catalyst)

(b) Potential Energy of the Products   (no change with catalyst)

(c) Potential Energy of the Activated Complex   (lower with catalyst)

Differences of two potential energies are shown with arrows d, e and f.
These arrows are always drawn between two energies of the diagram.

(d) Heat of Reaction, ΔH $(b - a)$ (no change with catalyst)

(e) Activation Energy for Forward Reaction $(c - a)$ (lower with catalyst)

(f) Activation Energy for Reverse Reaction $(c - b)$ (lower with catalyst)

Base your answers to practice questions 34 through 36 on the potential energy diagram below.

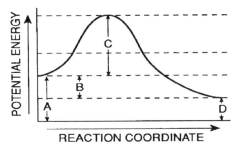

Practice 34
Which potential energy measurements will change if a catalyst is added to the reaction?
1) A and B only   2) C and E only   3) B, C, and E   4) A, B, and D

Practice 35
Which arrow represents the difference between the potential energy of the products and that of the reactants?
1) A   2) B   3) D   4) E

Practice 36
Potential energy of reactants for the forward reaction can be determined by the length of arrow
1) A   2) B   3) C   4) E

Base your answers to questions 37 through 40 on the potential energy diagram below.

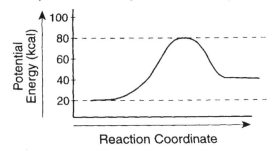

Practice 37
Which statement correctly describes the potential energy changes that occur in the forward uncatalyzed reaction?
1) The activation energy is 40 kJ and a ΔH of +20 kJ.
2) The activation energy is 40 kJ and a ΔH of -20 kJ.
3) The activation energy is 60 kJ and a ΔH of +20 kJ.
4) The activation energy is 60 kJ and a ΔH of -20 kJ.

Practice 38
Which reaction requires the lowest amount activation energy?
1) Forward uncatalyzed reaction.
2) Forward catalyzed reaction.
3) Reverse uncatalyzed reaction.
4) Reverse catalyzed reaction.

Practice 39
What is the heat of reaction (ΔH) for the reverse catalyzed reaction?
1) + 20 kJ   3) + 40 kJ
2) − 20 kJ   4) − 40 kJ

Practice 40
What is the energy of the activated complex for the uncatalyzed reaction?
1) 20 kJ   3) 60 kJ
2) 40 kJ   4) 80 kJ

©2017 E3 Scholastic Publishing. All Rights Reserved

Base your answers to practice questions 41 and 42 on the potential energy diagram below.

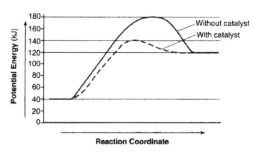

41. What is the heat of reaction with the catalyst?

42. Explain, in terms of the function of a catalyst, why the curves on the potential energy diagram for the catalyzed and uncatalyzed reactions are different.

Base your answers to practice questions 43 and 44 on the information below.

Given the reaction:

$$2NO_2(g) \; + \; 7H_2(g) \; \rightarrow \; 2NH_3(g) \; + \; 4H_2O(g) \; + \; 1127 \text{ kJ}$$

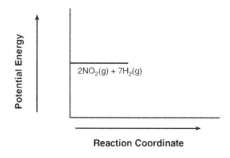

43. On the diagram to the left, complete the potential energy diagram for this reaction.

44. Determine the total amount of energy released when 0.5 moles of NO_2 is completely reacted with hydrogen.

---

45. On the potential energy diagram below, draw an arrow to represent the activation energy of the forward reaction.

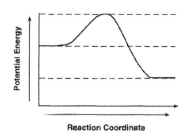

---

46. A potential energy diagram for a chemical reaction is shown below. On this diagram, use a dash-line to draw a curve to show how the potential energy diagram will change when a catalyst is added to the reaction.

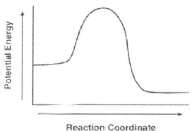

Lesson 3: Entropy
Randomness and Disorder

Particles (atoms, molecules, or ions) of a substance are arranged and organized differently in the solid, liquid, and gas states.

Entropy is a measure of randomness or disorder of particles in a substance or system.

A substance or system with low entropy has organized particles.

A substance or system with high entropy has disorganized particles.

Comparing Entropy: *Solids Have Lowest Entropy. Gases Have Highest Entropy.*

Entropy of chemical and physical systems is relative, meaning that the organization of a system is typically described in comparison to that of another system.

For examples:

$H_2O(\ell)$, water, has a ***greater entropy*** than $H_2O(s)$, ice.

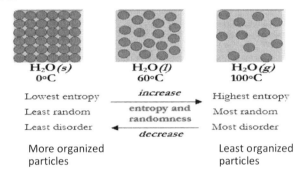

But

$H_2O(\ell)$, water, has a ***lower entropy*** than $H_2O(g)$, vapor.

$H_2O(\ell)$ at 60°C has a ***greater entropy*** than $H_2O(\ell)$ at 40°C.

But

$H_2O(\ell)$ at 60°C has a ***lower entropy*** than $H_2O(\ell)$ at 75°C.

Order of **increasing entropy** as related to phases of a substance is shown below.

Solid < aqueous < liquid < gas

Change in Entropy: *Less Organized Products, Increasing Entropy*

• **Systems in nature** tend to change in the direction of **higher entropy** and **lower energy.**

Entropy increases when a change leads to particles that are less organized or more random.

All *changes listed below* lead to ***increase in entropy.***

Physical Changes
• A solid *melting* to liquid or liquid *evaporating* to gas: **ex.** Au*(s)* → Au*(ℓ)*
• A solid *dissolving* in water to make a solution: **ex:** NaCl*(s)* → NaCl*(aq)*
• The temperature of a substance *increasing*: **ex:** $Br_2(\ell)$ at 30°C → $Br_2(\ell)$ at 45°C

Chemical Changes
• A solid reactant producing gaseous products.
• A compound reactant producing free element products.
• Fewer moles of reactants producing greater moles of products.

ex. $2Al_2O_3(s)$ → $4Al(s)$ + $3O_2(g)$

***Entropy decreases* if any of the above changes is reversed.**

©2017 E3 Scholastic Publishing. All Rights Reserved

Entropy: Practice Questions

Practice 47
Entropy measures which of the following about a chemical system?
1) Activation energy of the system
2) Intermolecular forces of the system
3) Energy change of the system
4) Disorder of the system

Practice 48
A system is most likely to undergo a reaction if the system after the reaction has
1) Lower energy and lower entropy
2) Lower energy and higher entropy
3) Higher energy and higher entropy
4) Higher energy and lower entropy

Practice 49
Under the same temperature and pressure, which sample of carbon dioxide contains particles with the highest entropy?
1) $CO_2(g)$ 3) $CO_2(\ell)$
2) $CO_2(s)$ 4) $CO_2(aq)$

Practice 50
Which 10-milliliter sample of water has the greatest degree of disorder?
1) $H_2O(g)$ at 120°C   3) $H_2O(\ell)$ at 20°C
2) $H_2O(\ell)$ at 80°C   4) $H_2O(\ell)$ at 0°C

Practice 51
Which temperature change of ethanol will lead to a decrease in randomness of its molecules?
1) 5°C to -10°C   3) 0°C to 5°C
2) -10°C to 5°C   4) -5°C to 0°C

Practice 52
Which of these changes produces the greatest increase in entropy?
1) $CaCO_3(s) \rightarrow CaO(s) + CO_2(g)$
2) $2Mg(s) + O_2(g) \rightarrow 2MgO(s)$
3) $H_2O(g) \rightarrow H_2O(\ell)$
4) $CO_2(g) \rightarrow CO_2(s)$

53. The compound KNO_3 is soluble in water. Compare the entropy of 30. grams of $KNO_3(s)$ at 20.°C with the entropy of 30. grams of KNO_3 dissolved in 100. grams of water at 20.°C.

Base your answer to practice question 54 on the information below.

The balanced equation below represents the decomposition of potassium chlorate.

$$2KClO_3(s) \rightarrow 2KCl(s) + 3O_2(g)$$

54. State why the entropy of the reactant is less than the entropy of the products.

Base your answer to the following question on the information below and on your knowledge of chemistry.

Fruit growers in Florida protect oranges when the temperature is near freezing by spraying water on them. It is the freezing of the water that protects the oranges from frost damage. When $H_2O(l)$ at 0°C changes to $H_2O(s)$ at 0°C, heat energy is released. This energy helps to prevent the temperature inside the orange from dropping below freezing, which could damage the fruit. After harvesting, oranges can be exposed to ethene gas, C_2H_4, to improve their color.

55. Explain, in terms of particle arrangement, why the entropy of the water decreases when the water freezes.

Lesson 4: Equilibrium

Equilibrium is the state of balance between two opposing processes taking place at the same time (simultaneously) and at equal rates. One example of two opposing processes is the freezing of water to ice and the melting of the ice back to water. Since both processes in equilibrium continue to take place, equilibrium is said to be dynamic.

When equilibrium is reached in a chemical or physical system:
- **Rates** of forward and reverse processes are **equal.**
- **Concentrations** (or amounts) of substances remain **constant.**

In this lesson, you will learn about physical and chemical equilibrium. You will also learn about Le Chatelier's Principle.

Equilibrium
Equal Rate, Constant Concentrations

Equilibrium can only occur in a closed system in which changes that are taking place are *reversible*. A closed system is a system in which nothing is allowed in or out. For example, if a soda can is left closed, carbon dioxide gas will not be able to get inside the can from the outside, or be able to escape out of the can to the outside. Inside the can, carbon dioxide will move in and out of the liquid of the soda can. If left undisturbed, equilibrium will be reached when movements of carbon dioxide gas into the liquid (*dissolving*) and out of the liquid (*undissolving*) is occurring at the same rate.

Closed can
Equilibrium process will occur in this can.

An equation that shows a reversible process at equilibrium always contain a double-headed arrow. (<——> or <====>). This means that the reaction can go in both the forward and reverse directions.

Open soda can
Equilibrium process CANNOT occur in this can.

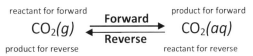

reactant for forward   product for forward

$$CO_2(g) \underset{\text{Reverse}}{\overset{\text{Forward}}{\rightleftarrows}} CO_2(aq)$$

product for reverse   reactant for reverse

Both physical and chemical changes can reach a state of equilibrium.

Physical Equilibrium

Physical equilibrium occurs in reversible physical changes. During a physical change, the composition of a substance does not change. Physical equilibrium, therefore, occurs in processes that do not change one substance to another. Two major types of physical equilibrium are:

Phase equilibrium
Solution equilibrium

Examples and descriptions of these equilibrium systems are discussed on the next page.

Topic 9   Kinetics and Equilibrium

Phase Equilibrium

A **phase equilibrium** occurs in a *closed system* in which a substance is changing from one phase to another. At a specific temperature of a substance, a state of balance or equilibrium can be reached between two opposing phase changes of the substance. The temperature at which a particular phase equilibrium is reached is different for different substances.
Phase equilibrium in water are described below.

Ice / water equilibrium occur at **0°C or 273 K** (melting and freezing points of water at 1 atm).
• Equilibrium exists between ice melting and liquid freezing
• *Rates* of melting and freezing are *equal*
• A*mounts* of ice and water remain *constant*

$$H_2O(s) \underset{\text{freezing}}{\overset{\text{melting}}{\rightleftarrows}} H_2O(\ell) \qquad \text{Ice/water equilibrium equation}$$

Water /steam (vapor) equilibrium occurs at **100°C or 373 K** (boiling point of water at 1 atm).
• Equilibrium exists between liquid evaporating and steam condensing.
• *Rates* of evaporation and condensation are *equal*.
• A*mounts* of liquid and steam remain *constant*.

$$H_2O(\ell) \underset{\text{condensation}}{\overset{\text{evaporation}}{\rightleftarrows}} H_2O(g) \qquad \text{water/steam equilibrium equation}$$

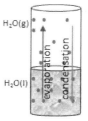

Solution Equilibrium

A **solution equilibrium** occurs in a closed system in which a substance is dissolving in a liquid. Two examples of solution equilibrium are described below.

Solid in liquid equilibrium: In a saturated solution
• Equilibrium exists between dissolved and undissolved particles
• *Rates* of dissolving of solid and crystallization of ions are equal
• A*mounts* of solids and ions remain *constant* in the solution

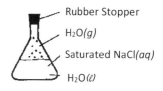

$$NaCl(s) \underset{\text{crystallizing}}{\overset{\text{dissolving}}{\rightleftarrows}} Na^+(aq) \ + \ Cl^-(aq)$$

Gas in liquid equilibrium: In a gaseous solution
• Equilibrium exists between dissolved gas in the liquid and undissolved gas above the liquid

• *Rates* of dissolving and undissolving of the gas are *equal*

• A*mounts* of undissolved gas (above liquid) and dissolved gas (in liquid) remain constant

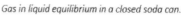

Gas in liquid equilibrium in a closed soda can.

$$CO_2(g) \underset{\text{undissolving}}{\overset{\text{dissolving}}{\rightleftarrows}} CO_2(aq)$$

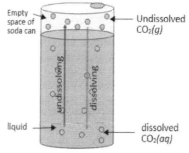

Physical Equilibrium: Practice Questions

Practice 56
Which changes can reach equilibrium?
1) Chemical changes, only
2) Physical changes, only
3) Both physical and chemical changes
4) Neither physical nor chemical changes

Practice 57
Given the phase change equation: $H_2O(g) \leftrightarrow H_2O(\ell)$

At 1 atm, at what temperature would equilibrium be reached?
1) 273 K   2) 0 K   3) 373 K   4) 298 K

Practice 58
Solution equilibrium always exists in a solution that is
1) unsaturated   2) saturated   3) concentrated   4) dilute

Practice 59
A sample of water in a sealed flask at 298 K is in equilibrium with its vapor. This is an example of
1) chemical equilibrium
2) phase equilibrium
3) solution equilibrium
4) energy equilibrium

Practice 60
Which of the following is NOT an example of a physical equilibrium?
1) The equilibrium process for the synthesis and the decomposition of ammonia
2) The equilibrium process dissolving and crystallization of salt in a saturated solution
3) The equilibrium process for the evaporation and condensation of water at 373 K and 1 atm
4) The equilibrium process for the freezing and melting of water at 273 K and 1 atm

Practice 61
Which description applies to a system in a sealed flask that is half full of water?
1) Only evaporation occurs, but it eventually stops
2) Only condensation occurs, but it eventually stops
3) Neither evaporation nor condensation occurs
4) Both evaporation and condensation occur

Practice 62
A solution equilibrium is reached in a saturated solution when
1) dissolving stops occurring
2) crystallization stops occurring
3) both dissolving and crystallization stop occurring
4) dissolving occurs at the same rate as crystallization is occurring

Practice 63
In the reaction: $Pb(NO_3)_2(s) \leftrightarrow Pb^{2+}(aq) + 2NO_3^-(aq)$

Equilibrium is reached when
1) the rate of dissolving of salt and the rate of crystallization of ions is constant
2) the concentration of $Pb(NO_3)_2(s)$, $Pb^{2+}(aq)$, and $NO_3^-(aq)$ are constant
3) the rate of dissolving of salt is slower than the rate of crystallization of ions
4) the concentration of Pb^{2+} is the same as the concentration of $Pb(NO_3)_2(s)$

Practice 64
The diagram below represents a sealed flask.

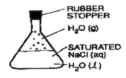

Which equation represents a system that will reach equilibrium in the flask?
1) $NaCl(s) \leftrightarrow NaCl(\ell)$
2) $NaCl(s) \leftrightarrow H_2O(\ell)$
3) $H_2O(g) \leftrightarrow NaCl(aq)$
4) $H_2O(g) \leftrightarrow H_2O(\ell)$

                                    ©2017 E3 Scholastic Publishing. All Rights Reserved

Chemical Equilibrium

A chemical equilibrium occurs in a closed system in which the chemical change is reversible.

A chemical equilibrium process is described below using the reaction of ammonia with hydrogen to make ammonia. The reaction is called *Haber process.*

$$N_2(g) \quad + \quad 3H_2(g) \quad \underset{\text{reverse}}{\overset{\text{forward}}{\rightleftharpoons}} \quad 2NH_3(g)$$

At the start of the reaction the reactants, N_2 and H_2, will combine to produce NH_3 in the forward reaction. As NH_3 is being produced, the reverse reaction in which NH_3 is decomposing to produce N_2 and H_2 will start. The speed or rate of this reverse reaction will be slow at first. As more NH_3 are being produced, the forward reaction slows down while the reverse reaction speeds up. Eventually, the forward and reverse reactions will be occurring at the same rate or equal speed. This means that if at a given time period 10 molecules of NH_3 are being produced, there will be 10 other molecules of NH_3 breaking up to produce N_2 and H_2. When the rates of forward and reverse are equal, the reaction is said to have reach a state of **equilibrium.**

At equilibrium:

• *Rates* of forward and reverse reactions are *equal.*

• *Concentrations* of N_2, H_2, and NH_3 remain *constant* or stay the same.

Stress and Le Chatelier's Principle

If a stress is introduced into the above reaction while at equilibrium, the reaction will change or shift. A **stress** is any change in the concentration, temperature or pressure to an equilibrium reaction. **Le Chatelier's Principle** states that when a stress is introduced into a reaction at equilibrium, the reaction will change by speeding up in one direction while slowing down in the other direction to bring back or re-establish the reaction to a new equilibrium point. The concentrations of the substances at the new equilibrium point will be different from those of the previous equilibrium point. There will be an increase in the concentrations of some substances, and a decrease in others.

Change in Concentration or Temperature

Given the reaction:
$$N_2(g) \quad + \quad 3H_2(g) \quad \underset{\text{endothermic}}{\overset{\text{exothermic}}{\rightleftharpoons}} \quad 2NH_3(g) \quad + \quad 92 \text{ KJ}$$

Increasing any Reactant (ex. ↑N_2)
• **Increases** forward reaction (shift right)
• **Increases** product concentrations (↑NH_3, ↑heat)
• **Decreases** reverse reaction
• **Decreases** the concentration of all other reactants (↓H_2)

Decreasing any Reactants has the same effect as **increasing any product.**

Increasing any Product (ex. ↑NH_3)
• **Increases** reverse reaction (shift left)
• **Increases** reactant concentrations (↑N_2, ↑H_2)
• **Decreases** forward reaction
• **Decreases** the concentration of all other products (↓heat)

Decreasing any products has the same effect as **increasing any reactant.**

Increasing Heat/Temperature: Favors or speeds up *endothermic* reaction
• In the above reaction, similar effect as increasing any product.

Decreasing Heat/Temperature: Favors or speeds up *exothermic* reaction
• In the above reaction, similar effect as increasing any reactant.

Kinetics and Equilibrium   Topic 9

Changes in Concentration and Temperature: Practice Questions

Concept Task: Be able to determine changes to an equilibrium reaction when the concentration of a substance is changed.

Practice 65
Given the reaction at equilibrium

$$SO_2(g) + NO_2(g) \leftrightarrow SO_3(g) + NO(g)$$

As NO(g) is removed from the system, the concentration of

1) $SO_3(g)$ will increase
2) $NO_2(g)$ will increase
3) $SO_2(g)$ will increase
4) $SO_2(g)$ and $NO_2(g)$ will both be equal

Practice 66
The reaction below is at equilibrium:

$$C(s) + O_2(g) \leftrightarrow CO_2(g)$$

If the concentration of C(s) is increased, the equilibrium point will shift
1) right, and the concentration of $O_2(g)$ will increase
2) right, and the concentration of $O_2(g)$ will decrease
3) left, and the concentration of $O_2(g)$ will increase
4) left, and the concentration of $O_2(g)$ will decrease

Practice 67
Given the reaction at equilibrium:

$$N_2(g) + 3H_2(g) \leftrightarrow 2NH_3(g)$$

Increasing the concentration of $NH_3(g)$ will cause
1) a decrease in the concentration of $N_2(g)$
2) a decrease in the concentration of $H_2(g)$
3) an increase in the rate of forward reaction
4) an increase in the rate of reverse reaction

Practice 68
Given the equilibrium reaction

$$A + B \leftrightarrow AB + heat$$

If the concentration of AB is decreased, the rate of forward reaction will
1) increase, and [B] will also increase
2) increase, and [B] will decrease
3) decrease, and [B] will also decrease
4) decrease, and [B] will increase

Concept Task: Be able to determine changes to an equilibrium reaction when the temperature is changed.

Practice 69
Given the reaction at equilibrium

$$2HBr(g) + 73 kJ \leftrightarrow H_2(g) + Br_2(g)$$

As the temperature decreases, the concentration of $H_2(g)$

1) increases
2) decreases
3) remains the same

Practice 70
Given the equilibrium reaction

$$2A(g) + B(g) \leftrightarrow C(g) + 42 kJ$$

If more heat is added to the reaction,
1) [A] and [C] will both decrease
2) [A] and [C] will both increase
3) [A] will decrease, but [C] will Increase
4) [A] will increase, but [C] will decrease

Practice 71
Given the system at equilibrium:

$$2NO_2(g) \leftrightarrow N_2O_4(g) + 58.1 kJ$$

When the temperature is increased at constant pressure, the concentration of
1) N_2O_4 will increase, because the forward rate increases
2) N_2O_4 will increase, because the reverse rate increases
3) NO_2 will increase, because the forward rate increases
4) NO_2 will increase, because the reverse rate increases

Practice 72
Given the following system at equilibrium:

$$2Cl + 2H_2O + energy \leftrightarrow 2HCl + O_2$$

If the temperature of the system is decreased, the concentration of O_2 will
1) decrease, and equilibrium will shift to the right
2) increase, and equilibrium will shift to the right
3) decrease, and equilibrium will shift to the left
4) increase, and equilibrium will shift to the left

©2017 E3 Scholastic Publishing. All Rights Reserved

Changes in Pressure
Increasing Pressure Favors the Side with Fewer Moles

When the pressure is changed on an equilibrium reaction, **moles** of gaseous reactants and products must be considered in order to correctly determine how the reaction will change.

Given the equilibrium reaction below.

$$CH_4 \; + \; H_2O \; \underset{\text{reverse}}{\overset{\text{forward}}{\rightleftharpoons}} \; 3H_2 \; + \; CO$$

number of moles	1	1	3	1
total moles	**2 moles**		**4 moles**	

Increasing pressure (by decreasing volume)
- Favors or speeds up production of substances that are on the side of the smaller number of moles.

In the above reaction, increasing pressure:
- **increases reverse reaction (shift the reaction left)**
- **increases** CH_4 and H_2O concentrations
- **decreases forward reaction**
- **decreases** H_2 and CO concentrations

Decreasing pressure (by increasing volume)
- Favors or speeds up production of substances that are on the side of greater moles.

In the above reaction, decreasing pressure:
- increases forward reaction (shift the reaction right)
- increases H_2 and CO concentrations
- decreases reverse reaction
- decreases CH_4 and H_2O concentrations

In reactions in which the total moles of gases on both sides of the equation are equal, a change in pressure has no effect on equilibrium; there will be no shift in either direction.

Practice 73
Given the reaction:

$2SO_2(g) \; + \; O_2(g) \; \leftrightarrow \; 2SO_3(g)$

If pressure is increased on the reaction, there will be
1) a decrease in concentration of SO_3
2) an increase in concentration SO_2
3) a shift of equilibrium to right
4) a shift in equilibrium to left

Practice 74
Given the reaction at equilibrium:
$4HCl(g) \; + \; O_2(g) \; \leftrightarrow \; 2Cl_2(g) \; + \; 2H_2O(g)$

If the volume on the system is decreased, the concentration of $Cl_2(g)$ will
1) decrease, because the reverse rate will decrease
2) decrease, because the reverse rate will increase
3) increase, because the forward rate will decrease
4) increase, because the forward rate will increase

Practice 75
Given the reaction at equilibrium

$2HCl(g) \;\;\;\; \leftrightarrow \;\;\; H_2(g) \; + \; Cl_2(g)$

As pressure is decreased at constant temperature, the concentration of HCl
1) decreases   2) increase   3) remains the same

Practice 76
Given the reaction below at equilibrium

$W(g) \; + \; 3X(g) \; \leftrightarrow \; 2Y(g) \; + \; 3Z(g)$

An increase in pressure at constant temperature will shift the equilibrium to the
1) left, and the concentration of W(g) will increase
2) left, and the concentration of W(g) will decrease
3) right, and the concentration of W(g) will increase
4) right, and the concentration of W(g) will decrease

Adding a Catalyst
When a catalyst is added to a reaction at equilibrium:
- Rates of both the **forward** and reverse reactions increase or speed up equally.

         As a result:
- There will be **no shift** to either direction of the reaction.
- There will be **no** overall change or effect on the equilibrium concentrations.

Chemical Equilibrium (Le Chatelier's Principle): Practice Questions

Most questions on equilibrium involve determining the stress that will cause a given change to a reaction.

Concept Task: Be able to determine which stress will cause a certain change to a reaction

Practice 77
Given the equilibrium reaction
$$H_2 \; + \; Cl_2 \; + \; energy \; \leftrightarrow \; 2HCl$$
Which change will cause the concentration of H_2 to decrease?
1) Decreasing Cl_2 3) Increasing temperature
2) Decreasing pressure   4) Increasing HCl

Practice 78
Given the equilibrium reaction below:
$$2SO_2(g) \; + \; O_2(g) \; \leftrightarrow \; 2SO_3(g) \; + \; heat$$

Which change at equilibrium will cause the rate of forward reaction to increase?
1) Decreasing concentration of $SO_2(g)$ 3) Increasing temperature
2) Decreasing concentration of $SO_3(g)$ 4) Decreasing pressure

Practice 79
Given the reaction
$$2C_2(g) \; + \; D_4(g) \; \leftrightarrow \; 4CD(g) \; + \; 20 \, kJ$$

Which change in the reaction will cause the equilibrium reaction to shift left?
1) Increase in pressure   3) Increase in concentration of $C_2(g)$
2) Decreasing heat   4) Adding a catalyst

Practice 80
Given the equilibrium reaction below:
$$SO_2(g) \; + \; NO_2(g) \; \leftrightarrow \; SO_3(g) \; + \; NO(g) \; + \; heat$$

Which stress will NOT shift the equilibrium point of this reaction?
1) Decreasing pressure   3) Increasing heat
2) Decreasing $SO_2(g)$ concentration   4) Increasing $NO(g)$ concentration

Practice 81
Given the reaction at equilibrium
$$2A(g) \; + \; 3B(g) \; \leftrightarrow \; A_2B_3(g) \; + \; heat$$
Which change will not affect the equilibrium concentrations of $A(g)$, $B(g)$, and $A_2B_3(g)$
1) Adding more $A(g)$ 3) Increase the temperature
2) Adding a catalyst   4) Increase the pressure

Practice 82
A saturated solution is represented by the equation below:
$$AgCl(s) \; + \; heat \; \leftrightarrow \; Ag^+(aq) \; + \; Cl^-(aq)$$

Which change will cause an increase in the amount of $AgCl(s)$?
1) A decrease in pressure   3) A decrease in the concentration of $Ag^+(aq)$
2) An increase in temperature   4) An increase in the concentration of $Cl^-(aq)$

Base your answer to the following question on the information below.

A beaker contains 100.0 milliliters of a dilute aqueous solution of ethanoic acid at equilibrium. The equation below represents this system.

$$HC_2H_3O_2(aq) \leftrightarrow H^+(aq) + C_2H_3O_2^-(aq)$$

83. Describe what happens to the concentration of $H^+(aq)$ when 10 drops of concentrated $HC_2H_3O_2(aq)$ are added to this system.

Base your answers to practice questions 84 and 85 on the information and balanced equation below.

Given the equation for a reaction at equilibrium:

$$2SO_2(g) + O_2(g) \leftrightarrow 2SO_3(g) + energy$$

84. Describe what happens to the concentration of $SO_2(g)$ when more $SO_3(g)$ is added to the reaction at equilibrium.

85. Explain, in terms of Le Chatelier's principle, why the equilibrium shifts to the right to relieve the stress when the pressure on the system is increased at constant temperature.

Base your answers to practice questions 86 and 87 on the information below.

In a laboratory, 0.100 mole of colorless hydrogen iodide gas at room temperature is placed in a 1.00-liter flask. The flask is sealed and warmed, causing the HI(g) to start decomposing to $H_2(g)$ and $I_2(g)$. Then the temperature of the contents of the flask is kept constant.

During this reaction, the contents of the flask change to a pale purple-colored mixture of HI(g), $H_2(g)$, and $I_2(g)$. When the color of the mixture in the flask stops changing, the concentration of $I_2(g)$ is determined to be 0.013 mole per liter. The relationship between concentration and time for the reactant and products is shown in the graph below.

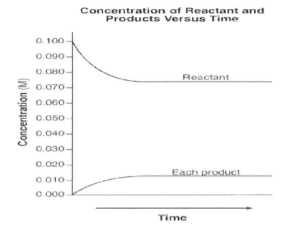

86. Calculate the mass of $I_2(g)$ in the flask at equilibrium. Your response must include *both* a correct numerical setup and the calculated result.

87. State, in terms of concentration, evidence that indicates the system in the flask has reached equilibrium.

Vocabulary

Lesson 1: Kinetics
Kinetics
Rate
Mechanism
Collision theory
Effective collision
Catalyst
Activation energy

Lesson 2: Energy in Reactions
Exothermic
Endothermic
Heat of reaction
Potential energy diagram

Lesson 3: Entropy
Entropy

Lesson 4: Equilibrium
Equilibrium
Stress
Le Chatelier's principle

 ©2017 E3 Scholastic Publishing. All Rights Reserved

1. 3

2. 4

3. 4

4. 3

5. 2

6. 4

7. 1

8. 1

9 and 10

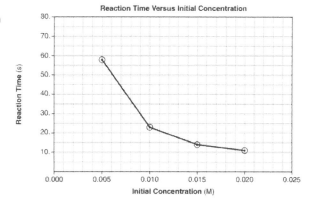

Reaction Time Versus Initial Concentration

11. As the concentration of the reactant increases, the rate of the reaction increases.
Reaction rate decreases as the concentration of reactants decreases.

12. The greater the kinetic energy of the reactant particles, the greater the frequency and effectiveness of the collisions.
Increasing the temperature causes more collisions.
more effective collisions

13. Increasing the concentration of HCl(aq) increases the reaction rate because frequency of effective collision will increase.

14. temperature, pressure, surface area of Zn, or amount of zinc

15. Concentration of HCl, HCl(aq), or [HCl(aq)]

16. 4

17. 2

18. 4

19. 3

20. 2

21. Heat is on the right side of the equation. Heat is a product.

22. The potential energy of the reactants is lower than the potential energy of the product.
Product has less energy than reactants.

23. 1	27. 3	31. 4	35. 2	39. 3
24. 4	28. 4	32. 3	36. 3	40. 4
25. 1	29. 2	33. 2	37. 3	
26. 4	30. 4	34. 2	38. 4	

41. +80 kJ

42. The catalyst lowers the activation energy.
The catalyst provides a different reaction pathway.

43.

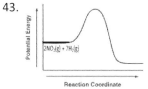

45.

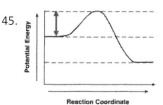

46.

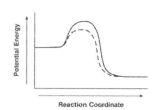

44. 281.75 kJ

47. 4
48. 4
49. 1
50. 1
51. 1
52. 1

53. The solid has a lower entropy than the dissolved solid in water.
The dissolved KNO_3 solid in water has a greater entropy than the solid itself.

54. The reactant is a solid, while the product contains a gas.

55. Because when water freezes, it is going from a less organized liquid state
to a more organized solid state.

56. 3	62. 4	68. 2	74. 2	80. 1
57. 3	63. 2	69. 2	75. 3	81. 2
58. 2	64. 4	70. 4	76. 1	82. 4
59. 2	65. 1	71. 4	77. 3	
60. 2	66. 2	72. 3	78. 2	
61. 4	67. 4	73. 3	79. 1	

83. The concentration of H^+ will increase.

84. The concentration of $SO_2(g)$ will increase.

85. Equilibrium shifts toward the fewer number of moles of gas.
The reaction shifts to the side that would result in a reduction of pressure.
fewer moles of gas, less pressure

86. mass = (0.100 mol) (127 g/mol) = 12.7 g

87. The concentration of reactant and products stays constant.

Topic 10
Organic Chemistry

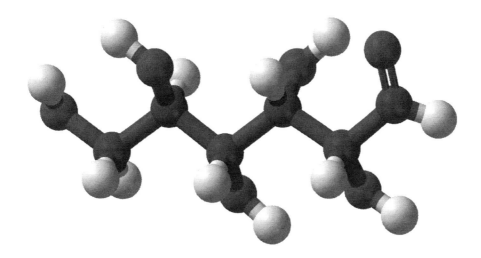

Lesson 1: Properties of Organic Compounds

Lesson 2: Classes of Organic Compounds

Lesson 3: Isomers

Lesson 4: Organic Reactions

Lesson 1 – Properties of Organic Compounds

Organic compounds are compounds of carbon. Chemical properties of a carbon atom make it possible for carbon to bond with each other and with other nonmetals to form an enormous number of organic compounds that can range from one to several hundred carbon atoms in length. Properties of organic compounds vary widely. In this lesson you will learn about general properties of a carbon atom and of organic compounds.

Bonding Properties of a Carbon Atom

Valence electrons are the electrons in the outermost electron shell of an atom. A carbon atom has four valence electrons and must form **four covalent or electron-sharing bonds.**

$$\cdot \overset{\displaystyle\cdot}{\underset{\displaystyle\cdot}{C}} \cdot \qquad -\overset{|}{\underset{|}{C}}- \qquad -\overset{|}{\underset{|}{C}}-\overset{|}{\underset{|}{C}}- \qquad -\overset{|}{C}=\overset{|}{C}- \qquad -C \equiv C-$$

electron-dot diagram for a carbon atom

All correctly drawn organic compound structures must have each C atom with exactly *four bonds* as shown above.

- Two carbon atoms can form a single (–), double (=), or triple (≡) covalent bond.

- Carbon atoms can join to form a straight chain, branched, or ring structure.

$$-C-C-C-C- \qquad\qquad \overset{\textstyle CH_3}{\underset{\textstyle}{-C-}}C-C-C- \qquad\qquad$$

straight chain   branched   ring (cyclic)

- Carbon bonds easily with other nonmetals such as H, O, N, and the halogens

General Properties of Organic Compounds
Covalent, Molecular, Low Melting and Boiling Points, Slow Reactions

General properties of organic compounds are listed below.
- They are molecular (covalent) substances.
- Bonding between atoms is covalent.
- Molecules are held together by weak intermolecular forces (IMFs).
- Low melting and boiling points, and high vapor pressure due to weak IMFs
- Solids decompose easily under heat.
- Most are nonelectrolytes, except for organic acids, which are weak electrolytes.
- Reactions are slow due to strong covalent bonding between atoms.
- Solubility in water varies depending if the compound is polar (soluble) or nonpolar (insoluble).

These properties vary within a class and between classes of organic compounds

Properties of Organic Compounds: Practice Questions

Concept Task: Be able to identify correctly drawn organic compound structures.
All correctly drawn structures of organic compounds must have each carbon atom with exactly four bonds.

Example 1

```
    H  H                        H  H  H
    |  |                        |  |  |
H – C = C – C – H          H – C = C – C – H
    |  |                              |
    H  H                              H
```

Incorrect organic structure
The Left C atom has only 3 bonds.
The middle C atom has 5 bonds .

Correct organic structure
All C atoms have exactly 4 bonds.

Example 2

```
    H  O  H                      H  O  H
    |  ||  |                     |  ||  |
H – C – C – C – H          H – C – C – C – H
    |  |  |                      |     |
    H  H  H                      H     H
```

Incorrect organic structure
The middle C atom has 5 bonds.

Correct organic structure
All C atoms have exactly 4 bonds.

Practice 1
Which organic structure is correctly drawn?

```
         H       H                    H        H
          \     /                      \      /
1)         C – C              3)         C = C
          /     \                      /      \
         H       H                    H        H

         H    H                       H        H
         |   /                         \      /
2)   H – C = C                4)        C ≡ C
         |   \\                        /      \
         H    O                       H        H
```

Practice 2
Which structural formula is incorrect?

```
         Cl
         |
1)   H – C – Cl              3)  H – C ≡ C – H
         |
         H

         O                          H    H
         ||                         |    |
2)   H – C – OH             4)  C = C = C
         |                          |    |
         H                          H    H
```

Practice 3
Which type of bonds and solids are characteristics of organic compounds?
1) Ionic bonds and ionic solid
2) Ionic bonds and molecular solids
3) Covalent bonds and ionic solids
4) Covalent bonds and molecular solids

Practice 4
In general, which property do organic compounds share?
1) High melting points
2) High electrical conductivity
3) High solubility in water
4) Slow reaction rate

Practice 5
Which best explains why there are more organic compounds than inorganic compounds?
1) The carbon atom readily forms covalent bonds with other carbon atoms
2) The carbon atom readily forms ionic bonds with other carbon atoms
3) The carbon atom readily combines with oxygen
4) The carbon atom readily dissolves in water

Practice 6
A carbon atom in any organic compound can form a total of
1) 1 covalent bond   3) 3 covalent bonds
2) 2 covalent bonds   4) 4 covalent bonds

Practice 7
A test tube contains a sample of solid stearic acid, an organic acid. Identify the element in stearic acid that makes it an organic compound.

Names of Organic Compounds

The IUPAC (International Union of Pure and Applied Chemistry) name of an organic compound has systematic components that reveal a lot about the compound.
Prefix (beginning root) of a name indicates the number of carbon atoms. See Table P below.
Suffix (ending root) of a name indicates the class that the substance belongs. See the Table below.
A **number** in a name indicate the position of a side chain, multiple bond, or functional group.
di- or tri- in a name indicates the presence of two or three of the same side chain or functional group.

Three IUPAC names of organic substances are given below. Different components of their names are explained under each substance. Understanding the components of their names will help you understand names, formulas and structures to several organic compounds given as examples as each class is discussed in the next few sections of this topic.

Prop*ane*

Prop: a 3 C-atom compound
ane: an alkane

2-Pentan*ol*

Pent: a 5 C-atom compound
ol: an alcohol
2: -OH functional group is on carbon number **2**

2,3-dimethyl, 1-but*ene*

but: 4 C atoms in the main chain
ene: an alkene
1: the double bond is on 1st bond position
2,3-dimethyl: 2 methyl side chains on carbons 2 and 3

Organic Prefixes: Table P

Prefix	Number of Carbon Atoms
meth-	1
eth-	2
prop-	3
but-	4
pent-	5
hex-	6
hept-	7
oct-	8
non-	9
dec-	10

Name Endings: See Reference Tables Q and R

Class of Compound	Name Ending (suffix)
Alkanes	- ane
Alkenes	- ene
Alkynes	-yne
Alcohols	-ol
Ethers	-yl
Aldehydes	-al
Ketones	-one
Organic acids	-oic
Esters	-oate
Amines	-amine
Amides	-amide

Halides are named with a *halogen* prefix.
Ex. *Chloro*butane

Concept Task: Be able to relate an organic compound name to the number of carbon atoms in the compound.

Practice 8
How many carbon atoms are in a molecule of a compound whose IUPAC name is pentanone?
1) 1   3) 3
2) 5   4) 7

Practice 9
Which is a correct name for an organic compound containing seven carbon atoms?
1) Butanol   3) Hexanal
2) Pentene   4) Heptanoic acid

Concept Task: Be able to relate IUPAC name of a substance to the class it belongs.

Practice 10
Which compound is an organic acid?
1) Pentanone   3) Hexanoic
2) Methanal   4) Propanamide

Practice 11
The compound hexanal is classified as
1) an alkene   3) an ester
2) an aldehyde   4) a halide

Practice 12
Methyl ethanoate is classified as
1) an organic acid   3) a halide
2) an alcohol   4) an ester

Lesson 2 – Classes of Organic Compounds

Homologous series are groups of related organic compounds in which each member of a class differs from the next member by a set number of atoms. Compounds belonging to the same homologous series always share the same general formula, same molecular name ending, and similar molecular structure.

In this lesson, you will learn about hydrocarbon compounds and functional group compounds.

Hydrocarbon Compounds
Compounds of Hydrogen and Carbon

Hydrocarbons are classes of organic compounds that are composed of just two elements: hydrogen (H) and carbon (C). Bonding between the carbon atoms in a hydrocarbon molecule could be single, double or triple covalent. Depending on the type of bond found between the carbon atoms, a hydrocarbon can be classified as saturated or unsaturated. Three homologous series of hydrocarbons are listed on Reference Table Q.

Saturated Hydrocarbons (Alkanes): *Single Covalent Bonds*

Saturated hydrocarbons are hydrocarbons in which the bonds between the carbon atoms are all single covalent bonds. A **single covalent** bond is formed between two C atoms when each atom shares one electron. Since each C atom shares one electron, a single covalent bond is formed by one pair of electrons or two total electrons.
Alkanes are classified as saturated hydrocarbons.

Table Q
Homologous Series of Hydrocarbons

Name	General Formula	Examples	
		Name	Structural Formula
alkanes	C_nH_{2n+2}	ethane	H–C–C–H (ethane)
alkenes	C_nH_{2n}	ethene	C=C (ethene)
alkynes	C_nH_{2n-2}	ethyne	H–C≡C–H

Note: *n* = number of carbon atoms

C •• C   C — C
1 pair (2 total) electrons   A single covalent bond

Unsaturated Hydrocarbons: *Multiple Covalent Bonds*
Unsaturated hydrocarbons are hydrocarbons that contain one or more multiple (double or triple) covalent bonds between two adjacent C atoms. *Alkenes* and *alkynes* are unsaturated hydrocarbons.

A **double covalent bond** is formed between two carbon atoms when each atom shares two electrons. Since each carbon atom shares two electrons, a double covalent bond contains two pairs of electrons or four total electrons.
Alkenes are unsaturated hydrocarbons with a double bond.

C :: C   C = C
2 pairs (4 total) electrons   A double covalent bond

A **triple covalent bond** is formed between two carbon atoms when each atom shares three electrons. Since each carbon atom shares three electrons, a triple covalent bond contains three pairs of electrons or six total electrons.
Alkynes are unsaturated hydrocarbons with a triple bond.

C ⋮⋮ C   C ≡ C
3 pairs (6 total) electrons   A triple covalent bond

Practice 13
Which formula represents an unsaturated hydrocarbon?

1) H–C=C–H
3) H–C–C–H (with O double bonded)

2) H–C–C–H
4) H–C–C–OH

Practice 14
What is the total number of electrons in the structure below?

H–C–C≡C–C–C–H

1) 12   3) 14
2) 24   4) *28*

Organic Chemistry   Topic 10

Alkanes – Saturated Hydrocarbons
All Single Bonds Between Carbons. Names End With -ane.

Alkanes are saturated hydrocarbons with all single bonds between the carbon atoms. The first three members of alkane series are methane, ethane and propane.

Ethane is given as an example on **Table R**. Propane is given below.

Molecular formula	C_3H_8
C_nH_{2n+2}	
Condensed formula	$CH_3CH_2CH_3$

Structural formula
all **single** bonds

$$\begin{array}{cccccc} & H & & H & & H \\ & | & & | & & | \\ H - & C & - & C & - & C & - H \\ & | & & | & & | \\ & H & & H & & H \end{array}$$

IUPAC name   prop*ane*
-ane ending

In both examples above, the number of H atoms is two more than twice the number of C atoms as indicated by the general formula.

Practice 15
Which name represents an alkane?
1) octane   3) propanal
2) octene   4) propanol

Practice 16
Which formula represents an alkane?
1) $C_{10}H_{10}$ 3) $C_{11}H_{22}$
2) $C_{10}H_{20}$ 4) $C_{11}H_{24}$

Practice 17
Which compounds is a saturated hydrocarbon?
1) CH_2CH_2 3) CH_3CH_3
2) CH_3CHO 4) CH_3CH_2OH

Practice 18
Which structure is correct for an alkane?

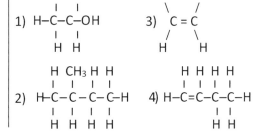

Alkenes – Unsaturated Hydrocarbons
One Double Bond Between Two Carbons. Names End With -ene.

Alkenes are unsaturated hydrocarbons with one double bond between two adjacent carbon atoms. The first two members of the alkene series are ethene and propene.

alkenes	C_nH_{2n}	ethene	

Ethene is given as an example on Table R. 2-Butene is shown below.

Molecular formula	C_4H_8
C_nH_{2n+2}	
Condensed formula	$CH_3CHCHCH_3$

Structural formula
one double bond

$$H - C - C = C - C - H$$

IUPAC name   2-butene
-ene ending

In both examples above, the number of H atoms is twice the number of C atoms as indicated by the general formula.

Practice 19
Which substance is an alkene?
1) heptyne   3) ethane
2) pentanol   4) pentene

Practice 20
Which formula represents an alkene?
1) C_5H_{10} 3) C_8H_{18}
2) C_5H_{12} 4) C_8H_{14}

Practice 21
Which compound is an alkene?
1) CHCH   3) CH_3CH_2Cl
2) CH_2CH_2 4) CH_2CHCl

Practice 22
Which structure is correct for an alkene?

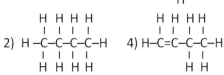

1) $H-C \equiv C-H$

210

©2017 E3 Scholastic Publishing. All Rights Reserved

Alkynes - Unsaturated Hydrocarbons
One Triple Bonds Between Two Carbons. Names End With -yne.

Alkynes are unsaturated hydrocarbons with one triple bond between two adjacent carbon atoms. The first two members of the alkyne series are ethyne and propyne.

Ethyne is given as an example on Table R. Propyne is shown below.

Molecular formula: C_3H_4
  C_nH_{2n-2}

Condensed formula CH_3CCH

Structural Formula
 one triple bond

$$H-\underset{\underset{H}{|}}{\overset{\overset{H}{|}}{C}}-C\equiv C-H$$

IUPAC name: 1- propy*ne* (propyne)
 -yne ending

In both examples above, the number of H atoms is two fewer than twice the number of C atoms, as indicated by the general formula.

Practice 23
Which name represents an alkyne?
1) heptanol   3) hexane
2) pentanoic   4) octyne

Practice 24
Which substance is an alkyne?
1) C_5H_{10} 3) C_6H_{14}
2) C_5H_8 4) C_6H_{12}

Practice 25
Which formula correctly represents an alkyne?
1) CH_3CHCl_2 3) CHCH
2) CH_3CH_2Cl 4) CH_2CH_2

Practice 26
Which structure represents an alkyne?

1) $H-\underset{\underset{H}{|}}{\overset{\overset{H}{|}}{C}}=\underset{\underset{H}{|}}{\overset{\overset{H}{|}}{C}}-\underset{\underset{H}{|}}{\overset{\overset{H}{|}}{C}}-\underset{}{\overset{\overset{H}{|}}{C}}-H$ 3) $N\equiv N$

2) $H-\underset{\underset{H}{|}}{\overset{\overset{H}{|}}{C}}-C\equiv C-\underset{\underset{H}{|}}{\overset{\overset{H}{|}}{C}}-H$ 4) $O=C=O$

Drawing and Naming Hydrocarbons

Draw the following hydrocarbon compounds.

Practice 27

Hexane

Practice 28

3-methyl, 2-pentene

Practice 29

$CH_3CH(CH_3)CH(CH_3)CH_3$

Name the following hydrocarbon compounds.

Practice 30

$$H-\underset{\underset{H}{|}}{\overset{\overset{H}{|}}{C}}-\underset{\underset{H}{|}}{\overset{\overset{H}{|}}{C}}-\underset{\underset{H}{|}}{\overset{\overset{H}{|}}{C}}-\underset{\underset{H}{|}}{C}=\underset{}{\overset{\overset{H}{|}}{C}}-H$$

Practice 31

$$H-\underset{\underset{H}{|}}{\overset{\overset{H}{|}}{C}}-\underset{\underset{CH_3}{|}}{\overset{\overset{CH_3}{|}}{C}}-\underset{\underset{H}{|}}{\overset{\overset{CH_3}{|}}{C}}-\underset{\underset{H}{|}}{\overset{\overset{H}{|}}{C}}-\underset{\underset{H}{|}}{\overset{\overset{H}{|}}{C}}-\underset{\underset{H}{|}}{\overset{\overset{H}{|}}{C}}-H$$

Practice 32

$CH_3 \ CH_2C(CH_3)_2CH_2CH_3$

Functional Group Compounds

A **functional group** is an atom, other than hydrogen, or a group of atoms that replaces one or more hydrogen atoms of a hydrocarbon compound. The element commonly found in most functional groups is oxygen (O). Nitrogen (N) and halogens (F, Cl, Br, or I) are also found in functional groups. Classes of compounds containing a functional group include:

Halides, alcohols, ethers, aldehydes, ketones, organic acids, esters, amines and amides.
Each class is briefly discussed below.

• Differences in physical and chemical properties between the classes are primarily due to differences in their functional groups.

Reference Table R lists classes of organic compounds and their functional groups. Example compound for each class is also given.

Each class of compound is further explained on the next few pages.

Table R
Organic Functional Groups

Class of Compound	Functional Group	General Formula	Example
halide (halocarbon)	— F (fluoro-) — Cl (chloro-) — Br (bromo-) — I (iodo-)	$R—X$ (X represents any halogen)	$CH_3CHClCH_3$ 2-chloropropane
alcohol	— OH	$R—OH$	$CH_3CH_2CH_2OH$ 1-propanol
ether	— O —	$R—O—R'$	$CH_3OCH_2CH_3$ methyl ethyl ether
aldehyde	$\overset{\text{O}}{\overset{\|}{—\text{C}}}—\text{H}$	$R—\overset{\text{O}}{\overset{\|}{\text{C}}}—H$	$CH_3CH_2\overset{\text{O}}{\overset{\|}{\text{C}}}—H$ propanal
ketone	$—\overset{\text{O}}{\overset{\|}{\text{C}}}—$	$R—\overset{\text{O}}{\overset{\|}{\text{C}}}—R'$	$CH_3\overset{\text{O}}{\overset{\|}{\text{C}}}CH_2CH_2CH_3$ 2-pentanone
organic acid	$—\overset{\text{O}}{\overset{\|}{\text{C}}}—\text{OH}$	$R—\overset{\text{O}}{\overset{\|}{\text{C}}}—OH$	$CH_3CH_2\overset{\text{O}}{\overset{\|}{\text{C}}}—OH$ propanoic acid
ester	$—\overset{\text{O}}{\overset{\|}{\text{C}}}—\text{O}—$	$R—\overset{\text{O}}{\overset{\|}{\text{C}}}—O—R'$	$CH_3CH_2COCH_3$ methyl propanoate
amine	$—\overset{\|}{\text{N}}—$	$R—\overset{\overset{\textstyle R'}{\|}}{N}—R''$	$CH_3CH_2CH_2NH_2$ 1-propanamine
amide	$—\overset{\text{O}}{\overset{\|}{\text{C}}}—\overset{\|}{\text{N}}\text{H}$	$R—\overset{\text{O}}{\overset{\|}{\text{C}}}—\overset{\overset{\textstyle R'}{\|}}{N}H$	$CH_3CH_2\overset{\text{O}}{\overset{\|}{\text{C}}}—NH_2$ propanamide

Note: *R* represents a bonded atom or group of atoms.

 ©2017 E3 Scholastic Publishing. All Rights Reserved

Alcohols: *Contain –OH group*

Alcohols are organic compounds with one or more -OH as the functional group. In alcohols, the –OH group replaces a hydrogen atom in the hydrocarbon chain (R).
The -OH of alcohols is called a hydroxyl group, which is different from OH⁻ (hydroxide ion) of bases.

alcohol	—OH	R—OH	$CH_3CH_2CH_2OH$ 1-propanol

(Table R)

1-propanol is given as an example on Table R. Ethanol is shown below.

Molecular formula	C_2H_5OH
Condensed formula	$CH_3\mathbf{CH_2}OH$
Structural formula	$H - \underset{\underset{H}{\mid}}{\overset{\overset{H}{\mid}}{C}} - \underset{\underset{H}{\mid}}{\overset{\overset{H}{\mid}}{\mathbf{C}}} - OH$
IUPAC name: **-ol** *ending*	Ethanol

Types of Alcohols

Monohydroxy alcohols are alcohols with just one -OH group. Depending on how many other C atoms are bonded to the C atom with the -OH group, a monohydroxy alcohol can also be classified as a primary, secondary or tertiary alcohol.

Primary alcohols are alcohols in which the **C** atom with the -OH is bonded to just one other C atom.

Secondary alcohols are alcohols in which the **C** atom with the -OH is bonded to two other C atoms.

Tertiary alcohols are alcohols in which the **C** atom with the -OH is bonded to three other C atoms.

primary	secondary	tertiary
$-C-\underset{\underset{OH}{\mid}}{C}-C-$	$-C-\underset{\underset{OH}{\mid}}{\mathbf{C}}-C-$	$-C-\underset{\underset{OH}{\mid}}{\overset{\overset{CH_3}{\mid}}{C}}-C-$
1-propanol	**2**-propanol	2-methyl, 2-propanol

Dihydroxy alcohols are alcohols with two -OH groups.

$-C-\underset{\underset{OH}{\mid}}{C}-\underset{\underset{OH}{\mid}}{C}-$ 1,3-propane*diol*

Trihydroxy alcohols are alcohols with three -OH groups.

$-\underset{\underset{OH}{\mid}}{C}-\underset{\underset{OH}{\mid}}{C}-\underset{\underset{OH}{\mid}}{C}-$ 1,2,3-propane*triol* (glycerol)

Practice 33
Which IUPAC name is of a compound of alcohol?
1) 2-butanal
2) methanoic
3) heptane
4) octanol

Practice 34
Which molecular formula represents an alcohol?
1) CH_3CH_2OH
2) CH_3CHO
3) NH_4OH
4) $CH_3CH_2CH_2COOH$

Practice 35
Which IUPAC name is of a primary alcohol?
1) 2-butanal
2) 1-chloropropane
3) 2-butanol
4) heptanol

Practice 36
Which formula represents a dihydroxy alcohol?
1) $CH_3CH_2CH_2COOH$
2) $CH_3CHOHCH_2OH$
3) CH_3COOCH_3
4) CH_3CHO

Practice 37
Which formula represents a secondary alcohol?

1)
$H-\underset{\underset{H}{\mid}}{\overset{\overset{H}{\mid}}{C}}-\underset{\underset{H}{\mid}}{\overset{\overset{CH_3}{\mid}}{C}}-\underset{\underset{OH}{\mid}}{\overset{\overset{H}{\mid}}{C}}-\underset{\underset{H}{\mid}}{\overset{\overset{H}{\mid}}{C}}-H$

2)
$H-\underset{\underset{H}{\mid}}{\overset{\overset{H}{\mid}}{C}}-\underset{\underset{H}{\mid}}{\overset{\overset{H}{\mid}}{C}}-\underset{\underset{OH}{\mid}}{\overset{\overset{CH_3}{\mid}}{C}}-\underset{\underset{H}{\mid}}{\overset{\overset{H}{\mid}}{C}}-H$

3)
$H-\underset{\underset{H}{\mid}}{\overset{\overset{H}{\mid}}{C}}-\underset{\underset{H}{\mid}}{\overset{\overset{OH}{\mid}}{C}}-\underset{\underset{H}{\mid}}{\overset{\overset{OH}{\mid}}{C}}-\underset{\underset{H}{\mid}}{\overset{\overset{H}{\mid}}{C}}-H$

4)
$H-\underset{\underset{H}{\mid}}{\overset{\overset{H}{\mid}}{C}}-\underset{\underset{H}{\mid}}{\overset{\overset{H}{\mid}}{C}}-\underset{\underset{H}{\mid}}{\overset{\overset{OH}{\mid}}{C}}-C=O$

Halides: *Contain Halogen Atom (Group 17)*

Halides or halocarbons are organic compounds that contain one or more halogen (Group 17) atoms as the functional group. Compounds of halides share the following characteristics:

Table R	halide (halocarbon)	—F (fluoro-) —Cl (chloro-) —Br (bromo-) —I (iodo-)	R—X (X represents any halogen)	$CH_3CHClCH_3$ 2-chloropropane

2-chloropropane is given as an example on Table R. Two more examples are shown below.

Molecular formula	C_3H_7F	$C_3H_6F_2$
Condensed formula	$CH_3CH_2CH_2F$	$CH_2FCHFCH_3$

Structural formula

$$H-\overset{\overset{\displaystyle H}{|}}{\underset{\underset{\displaystyle H}{|}}{C}}-\overset{\overset{\displaystyle H}{|}}{\underset{\underset{\displaystyle H}{|}}{C}}-\overset{\overset{\displaystyle H}{|}}{\underset{\underset{\displaystyle H}{|}}{C}}-F \qquad H-\overset{\overset{\displaystyle H}{|}}{\underset{\underset{\displaystyle F}{|}}{C}}-\overset{\overset{\displaystyle H}{|}}{\underset{\underset{\displaystyle F}{|}}{C}}-\overset{\overset{\displaystyle H}{|}}{\underset{\underset{\displaystyle H}{|}}{C}}-H$$

IUPAC name   **1**- fluoropropane   **1,2**-difluoropropane
- **halogen prefix**

Practice 38
Which substance is a halide?
1) 2-butene
2) Methyl propanoate
3) 2-Iodomethane
4) Hexanol

Practice 39
Which molecular formula represents a halide?
1) CH_3CH_2OH
2) CH_2Cl_2
3) CH_3CHN_2
4) $HClO_3$

Ethers: *Contain $-O-$ group*

Ethers are organic compounds that contain the –O– functional group. A common member of this class is diethyl ether, which was widely used as surgical anesthesia up until the 19th century. Compounds of ethers share the following characteristics:

Table R	ether	—O—	R—O—R'	$CH_3OCH_2CH_3$ methyl ethyl ether

Methyl ethyl ether is given as an example on Table R.
Methyl methyl (dimethyl) ether is shown below.

Molecular formula	C_2H_6O
Condensed formula	CH_3OCH_3

Structural formula

$$H-\overset{\overset{\displaystyle H}{|}}{\underset{\underset{\displaystyle H}{|}}{C}}-O-\overset{\overset{\displaystyle H}{|}}{\underset{\underset{\displaystyle H}{|}}{C}}-H$$

IUPAC name: methyl   methyl ether
                (dimethyl ether)

*Names include both alkyl (**-yl**) chains.*
The shorter chain is always named first; ex. methyl ethyl ether.

Practice 40
Which molecular formula represents a member of the ether family?
1) $CH_3OCH_2CH_2CH_3$ 3) HCHO
2) $CH_3COOCH_2CH_3$ 4) $CH_2(OH)_2$

Practice 41
Which structural formula represents an ether?

1) 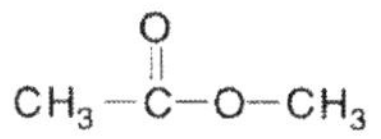
$$CH_3-\overset{\overset{\displaystyle O}{\|}}{C}-O-CH_3$$

2) 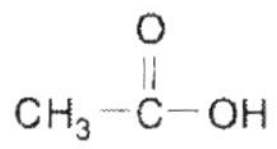
$$CH_3-\overset{\overset{\displaystyle O}{\|}}{C}-OH$$

3) CH_3-O-CH_3

4) CH_3-OH

Aldehydes: *Contain – CHO group*

Aldehydes are organic compounds that contain the –CHO functional group. Methanal, which is commonly known as formaldehyde, is the first member of this class. Methanal is used as a preservative for dead animals. Compounds of aldehydes share the following characteristics:

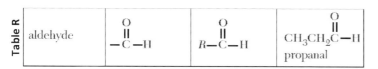

| Table R | aldehyde | $-\overset{\overset{\displaystyle O}{\|\|}}{C}-H$ | $R-\overset{\overset{\displaystyle O}{\|\|}}{C}-H$ | $CH_3CH_2\overset{\overset{\displaystyle O}{\|\|}}{C}-H$
 propanal |

Propanal is given as an example on Table R.
Methanal is shown below.

Molecular formula	CH_2O
Condensed formula	H**CHO**
Structural formula	$H-\overset{\overset{\displaystyle O}{\|\|}}{C}-H$
IUPAC name: -al ending	Methanal

Practice 42
Which IUPAC name is of a compound of an aldehyde?
1) butanol   3) butanal
2) butanoate   4) butanoic

Practice 43
Which compound is an aldehyde?
1) CH_3CH_2OH 3) CH_3COOH
2) CH_3OCH_3 4) CH_3CHO

Practice 44
Which structure represents an aldehyde?

1) $\overset{H}{\underset{H}{}}C=C\overset{H}{\underset{H}{}}$
    3) $H-\overset{\overset{\displaystyle O}{\|\|}}{C}-OH$

2) $H-\overset{H}{\underset{H}{C}}-C\overset{H}{\underset{O}{}}$
    4) $\overset{H-O}{\underset{H}{}}$

Organic Acids: *Contain –COOH group*

Organic acids are compounds that contain –COOH, carboxyl functional group.
Organic acids, unlike other organic compounds, ionize weakly in water. They are weak electrolytes, therefore will conduct electrical current. Their properties are the same as those of inorganic acids discussed in the acid-base topic. These properties include producing H^+ in solutions, changing litmus to red, and pH below 7.

| Table R | organic acid | $-\overset{\overset{\displaystyle O}{\|\|}}{C}-OH$ | $R-\overset{\overset{\displaystyle O}{\|\|}}{C}-OH$ | $CH_3CH_2\overset{\overset{\displaystyle O}{\|\|}}{C}-OH$
 propanoic acid |

Propanoic acid is given as an example on Table R.
Ethanoic acid is shown below.

Molecular formula	$C_2H_4O_2$
Condensed formula	CH_3 **COOH**
Structural formula	$H-\overset{\overset{\displaystyle H}{\|}}{\underset{\underset{\displaystyle H}{\|}}{C}}-\overset{\overset{\displaystyle O}{\|\|}}{C}-OH$
IUPAC name: -oic ending *Common name*	Ethanoic acid (acetic acid, vinegar)

Practice 45
Which substance is an organic acid?
1) butanoic   3) iodomethane
2) methylamine   4) heptanone

Practice 46
Which molecular formula belongs to an organic acid?
1) CH_3COCH_3 3) CH_3CH_2COOH
2) CH_3COOCH_3 4) $OHCH_2CH_2OH$

Practice 47
Which is a structure of an organic acid?

1) $H-\overset{\overset{\displaystyle H}{\|}}{\underset{\underset{\displaystyle H}{\|}}{C}}-\overset{\overset{\displaystyle O}{\|\|}}{C}-\overset{\overset{\displaystyle H}{\|}}{\underset{\underset{\displaystyle H}{\|}}{C}}-H$

2) $H-\overset{\overset{\displaystyle H}{\|}}{\underset{\underset{\displaystyle OH}{\|}}{C}}-\overset{\overset{\displaystyle H}{\|}}{\underset{\underset{\displaystyle OH}{\|}}{C}}-\overset{\overset{\displaystyle H}{\|}}{\underset{\underset{\displaystyle OH}{\|}}{C}}-H$

3) $H-\overset{\overset{\displaystyle H}{\|}}{\underset{\underset{\displaystyle H}{\|}}{C}}-\overset{\overset{\displaystyle H}{\|}}{\underset{\underset{\displaystyle H}{\|}}{C}}-C=O$

4)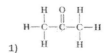

Ketones: *Contain –CO– group*

Ketones are organic compounds that contain the – CO – functional group. Propanone, which is commonly known as acetone, is the first member of this class. Acetone is the main chemical in most nail polish removers.

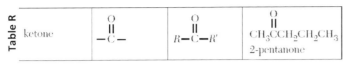

2-pentanone is given as an example on Table R.
Propanone is shown below.

Molecular formula	C_3H_6O
Condensed formula	CH_3COCH_3

Structural formula

$$\begin{array}{ccc} H & O & H \\ | & || & | \\ H-C-&C-&C-H \\ | & & | \\ H & & H \end{array}$$

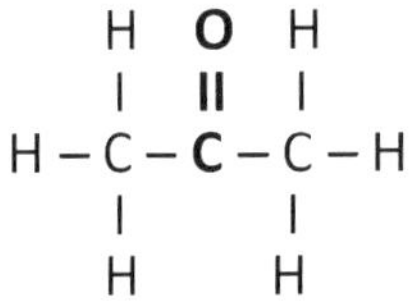

IUPAC name ending: **-one**   Propan*one*
Common name   (acetone, nail polish remover)

Practice 48
Which IUPAC name represents a compound of a ketone?
1) chlorogenate
2) pentanoate
3) 3-hexanol
4) 3-hexanone

Practice 49
Which structure represents a ketone?
1) $CH_3CH_2CH_2COCH_3$
2) CH_3COOH
3) $CH_3CH_2OOCH_3$
4) $CH_3CH(OH)CH_3$

Esters: *Contain –COO– group*

Esters are organic compounds that contain the –COO– functional group. *Esters are found naturally in fruits and flowers and are responsible for their odors. Synthetic esters are used as scents in cologne and perfume and flavoring in food.* Esters are synthesized or made by reacting an organic acid with an alcohol.

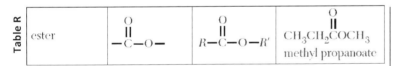

Methyl propanoate is given as an example on Table R.
Methyl ethanoate is shown below.

Molecular formula	$C_3H_6O_2$
Condensed formula	CH_3COOCH_3

Structural formula

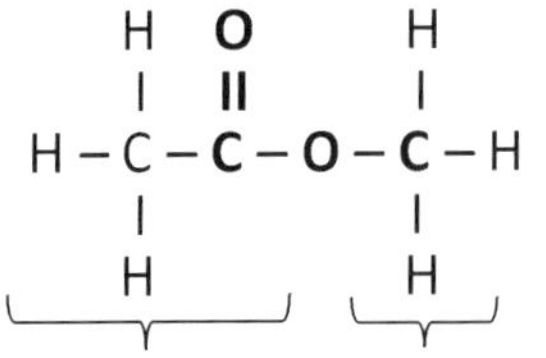

$$\begin{array}{cccc} H & O & & H \\ | & || & & | \\ H-C-&C-&O-&C-H \\ | & & & | \\ H & & & H \end{array}$$
$$\underbrace{}_{\text{ethanoate}} \quad \underbrace{}_{\text{methyl}}$$

IUPAC name ending: **-oate**   methyl ethan*oate*
The alkyl chain after the -O- (methyl) is always named first.

Practice 50
Which substance is an ester?
1) 1,2-ethanediol   3) pentanal
2) ethyl propanoate   4) heptanoic

Practice 51
Which formula represents an ester?
1) CH_3CH_2COOH 3) CH_3CH_2CHO
2) $HCOOCH_2CH_2CH_3$ 4) CH_3COCH_3

Practice 52
The formula of which compound is an ester?

1) CH_3CH_2OH

2) CH_3-O-CH_3

3) $CH_3OCH_2CH_3$ with O double bond above

4)

Amines, Amides and Amino Acids: *Contain N atom in their functional group*

Amines, amides, and amino acids are classes of organic compounds containing a nitrogen atom in their functional group.

Amines are classes of organic compounds with just a nitrogen atom, $-N-$, as the functional group.

Amides are classes of organic compounds containing both nitrogen and oxygen as part of the functional group.

Amino acids are classes of organic compounds that contain two functional groups: An amine group, $-N-$, and an acid group, -COOH. Amino acids join together to make proteins in cells.

Table R				
amine	$-N-$	$R-\overset{\overset{R'}{\mid}}{N}-R''$	$CH_3CH_2CH_2NH_2$ 1-propanamine	
amide	$\overset{O}{\overset{\parallel}{-C}}-NH$	$R-\overset{O}{\overset{\parallel}{C}}-\overset{R'}{\overset{\mid}{N}}H$	$CH_3CH_2\overset{O}{\overset{\parallel}{C}}-NH_2$ propanamide	

Condensed formula	$CH_3\mathbf{NH_2}$	$CH_3\mathbf{CONH_2}$
Structural formula	$\begin{array}{c} H \quad H \\ \mid \quad \mid \\ H-C-\mathbf{N}-H \\ \mid \\ H \end{array}$	$\begin{array}{c} H \quad \mathbf{O} \quad\quad H \\ \mid \quad \parallel \quad\; / \\ H-C-\mathbf{C}-\mathbf{N} \\ \mid \quad\quad\quad \backslash \\ H \quad\quad\quad H \end{array}$
IUPAC name	methylamine	ethanamide

Draw the following functional group compounds.

Practice 53
3- iodohexane

Practice 54
dipropyl ether

Practice 55
$CH_3CH(NH_2)COOH$

Name the following functional group compounds.

Practice 56
$$\begin{array}{c} H \quad H \quad OH \; H \\ \mid \quad\; \mid \quad\; \mid \quad\; \mid \\ H-C-C-C-C-H \\ \mid \quad\; \mid \quad\; \mid \quad\; \mid \\ H \quad H \quad H \quad H \end{array}$$

Practice 57
$$\begin{array}{c} H \quad O \quad\quad\quad H \quad H \\ \mid \quad\; \parallel \quad\quad\quad \mid \quad\; \mid \\ H-C-C-O-C-C-H \\ \mid \quad\quad\quad\quad\; \mid \quad\; \mid \\ H \quad\quad\quad\quad H \quad H \end{array}$$

Practice 58
$CH_3COCH_2CH_3$

Base your answers to questions 59 and 60 on the information below and on your knowledge of chemistry.

Natural gas and coal are two fuels burned to produce energy. Natural gas consists of approximately 80% methane, 10% ethane, 4% propane, 2% butane, and other components.

59. Draw a structural formula for the hydrocarbon that is approximately 2% of natural gas.

60. Write the general formula for the homologous series that includes the components of the natural gas listed in this passage.

Base your answers to the questions 61 and 62 on the information below.

Two hydrocarbons that are isomers of each other are represented by the structural formulas and molecular formulas below.

Hydrocarbon 1   Hydrocarbon 2

$$H-C=C-C=C-C-H \qquad H-C-C-C-C\equiv C-H$$

C_5H_8 C_5H_8

61. Explain, in terms of bonds, why these hydrocarbons are unsaturated.

62. What is the IUPAC name for Hydrocarbon 2?

Base your answers to practice questions 63 and 64 on the information below.

Many esters have distinctive odors, which lead to their widespread use as artificial flavorings and fragrances. For example, methyl butanoate has an odor like pineapple and ethyl methanoate has an odor like raspberry. Esters are produced by reacting an organic acid with an alcohol. Methyl butanoate is produced by reacting methanol with butanoic acid.

63. Draw a structural formula for the ester that has an odor like pineapple.

64. Draw a structural formula for the acid that produce methyl butanoate.

©2017 E3 Scholastic Publishing. All Rights Reserved

Isomers
Same Molecular Formula, Different Structural Formulas.

Isomers are organic compounds with the same molecular formula but different structural formulas. Isomers have the same type and number of atoms, but different arrangements of the atoms.
• All hydrocarbons with four or more carbon atoms have isomers.
• The higher the number of carbon atoms, the greater the number of possible isomers.

The two compounds below are isomers of each other.

C_3H_7Br C_3H_7Br *Same molecular formula*

$CH_3CH_2CH_2Br$ $CH_3CHBrCH_3$ *Same percent composition*

Same number of covalent bonds

```
   H   H   H              H   H   H
   |   |   |              |   |   |
H– C – C – C –H        H– C – C – C –H
   |   |   |              |   |   |
   H   H   Br             H   Br  H
```
                                     Different structural formulas

1- bromopropane   *2*-bromopropane

                                       Different names, different substances.
                                       Different physical and chemical properties

Practice 65
Two isomers must have the same
1) percent composition   3) physical properties
2) arrangement of atoms   4) chemical properties

Practice 66
2-methyl butane and 2,2-dimethyl propane are isomers. Molecules of these two compounds have different
1) number of covalent bonds   3) molecular formulas
2) structural formulas   4) number of carbon

Practice 67
What is the minimum number of carbon atoms a hydrocarbon must have in other to have an isomer?
1) 1   2) 2   3) 3   4) 4

Practice 68
As the number of carbon atoms in each successive member of a homologous series of hydrocarbon series increases, the number of possible isomers
1) increases   2) decreases   3) remains the same

Practice 69
Which alkane compound will have the most number of isomers?
1) C_7H_{16} 2) C_6H_{14} 3) C_5H_{12} 4) C_4H_{10}

Practice 70
Which compound has no isomer?
1) C_2H_5Cl 2) C_3H_7Cl 3) C_4H_9Cl 4) $C_5H_{11}Cl$

Concept Task: Be able to determine formulas of compounds that are isomers.

Practice 71
Which two condensed formulas are isomers of each other?
1) $CH_3CH_2CH(Cl)CH_3$ and $CH_3CH(Cl)CH_2CH_3$
2) CH_2CH_2 and CH_3COCH_3
3) $CH_3CH_2CH_3$ and CH_2CHCH_3
4) $CH_3CH(OH)CH_3$ and $CH_3CH(OH)CH_2CH_3$

Practice 72
Which compound is isomer of 2-methyl butane?
1) 2,2-dimethyl propane   3) 2-methyl butene
2) 2,2-dimethyl butane   4) 3-methyl pentane

Practice 73
Which structural formula represents an isomer of the compound given below?

```
     Br  H  H  H  H
     |   |  |  |  |
  H– C – C –C –C –C –H
     |   |  |  |  |
     Br  H  H  H  H
```

1)
```
   H  H  H  Br
   |  |  |  |
H– C –C –C –C –H?
   |  |  |  |
   H  H  H  Br
```

2)
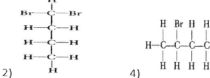

3)
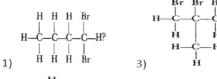

4)
```
   H  Br H  H
   |  |  |  |
H– C –C –C –C –Br
   |  |  |  |
   H  H  H  H
```

Isomers of Hydrocarbons

Alkane Isomers
Isomers of an alkane usually have different arrangements of the carbon chain, with the structures having one or more alkyl side chains.

An **alkyl** is a hydrocarbon group with one fewer hydrogen atom than the corresponding alkane.

CH_4 (methane, an alkane) CH_3 (methyl, an alkyl)

C_2H_6 (ethane, an alkane) C_2H_5 (ethyl, an alkyl)

Examples of Alkane Isomers

C_4H_{10}

$CH_3CH_2CH_2CH_3$

```
  H   H   H   H
  |   |   |   |
H-C - C - C - C-H
  |   |   |   |
  H   H   H   H
```
butane

C_4H_{10}

$CH_3CH(CH_3)CH_3$

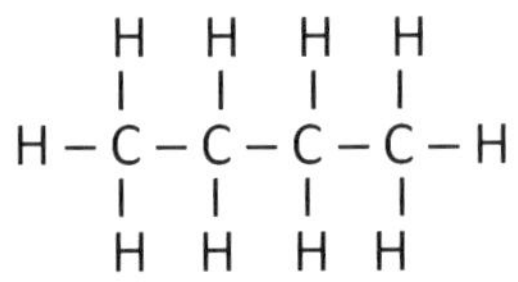

```
  H  CH3  H
  |   |   |
H-C - C - C-H
  |   |   |
  H   H   H
```
2-methyl prop*ane*
(methyl propane)

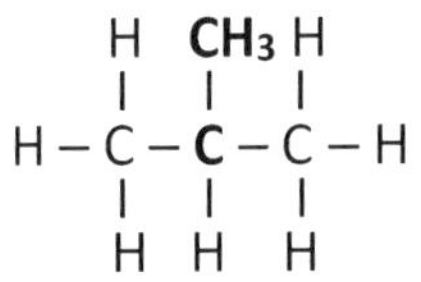

Butane and 2-methyl propane are isomers.
They have the same molecular formula but different structural formulas and properties.

Alkene and Alkyne Isomers
Isomers of alkenes and alkynes typically have the double or triple bond between different adjacent carbon atoms. Some may even have alkyl side chains along with the multiple covalent bond.

Examples of Alkene Isomers

C_4H_8

$CH_2CHCH_2CH_3$

```
  H   H   H   H
  |   |   |   |
H-C = C - C - C-H
          |   |
          H   H
```
1-butene

C_4H_8

$CH_3CHCHCH_3$

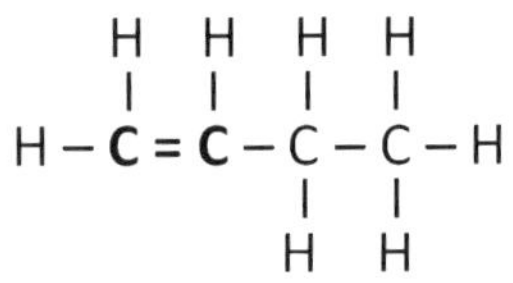

```
  H   H   H   H
  |   |   |   |
H-C - C = C - C-H
  |           |
  H           H
```
2-butene

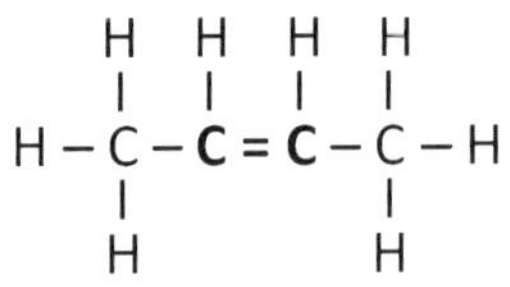

1-butene and 2-butene are isomers

Concept Task: Be able to draw and name isomers of hydrocarbons.

Practice 74
Draw octane, and then draw and name any two isomers of octane.

Practice 75
Draw pentene, and then draw and name any two isomers of pentene.

Practice 76
Draw heptyne, and then draw and name any two isomers of heptyne.

 ©2017 E3 Scholastic Publishing. All Rights Reserved

Isomers of Functional Group Compounds

Functional group compounds that are isomers usually have the functional group attached to different carbon atoms. In some cases, a compound from two different functional group classes may be isomers of each other.

Halide Isomers

C_4H_9Br	C_4H_9Br	C_4H_9Br
$CH_3CH_2CH_2CH_2Br$	$CH_3CH_2CHBrCH_3$	$CH_2BrCH(CH_3)CH_3$

| 1- bromobutane | 2-bromobutane | 1-bromo, 2-methyl propane |

Alcohol and Ether Isomers

A monohydroxy alcohol and an ether of the same number of carbon atoms are always isomers.

C_3H_8O	C_3H_8O	C_3H_8O
$CH_3CH_2C H_2OH$	$CH_3CH(OH)CH_3$	$CH_3OCH_2CH_3$

| 1-propanol | 2-propanol | methyl ethyl ether |

Ketone and Aldehyde Isomers

A ketone and an aldehyde of the same number of carbon atoms are always isomers.

$C_5H_{10}O$	$C_5H_{10}O$	$C_5H_{10}O$
$CH_3COCH_2CH_2CH_3$	$CH_3CH_2COCH_2CH_3$	$CH_3CH_2CH_2CH_2CHO$

| 2-pentanone | 3-pentanone | pentanal |

Ester and Organic Acid Isomers

An ester and organic acid of the same number of carbon atoms are always isomers

methyl propanoate	ethyl ethanoate	butanoic acid
$CH_3CH_2COOCH_3$	$CH_3COOCH_2CH_3$	$CH_3CH_2CH_2COOH$

Practice 77
Draw 1,1-difluoropropane, then draw and name two isomers of 1,1-difluoropropane.

Practice 78

Draw butanol, and then draw and name two isomers of butanol. Include an ether as one of the isomers.

Practice 79

Draw 2-hexanone, and then draw and name two isomers of 2-hexanone. Include an aldehyde as one of the isomers.

Base your answers to practice questions 80 through 82 on the information below.

The equation below represents a reaction between propene and hydrogen bromide.

```
  H  H                          H   H   H
  |  |                          |   |   |
H-C-C=C-H  +  H-Br  ⟶   H-C-C-C-H
  |     |                       |   |   |
  H     H                       H  Br   H
```

80. Draw and name a structural formula for an isomer of the product.

81. How many electrons are shared in the propene molecule?

82. Identify the class of organic compounds to which the product of this reaction belongs.

Base your answer to practice question 83 on the information below.

Cyclopropane, an isomer of propene, has a boiling point of −33°C at standard pressure and   is represented by the formula below.

```
  H      H
   \    /
    C
   / \
H    \
 \    \
  C — C
 /     \
H   H    H
```

83. Explain, in terms of molecular formulas and structural formulas, why cyclopropane is an isomer of propene.

Lesson 5: Reactions of Organic Compounds

There are many types of organic reactions. Organic compounds can react with each other, as well as with inorganic compounds to form a wide range of organic products. Organic reactions are generally slower than reactions of inorganic compounds because strong covalent bonds within organic molecules must first be broken before a reaction can occur.

Organic reactions discussed in this lesson include:
substitution, addition, esterification, polymerization, fermentation, saponification and combustion

Substitution Reactions
Replacing a hydrogen atom of an alkane with a halogen.

Substitution reactions typically involve the removing of a hydrogen atom from an alkane and replacing it with a halogen. The main organic product in substitution reactions is a halide.

Organic reactant   Organic product
Alkane (saturated hydrocarbon)   Halide (with 1 halogen attached)

An example of a substitution reaction is shown below.

| Alkane | + | Halogen | → | Halide | + | Acid |

$$\begin{array}{cccccc}
& H\ \ H\ \ H & & & H\ \ H\ \ H & & \\
& |\ \ \ |\ \ \ | & & & |\ \ \ |\ \ \ | & & \\
H-C-C-C-H & + & F-F & \rightarrow & H-C-C-C-F & + & H-F \\
& |\ \ \ |\ \ \ | & & & |\ \ \ |\ \ \ | & & \\
& H\ \ H\ \ H & & & H\ \ H\ \ H & &
\end{array}$$

Propane   Fluorine   Fluoropropane   Hydrogen fluoride

Practice 84
Which substance will likely undergo a substitution reaction with iodine?
1) 2-hexene   3) 2 - methyl pentane
2) 2-pentanol   4) 2 - methyl hexyne

Practice 85
Which equation represents a substitution reaction?
1) $CH_2CH_2 + H_2 \rightarrow CH_3CH_3$
2) $CH_3CH_3 + O_2 \rightarrow CO_2 + H_2$
3) $CH_2CH_2 + Br_2 \rightarrow CH_2BrCH_2Br$
4) $CH_3CH_3 + Br_2 \rightarrow BrCH_2CH_3 + HBr$

Practice 86
Draw and name the structural formula of the organic product.

$CH_3CH_2CH(CH_3)CH_3 + I_2 \rightarrow CH_2ICH_2CH(CH_3)CH_3 + HI$

Practice 87
Draw and name the structural formula of the product that will form.

$$\begin{array}{c}
H\ \ H\ \ H\ \ H\ \ H \\
|\ \ \ |\ \ \ \ |\ \ \ \ |\ \ \ \ | \\
H-C-C-C-C-C-H \ \ +\ \ Cl_2 \rightarrow HCl\ + \\
|\ \ \ |\ \ \ \ |\ \ \ \ |\ \ \ \ | \\
H\ \ H\ \ H\ \ H\ \ H
\end{array}$$

Addition Reactions

An **addition** reaction usually involves the breaking of a double or triple bond in an unsaturated hydrocarbon, and adding hydrogen or halogen atoms to the free electrons. The organic reactant in an addition reaction is an alkene or alkyne. Two types of addition reactions are given below.

Hydrogen Addition (**Hydrogenation**): *Adding H atoms to the double bond of an alkene*
In hydrogenation, hydrogen atoms are added to a double bond of an alkene. The unsaturated hydrocarbon (alkene) is changed to a saturated hydrocarbon (alkane).

Organic reactant				*Organic product*
Alkene (unsaturated)	+	Hydrogen	→	Alkane (saturated)
C_3H_6	+	H_2	→	C_3H_8

```
   H H H                          H H H
   | | |                          | | |
 H-C=C-C-H    +    H-H     →     H-C-C-C-H
       |                            | | |
       H                            H H H
  propene        hydrogen           propane
```

Halogen Addition (**Halogenation**): *Adding halogen atoms to the double bond of an alkene.*
In halogenations, halogen atoms are added to a double bond of an alkene. The alkene is changed to a halide compound with two attached halogen atoms.

Organic reactant				*Organic product*
Alkene (unsaturated)	+	Halogen	→	Halide (with 2 halogen atoms attached)
C_3H_6	+	Br_2	→	$C_3H_6Br_2$

```
   H  H H                         H  H  H
   |  | |                         |  |  |
 H-C = C-C-H    +   Br-Br   →   H-C-C-C-H
          |                        |  |  |
          H                        Br Br H
  propene        bromine       1,2-dibromopropane
```

Practice 88
Which substance will likely undergo addition reaction with iodine?

1) 2-methyl butene   3) 2-methyl butane
2) 3-pentanone   4) 2-fluoro pentane

Practice 89
Which equation represents addition reaction?
1) C_2H_4 + H_2 → C_2H_6
2) C_2H_4 + O_2 → CO_2 + H_2
3) C_2H_6 + Cl_2 → C_2H_5Cl + HCl
4) $C_6H_{12}O_6$ → $2C_2H_5OH$ + $2CO_2$

Practice 90
Draw and name the organic reactant.
$CH_3CH_2CHCH_2$ + H_2 → $CH_3CH_2CH_2CH_3$

Practice 91
Draw and name the structural formula of the product that is formed in the reaction below.

```
   H H        H
   | |        |
 H-C-C-C = C-C-H  + F_2  →
   | | | | |
   H H H H H
```

Esterification
Reacting an organic acid with an alcohol to make ester.

Esterification is the process of making an ester by reacting an organic acid with a primary alcohol. In esterification processes, water is formed from the H^+ ion of the acid and the -OH group of the alcohol.

Example of an ester reaction is shown below. Pay attention to the atoms in the structures to help you see and understand how the products are formed from the reactants.

Organic acid	+	Alcohol	→	Ester	+	Water
CH_3COOH	+	$HOCH_2CH_2CH_3$	→	$CH_3COOCH_2CH_2CH_3$	+	H_2O

$$H-\underset{\underset{H}{|}}{\overset{\overset{H}{|}}{C}}-\overset{\overset{O}{||}}{C}-OH \;+\; HO-\underset{\underset{H}{|}}{\overset{\overset{H}{|}}{C}}-\underset{\underset{H}{|}}{\overset{\overset{H}{|}}{C}}-\underset{\underset{H}{|}}{\overset{\overset{H}{|}}{C}}-H \;\rightarrow\; H-\underset{\underset{H}{|}}{\overset{\overset{H}{|}}{C}}-\overset{\overset{O}{||}}{C}-O-\underset{\underset{H}{|}}{\overset{\overset{H}{|}}{C}}-\underset{\underset{H}{|}}{\overset{\overset{H}{|}}{C}}-\underset{\underset{H}{|}}{\overset{\overset{H}{|}}{C}}-H \;+\; H_2O$$

ethanoic acid   propanol   propyl ethanoate

Note: The first part of the ester's name (*prop-*) comes from the alcohol (*propanol*).
The second part of the ester's name (*eth-*) comes from the organic acid (*ethanoic*).

Practice 92
A structure of which organic compound is a product of a reaction between an organic acid and alcohol?

1) 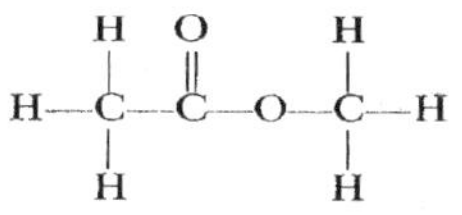 $H-\overset{\overset{H}{|}}{\underset{\underset{H}{|}}{C}}-\overset{\overset{O}{||}}{C}-O-\overset{\overset{H}{|}}{\underset{\underset{H}{|}}{C}}-H$

2) 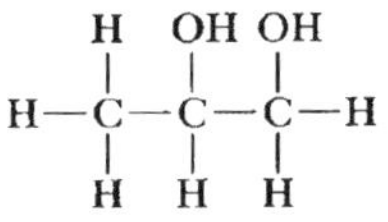 $H-\overset{\overset{H}{|}}{\underset{\underset{H}{|}}{C}}-\overset{\overset{OH}{|}}{\underset{\underset{H}{|}}{C}}-\overset{\overset{OH}{|}}{\underset{\underset{H}{|}}{C}}-H$

3) 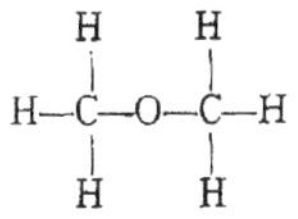 $H-\overset{\overset{H}{|}}{\underset{\underset{H}{|}}{C}}-O-\overset{\overset{H}{|}}{\underset{\underset{H}{|}}{C}}-H$

4) 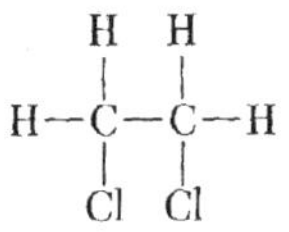 $H-\overset{\overset{H}{|}}{\underset{\underset{Cl}{|}}{C}}-\overset{\overset{H}{|}}{\underset{\underset{Cl}{|}}{C}}-H$

Practice 93
Which compound will react with methanol to form methyl propanoate?
1) Methyl Propyl ether
2) Propanoic acid
3) Propanone
4) Propanol

Practice 94
Draw and name the organic substance that reacts with ethanol in the reaction shown below.

$$+\; OH-CH_2-CH_3 \;\rightarrow\; CH_3-CH_2-CH_2-\overset{\overset{O}{||}}{C}-O-CH_2-CH_3 \;+\; H_2O$$

Practice 95
Draw and name the structure of the organic product that will form in the reaction below.

$$H-\underset{\underset{H}{|}}{\overset{\overset{H}{|}}{C}}-\underset{\underset{H}{|}}{\overset{\overset{H}{|}}{C}}-\underset{\underset{H}{|}}{\overset{\overset{H}{|}}{C}}-\underset{\underset{H}{|}}{\overset{\overset{H}{|}}{C}}-\overset{\overset{O}{||}}{C}-OH \;+\; H-\underset{\underset{H}{|}}{\overset{\overset{H}{|}}{C}}-OH \;\rightarrow\; H_2O \;+\;$$

$$H-\underset{\underset{}{}}{\overset{\overset{H}{|}}{C}}-\underset{\underset{H}{|}}{\overset{\overset{H}{|}}{C}}-\underset{\underset{H}{|}}{\overset{\overset{H}{|}}{C}}-\underset{\underset{H}{|}}{\overset{\overset{H}{|}}{C}}-\overset{\overset{O}{||}}{C}-O-\underset{\underset{H}{|}}{C}-OH$$

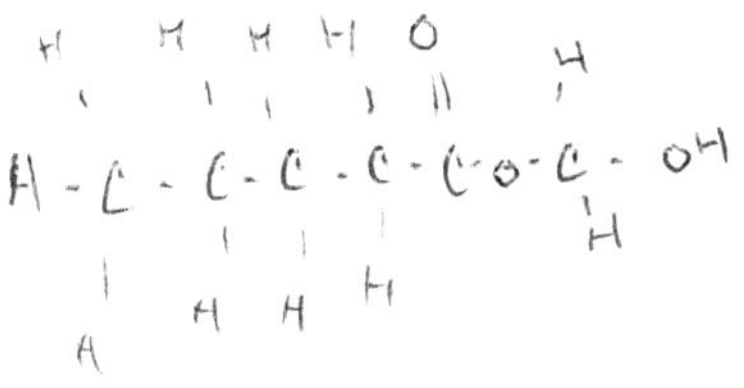

Polymerization

Polymerization is a process of joining small organic molecules together to make a longer chain molecule. *Monomers* are small unit molecules that are joined together by covalent bonds to form a polymer.

Two types of polymerization reactions are discussed below.

Condensation Polymerization: *Joining small molecules by removing water.*
In condensation polymerization reactions, monomers with -**OH** groups are joined together as water is removed. *Ethers* and *proteins* are substances commonly produced by condensation polymerization.

An example of a condensation polymerization reaction is given below:

Monomer	+	Monomer	→	Polymer	+	water

CH_3**OH**   +   **HO**CH_2CH_3 → CH_3**O**CH_2CH_3 +   **H_2O**

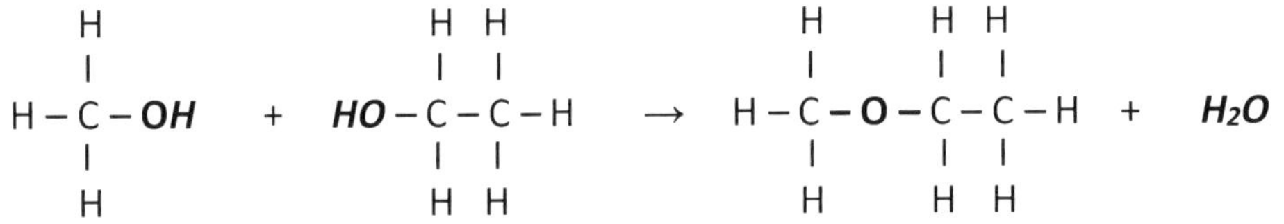

```
    H                 H  H              H       H  H
    |                 |  |              |       |  |
H – C – OH  +  HO – C – C – H  →  H – C – O – C – C – H  +  H₂O
    |                 |  |              |       |  |
    H                 H  H              H       H  H
  Methanol          Ethanol         Methyl ethyl  ether      water
```

Addition Polymerization: *Joining small unsaturated molecules together*
In addition polymerization reactions, several identical small alkene molecules with double bonds are joined together to create a larger saturated polymer.

Example of an addition polymerization process is shown below:

$n(CH_2=CH_2)$ → $(-CH_2-CH_2-)_n$ n represents several repeated units of the monomer.

monomers   Polymer

Common polymers that are produced by natural and synthetic polymerization processes are listed below.

Natural polymers (condensation polymerization): Protein, starch, and cellulose .

Synthetic polymers (addition polymerization): Nylon, plastic, polyethylene, and polyvinyl .

Practice 96
Given the incomplete reaction below, draw and name the organic product of the reaction.

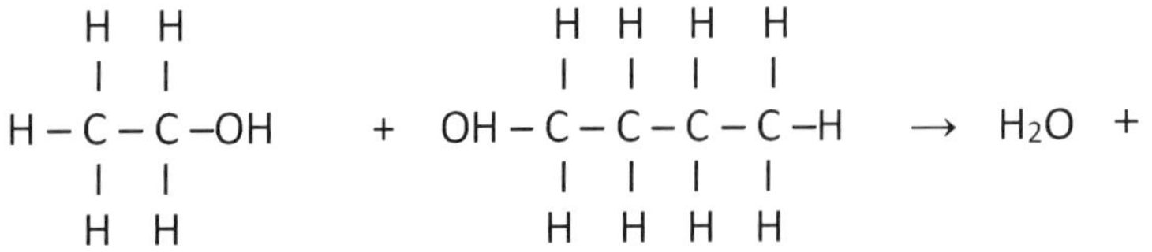

```
    H  H              H  H  H  H
    |  |              |  |  |  |
H – C – C –OH  +  OH – C – C – C – C –H  →  H₂O  +
    |  |              |  |  |  |
    H  H              H  H  H  H
```

 ©2017 E3 Scholastic Publishing. All Rights Reserved

Fermentation
Making ethanol from sugar

Fermentation is an organic process of making ethanol, an alcohol, from sugar.
• Carbon dioxide, CO_2, is also produced.
• Enzyme catalyst is required for this process.

Fermentation reaction is shown below:

sugar $\xrightarrow{\text{enzyme}}$ ethanol + carbon dioxide

$C_6H_{12}O_6 \xrightarrow{\text{zymase}}$ $2C_2H_5OH$ + $2CO_2$

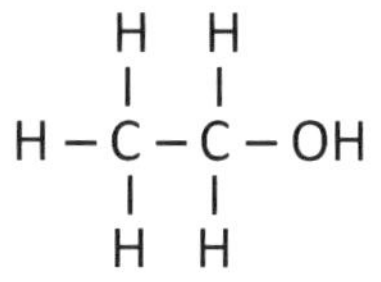

```
      H  H
      |  |
  H – C – C – OH
      |  |
      H  H
    ethanol
```

Saponification
Making soap from fat and base

Saponification is an organic process of making soap.
Glycerol, a tertiary alcohol, is also produced during a saponification process.

Saponification reaction is shown below:

Fat + Base → Soap + Glycerol (an alcohol)

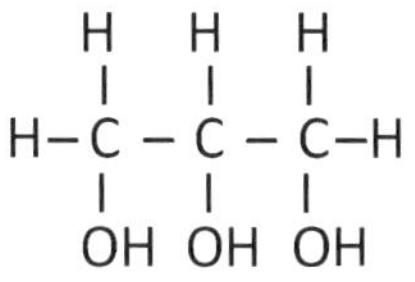

```
      H   H   H
      |   |   |
  H – C – C – C–H
      |   |   |
      OH  OH  OH
```

1,2,3-propanetri*ol* (glycerol)

Combustion
Burning of an organic substance with oxygen.

Combustion is a process of burning an organic compound (fuel) in the presence of oxygen.
Carbon dioxide (CO_2) and water (H_2O) are the two main products of a combustion reaction.

A combustion reaction is shown below.:

Organic compound + Oxygen → Carbon dioxide + water

$2C_8H_{18}$ + $25O_2$ → $16CO_2$ + $18H_2O$
octane (car fuel)

Organic Reactions: Summary Table

Use this table for a quick review of organic reactions.

Organic Reactions	Reactants		Products	
1. **Substitution**	Alkane (saturated hydrocarbon)	Halogen	1 – Halide a one-halogen halide	Acid inorganic
2. **Addition** **Hydrogenation**	Alkene (unsaturated hydrocarbon)	Hydrogen	Alkane	
Halogenation	Alkene	Halogen	1,2 – Halide (a two-halogen halide)	
3. **Saponification**	Fat	Base	1,2,3-propanetriol (glycerol)	Soap
4. **Fermentation** (requires enzyme)	$C_6H_{12}O_6$ (sugar)		C_2H_5OH (ethanol)	CO_2 (Carbon dioxide)
5. **Combustion**	Hydrocarbon	O_2	Carbon dioxide	Water
6. **Esterification**	Organic Acid	Alcohol	Ester	Water
7. **Polymerization** **Condensation** **Polymerization**	Alcohol (monomers)	Alcohol	Ether (a polymer)	Water
	Amino acid (monomers)	Amino acid	Protein (a polymer)	Water
Addition **Polymerization**	$n(CH_2=CH_2)$ (ethene monomers)		$(-CH_2-CH_2-)_n$ (polyethylene polymer)	
8. **Cracking**	$C_{14}H_{30}$ (long chain hydrocarbon		C_7H_{16} (shorter chains hydrocarbons)	C_7H_{14}

©2017 E3 Scholastic Publishing. All Rights Reserved

Organic Reactions: **Practice Questions**

Concept Task: Be able to determine or recognize organic reaction from a given equation.

Practice 97
Which reaction is used to produce polyethylene from ethylene?
1) Addition polymerization
2) Condensation polymerization
3) Substitution
4) Combustion

Practice 98
Carbon dioxide and water are two products formed from which organic reaction?
1) Combustion
2) Esterification
3) Fermentation
4) Saponification

Practice 99
Chloromethane is likely a product of
1) addition
2) fermentation
3) substitution
4) neutralization

Practice 100
Consider the equation

$$C_5H_{10} \quad + \quad H_2 \quad \rightarrow \quad C_5H_{12}$$

This reaction can be best described as
1) hydrogen addition
2) hydrogen substitution
3) polymerization
4) combustion

Practice 101
The organic reaction below can be described as

$$CH_3COOH \quad + \quad CH_3OH \quad \rightarrow \quad CH_3COOCH_3 \quad + \quad H_2O$$

1) addition polymerization
2) substitution
3) saponification
4) esterification

Practice 102
The reaction below is an example of

$$C_2H_4(g) \quad + \quad 3O_2(g) \quad \rightarrow \quad H_2O(\ell) \quad + \quad CO_2(g)$$

1) substitution
2) combustion
3) addition
4) saponification

Practice 103

The reaction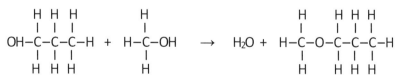

is best classified as
1) polymerization
2) combustion
3) saponification
4) substitution

Base your answers to practice questions 104 through 106 on the information below.
A reaction between bromine and a hydrocarbon is represented by the balanced equation below.

$$Br_2 + H-\underset{\underset{H}{|}}{\overset{\overset{H}{|}}{C}}=\underset{\underset{H}{|}}{\overset{\overset{H}{|}}{C}}-\underset{\underset{H}{|}}{\overset{\overset{H}{|}}{C}}-H \longrightarrow H-\underset{\underset{Br}{|}}{\overset{\overset{H}{|}}{C}}-\underset{\underset{Br}{|}}{\overset{\overset{H}{|}}{C}}-\underset{\underset{H}{|}}{\overset{\overset{H}{|}}{C}}-H$$

104. Write the name of the homologous series to which the hydrocarbon belongs.

105. Write the name of the product. *1,2 dibropropanise*

106. Identify the type of organic reaction represented by the equation.

Base your answers to questions 107 through 109 on the information below and on your knowledge of chemistry.

The unique odors and flavors of many fruits are primarily due to small quantities of a certain class of organic compounds. The equation below represents the production of one of these compounds.

$$H-\underset{\underset{H}{|}}{\overset{\overset{H}{|}}{C}}-\underset{\underset{H}{|}}{\overset{\overset{H}{|}}{C}}-OH + H-\overset{\overset{O}{\|}}{C}-O-H \longrightarrow H-\overset{\overset{O}{\|}}{C}-O-\underset{\underset{H}{|}}{\overset{\overset{H}{|}}{C}}-\underset{\underset{H}{|}}{\overset{\overset{H}{|}}{C}}-H + HOH$$

Reactant 1   Reactant 2   Product 1   Product 2

107. State the class of organic compounds to which Reactant 2 belongs.

108. Identify the type of organic reaction represented by the equation.

109. Draw and name a structural formula for an isomer of Product 1.

Base your answers to questions 110 and 111 on the information below.

One type of soap is produced when ethyl stearate and sodium hydroxide react. The soap produced by this reaction is called sodium stearate. The other product of the reaction is ethanol. This reaction is represented by the balanced equation below.

$$C_{17}H_{35}-\overset{\overset{O}{\|}}{C}-O-C_2H_5 + NaOH \longrightarrow C_{17}H_{35}-\overset{\overset{O}{\|}}{C}-O^- Na^+ + C_2H_5OH$$

Ethyl stearate   Sodium hydroxide   Sodium stearate   Ethanol

110. To which class of organic compounds does ethyl stearate belong?

111. Identify the type of organic reaction used to make soap.

                                    ©2017 E3 Scholastic Publishing. All Rights Reserved

Vocabulary

Lesson 1: Properties of Organic Compounds

Organic compound

Lesson 2: Classes of Organic Compounds

Homologous series	Alkyne	Ketone
Hydrocarbon	Functional group	Organic acid
Saturated hydrocarbon	Halide	Ester
Unsaturated hydrocarbon	Alcohol	Amine
Alkane	Ether	Amide
Alkene	Aldehyde	

Lesson 3: Isomers

Isomer

Lesson 4: Organic Reactions

Substitution	Combustion
Addition	Esterification
Hydrogenation	Polymerization
Halogenation	Addition polymerization
Fermentation	Condensation polymerization

1. 3	5. 1	9. 4	13. 2	17. 3	21. 2	25. 3
2. 2	6. 4	10. 3	14. 4	18. 2	22. 4	26. 2
3. 4	7. carbon, C	11. 2	15. 1	19. 4	23. 4	
4. 4	8. 2	12. 4	16. 3	20. 1	24. 2	

27.

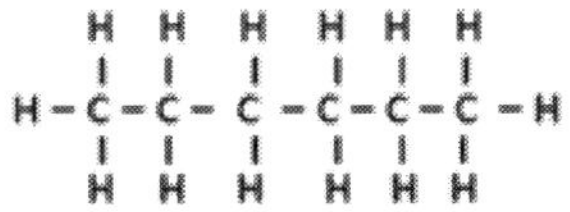

28.

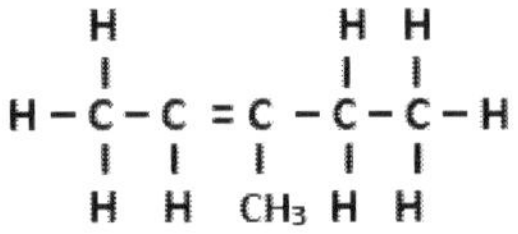

29.

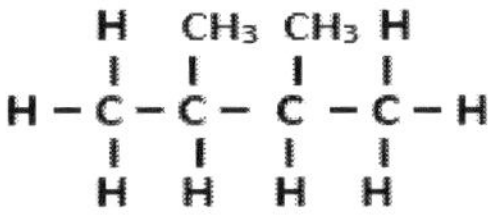

30. 1 – pentene, pentene

31. 2,2,3-trimethyl hexane

32. 3,3-dimethyl pentane

33. 4	36. 2	39. 2	42. 3	45. 1	48. 4	51. 2
34. 1	37. 1	40. 1	43. 4	46. 3	49. 1	52. 3
35. 4	38. 3	41. 3	44. 2	47. 4	50. 2	

53.

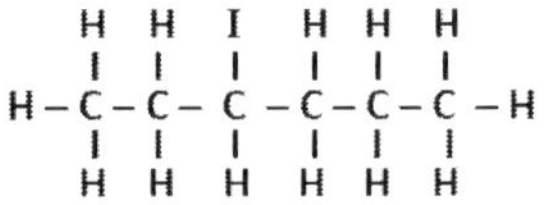

54.

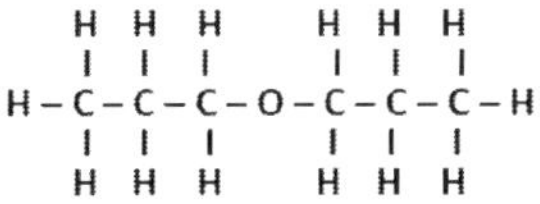

55.

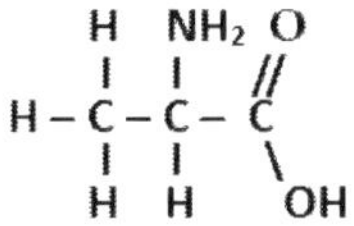

56. 2-butanol

57. ethyl ethanoate

58. butanone

59.

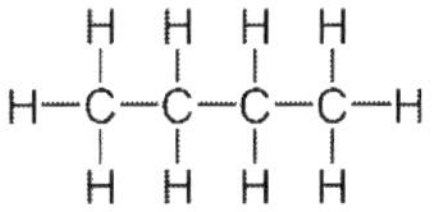

60. C_nH_{2n+2}

61. They contain multiple covalent bonds.
They have double and triple bonds.

62. pentyne

63.

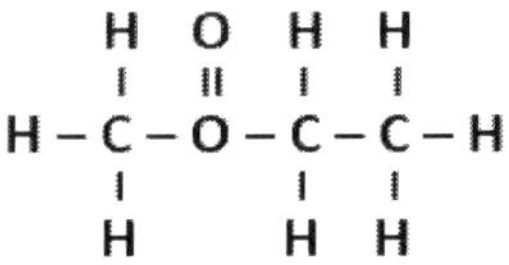

64

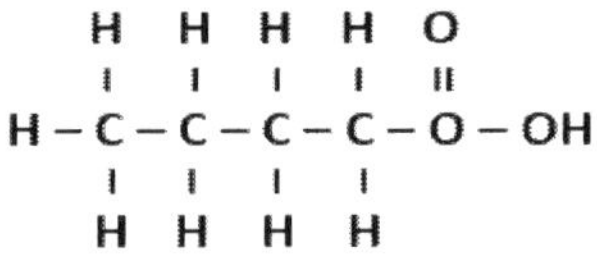

65. 1
66. 2
67. 4
68. 1
69. 1
70. 1
71. 1
72. 1
73. 4

74

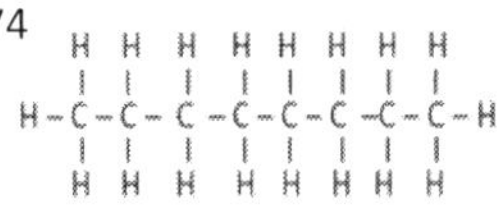

octane

There are 17 possible isomers of octane.
Two are shown below.

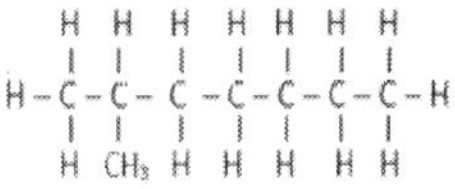

2- methyl heptane

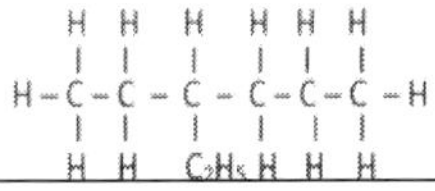

3-ethyl hexane

75

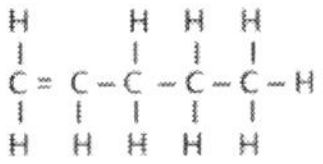

pentene (1-pentene)

There are 4 possible isomers of pentene.
Two are shown below.

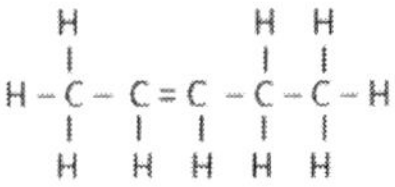

2-pentene

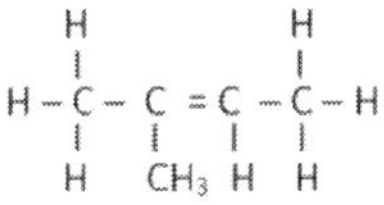

2 –methyl, 2-butene

76

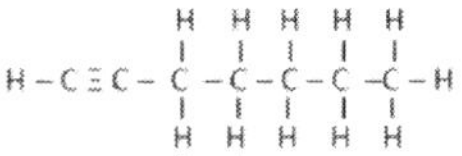

heptyne

There are 13 possible somers of heptyne.
Two are shown below.

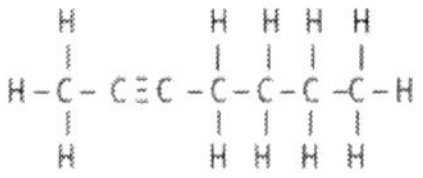

2- heptyne

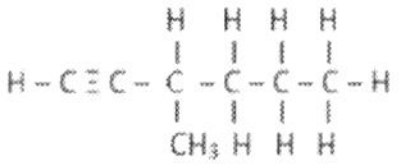

3-methyl hexyne

77

1,1-difluoropropane

1,2-difluoropropane

1,3-difluoropropane

2,2-difluoropropane

All three isomers are shown above.

78

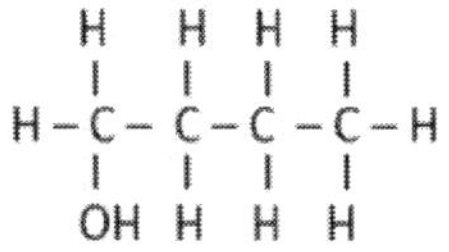

butanol (1–butanol)

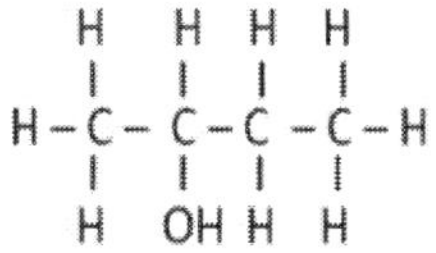

2–butanol

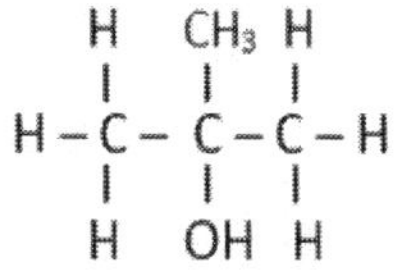

2-methyl, 2-propanol

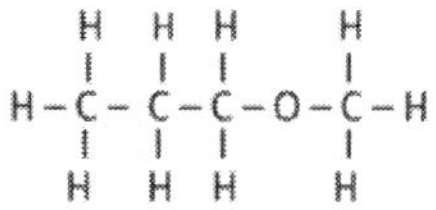

methyl propyl ether

79.

2-hexanone

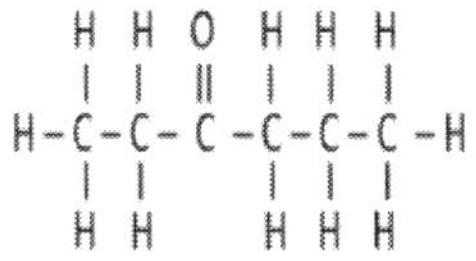

3-hexanone

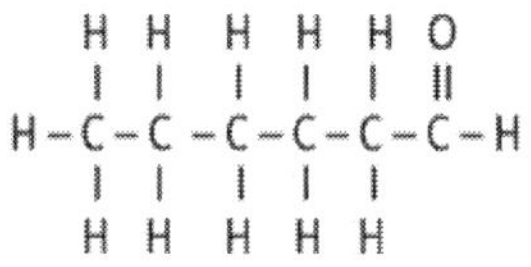

hexanal

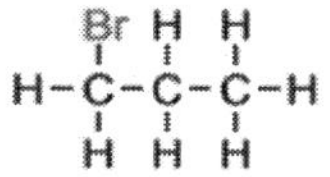

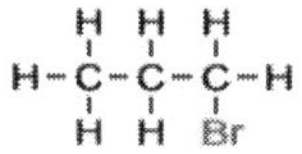

81. 18 electrons

82. halide, halocarbon

83. Cyclobutane and butene have the same molecular formula, but their structural formulas are different.

Cyclobutane has the same molecular formula as butene, but its structure is different.

84. 3

85. 4

86.

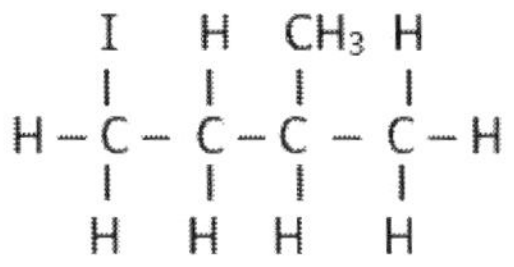

2-methyl, 4-iodobutane

87.

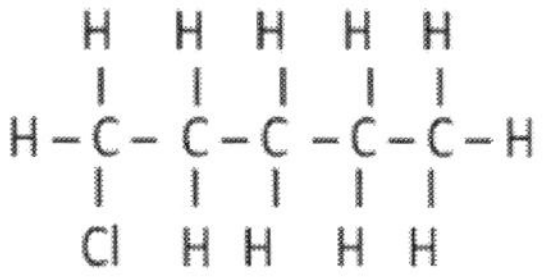

1-chloropentane

88. 1

89. 1

90.

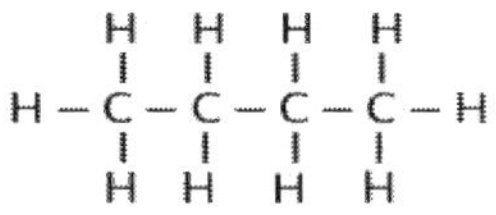

butane

91.

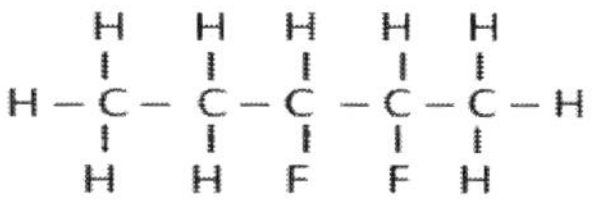

2,3-difluoropentane

92. 1

93. 2.

94.

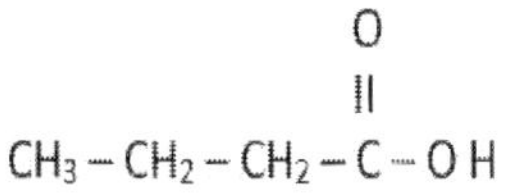

$$CH_3 - CH_2 - CH_2 - C - OH$$

butanoic acid

95.

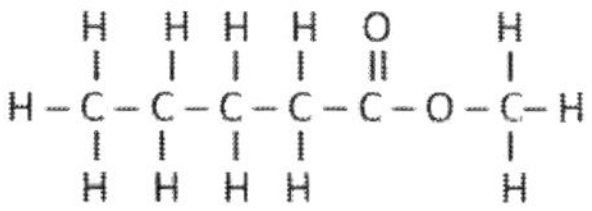

methyl pentanoate

96.

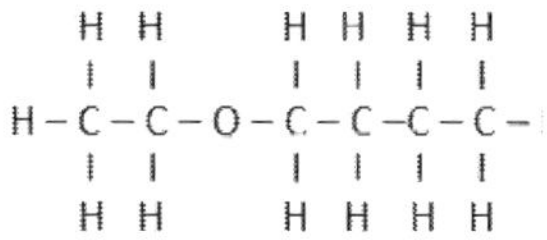

ethyl butyl ether

97. 1

98. 1

99. 3

100. 1

101. 4

102. 2

103. 1

104. alkene

105. 1,2-dibromopropane

106. addition, halogenation

107. organic acid, acid

108. esterification, polymerization

109.

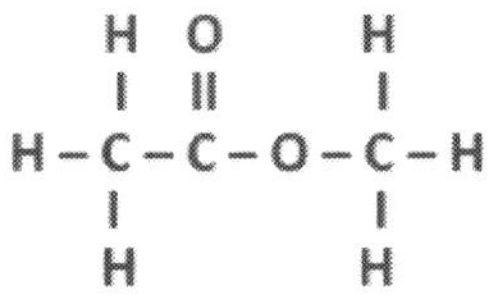

```
    H  O     H                    H  H  O
    |  ||    |                    |  |  ||
H – C – C – O – C – H        H – C – C – C – OH
    |        |                    |  |
    H        H                    H  H
   methyl ethanoate             propanoic acid
```

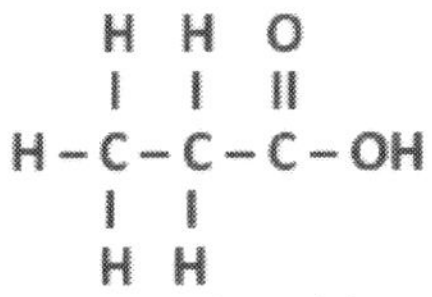

110, ester

111. saponification

©2017 E3 Scholastic Publishing. All Rights Reserved

Topic 11
Redox and Electrochemistry

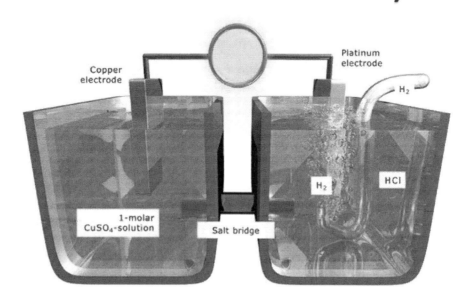

Lesson 1: Oxidation Numbers

Lesson 2: Redox - Oxidation and Reduction Reactions

Lesson 3: Electrochemistry (Voltaic and Electrolytic cells)

Lesson 4: Spontaneous Reactions

Lesson 1 – Oxidation Numbers

Certain chemical reactions involve the transfer of electrons between species (molecules, atoms, or ions) in the reaction.

Oxidation is the **loss** of electrons in a reaction.

Reduction is the **gain** of electrons in a reaction.

Redox is any chemical reaction that involves both oxidation and reduction.

The losing and gaining of electrons in these reactions occur simultaneously (at the same time).
• *The number of electrons lost is equal to the number of electrons gained*

Species that gain and lose electrons undergo changes in their oxidation numbers. Understanding oxidation numbers, as well as being able to correctly assign oxidation numbers to elements in a reaction, are keys to answering many redox-related questions in this topic.

Oxidation Number
Charge of an Atom

An **oxidation number** is the charge of an atom when it has lost or gained electrons.
Oxidation number of an element can be 0, negative (-), or positive(+).

For example:
The neutral K atom has an oxidation number of **0.**
The O^{2-} ion has an oxidation number of **-2.**
The Al^{3+} ion has an oxidation number of **+3.**

In all compounds, the sum of all oxidation numbers is equal to **zero.**
In the compound Na_2SO_4 , the sum of oxidation numbers of Na, S and O is Zero (0).

In polyatomic ions (Table E), the sum of all oxidation numbers is equal to the **charge** of the ion.
In the polyatomic ion CO_3^{2-}, the sum of oxidation numbers of C and O is equal to **-2.**

Determining Oxidation Numbers

When an atom in a formula has a few possible positive oxidation numbers, the actual oxidation number of the atom in that formula can be determined using simple math.
Two examples are given below.

Example 1: What is the oxidation number of **S** in the compound Na_2SO_4?

     Na = +1 charge: 2Na = 2(+1) = +2   *total positive charge in the formula.*
     O = -2 charge: 4O = 4(-2) = - 8   *total negative charge in the formula*
     S oxidation number must be a **+6** for charges to add up to **0**   **(+2 − 8 +6 = 0)**

Example 2: What is the oxidation number of **C** in the polyatomic ion CO_3^{2-} ?

     1C + 3O = -2
     C + 3(-2) = -2
         C = -2 + 6 = **+4**

Rules for Assigning Oxidation Numbers

In redox equations, oxidation numbers are assigned to the elements to help determine the oxidized and reduced species, as well as the number of electrons that are lost and gained. A few simple rules must be followed to correctly assign oxidation numbers to all elements in a reaction equation.

1. The oxidation number of a free element is always zero (0). Ex. Na, O_2, S_8.
2. The oxidation number of a monatomic ion is the charge of the ion. Ex. Na^+, O_2^-
3. The sum of all the oxidation numbers in a neutral compound is zero.
4. The sum of all the oxidation numbers in a polyatomic ion is the charge of the ion.
5. The common oxidation state of an element in a compound can be found on the Periodic Table. The table below lists categories of elements and their common oxidation states, as well as exceptions in which the charge of the element is different.

Element	Common Oxidation State	Exceptions
Group 1 metals	always +1	
Group 2 metals	always +2	
Oxygen	usually -2	In peroxides (ex. N_2O_2), O is a -1. In a compound with fluorine (OF_2), O is a +2.
Hydrogen	usually +1	In metal hydrides (ex. NaH, CaH_2), H is a -1.
Fluorine	always -1	
Chlorine Bromine Iodine	usually -1	In compounds and polyatomic ions with O (ex. NaClO, $LiBrO_3$), these halogens can have one of many positive values. The actual positive charge value of Cl, Br, or I can be determined mathematically.

Redox and Electrochemistry

Oxidation Numbers: Practice Questions

Practice 1
What is the oxidation number of oxygen in ozone, O_3?
1) +1   2) 0   3) -2   4) -6

Practice 2
The oxidation number of hydrogen in BeH_2 is
1) +1   2) -1   3) 0   4) +2

Practice 3
What is the oxidation number of Pt in K_2PtCl_6?
1) +4   2) -4   3) +2   4) -2

Practice 4
Below, two compounds of chlorine are given:
         Compound A: Cl_2O Compound B: HClO
Which is true of the oxidation number of chlorine in compounds A and B?
1) Chlorine's oxidation number is +2 in A, but +1 in B
2) Chlorine's oxidation number is +1 in A, but +2 in B
3) Chlorine's oxidation number is +2 in both A and B
4) Chlorine's oxidation number is +1 in both A and B

Practice 5
What is the oxidation number of Cr in the polyatomic ion, $Cr_2O_7^{2-}$?
1) +7   2) +6   3) -2   4) +2

Practice 6
In which substance does bromine have an oxidation number of +3?
1) KBrO   2) $KBrO_3$ 3) $KBrO_2$ 4) $KBrO_4$

Practice 7
Sulfur has an oxidation number of +6 in which two formulas?
1) SO_3 and SO_4^{2-} 3) SO_2 and SO_4^{2-}
2) H_2SO_4 and SO_2 4) HSO_4^- and $S_2O_3^{2-}$

Base your answers to practice questions 8 and 9 on the information below.
Litharge, PbO, is an ore that can be roasted (heated) in the presence of carbon monoxide, CO, to produce elemental lead. The reaction that takes place during this roasting process is represented by the balanced equation below.

     $PbO(s) + CO(g) \rightarrow Pb(s) + CO_2(g)$

8. Determine the oxidation number of lead in litharge.

9. In which compound does carbon have the greater oxidation number?

Base your answers to practice questions 10 and 11 on the information below.
The head of matches contains an oxidizing agent such as potassium chlorate, $KClO_3$, together with tetraphosphorus trisulfide, P_4S_3, glass and binder. When struck either by an object or on the side of a box of matches, the phosphorus sulfide compound is easily ignited, causing the potassium chlorate to decompose into potassium chloride and oxygen. The oxygen in turn causes the phosphorus sulfide to burn more vigorously.

10. Determine the oxidation number of chlorine in potassium chlorate.

11. In terms of charges, explain why potassium chloride, KCl, is neutral.

238
©2017 E3 Scholastic Publishing. All Rights Reserved

Lesson 2 – Oxidation and Reduction (Redox) Reactions

In redox reactions, electrons are lost (oxidation) and gained (reduction).
The number of moles of electrons lost and gained must be the same (equal).

In this lesson you will learn about redox reactions, as well as oxidation and reduction half-reactions.

Redox Reactions
Involve Transfer of Electrons

All single replacement reactions are redox reactions. Most synthesis and decomposition reactions are also redox reactions. Double replacement reactions are non-redox reactions. Types of reactions were discussed in topic 5. Examples of redox and non-redox reactions are given below.

The equations below represent redox reactions

Synthesis	$N_2 + O_2 \rightarrow 2NO$
Decomposition	$2H_2O_2 \rightarrow 2H_2O + O_2$
Single replacement	$Cu + 2AgNO_3 \rightarrow Cu(NO_3)_2 + 2Ag$
Simplified redox	$Cu + 2Ag^+ \rightarrow Cu^{2+} + 2Ag$

These and similar reactions represent redox because:

• Two elements in each reaction have a change in oxidation number.

Therefore, electrons are lost and gained in each reaction.

The equations below do not represent redox reactions.

Double replacement:	$KI + AgNO_3 \rightarrow AgI + KNO_3$
Ions combining:	$Na^+ + Cl^- \rightarrow NaCl$
Ionization:	$H_2O \rightarrow H^+ + OH^-$

These and similar reactions are not redox because:

• **None of the elements in the reactions have a change in oxidation number**

Therefore, electrons are neither lost nor gained in any of the reactions.

Redox Equations: Practice Questions

Practice 12
Which equation represents a redox reaction?
1) $AgNO_3 + LiBr \rightarrow AgBr + LiNO_3$
2) $KI \rightarrow K^+ + I^-$
3) $4Na + O_2 \rightarrow 2Na_2O$
4) $2Na^+ + SO_4^{2-} \rightarrow Na_2SO_4$

Practice 13
Which equation represents a redox reaction?
1) $PbSO_4 + Zn \rightarrow ZnSO_4 + Pb$
2) $3O_2 \rightarrow 2O_3$
3) $H_3PO_4 + 3KOH \rightarrow K_3PO_4 + 3H_2O$
4) $H^+ + Cl- \rightarrow HCl$

Practice 14
Given the four equations below.
I: $AgNO_3 + NaCl \rightarrow AgCl + NaNO_3$
II: $Cl_2 + H_2O \rightarrow HClO + HCl$
III: $CuO + CO \rightarrow CO_2 + Cu$
IV: $LiOH + HCl \rightarrow LiCl + H_2O$

Oxidation-reduction reactions are shown in which two equations?
1) I and II
2) II and III
3) III and I
4) IV and II

Oxidation and Reduction
Redox reactions involve oxidation and reduction.

Oxidation: *Loss of Electrons is Oxidation* **(LEO).**
An **oxidized substance** is the substance or ion that is losing or transferring its electrons in a reaction. The oxidized substance is also known as a *reducing agent* because it causes another substance in the reaction to gain electrons. The oxidation number of an oxidized substance always increases (becomes more positive) because the substance has lost negative particles (electrons).

Reduction: *Gain of Electrons is Reduction* **(GER).**
A **reduced substance** is the substance or ion in a reaction that is gaining or accepting electrons. The reduced substance is also known as an *oxidizing agent* because it causes another substance in the reaction to lose electrons. The oxidation number of a reduced substance always decreases (becomes more negative) because the substance has gained negative particles (electrons).

Half-reactions: *Witten for Oxidation or Reduction*
A **half-reaction** shows the oxidation or reduction portion of a redox reaction. A correct half-reaction must show conservation of atoms, mass, and charge; It must be balanced.

Consider the redox reaction below:

$$2Na + Cl_2 \rightarrow 2NaCl$$

An **oxidation half-reaction** shows the loss of electrons by a substance in a redox reaction. In the above redox reaction, sodium is the species that is losing electrons. The electrons that are lost are always shown on the right side of the half-reaction equation as given below.

$$2Na^0 \rightarrow 2Na^+ + 2e^- \quad \textbf{oxidation half-reaction}$$

A **reduction half-reaction** shows the gain of electrons by a substance in a redox reaction. In the above redox reaction, chlorine is the species that is gaining electrons. The electrons that are lost are always shown on the left side of the half-reaction equation as given below.

$$Cl_2^0 + 2e^- \rightarrow 2Cl^- \quad \textbf{reduction half-reaction}$$

Note:
Both half-reaction equations demonstrate conservation of atoms and charge. Both half-reactions are balanced.

Practice 15
Which half-reaction equation correctly represents a reduction reaction?
1) $Li^0 + e^- \rightarrow Li^+$
2) $Na^0 + e^- \rightarrow Na^+$
3) $Br_2^0 + 2e^- \rightarrow 2Br^-$
4) $Cl_2^0 + e^- \rightarrow 2Cl^-$

Practice 16
Which is a correct oxidation-half equation?
1) $F_2^0 \rightarrow 2F^- + 2e^-$
2) $Ca^0 \rightarrow Ca^{2+} + 2e^-$
3) $Ca^{2+} + 2e^- \rightarrow Ca^0$
4) $2F^- + 2e^- \rightarrow F_2^0$

Practice 17
Which half-reaction correctly represents an oxidation reaction?
1) $Nb^{5+} + 2e^- \rightarrow Nb^{3+}$
2) $Mn^{4+} + 3e- \rightarrow Mn^{7+}$
3) $Nb^{3+} \rightarrow Nb^0 + 3e^-$
4) $Mn^{4+} \rightarrow Mn^{7+} + 3e^-$

Practice 18
Which half-reaction correctly represents reduction?
1) $Al(s) \rightarrow Al^{3+}(aq) + 3e^-$
2) $H_2(g) + 2e- \rightarrow 2H^+(aq)$
3) $I_2(s) \rightarrow 2I^-(aq) + 2e-$
4) $Cu^{2+}(aq) + 2e^- \rightarrow Cu(s)$

Interpreting Half-reaction Equations

A **half-reaction** provides several information about changes that a substance is going through in a redox reaction. Below, two different half-reaction equations are given. One has electrons on the left and one has electrons on the right. Each half-reaction equation is interpreted by describing the changes that the species is going through.

Reduction half-reaction
Equation with electrons on the LEFT

$$C^0 + 4e^- \rightarrow C^{4-}$$

C^0 atom gains 4 electrons to become C^{4-} ion.

C^0 oxidation number decreases from 0 to -4

C^0 is the reduced substance, and also the oxidizing agent.

The number of electrons gained (4) is the difference between the two oxidation states: $0 - (-4) = 4$ electrons

Oxidation half-reaction
Equation with electrons on the RIGHT

$$Sb^{3+} \rightarrow Sb^{5+} + 2e^-$$

Sb^{3+} loses 2 electrons to become Sb^{5+}.

Sb^{3+} oxidation number increases from +3 to +5

Sb^{3+} is the oxidized substance, and also the reducing agent.

The number of electrons lost (2) is the difference between the two oxidation states: $+5 - +3 = 2$ electrons

---

Practice 19
A reduced substance in oxidation and reduction reactions
1) gains electrons and has a decrease in oxidation number
2) gains electrons and has an increase in oxidation number
3) loses electrons and has a decrease in oxidation number
4) loses electrons and has an increase in oxidation number

Practice 20
Which change in oxidation number represents oxidation?
1) 0 to -1   3) -2 to -1
2) 0 to -2   4) -2 to -3

Practice 21
In which oxidation number change would a species in a redox reaction gains the most number of electrons?
1) +3 to -1   3) 0 to +4
2) +5 to +3   4) +3 to +7

Practice 22
When Cr^{4+} changes to Cr^{2+}, there will be
1) 6 electrons gained   3) 2 electrons gained
2) 6 electrons lost   4) 2 electrons lost

Practice 23
Given the half reaction equation below

$$Fe^{3+} + 3e^- \rightarrow Fe$$

Fe^{3+} is
1) reduced by gaining 3 electrons
2) reduced by losing 3 electrons
3) oxidized by gaining 3 electrons
4) oxidized by losing 3 electrons

Practice 24
Complete the equations below

$$2N^{3-} \rightarrow N_2^0 + \underline{\hspace{3cm}}$$

$$\underline{\hspace{3cm}} + 4e^- \rightarrow Cr^{2+}$$

Interpreting Redox Reactions

A redox equation can be given in one of two forms as shown below.

Redox equation 1 $Mg^0 + Al^{3+} \rightarrow Mg^{2+} + Al^0$ Oxidation numbers are already assigned to the elements.

Redox equation 2 $Ca + H_2SO_4 \rightarrow CaSO_4 + H_2$ Oxidation number must be assigned to each element.

Many different questions can be asked about a given redox reaction. You may be asked to determine the oxidized or reduced species of a reaction, or the number of electrons lost or gained.

TIP: When determining oxidized or reduced species in a redox reaction, consider the following about the equation given:

Oxidized substance: The substance *left* of the arrow with the *smaller charge.*

Reduced substance: The substance *left* of the arrow with the *greater charge.*

The above two redox reactions are interpreted below.

3Mg⁰ + **2Al³⁺**		⟶ **3Mg²⁺** + **2Al⁰**
Mg^0 has a *smaller* charge than Al^{3+}.	Al^{3+} has a *larger* charge than Mg^0	Species to the *right* of the arrow in a redox equation (ex. Mg^{2+} and Al^0) are the results of species on the *left* losing and gaining electrons. Therefore, species on the *right* are neither oxidized nor reduced.
Therefore:	*Therefore:*	
Mg^0 is oxidized.	Al^{3+} is reduced.	
Mg^0 loses 2 electrons.	Al^{3+} gains 3 electrons.	
Mg^0 is also the reducing agent.	Al^{3+} is also the oxidizing agent.	
Mg^0 oxidation number increases from 0 to +2.	Al^{3+} oxidation number decreases from +3 to 0 .	
Oxidation half-reaction: $Mg^0 \rightarrow Mg^{2+} + 2e\text{-}$	*Reduction half-reaction:* $Al^{3+} + 3e\text{-} \rightarrow Al^0$	

Note: For the equation below, oxidation numbers are **correctly assigned** (according to rules) to elements before it can be interpreted.

Ca + H_2SO_4 ⟶ $CaSO_4$ + H_2		
Assigned oxidation numbers 0 +1 +6 -2 +2 +6 -2 0		
Ca + H_2SO_4 ⟶ $CaSO_4$ + H_2		
Ca^0 has a *smaller* charge than H^+.	H^+ has a *greater* charge than Ca^0.	Species to the *right* of the arrow in a redox equation (ex. Ca^{2+} and H_2^0) are the results of species on the *left* losing and gaining electrons. Therefore, species on the *right* are neither oxidized nor reduced.
Therefore:	*Therefore:*	
Ca^0 is oxidized.	H^+ is reduced.	
Ca^0 loses 2 electrons.	H^+ gains 1 electron.	
Ca^0 is also the reducing agent.	H^+ is also the oxidizing agent.	
Ca^0 oxidation number increases from 0 to +2.	H^+ oxidation number decreases from +1 to 0.	The oxidation numbers of S and O did not change. Therefore, S and O are neither oxidized nor reduced.
Oxidation half-reaction: $Ca^0 \rightarrow Ca^{2+} + 2e\text{-}$	*Reduction half-reaction:* $2H^+ + 2e\text{-} \rightarrow H_2^0$	

                           ©2017 E3 Scholastic Publishing. All Rights Reserved

Interpreting Redox Reactions: Practice Questions

Practice 25

Consider the oxidation-reduction reaction: Co^0 + Cu^{2+} $\rightarrow$ Co^{2+} + Cu
Which species is reduced?
1) Co^0 2) Cu^0 3) Co^{2+} 4) Cu^{2+}

Practice 26

In the oxidation-reduction reaction, Zn + Ni^{2+} $\rightarrow$ Zn^{2+} + Ni ,
Which species is losing electrons?
1) Zn 2) Ni^{2+} 3) Zn^{2+} 4) Ni

Practice 27

Given the reaction: Pb + $2Ag^+$ $\rightarrow$ Pb^{2+} + $2Ag$
The lead atom is
1) reduced by losing 1 electrons   3) oxidized by losing 2 electrons
2) reduced by gaining 1 electrons   4) oxidized by gaining 2 electrons

Practice 28

In the redox reaction: $3Cu^{2+}$ + $2Al$ $\rightarrow$ $3Cu$ + $2Al^{3+}$
The reduction half-reaction is
1) Cu^{2+} + $2e^-$ $\rightarrow$ Cu 3) Al + $3e^-$ $\rightarrow$ Al^{3+}
2) Cu^{2+} $\rightarrow$ Cu + $2e^-$ 4) Al $\rightarrow$ Al^{3+} + $3e^-$

Practice 29

In the oxidation-reduction reaction: Fe + $2AgCl$ $\rightarrow$ $2Ag$ + $FeCl_2$
Which species is oxidized?
1) Fe^{3+} 2) Fe^0 3) Cl^- 4) Ag^+

Practice 30

Given the balanced equation representing a reaction:
     Fe_2O_3 + $2Al$ $\rightarrow$ Al_2O_3 + $2Fe$
During this reaction, the oxidation number of Fe changes from
1) +2 to 0 as electrons are transferred   3) +3 to 0 as electrons are transferred
2) +2 to 0 as protons are transferred   4) +3 to 0 as protons are transferred

Practice 31

Given the oxidation-reduction reaction: $Co(s)$ + $PbCl_2(aq)$ $\rightarrow$ $CoCl_2(aq)$ + $Pb(s)$
Which statement correctly describes the oxidation and reduction that occur?
1) $Co(s)$ is oxidized and $Cl^-(aq)$ is reduced.   3) $Co(s)$ is reduced and $Cl^-(aq)$ is oxidized.
2) $Co(s)$ is oxidized and $Pb^{2+}(aq)$ is reduced.   4) $Co(s)$ is reduced and $Pb^{2+}(aq)$ is oxidized.

Practice 32

In the chemical reaction: $2AgNO_3(aq)$ + $Cu(s)$ $\rightarrow$ $Cu(NO_3)_2(aq)$ + $2Ag(s)$
Which half-reaction equation correctly shows oxidation?
1) $2Ag^+(aq)$ $\rightarrow$ $2Ag(s)$ + $2e^-$ 3) $Cu(s)$ $\rightarrow$ $Cu^{2+}(aq)$ + $2e^-$
2) $2Ag(s)$ $\rightarrow$ $2Ag^+(aq)$ + $2e^-$ 4) $Cu^{2+}(aq)$ $\rightarrow$ $Cu(s)$ + $2e^-$

Base your answers to questions 33 and 34 on the following redox reaction, which occurs spontaneously.

$$Zn + Fe^{3+} \rightarrow Zn^{2+} + Fe$$

33. State what happens to the number of protons in a Zn atom when it changes to Zn^{2+} as the redox reaction occurs.

34. Which species in this reaction is losing electrons?

Base your answers to practice questions 35 and 36 on the information below.

In a laboratory investigation, magnesium reacts with hydrochloric acid to produce hydrogen gas and magnesium chloride. This reaction is represented by the unbalanced equation below.

$$Mg(s) + HCl(aq) \rightarrow H_2(g) + MgCl_2(aq)$$

35. Write a balanced half-reaction equation for the reduction that occurs.

36. Compare the number of electrons lost and gained by species in this reaction.

Base your answers to practice questions 37 through 39 on the information below.

In a laboratory investigation, a student constructs a voltaic cell with iron and copper electrodes. Another student constructs a voltaic cell with zinc and iron electrodes. Testing the cells during operation enables the students to write the balanced ionic equations below.

Cell with iron and copper electrodes: $Cu^{2+}(aq) + Fe(s) \rightarrow Cu(s) + Fe^{2+}(aq)$

Cell with zinc and iron electrodes: $Fe^{2+}(aq) + Zn(s) \rightarrow Fe(s) + Zn^{2+}(aq)$

37. State evidence from the balanced equation for the cell with iron and copper electrodes that indicates the reaction in the cell is an oxidation-reduction reaction.

38. Identify the particles transferred between Fe^{2+} and Zn during the reaction in the cell with zinc and iron electrodes.

39. Write a balanced half-reaction equation for the reduction that takes place in the cell with zinc and iron electrodes.

©2017 E3 Scholastic Publishing. All Rights Reserved

Lesson 3 - Electrochemistry

Electrochemistry is the study of relationships between redox chemical reactions and electrical energy. When a substance in a redox reaction is oxidized, the electrons that are lost are gained by the reduced substance. If a redox reaction system is set up so that there are paths for the electrons and ions to flow, electrical current can be produced. A *battery* is a good example of a system that is set up to produce electrical energy from a redox reaction.

In this lesson of topic 11, you will learn about redox reactions that produce electrical energy and those that use electrical energy.

Electrochemical Cells
Voltaic and Electrolytic Cells

An **electrochemical cell** is a device or system that can either produce electrical energy from a chemical reaction or use electrical energy to force a chemical reaction. Voltaic and electrolytic cells are types of electrochemical cells.

Voltaic Cells: *Chemical to Electrical Energy*

A **voltaic cell** is a type of cell in which a spontaneous redox reaction occurs to produce electrical energy.

In voltaic cells:
• Chemical energy is converted to electrical energy.
• Reaction is spontaneous and exothermic.
• Oxidation and reduction occur in two separate cells.
• A salt bridge connects the two half-cells and provides a path for ions to flow between cells.
• A battery is an example of a voltaic cell.

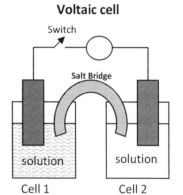

Electrolytic Cells: *Electrical to Chemical Energy*

An **electrolytic cell** is a type of cell in which electrical energy is used to force a nonspontaneous redox reaction to occur.

In electrolytic cells:
• Electrical energy is converted to chemical energy.
• External energy source (such as a battery) provides the energy needed to force the reaction.
• Reaction is nonspontaneous and endothermic.
• Both oxidation and reduction occur in one cell.
• Electrolytic reduction, electroplating of metals, and electrolysis of water use electrolytic cell processes.

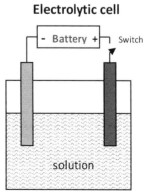

Anode, Cathode, and Salt Bridge.

Oxidation and reduction reactions that occur in electrochemical cells take place at specific sites called electrodes.

Electrodes are sites on electrochemical cells where oxidation and reduction take place. Anode and cathode are the two electrodes in electrochemical cells. The anode and cathode of a cell are labeled with positive (+) and negative (-) signs. The type of cell determines which electrode is positive and which electrode is negative.

Anode: *Oxidation Site*
The anode is the electrode where oxidation occurs in both the voltaic and electrolytic cells.
The anode, therefore, is the site on electrochemical cells where *electrons are lost.*

Voltaic cells: Anode is Negative (-).

Electrolytic cells: Anode is Positive (+).

Cathode: *Reduction Site*
The cathode is the electrode where reduction occurs in both voltaic and electrolytic cells.
The cathode, therefore, is the site on electrochemical cells where *electrons are gained.*

Voltaic cells: Cathode is Positive (+).

Electrolytic cells: Cathode is Negative (-).

External conduit (Wire): *Permits the Flow of Electrons from Anode to Cathode*
The electrons that are lost at the anode flow to the cathode via the external conduit, which is usually any electrical wire that connects the two electrodes. The external conduit is present in both the voltaic and electrolytic cells.

Salt bridge: *Permits Flow of Ions (Voltaic only).*
The salt bridge is any porous substance that connects the solutions in the two half-cells of a voltaic cell. Positive and negative ions flow (migrate) between the two cells via the salt bridge. The flow of ions is necessary to keep the two half-cells neutral, and for the appropriate functioning of a voltaic cell. A salt bridge is not present in electrolytic cells.

Battery or Power Source: *Provides Energy (Electrolytic, only).*
In electrolytic cell processes, energy is needed to force the non-spontaneous redox reaction to occur. Without an external energy source, half-reactions will not occur in electrolytic cells.

Use these codes to help you remember key information:

LEO:	Loss of Electrons is Oxidation	**APE:**	Anode is Positive in Electrolytic
GER:	Gain of Electrons is Reduction.	**VAN:**	Voltaic, Anode is Negative
An Ox:	Anode is for Oxidation	**CVP:**	Cathode in Voltaic is Positive
Red Cat:	Reduction at Cathode	**CEN:**	Cathode in Electrolytic is Negative

         ©2017 E3 Scholastic Publishing. All Rights Reserved

Electrochemical Cells: Practice Questions

Practice 40
Which is true of anode in any electrochemical cell?
1) The anode is the site for oxidation.
2) The anode is the site for reduction.
3) The anode is the site for both oxidation and reduction.
4) The anode is the site where protons are lost and gained.

Practice 41
The negative electrode in all electrolytic cells is the
1) cathode, at which oxidation occurs
2) cathode, at which reduction occurs
3) anode, at which oxidation occurs
4) anode, at which reduction occurs

Practice 42
An electrochemical cell setup consists of two half cells connected by an external conductor and salt bridge. The function of the salt bridge is to
1) block a path for the flow of electrons
2) block a path for the flow of ions
3) provide a path for the flow of electrons
4) provide a path for the flow of ions

Practice 43
What kind of reaction occurs in an operating electrolytic cell?
1) Non-spontaneous oxidation-reduction.
2) Spontaneous oxidation-reduction.
3) Non-spontaneous oxidation, only.
4) Spontaneous reduction, only.

Practice 44
In both the voltaic and the electrolytic cell, the anode is the electrode at which
1) reduction occurs and electrons are lost
2) reduction occurs and electrons are gained
3) oxidation occurs and electrons are lost
4) oxidation occurs and electrons are gained

Practice 45
In an electrolytic cell, the positive electrode is the
1) anode, at which reduction occurs
2) anode, at which oxidation occurs
3) cathode, at which reduction occurs
4) cathode, at which oxidation occurs

Practice 46
Which energy conversion occurs during the operation of a voltaic cell?
1) Chemical energy is spontaneously converted to electrical energy.
2) Chemical energy is converted to electrical energy only when an external power source is provided.
3) Electrical energy is spontaneously converted to chemical energy.
4) Electrical energy is converted to chemical energy only when an external power source is provided.

Voltaic Cells: *Convert Chemical Energy to Electrical Energy*

Below is a diagram representing a voltaic cell. The components of the cell are labeled on the diagram. All components must be present and correctly connected for a voltaic cell to operate. The redox equation representing the reaction taking place in this cell is given at the bottom of the diagram. Table J (Activity Series) can be used to determine the anode and cathode of a voltaic cell.

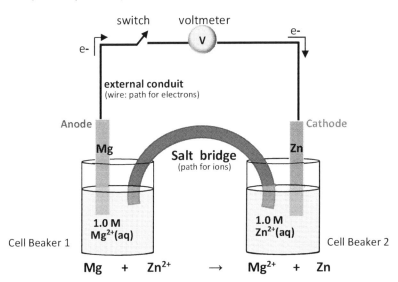

$$Mg \;+\; Zn^{2+} \;\rightarrow\; Mg^{2+} \;+\; Zn$$

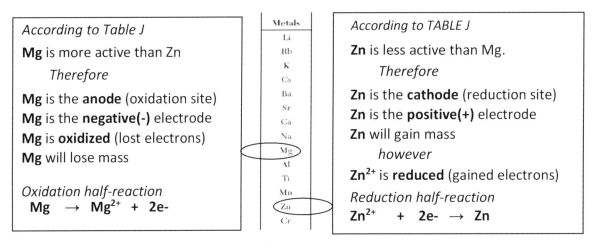

According to Table J

Mg is more active than Zn

   Therefore

Mg is the **anode** (oxidation site)
Mg is the **negative(-)** electrode
Mg is **oxidized** (lost electrons)
Mg will lose mass

Oxidation half-reaction
  $Mg \;\rightarrow\; Mg^{2+} \;+\; 2e\text{-}$

According to TABLE J

Zn is less active than Mg.

   Therefore

Zn is the **cathode** (reduction site)
Zn is the **positive(+)** electrode
Zn will gain mass
   however
Zn^{2+} is **reduced** (gained electrons)

Reduction half-reaction
$Zn^{2+} \;+\; 2e\text{-} \;\rightarrow\; Zn$

How the Voltaic Cell Works

When the switch is closed:
In Cell 1: The more active of the two metals, **Mg (the anode),** will be oxidized by losing its electrons.
   The *oxidation-half* reaction at the anode is: $Mg \;\rightarrow\; Mg^{2+} \;+\; 2e^-$

The wire (external conduit) carries the electrons from Mg anode to Zn cathode.

In Cell 2: The ion of the less active metal, **Zn^{2+},** will be reduced by gaining the electrons lost by Mg.
   Although reduction occurs at **Zn (the cathode)**, it is the Zn^{2+} that is reduced.
   The *reduction-half* reaction at the cathode is: $Zn^{2+} \;+\; 2e\text{-} \;\rightarrow\; Zn$

Electrical energy that is produced is the flow of electrons in the wire from the anode to cathode.

The voltmeter registers the amount of electrical potential energy (voltage) produced by the reaction.
The salt bridge allows ions in the solutions to flow back and forth between Cell 1 and Cell 2 to maintain neutrality of the cell. This is necessary for the voltaic cell to operate.

Voltaic Cells: Practice Questions

Base your answers to practice questions 47 to 53 on the cell diagram below.

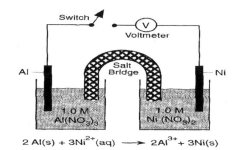

$2 Al(s) + 3Ni^{2+}(aq) \longrightarrow 2Al^{3+} + 3Ni(s)$

47. The cathode in this electrochemical cell is
1) Al atoms   3) Ni atoms
2) Al^{3+} ions   4) Ni^{2+} ions

48. Which particles in this electrochemical cell undergo reduction?
1) Al^{3+} 3) Al
2) Ni^{2+} 4) Ni

49. The loss of electrons occurs at
1) aluminum electrode, because it is the anode
2) aluminum electrode, because it is the cathode
3) nickel electrode, because it is the anode
4) nickel electrode, because it is the cathode

50. Which is true of the electrochemical cell when the switch is closed?
1) Electrons will flow from Ni^{2+} to Ni.
2) Electrons will flow from Al^{3+} to Al .
3) Electrons will flow from Ni to Al.
4) Electrons will flow from Al to Ni.

51. The salt bridge in the electrochemical cell connects
1) Al atom to Ni atom   3) Ni atom to Ni^{2+}ion
2) Al^{3+} ions to Ni^{2+} ions   4) Ni^{2+} ion to Al atom

52. When the switch is closed, which correctly shows the reduction process that takes place?
1) $Al + 3e^- \rightarrow Al^{3+}$ 3) $Ni^{2+} + 2e^- \rightarrow Ni$
2) $Al \rightarrow Al^{3+} + 3e^-$ 4) $Ni^{2+} \rightarrow Ni + 2e^-$

53. Which is true of this cell as the redox reaction is taking place?
1) The mass of Al electrode will increase, and the mass of Ni electrode will decrease.
2) The mass of Al electrode will decrease, and the mass of Ni electrode will increase.
3) The mass of Al electrode will increase, and the mass of Ni electrode will remain the same.
4) The mass of Al electrode will remain the same, and the mass of Ni electrode will increase.

Base your answers to practice questions 54 to 58 on the cell diagram below.

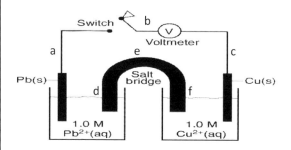

54. This reaction that will occur in this cell is
1) redox, and non-spontaneous
2) redox, and spontaneous
3) non-redox and spontaneous
4) non-redox and nonspontaneous

55. In the electrochemical diagram, Pb(s) is the
1) cathode, where oxidation occurs
2) cathode, where reduction occurs
3) anode, where oxidation occurs
4) anode, where reduction occurs

56. In the given electrochemical diagram, the Cu^{2+} ions
1) gain protons
2) lose protons
3) gains electrons
4) lose electrons

57. Which is true of the Pb^{2+} ion in this cell?
1) It is reduced.
2) It is oxidized.
3) It migrates across the salt bridge.
4) it migrates across the external conductor.

58. When the switch is closed, which letters show the path and direction of the electrons?
1) abc
2) def
3) cba
4) fed

Electrolytic Cells: *Converts Electrical Energy to Chemical Energy*

An electrolytic cell is set up to use electrical energy to force a nonspontaneous chemical reaction to occur. A battery provides the energy needed to force the reaction. Three common electrolytic processes are described below.

Electrolysis of water is a process that splits water molecules to produce oxygen and hydrogen.

$$2H_2O(\ell) \quad + \quad electricity \quad \rightarrow \quad 2H_2(g) \quad + \quad O_2(g)$$

Electrolytic reduction process is used to obtain a reactive metal from its fused salt. Elements in Group 1 and Group 2 of the Periodic Table, because of their high reactivity, are generally obtained from this process.

$$2NaBr(\ell) \quad + \quad electricity \quad \rightarrow \quad 2Na(s) \quad + \quad Br_2(g)$$

     fused salt   *a highly reactive*
                                                     element is obtained

Electroplating is a process by which ion of a desired metal is reduced to produce the metal. The metal that is produced is coated onto the surface of another object.

$$Au^+(aq) \quad + \quad e\text{-} \quad \rightarrow \quad Au(s)$$

Electrolytic reduction cell diagram   *Electroplating cell diagram*

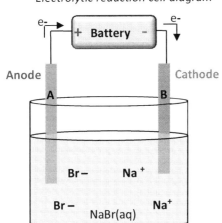
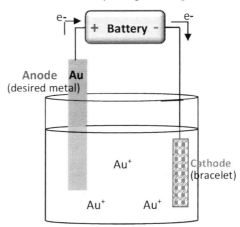

In any given electrolytic cell, you should be able to identify the different components of the cell. You should also be able to identify the oxidized and reduced substances based on the elements and ions taking parts in the reaction. The components for above two diagrams are identified below. Follow these examples for similar cells.

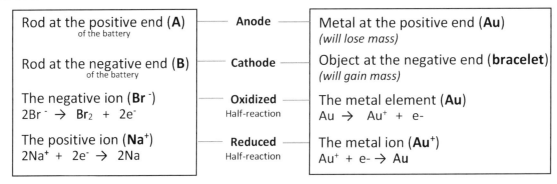

Rod at the positive end (**A**) *of the battery*	— **Anode** —	Metal at the positive end (**Au**) *(will lose mass)*
Rod at the negative end (**B**) *of the battery*	— **Cathode** —	Object at the negative end (**bracelet**) *(will gain mass)*
The negative ion (**Br⁻**) $2Br^- \rightarrow Br_2 + 2e^-$	— **Oxidized** — Half-reaction	The metal element (**Au**) $Au \rightarrow Au^+ + e\text{-}$
The positive ion (**Na⁺**) $2Na^+ + 2e^- \rightarrow 2Na$	— **Reduced** — Half-reaction	The metal ion (**Au⁺**) $Au^+ + e\text{-} \rightarrow Au$

©2017 E3 Scholastic Publishing. All Rights Reserved

Electrolytic Cells: **Practice Questions**

Base your answers to practice questions 59 to 64 on the cell diagram below.

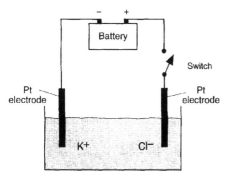

59. Which is reduced?
   1) K^+ 2) Cl^- 3) K   4) Pt

60. The cathode in this diagram is the
   1) positive electrode, where oxidation occurs
   2) negative electrode, where oxidation occurs
   3) positive electrode, where reduction occurs
   4) negative electrode, where reduction occurs

61. When the switch is closed in this cell, the
   1) Cl^- ions migrate toward the cathode, where they will lose electrons
   2) Cl^- ions migrate toward the cathode, where they will gain electrons
   3) Cl^- ions migrate toward the anode, where they will lose electrons
   4) Cl^- ions migrate toward the anode, where they will gain electrons

62. Which equation best represents the reaction at the negative electrode?
   1) $K^+(aq) \rightarrow K(s) + e^-$
   2) $K^+(aq) + e^- \rightarrow K(s)$
   3) $2Cl^-(aq) \rightarrow Cl_2(g) + 2e^-$
   4) $2Cl^-(aq) + 2e^- \rightarrow Cl_2(g)$

63. The redox reaction that occurs in this cell is best described as
   1) spontaneous and endothermic
   2) spontaneous and exothermic
   3) non-spontaneous and endothermic
   4) non-spontaneous and exothermic

64. When the switched is closed in the cell, what will be the direction of electrons flow?
   1) abc   3) adc
   2) cba   4) cda

Base your answers to practice questions 65 to 70 on the cell diagram below.

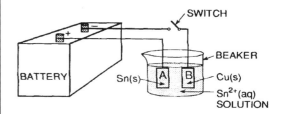

65. Which species are oxidized and reduced in this cell?
   1) Sn^{2+} is oxidized, and Sn is reduced.
   2) Sn is oxidized, and Sn^{2+} is reduced.
   3) Cu is oxidized, and Sn is reduced.
   4) Sn is oxidized, and Cu is reduced.

66. When the switch is closed, Sn^{2+} is
   1) oxidized, and Sn will be coated with Cu
   2) reduced, and Sn will be coated with Cu
   3) oxidized, and Cu will be coated with Sn
   4) reduced, and Cu will be coated with Sn

67. Which best explains why the mass of electrode B increases as a redox reaction occurs in this cell?
   1) Electrode B is oxidized.
   2) Electrode B is losing electrons.
   3) Electrode B is coated with more copper.
   4) Electrode B is coated with tin.

68. Which statement is true of electrode A when the switch is closed in this cell diagram?
   1) A is the cathode, where oxidation is occurring.
   2) A is the cathode, where reduction is occurring.
   3) A is the anode, where oxidation is occurring.
   4) A is the anode, where reduction is occurring.

69. When the switch is closed, the half-reaction that occurs at electrode B is represent by which equation?
   1) $Sn(s) + 2e^- \rightarrow Sn^{2+}(aq)$
   2) $Sn^{2+}(aq) + 2e^- \rightarrow Sn(s)$
   3) $Sn(s) \rightarrow Sn^{2+}(aq) + 2e^-$
   4) $Sn^{2+}(aq) \rightarrow Sn(s) + 2e^-$

70. The battery in this cell acts as the
   1) external conduit   3) salt bridge
   2) external energy source   4) voltmeter

Electrochemical Cells: **Summary Table**

Below is a summary of voltaic and electrolytic cells. Use this table for a quick review and comparisons of the two electrochemical cells.

Concept Facts: Study to remember

		Voltaic	Electrolytic
	Diagrams		
D i f f e r e n c e s	**Example redox equation**	$Pb + Cu^{2+} \rightarrow Pb^{2+} + Cu$	$2H_2O + electricity \rightarrow 2H_2 + O_2$
	Type of reaction	Spontaneous redox. Exothermic	Non-spontaneous redox. Endothermic
	Energy conversion	Chemical to electrical energy	Electrical to chemical energy
	Anode (site for oxidation)	Negative (-) electrode	Positive (+) electrode
	Cathode (site for reduction)	Positive (+) electrode	Negative (-) electrode
	Half-Reactions occur in	Two separate cells	One cell
	Salt bridge present?	Yes (connects the two half-cells and permits flow of ions).	No
	Usages and examples	Battery	Electroplating Electrolytic reduction Electrolysis
S i m i l a r i t i e s	**Oxidation** (losing of electrons) at	Anode (-) (loses mass)	Anode (+) (loses mass)
	Reduction (gaining of electrons) at	Cathode (+) (gains mass)	Cathode (-) (gains mass)
	Direction of electron flow	Anode to Cathode	Anode to Cathode

Practice 71
Given the reaction:

$$Mg(s) + FeSO_4(aq) \rightarrow Fe(s) + MgSO_4(aq)$$

The reaction would most likely occur in
1) a voltaic cell, and will produce energy
2) a voltaic cell, and will absorb energy
3) an electrolytic cell, and will produce energy
4) an electrolytic cell, and will absorb energy

Base your answers to practice questions 72 through 75 on the information below and on your knowledge of chemistry.

A small digital clock can be powered by a battery made from two potatoes and some household materials. The "potato clock" battery consists of two cells connected in a way to produce enough electricity to allow the clock to operate. In each cell, zinc atoms react to form zinc ions. Hydrogen ions from phosphoric acid in the potatoes react to form hydrogen gas. The labeled diagram and balanced ionic equation below show the reaction, the materials, and connections necessary to make a "potato clock" battery.

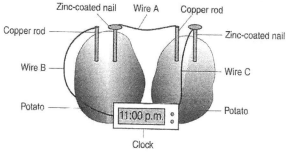

$$Zn(s) + 2H^+(aq) \rightarrow Zn^{2+}(aq) + H_2(g)$$

72. What type of an electrochemical cell is a "potato clock" battery?

73. State the direction of electron flow in wire A as the two cells operate.

74. Write a balanced half-reaction equation for the oxidation that occurs in the "potato clock" battery.

75. Explain why phosphoric acid is needed for the battery to operate.

Base your answers to practice questions 76 through 78 on the information below.

Metallic elements are obtained from their ores by reduction. Some metals, such as zinc, lead, iron, and copper, can be obtained by heating their oxides with carbon.

More active metals, such as aluminum, magnesium, and sodium, cannot be reduced by carbon. These metals can be obtained by the electrolysis of their molten (melted) ores. The diagram below represents an incomplete cell for the electrolysis of molten NaCl. The equation below represents the reaction that occurs when the completed cell operates.

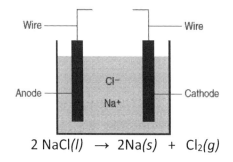

$$2\,NaCl(l) \rightarrow 2Na(s) + Cl_2(g)$$

76. Identify the component required for the electrolysis of molten NaCl that is missing from the cell diagram.

77. When the completed cell operates, which species will be oxidize?

78. Write a balanced half-reaction equation for the reduction that will occur when the completed cell operates.

Lesson 4 – Spontaneous Reactions and the Activity Series

A **spontaneous reaction** is a reaction that will take place (occur) on its own under a specific set of conditions.

In Topic 8 (Acids and Bases) you learned that certain metals will react spontaneously with an acid to produce hydrogen gas.

In Topic 9 (Kinetics and Equilibrium), you learned that a reaction is spontaneous if the reaction will lead to a lower energy and higher entropy products.

In this lesson you will learn how to use the Activity Series Reference Table J to predict which reactions will occur spontaneous.

Spontaneous and Non-spontaneous Reactions

Spontaneous Redox Reactions
Single replacement reactions are redox reactions. A single replacement reaction will occur spontaneously when the **free element** reactant is more reactive than the **similar element** of the compound.

Examples of spontaneous redox reactions.

Zn   +   **Fe(NO$_3$)$_2$**   →   **Zn(NO$_3$)$_2$**   +   **Fe**
                  ↓
free element   *similar element to Zn*

Cl$_2$ +   **SnBr$_2$**   →   **SnCl$_2$**   +   **Br$_2$**
                  ↓
free element   *similar element to Cl$_2$*

In each reaction above, the free element is more reactive (higher up on Table J) than the similar element. Zn can replace Fe and Cl can replace Br. These reactions will occur spontaneously under normal conditions.

Nonspontaneous Redox Reactions
A reaction is nonspontaneous if the free element is less reactive than the element it is supposed to replace in the compound.

Example of nonspontaneous reactions

Fe   +   **Zn(NO$_3$)$_2$**   →   **Fe(NO$_3$)$_2$**   +   **Zn**
                  ↓
free element   *similar element to Fe*

Br$_2$ +   **SnCl$_2$**   →   **SnBr$_2$**   +   **Cl$_2$**
                  ↓
free element   *similar element to Br$_2$*

In each reaction above, the free element is less reactive (lower down on Table J) than the similar element to be replaced. Fe cannot replace Zn and Br cannot replace Cl. These reactions *will not* occur spontaneously under normal conditions.

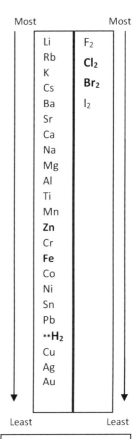

Reference Table J
Activity Series

Most	Most
Li	F$_2$
Rb	Cl$_2$
K	Br$_2$
Cs	I$_2$
Ba	
Sr	
Ca	
Na	
Mg	
Al	
Ti	
Mn	
Zn	
Cr	
Fe	
Co	
Ni	
Sn	
Pb	
**H$_2$	
Cu	
Ag	
Au	
Least	Least

** **Activity series based on Hydrogen standard**

         ©2017 E3 Scholastic Publishing. All Rights Reserved

Spontaneous Reactions: **Practice Questions**

Concept Task: Be able to predict spontaneous and nonspontaneous reactions based on the Activity Series Table J.

Practice 79

Based on Reference Table J, which reaction will take place spontaneously?

1) $Ni^{2+}(aq) + Pb(s) \rightarrow Ni(s) + Pb^{2+}(aq)$
2) $Sr^{2+}(aq) + Sn(s) \rightarrow Sr(s) + Sn^{2+}(aq)$
3) $Au^{3+}(aq) + Al(s) \rightarrow Au(s) + Al^{3+}(aq)$
4) $Fe^{2+}(aq) + Cu(s) \rightarrow Fe(s) + Cu^{2+}(aq)$

Practice 80

According to information from Reference Table J, which redox reaction occurs spontaneously?

1) $Cu(s) + 2H^{+}(aq) \rightarrow Cu^{2+}(aq) + H_2(g)$
2) $Mg(s) + 2H^{+}(aq) \rightarrow Mg^{2+}(aq) + H_2(g)$
3) $2Ag(s) + 2H^{+}(aq) \rightarrow 2Ag^{+}(aq) + H_2(g)$
4) $2Au(s) + 2H^{+}(aq) \rightarrow 2Au^{+}(aq) + H_2(g)$

Practice 81

Based on Reference Table J, which redox reaction will occur spontaneously?

1) $Br_2 + 2KI \rightarrow 2Br + I_2$
2) $I_2 + 2KCl \rightarrow 2KI + Cl_2$
3) $Cl_2 + 2KF \rightarrow 2KCl + F_2$
4) $I_2 + 2KBr \rightarrow 2KI + Br_2$

Practice 82

Referring to the Activity Series on Reference Table J, which reaction will not occur spontaneously under standard conditions?

1) $Sn(s) + 2HF(aq) \rightarrow SnF_2(aq) + H_2(g)$
2) $Mg(s) + 2HF(aq) \rightarrow MgF_2(aq) + H_2(g)$
3) $Ba(s) + 2HF(aq) \rightarrow BaF_2(aq) + H_2(g)$
4) $2Cu(s) + 2HF(aq) \rightarrow CuF_2(aq) + H_2(g)$

Practice 83

Which metal, according to Reference Table J, will react spontaneously with Al^{3+}?

1) Ca(s)   2) Cu(s)   3) Cr(s)   4) Co(s)

Using the Activity Series Table J to Determine Most Easily Oxidized and Reduced

Some elements are more easily oxidized, others are more easily reduced. The Activity Series Table J can be used to determine which element or ion is most likely to be oxidized or reduced. On the information below, the element or ion in parentheses is in comparison to all the elements listed on Table J.

Metals

Most easily oxidized: The metal closest to the top of Table J (Li).

Most easily reduced: Ion of the metal closest to the bottom (Au^+).

• An element on the top will react spontaneously with an ion of an element below it.
  For example: Zn will react spontaneously with Fe^{2+}. When the reaction occurs:
            Zn will cause Fe^{2+} to be reduced to Fe atoms.
            Fe^{2+} will cause Zn to be oxidized to Zn^{2+} .

Nonmetals

Most easily oxidized: Ion of the nonmetal closest to the bottom (I^-).

Most easily reduced: Nonmetal closest to the top (F_2).

Using Activity Series Table J: **Practice Questions**

Practice 84
According to Reference Table J, which of these ions is most easily reduced?
1) Ca^{2+} 2) Cr^{3+} 3) Co^{2+} 4) Cs^+

Practice 85
Based on Reference Table J, which most easily oxidized?
1) Ba   2) Sr   3) Ca   4) Mg

Practice 86
According to Table J, which ion is least easily oxidized?
1) Br^- 2) Cl^- 3) F^- 4) I^-

Practice 87
Which metal will reduce Zn^{2+} to Zn?
1) Mn   2) Cr   3) H_2 4) Ag

Practice 88
Which ion is most likely to oxidize Cs to Cs^+?
1) Li^+ 2) Rb^+ 3) K^+ 4) Na^{2+}

Base your answers to practice questions 89 and 90 on the information below.

The outer structure of the Statue of Liberty is made of copper metal. The framework is made of iron. Over time, a thin green layer (patina) forms on the copper surface. When copper oxidized to form this patina layer, the copper atoms became copper(II) ions (Cu^{2+}).

89. Write a balanced half-reaction for this oxidation of copper.

90. Where the iron framework came in contact with the copper surface, a reaction occurred in which iron was oxidized. Using information from Reference Table *J*, explain why the iron was oxidized.

Base your answer to the following question on the information below.

Because tap water is slightly acidic, water pipes made of iron corrode over time, as shown by the balanced ionic equation below:

$$2Fe + 6H^+ \rightarrow 2Fe^{3+} + 3H_2$$

91. Explain, in terms of chemical reactivity, why copper pipes are *less* likely to corrode than iron pipes.

Base your answers to practice questions 92 through 94 on the voltaic cell diagram below.

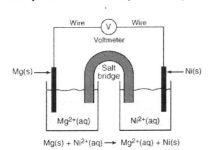

Mg(s) + Ni²⁺(aq) → Mg²⁺(aq) + Ni(s)

92. Identify *one* metal from your Reference Tables that is more easily oxidized than Mg(s).

93. Identify one piece of information in the diagram that indicates this system is a voltaic cell.

94. Compare the number of moles of electrons lost to the number of moles of electrons gained during the reaction in the cell.

       ©2017 E3 Scholastic Publishing. All Rights Reserved

Vocabulary

Lesson 1: Oxidation Number

Oxidation number

Lesson 2: Redox Reactions

Redox

Oxidation

Reduction

Oxidized substance

Reduced substance

Oxidizing agent

Reducing agent

Half-reaction

Lesson 3: Electrochemistry

Electrochemical cell

Voltaic cell

Electrolytic cell

Electroplating

Electrolytic reduction

Electrolysis

Electrode

Anode

Cathode

Salt Bridge

External conduit

Lesson 4: Spontaneous Reactions and the Activity Series

Spontaneous reaction

©2017 E3 Scholastic Publishing. All Rights Reserved

1. 2

2. 2

3. 1

4. 4

5. 2

6. 3

7. 1

8. +2, 2

9. CO_2

10. +5, 5

11. It contains one K^+ and one Cl^- ions.
The sum of positive and negative charges is equal to zero.

12. 3

13. 1

14. 2

15. 3

16. 2

17. 4

18. 4

19. 1

20. 3

21. 1

22. 3

23. 1

24. $2N^{3-} \rightarrow N_2^0 + \underline{6e^-}$

$\underline{Cr^{6+}} + 4e^- \rightarrow Cr^{2+}$

25. 4

26. 1

27. 3

28. 4

29. 4

30. 3

31. 2

32. 3

33. The number of protons stays the same.

34. zinc, Zn

35. $2H^+ + 2e^- \rightarrow H_2$

36. The number of electrons lost *is the same* as the number of electrons gained.
Equal. The same.

37. The oxidation number of Cu^{2+} changes to 0. **Iron's oxidation state changes from zero to +2.**
Oxidation numbers change during the reaction because electrons are transferred.

38. electrons

39. $Zn(s) \rightarrow Zn^{2+}(aq) + 2e^-$

40. 1

41. 2

42. 4

43. 1

44. 3

45. 2

46. 1

47. 3

48. 2

49. 1

50. 4

51. 2

52. 3

53. 2

54. 1

55. 3

56. 3

57. 3

58. 1

59. 1

60. 4

61. 3

62. 3

63. 3

64. 2

65. 4

66. 4

67. 4

68. 2

69. 2

70. 2

71. 1

72. Voltaic cell. Galvanic cell.

73. zinc-coated nail to copper rod
zinc to copper
Zn to Cu

74. $Zn \rightarrow Zn^{2+} + 2e^-$

75. Phosphoric acid provides the H^+ ion that is needed.

76. battery, power source

77. Na^+, sodium ion

78. $2Cl^- + 2e^- \rightarrow Cl_2$

79. 3

80. 2

81. 4

82. 4

83. 1

84. 3

85. 1

86. 3

87. 1

88. 4

89. $Cu \rightarrow Cu^{2+} + 2e^-$

90. The iron was oxidized because it is more reactive than copper.
Fe is more reactive than Cu.

91. Copper is less reactive than iron. Cu is less likely to react with the acidic water.

92. Any element from Li to Na on Table J.

93. The presence of a salt bridge. The presence of a voltmeter (V).
Two cells. Two beakers.

94. The number of moles of electrons lost and gained is the same.
Equal moles of electrons are lost and gained.

©2017 E3 Scholastic Publishing. All Rights Reserved

Topic 12
Nuclear Chemistry

Lesson 1: Nuclear Particles

Lesson 2: Types of Nuclear Reactions

Lesson 3: Half-life and Half-life Calculations

Lesson 1 – Nuclear Particles and Stability of the Nucleus

Nuclear chemistry is the study of changes that occur in the nucleus of atoms.

The nucleus and nuclear particles of an atom were discussed in Topic 3; The Atomic Structure.

The information below is important to understanding nuclear reactions.

• Protons and neutrons are found in the nucleus of atoms.

• The number of protons or atomic number identifies each element.

• The number of neutrons plus protons determines the mass number of an atom.

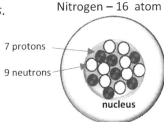

Nitrogen – 16 atom

7 protons

9 neutrons

nucleus

Any change to the nucleus of an atom likely involves a change in the number of protons and/or neutrons. Any change to the nucleus of an atom will change that atom to a different atom. These changes occur by way of nuclear reactions.

A **nuclear reaction** leads to changes in the contents of the nucleus of one or more atoms. *Transmutation, fission* and *fusion* are types of nuclear reactions. These reactions are discussed in lesson 2.

Nuclear Equation

A **nuclear equation** is used to show changes that are taking place during a nuclear reaction.

Information about the nucleus of an atom can be represented using nuclear particle symbols.

Below, a nuclear symbol for an atom of strontium (Sr) is given.

$$^{90}_{38}\text{Sr}$$

90 = mass number = number of protons + neutrons	
Sr symbol for strontium	
38 = atomic number = number of protons	

Nuclear symbols are used in nuclear reaction equations. An example is given below. Note the difference in the three types of equations.

Nuclear change equation: $^{90}_{38}\text{Sr} \longrightarrow \ ^{86}_{36}\text{Rn} \ + \ ^{4}_{2}\text{He}$

Chemical change equation: $\text{KClO}_3(s) \rightarrow 2\text{KCl}(s) \ + \ 3\text{O}_2(g)$

Physical change equation: $\text{CO}_2(s) \ \longrightarrow \ \text{CO}_2(g)$

In this topic, only nuclear changes will be discussed.

Concept Task: Be able to recognize a nuclear reaction equation.

Practice 1
Which of the equation represents a nuclear change?
1) $\text{H}^+ \ + \text{OH}^- \ \longrightarrow \ \text{H}_2\text{O}$
2) $\text{H}_2\text{O} + \text{Na} \longrightarrow \ \text{NaOH} \ + \ \text{H}_2$
3) $\text{NaCl}(s) \ \longrightarrow \ \text{Na}^+(aq) \ + \ \text{Cl}^-(aq)$
4) $^{4}\text{He} \ + \ ^{12}\text{C} \ \longrightarrow \ ^{16}\text{N} \ + \ ^{0}\text{n}$

Practice 2
Which equation is an example of a transmutation?
1) $^{9}\text{Be} \ + \ ^{4}\text{He} \ \longrightarrow \ ^{12}\text{C} \ + \ ^{1}\text{n}$
2) $\text{U} \ + \ 3\text{F}_2 \ \longrightarrow \ \text{UF}_6$
3) $\text{Mg(OH)}_2 \ + \ 2\text{HCl} \longrightarrow 2\text{H}_2\text{O} \ + \ \text{MgCl}_2$
4) $\text{Ca} \ + 2\text{H}_2\text{O} \ \longrightarrow \ \text{Ca(OH)}_2 \ + \ \text{H}_2$

                                                    ©2017 E3 Scholastic Publishing. All Rights Reserved

Nuclear Particles

During nuclear transmutations, particles are absorbed and/or released by the nucleus. The change or transmutation that occur depends on which nuclear particle is absorbed and/or released. *Radiation* or energy are also released during nuclear changes.

Particles and radiation commonly involved in nuclear changes are given on the Table below. Some information on this table can also be found on **Reference Table O.** More information about each particle is further given below the table.

Nuclear Particle	Symbol	Mass	Charge	Penetrating power	Able to be accelerated
Alpha	^4_2He , α	4 amu	+2	Low (weakest)	Yes
Beta	$^0_{-1}e$, $-\beta$	0 amu	-1	Medium	Yes
Positron	$^0_{+1}e$, $+\beta$	0 amu	+1	Medium	Yes
Proton	^1_1p	1 amu	1	Medium	Yes
Gamma	^0_0y	0 amu	0	High (strongest)	No
Neutron	^1_0n	1 amu	0	------	No

Nuclear Chemistry Particles and Radiation

Alpha particle ^4_2He or α

Alpha particles are similar to helium nuclei.
Alpha particles have a mass of 4 amu and a charge of +2.
Alpha particles have the lowest penetrating power of all radiation.

Beta particles $^0_{-1}e$ or $\beta-$

Beta particles are similar to a high-speed electron.
Beta particles have a mass of 0 amu and a charge of -1.
A beta particle is produced when a neutron is converted to a proton.

Positrons $^0_{+1}e$ or $\beta+$

Positrons have a mass of 0 and a charge of +1.
A positron is produced when a proton is converted to a neutron.

Gamma rays ^0_0y

Gamma rays are similar to high energy x-rays.
Gamma rays have a mass of 0 amu and a charge of 0.
Gamma rays have the highest penetrating power of all radiation.

Neutrons ^1_0n

Neutrons have a mass of 1 amu and a charge of 0.
Neutrons are found in the nucleus of atoms.

An **accelerator** is a device that moves charged particles to a high speed. Only charged particles (*alpha, beta, and positron*) can be accelerated.

Penetrating power refers to the strength of a particle to go through a given object. See diagram below.

• Alpha particles have the weakest penetrating power. They can be stopped by a piece of paper.

• Gamma rays have the strongest penetrating power. They can be stopped only by a high-density metal, like lead.

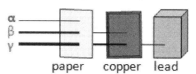

Separation of Particles
Opposites Attract

Nuclear emanations or particles released from a radioactive source can be separated through an electric or a magnetic field. An **electric field** contains positive and negative charged plates as shown below.

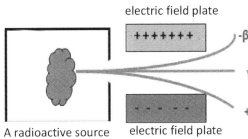

electric field plate

A radioactive source in a lead box.

electric field plate

As particles are released from a radioactive source:

- **Negative particles (β-)** will attract or deflect toward the positive plate(+) of the electric field.

- **Particles with no charge (γ)** will be unaffected by the electric field, and will go straight through.

- **Positive particles (α+)** will attract or deflect toward the negative plate(-) of the electric field.

Nuclear Particles: **Practice Questions**

Practice 3
Which nuclear radiation is similar to high energy X-ray?
1) Beta   3) Alpha
2) Gamma   4) Neutron

Practice 4
Alpha particles and beta particles differ in
1) mass only   3) both mass and charge
2) charge only   4) neither mass nor charge

Practice 5
Which nuclear emission has neither mass nor charge?
1) α   3) β+
2) β-   4) γ

Practice 6
Which list of particles is in order of increasing mass?
1) Proton → Beta → Alpha
2) Alpha → Beta → Proton
3) Beta → Proton → Alpha
4) Proton → Alpha → Beta

Practice 7
Which list is showing the particles arranged in order of increasing penetrating power?
1) Gamma → Beta → Alpha
2) Alpha → Beta → Gamma
3) Beta → Gamma → Alpha
4) Gamma → Alpha → Beta

Practice 8
In which list can all particles be accelerated by an electric field?
1) Alpha, beta, and neutrons.
2) Alpha, protons, and neutrons.
3) Alpha, beta, and protons.
4) Beta, protons, and neutrons.

Practice 9
Which nuclear emission moving through an electric field would be attracted toward a positive electrode?
1) Proton   3) Gamma radiation
2) Beta Particle   4) Alpha particle

Base your answers to practice questions 10 through 12 on the diagram below.

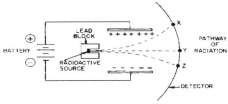

10. Identify radiation Z.

11. List the radiation in the order of increasing charge.

12. Which radiation has the strongest penetrating power?

 ©2017 E3 Scholastic Publishing. All Rights Reserved

Stability of Nucleus
Depends on Neutron to Proton Ratio

Most atoms, especially those found in nature, have stable nuclei.

The ratio of neutrons to protons determines the stability of an atom.

• *Stable nuclei* generally have *equal* number of neutrons and protons (1 : 1 ratio).
  Stable nuclei are not radioactive and do not spontaneously decay.

• *Unstable nuclei* generally have *unequal* number of neutrons to protons.
  Unstable nuclei are radioactive and spontaneously decay in their natural state.

• Radioactive atoms of small atomic numbers are "proton rich," meaning they have more protons than neutrons.

• Radioactive atoms of high atomic numbers are "neutron rich," meaning they have more neutrons than protons.

• **Elements with atomic number 84 and above have no stable isotopes.**
  Nuclei of these elements contain many more neutrons than protons.
  For example: Francium (atomic number 87) has no stable isotopes.
            All 33 known isotopes of francium are radioactive.

Radioisotopes and Decay Modes: Reference Table N

Decay mode refers to the type of particle that a radioisotope will release when it decays.
Reference Table N lists selected radioisotopes and their decay modes.

Table N
Selected Radioisotopes

Nuclide	Half-Life	Decay Mode	Nuclide Name	
^{198}Au	2.695 d	β^-	gold-198	*positron emitter*
^{14}C	5715 y	β^-	carbon-14	*alpha emitter*
^{37}Ca	182 ms	β^+	calcium-37	*beta emitter*

A **radioisotope** is any radioactive isotope of an element. A radioisotope can be described as one of the following depending on its decay mode.

An **alpha emitter** is a radioisotope that releases *alpha particles* (α^+) as it decays.
Radioisotopes with atomic number 84 and above tend to be alpha emitters.
  Ex. Francium–220 and uranium–238 are alpha emitters.

A **beta emitter** is a radioisotope that releases *beta particles* (β^-) as it decays.
  Ex. Hydrogen–3 and strontium–90 are beta emitters.

A **positron emitter** is a radioisotope that releases *positrons* (β^+) as it decays.
  Ex. Iron–53 and neon–19 are positron emitters.

Radioisotopes of small atomic numbers tend to be beta and positron emitters.

Radioisotopes and Stability of Nucleus: Practice Questions.

Practice 13
Spontaneous decay of certain elements in nature occurs because these elements have
1) disproportionate ratios of electrons to protons   3) high reactivity with oxygen
2) disproportionate ratios of neutrons to protons   4) low reactivity with oxygen

Practice 14
Atoms of I-131 spontaneously decay when the
1) stable nuclei emit alpha particles   3) unstable nuclei emit alpha particles
2) stable nuclei emit beta particles   4) unstable nuclei emit beta particles

Practice 15
Which Group 18 element is naturally radioactive and has no known stable isotope?
1) Rn   2) Xe   3) Kr   4) He

Practice 16
Which radioisotope decays by releasing a particle with a mass of 4?
1) ^{32}P   2) ^{239}Pu   3) ^{14}C   4) ^{3}H

Practice 17
Which particle is spontaneously emitted in the nucleus of Calcium-37?
1) Alpha   2) Positron   3) Beta   4) Electron

Practice 18
Which notation of a radioisotope is correctly paired with the notation of its emission particle?
1) ^{37}K and β-   3) ^{222}Rn and α
2) ^{16}N and β+   4) ^{99}Tc and β-

Practice 19
Which two radioisotopes have the same decay mode?
1) ^{37}K and ^{42}K   3) ^{220}Fr and ^{239}Pu
2) ^{232}Th and ^{32}P   4) ^{233}U and ^{99}Tc

Practice 20
Explain why it is more difficult to cause an artificial transmutation with an alpha particle than with a neutron.

Base your answers to practice questions 21 through 23 on the information below, which relates the numbers of neutrons and protons for specific nuclides of C, N, Ne, and S.

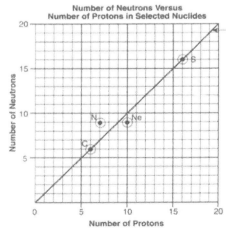

Number of Neutrons Versus
Number of Protons in Selected Nuclides

This line connects points where the neutron-to-proton ratio is 1:1.

21. Using the point plotted on the graph for nitrogen, what is the neutron-to-proton ratio of this nuclide?

22. Explain, in terms of atomic particles, why S-32 is a stable nuclide.

23. What is the mass number of the carbon isotope represented on the graph?

Lesson 2 – Nuclear Reactions

Transmutation, fission and **fusion** are types of nuclear reactions. Nuclear reactions release tons more energy than any ordinary chemical reaction.

Transmutation
Converts One Atom to Another

Transmutation is a nuclear reaction that changes or converts one atom to a different atom. A nuclear transmutation can be natural or artificial.

Natural transmutation occurs when a single unstable radioactive nucleus spontaneously decays by breaking down and emitting particles.
• Alpha decay, beta decay, and positron emission are natural transmutation.

Artificial transmutation occurs when an atom is intentionally hit (bombarded) with high speed particles and is changed to another atom.

Alpha Decay: *A Natural Transmutation*

Alpha decay occurs when a radioactive nucleus spontaneously breaks down to emit an alpha particle. The equation below shows the decay of uranium-238, an alpha emitter.

$$^{238}_{92}U \longrightarrow {}^{4}_{2}He + {}^{234}_{90}Th$$

alpha emitter   *alpha particle*   *new atom*
(unstable nucleus)   *is emitted*   *is formed*

After an alpha decay, the new atom contains different amounts of particles than were in the radioactive atom, as shown below.

	Radioactive atom $^{238}_{92}U$	New atom $^{234}_{90}Th$
mass number	238	234
protons (atomic number)	92	90
neutrons (mass number - atomic number)	146	144

• **Mass number is decreased by 4** *(alpha particle is produced)*
• **Number of protons** is decreased by 2 *(two protons were converted)*
• **Number of neutrons is decreased by 2** *(two neutrons were converted)*

Practice 24
Compared to an atom before an alpha decay, the number of protons of the atom after alpha decay will be
1) greater by 4   3) lesser by 2
2) greater by 2   4) the same

Practice 25
Which of the following equations represents an alpha decay?

1) $^{19}_{10}Ne \longrightarrow {}^{19}_{11}Na + {}^{0}_{-1}e$

2) $^{228}_{89}Ac \longrightarrow {}^{228}_{88}Ra + {}^{0}_{+1}e$

3) $^{232}_{90}Th \longrightarrow {}^{228}_{88}Ra + {}^{4}_{2}He$

4) $^{220}_{87}Fr + {}^{4}_{2}He \longrightarrow {}^{224}_{89}Ac$

Nuclear Chemistry

Beta Decay: *A Natural Transmutation*

Beta decay occurs when a radioactive nucleus converts a neutron to a proton and an electron. The electron is then released from the nucleus. The equation below shows the decay of carbon-14, a beta emitter.

$$^{14}_{6}C \longrightarrow \ ^{0}_{-1}e \ + \ ^{14}_{7}N$$

beta emitter   beta particle   new atom
(unstable nucleus)   is emitted   is formed

After a beta decay, the new atom contains different amounts of particles than were in the radioactive atom, as shown below.

	Radioactive atom $^{14}_{6}C$	New atom $^{14}_{7}N$
mass number	14	14
protons (atomic number)	6	7
neutrons (mass number - atomic number)	8	7

• **Mass number remains the same** *(because the electron produced has no mass)*
• **Number of protons is increased by 1** *(because a proton was produced)*
• **Number of neutrons is decreased by 1** *(because a neutron was converted)*

Practice 26
As a radioactive isotope undergoes a beta decay, the mass number of the atom
1) increases by 2
2) increases by 1
3) decreases by 1
4) remains unchanged

Practice 27
Which of the following equations represents a beta decay?

1) $^{220}_{87}Fr \ + \ ^{4}_{2}He \ \longrightarrow \ ^{224}_{89}Ac$

2) $^{43}_{21}Sc \ \longrightarrow \ ^{43}_{20}Ca \ + \ ^{0}_{+1}e$

3) $^{198}_{79}Au \ \longrightarrow \ ^{198}_{80}Hg \ + \ ^{0}_{-1}e$

4) $^{42}_{19}K \ + \ ^{0}_{-1}e \ \longrightarrow \ ^{42}_{18}Ar$

Positron Emission: *A Natural Transmutation*

Positron emission occurs when a radioactive nucleus converts a proton to a neutron and positron. The positron is then released from the nucleus. The equation below shows the decay of calcium-37, a positron emitter.

$$^{37}_{20}Ca \ \longrightarrow \ ^{0}_{+1}e \ + \ ^{37}_{19}K$$

positron emitter   positron   new atom
(unstable nucleus)   is emitted   is formed

After a positron emission, the new atom contains different amounts of particles than were in the radioactive atom, as shown below.

	Radioactive atom $^{37}_{20}Ca$	New atom $^{37}_{19}K$
mass number	37	37
protons (atomic number)	20	19
neutrons (mass number - atomic number)	17	18

• **Mass number remains the same** *(because the positron produce has no mass)*
• **Number of protons is decreased by 1** *(because a proton was converted)*
• **Number of neutrons is increased by 1** *(because a neutron was produced)*

Practice 28
Compared to an atom after a positron emission, the number of protons of the atom before the decay is
1) 1 greater   3) 2 fewer
2) 1 fewer   4) the same

Practice 29
Which of the following equations represents a positron emission?

1) $^{19}_{10}Ne \ \longrightarrow \ ^{19}_{9}F \ + \ ^{0}_{+1}e$

2) $^{137}_{55}Ac \ \longrightarrow \ ^{137}_{56}Ba \ + \ ^{0}_{-1}e$

3) $^{232}_{90}Th \ \longrightarrow \ ^{4}_{2}He \ + \ ^{228}_{88}Ra$

4) $^{16}_{7}N \ + \ ^{0}_{+1}e \ \longrightarrow \ ^{15}_{7}O \ + \ ^{1}_{1}p$

 ©2017 E3 Scholastic Publishing. All Rights Reserved

Decay Series

A decay series is a chain of decays of one radioactive element after another until a stable isotope, usually lead, is produced. The graph below shows the decay series of Th-230. Each disintegration by alpha (⤢) or beta (→) leads to a new radioisotope until a stable Pb-206 isotope is produced.

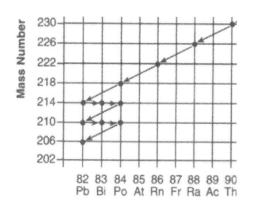

Practice 30

The chart below shows the spontaneous decay of U-238 to Th-234 to Pa-234 to U-234.

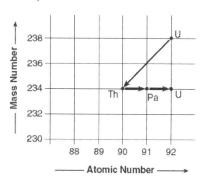

What is the correct order of nuclear decay modes for the change from U-238 to U-234?
1) β- decay, γ decay, β-decay
2) β-decay, β-decay, α decay
3) α decay, α decay, β-decay
4) α decay, β-decay, β-decay

Artificial Transmutation
A Stable Nucleus is Intentionally Hit with a High-speed Particle

Artificial transmutation occurs when an atom is *intentionally* bombarded (hit) with particles to change it to a different atom. Artificial transmutation is done in a particle accelerator because the particles must move at the speed of light to be able to penetrate the nucleus of the atom. The equation below shows an artificial transmutation of beryllium-9 nuclide through alpha bombardment.

$$^{4}_{2}He \quad + \quad ^{9}_{4}Be \quad \rightarrow \quad ^{12}_{6}C \quad + \quad ^{1}_{0}n$$

| accelerated high speed particles | nuclide to be converted | new atom is produced | neutron is released |

Practice 31
Which equation is an example of artificial transmutation?

1) $^{1}_{0}n \ + \ ^{14}_{7}N \ \rightarrow \ ^{14}_{6}C \ + \ ^{1}_{1}H$

2) $^{38}_{19}K \ \rightarrow \ ^{37}_{18}Ar \ + \ ^{1}_{1}p$

3) $^{212}_{84}Po \ \rightarrow \ ^{208}_{82}Pb \ + \ ^{4}_{2}He$

4) $^{2}_{1}H \ + \ ^{2}_{1}H \ \rightarrow \ ^{3}_{2}He$

Practice 32
Artificial transmutation is represented by which equation?

1) $^{43}_{21}Sc \ \rightarrow \ ^{43}_{20}Ca \ + \ ^{0}_{+1}e$

2) $^{10}_{4}Be \ \rightarrow \ ^{10}_{5}B \ + \ ^{0}_{-1}e$

3) $^{235}_{92}U \ + \ ^{1}_{0}n \ \rightarrow \ ^{139}_{56}Ba \ + \ ^{94}_{36}Kr \ + \ 3^{1}_{0}n$

4) $^{32}_{16}S \ + \ ^{1}_{0}n \ \rightarrow \ ^{32}_{15}P \ + \ ^{1}_{1}H$

Fission and Fusion
Convert Mass to Energy

Fission and *fusion* reactions are two types of nuclear reactions that produce tremendous amounts of energy and radiation. During these nuclear processes, it is known that the mass of the new atom is slightly less than that of the reactants. The result of this is called the **mass defect.** The relationship between the missing mass and the tremendous amounts of energy produced from nuclear reactions is given by this well-known equation:

$$E = mc^2$$

Where **E** is the energy produced

m is the mass defect (missing mass)

c is the speed of light

According to the above equation, it can be concluded that during a nuclear reaction:
- **Energy is converted from mass (or mass is converted to energy).**

  The amount of energy that is released is much higher in comparison to that of an ordinary chemical reaction.

When the energy that is released in three types of reactions are compared:

Fusion reactions produce the greatest amount of energy.

Fission reactions produce the second most energy.

Chemical reactions produce the least amount of energy.

Fission
A Large Nucleus Splits into Fragments. Mass is Converted to Energy.

Fission is a nuclear reaction in which a large nucleus is split into smaller nuclei.
The diagram and equation below show nuclear fission of uranium-235. In the reaction, a neutron hits a uranium nucleus, causing it to break into two smaller fragments. Three neutrons and tremendous amount of energy and radiation are also produced in the reaction.

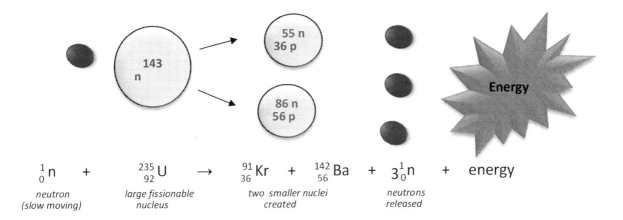

$$\underset{0}{\overset{1}{n}} + \underset{92}{\overset{235}{U}} \longrightarrow \underset{36}{\overset{91}{Kr}} + \underset{56}{\overset{142}{Ba}} + 3\underset{0}{\overset{1}{n}} + \text{energy}$$

neutron (slow moving)	large fissionable nucleus	two smaller nuclei created	neutrons released	

In a fission reaction:

- A large fissionable nucleus absorbs a slow-moving neutron.
  The large nucleus is split into smaller fragments, with the release of more neutrons.

- Tons of nuclear energy is released. Energy is converted from mass.
  The energy that is released is less than that of a fusion reaction.

- In nuclear power plants, the fission process is well controlled.
  The energy is used to produce electricity, which benefits us.

- In nuclear bombs, the fission process is uncontrolled.
  Energy and radiation released are used to cause destruction.

- Dangerous nuclear waste is also produced.
  Nuclear wastes must be stored and disposed of properly.

Fusion
Two Small Nuclei Join. Mass is Converted to Energy

Fusion is a nuclear reaction in which small nuclei are joined (fused) to create a larger nucleus. Only small atoms like those of hydrogen and helium can be fused in a nuclear fusion reaction.
The diagram and equation below show a nuclear fusion reaction. In the reaction, two small hydrogen nuclei join to produce a larger helium nucleus. A tremendous amount of energy is also produced.

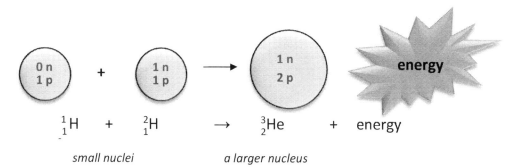

$$_1^1H \;+\; _1^2H \;\rightarrow\; _2^3He \;+\; energy$$

small nuclei   *a larger nucleus*

In a fusion reaction:

- Two small nuclei are brought together under extreme high temperature and pressure.
  The two nuclei join to create a slightly larger nucleus.

- Tons of nuclear energy is released. Energy is converted from mass.
  Energy released is much greater than that of a fission or chemical reaction.

- No nuclear waste is produced, unlike fission.

- Energy from the sun is due to fusion reactions that occur in the core of the sun.

- *High temperature* and *high pressure* are required to overcome the repelling force of the two positive nuclei that are to be fused.

Fission and Fusion: Practice Questions

Practice 33
Which statement explains why fusion reactions are difficult to start?
1) Positive nuclei attract each other
2) Positive nuclei repel each other
3) Negative nuclei attract each other
4) Negative nuclei repel each other

Practice 34
The amount of energy released from a fission reaction is much greater than the energy from a chemical reaction because in a fission reaction
1) energy is converted to mass
2) ionic bonds are broken
3) mass is converted to energy
4) covalent bonds are broken

Practice 35
Which nuclear equation represents fission reaction?

1) $^{1}_{0}n + {}^{14}_{7}N \rightarrow {}^{14}_{6}C + {}^{1}_{1}H$

2) $^{238}_{92}U + {}^{4}_{2}He \rightarrow {}^{241}_{94}Pu + {}^{1}_{0}n$

3) $^{38}_{19}K \rightarrow {}^{37}_{18}Ar + {}^{1}_{1}p$

4) $^{239}_{94}Pu + {}^{1}_{0}n \rightarrow {}^{91}_{38}Br + {}^{146}_{56}La + 3{}^{1}_{0}n$

Practice 36
Which nuclear equation represents a fusion reaction?

1) $^{14}_{7}N + {}^{1}_{0}n \rightarrow {}^{14}_{6}C + {}^{1}_{1}H$

2) $^{238}_{92}U + {}^{4}_{2}He \rightarrow {}^{241}_{94}Pu + {}^{1}_{0}n$

3) $^{1}_{1}H + {}^{3}_{2}He \rightarrow {}^{4}_{2}He + {}^{0}_{+1}e$

4) $^{235}_{92}U + {}^{1}_{0}n \rightarrow {}^{87}_{35}Br + {}^{146}_{57}La + 3{}^{1}_{0}n$

Base your answers to practice questions 37 through 39 on in the information below.

A breeder reactor is one type of nuclear reaction. In a breeder reactor, uranium-238 is transformed in a series of nuclear reactions into plutonium-239.

The plutonium-239 can undergo fission as shown in the equation below. The *X* represents a missing product in the equation.

$$^{1}_{0}n + {}^{239}_{94}Pu \rightarrow X + {}^{94}_{36}Kr + 2{}^{1}_{0}n$$

37. Write a notation for the nuclide represented by missing product *X* in this equation.

38. Compare the amount of energy released by 1 mole of completely fissioned plutonium-239 to the amount of energy released by the complete combustion of 1 mole of methane.

39. State one problem or risk that is associated with the fission of plutonium-239.

Nuclear Reactions: Summary Table

Below is a summary of the five types of nuclear processes discussed in the last few pages.

Use this table for quick study and comparison of the five nuclear reactions

Nuclear Process and Equation	Mass number *after decay*	Protons (atomic number) *after decay*	Neutrons *after decay*
Alpha decay (natural transmutation) $^{226}_{88}Ra \rightarrow\ ^{222}_{86}Rn\ +\ ^{4}_{2}He$	$\downarrow 4$	$\downarrow 2$	$\downarrow 2$
Beta decay (natural transmutation) $^{14}_{6}C \rightarrow\ ^{14}_{7}N\ +\ ^{0}_{-1}e$	same	$\uparrow 1$	$\downarrow 1$
Positron emission (natural transmutation) $^{226}_{88}Ra \rightarrow\ ^{226}_{87}Fr\ +\ ^{0}_{+1}e$	same	$\downarrow 1$	$\uparrow 1$
Artificial Transmutation $^{40}_{18}Ar\ +\ ^{1}_{1}H \rightarrow\ ^{40}_{19}K\ +\ ^{1}_{0}n$	Bombarding nucleus with high speed particles.		
Fission (nuclear energy) $^{235}_{92}U\ +\ ^{1}_{0}n \rightarrow\ ^{142}_{56}Ba\ +\ ^{91}_{36}Kr\ +\ 3^{1}_{0}n$	Nucleus splits into smaller nuclei. Mass is converted to energy. More energy is produced than in chemical reactions. *Problems:* Produces dangerous radioactive wastes.		
Fusion (nuclear energy) $^{2}_{1}H\ +\ ^{2}_{1}H \rightarrow\ ^{4}_{2}He\ +\ energy$	Nuclei join to make a larger nucleus. Mass is converted to energy. Energy produced is greater than that of fission. No radioactive waste is produced. *Problem:* High energy and high pressure are needed to overcome the repelling nuclei.		

Balancing Nuclear Equations

A nuclear equation is balanced when the mass numbers (top numbers) and charges (bottom numbers) are equal on both sides as in the equation below.

$$^{222}_{86}Rn \rightarrow\ ^{4}_{2}He\ +\ ^{218}_{84}Po$$

An incomplete equation typically contains an X or a blank as in Example 1.
The X or blank represents the missing particle in the equation.

Top and bottom numbers for X can be determined mathematically.

Example 1
Which particle is represented by the X in the equation below?

$$X\ +\ ^{0}_{-1}e\ \rightarrow\ ^{37}_{17}Cl$$

$$\overbrace{^{37}_{18}X\ +\ ^{0}_{-1}e}^{37}\ \rightarrow\ ^{37}_{17}Cl$$
$$\underbrace{\phantom{^{37}_{18}X\ +\ ^{0}_{-1}e}}_{17}$$

Top number for X must be **37**

Bottom number for X must be **18**

The symbol for X can be determined from the **Periodic Table** (if X is an element) or **Table O** (if X is a particle).

Practice 40
In the nuclear equation:

$$^{234}_{91}Pa\ \rightarrow\ X\ +\ ^{0}_{-1}e$$

Which particle is represented by the X?

1) $^{234}_{92}U$ 2) $^{234}_{93}Np$ 3) $^{235}_{92}U$ 4) $^{235}_{93}Np$

Practice 41
Which particle is represented by X in the nuclear equation below?

$$^{75}_{33}As\ +\ X\ \rightarrow\ ^{78}_{35}Br\ +\ ^{1}_{0}n$$

1) $^{1}_{1}H$ 2) $^{1}_{0}n$ 3) $^{0}_{+1}e$ 4) $^{4}_{2}He$

Practice 42
Which nuclear reaction involves the emission of a positron?

1) $^{9}_{4}Be\ +\ ^{1}_{1}H\ \rightarrow\ ^{6}_{3}Li\ +\ X$

2) $^{18}_{9}F\ \rightarrow\ ^{18}_{8}O\ +\ X$

3) $^{234}_{90}Th\ \rightarrow\ ^{234}_{91}Pa\ +\ X$

4) $^{14}_{7}N\ +\ ^{1}_{0}n\ \rightarrow\ ^{14}_{6}C\ +\ X$

---

43. When a uranium-235 nucleus absorbs a slow-moving neutron, different nuclear reactions may occur. One of these possible reactions is represented by the incomplete, balanced equation below.

$$^{235}_{92}U\ +\ ^{1}_{0}n\ \rightarrow\ ^{92}_{38}Sr\ +\ \underline{\hspace{2cm}}\ +\ 2\,^{1}_{0}n$$

Write the notation for the missing product in this reaction.

44. The incomplete equation below shows the beta decay of iron-59, which is used to study red blood cells.

$$^{59}_{26}Fe\ \rightarrow\ ^{0}_{-1}e\ +\ \underline{\hspace{1.5cm}}\ +\ energy$$

Write the notation for the missing product in this reaction.

Writing Decay Equations

A balance nuclear reaction equation can be written for a radioisotope if its decay mode is known. This is generally done by piecing together information from Reference Tables N and O, and the Periodic Table.

Concept Task: Be able to write or determine a balance nuclear equation for the decay of a radioisotope.

Example 2

Write nuclear decay equations for the decay of plutonium-239 and iodine-131.

	Step 1: Write		Step 2: Write		Step 3: Determine missing
	Nuclide symbol (Use Table N)	$\rightarrow$	Decay mode symbol (Use Table N and O)	+	Top #, bottom #, and atom's symbol (numbers must make for a balanced equation)

Plutotonium-239 $^{239}_{94}\text{Pu}$ $\rightarrow$ $^{4}_{2}\text{He}$ + $^{235}_{92}\text{U}$

Iodine-131 $^{131}_{53}\text{I}$ $\rightarrow$ $^{0}_{-1}\text{e}$ + $^{131}_{54}\text{Xe}$

Note:
The bottom number of each symbol is the atomic number. (see the Periodic Table)

Practice questions 45 through 49
Use the information provided on Reference Table N to write balanced nuclear equations for the decay of the following radioisotopes.

45. Krypton – 85

46. Uranium – 233

47. Neon – 19

48. Radon – 222

49. Gold – 198

Practice questions 50 through 55
Write a balanced nuclear equation for each reaction based on the information provided.

50. Alpha emission by ^{214}Po

51. Electron absorption by ^{116}Sb

52. Neutron emission by ^{107}Ag

53. Positron absorption by ^{40}Ar

54. Alpha absorption by ^{14}N with neutron emission

55. Neutron absorption by ^{209}Bi with alpha emission

Lesson 3 – Half-life

Half-life is the length of time it takes for a sample of a radioactive element to decay to half of its original mass. During a radioactive decay, the radioisotope is converted to a different element. Over time, less and less of the radioactive element remains as a new element is formed. At a certain time in the decay process, exactly half of the original mass or atoms of the radioactive element will remain unchanged. The time (seconds, minutes, hours, or years) it takes the substance to decay to half its original mass is the half-life of that element.

This diagram below shows a 10-gram sample of a radioisotope decaying to 5 grams after 3 days, and to 2.5 grams after another 3 days.

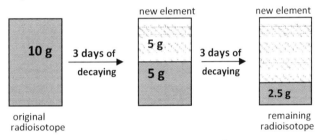

original radioisotope

remaining radioisotope

The half-life of the radioisotope is 3 days.
The number of half-life periods (how many halves) is 2.
The total length of time is 6 days

• The decaying of a radioisotope is at a constant rate. Therefore, half-life of a radioisotope is constant.

• Temperature, pressure, or amount of a radioisotope does not change its half-life.

• Each radioisotope has its own half-life

Reference Table N lists selected radioisotopes, their decay modes and half-lives.

Table N
Selected Radioisotopes

Nuclide	Half-Life	Decay Mode	Nuclide Name
^{198}Au	2.695 d	β^-	gold-198
^{14}C	5715 y	β^-	carbon-14
^{37}Ca	182 ms	β^+	calcium-37
^{60}Co	5.271 y	β^-	cobalt-60
^{137}Cs	30.2 y	β^-	cesium-137
^{53}Fe	8.51 min	β^+	iron-53
^{220}Fr	27.4 s	α	francium-220
^{3}H	12.31 y	β^-	hydrogen-3
^{131}I	8.021 d	β^-	iodine-131
^{37}K	1.23 s	β^+	potassium-37
^{42}K	12.36 h	β^-	potassium-42
^{85}Kr	10.73 y	β^-	krypton-85
^{16}N	7.13 s	β^-	nitrogen-16
^{19}Ne	17.22 s	β^+	neon-19
^{32}P	14.28 d	β^-	phosphorus-32
^{239}Pu	2.410×10^4 y	α	plutonium-239
^{226}Ra	1599 y	α	radium-226
^{222}Rn	3.823 d	α	radon-222
^{90}Sr	29.1 y	β^-	strontium-90
^{99}Tc	2.13×10^5 y	β^-	technetium-99
^{232}Th	1.40×10^{10} y	α	thorium-232
^{233}U	1.592×10^5 y	α	uranium-233
^{235}U	7.04×10^8 y	α	uranium-235
^{238}U	4.47×10^9 y	α	uranium-238

Source: CRC Handbook of Chemistry and Physics, 91st ed., 2010–2011, CRC Press

---

Practice 56
As a sample of Iodine-131 decays, its half-life
1) increases
2) decrease
3) remains the same

Practice 57
Which of the following radioisotope has the longest half-life?
1) Fr-220   3) N-16
2) K -37   4) Ne-19

Practice 58
Which radioisotope has a half-life that is less than 1 minute?
1) K – 37   3) P-32
2) K – 42   4) Fe-53

Practice 59
Compared to K-37, the isotope of K-42 has a
1) shorter half-life and the same decay mode
2) longer half-life and the same decay mode
3) shorter half-life and a different decay mode
4) longer half-life and a different decay mode

Practice 60
Compared to U – 238, U – 235 has a
1) shorter half-life and the same decay mode
2) shorter half-life and a different decay mode
3) longer half-life and the same decay mode
4) longer half-life and a different decay mode

©2017 E3 Scholastic Publishing. All Rights Reserved

Half-Life Problems

Solving a half-life problem quickly, easily and correctly depends on your understanding of the half-life concept. Most half-life problems can be solved with little or no set up if you have a clear understanding of the concept. When solving any half-life problem, the one key piece of information that must be known is the number of half-life periods.

Half-life is the time it takes for half the amount of the substance to decay to a new substance.

Half-life period of a decay is the number of times a radioactive substance decays in half to go from one mass to another. In all half-life problems, the number of half-life periods must be known in order to solve the problem.

Length of time of a decaying process is the total time it takes for a radioisotope to decay from one mass to another.

The relationship between these three factors of decaying process is given by the equation below.

$$\text{Half-life} \;=\; \frac{\textbf{Length of Time}}{\textbf{Number of Half-life Periods}}$$

Example 3: Calculating Half-life Using Equation

What is the half-life of an unknown radioisotope if it takes 12 years for the radioisotope to undergo 5 half-life periods?

$$\text{Half-life} \;=\; \frac{\text{Length of Time}}{\text{Half-life Periods}} \;=\; \frac{12 \text{ years}}{5} \;=\; \textbf{2.4 years}$$

setup   calculated result

Example 4: Calculating Half-life Periods Using Equation

The half-life of a radioisotope is 15 minutes. In 75 minutes, how many half-life periods of decay would the substance had gone through?

$$\text{Half-life Periods} \;=\; \frac{\text{Length of Time}}{\text{Half-life}} \;=\; \frac{75 \text{ min.}}{15 \text{ min.}} \;=\; \textbf{5}$$

setup   calculated result

Example 5: Calculating Length of Time Using Equation

Approximately how long will it take for a radioactive ^{42}K to undergo 6 half-life periods?

Length of Time = Half-life Periods x Half-life

Length of Time = 6 x 12.4 hours = **74.4 hours**   The half-life of ^{42}K is 12.4 hours (see Table N)

setup   calculated result

Original and Remaining Mass Calculations

Original mass of a radioisotope is the mass or number of atoms of the sample that was present at the beginning of a decaying process. **Remaining mass** is the amount that remained after a given length of time or half-life periods of decaying. When both of these masses are given in a half-life problem, the number of half-life period, length of time, or half-life of the radioisotope can be determined. If one of these masses are given in a problem, the other can be determined.

Example 4: Half-life Periods from Original and Remaining Masses

How many half-life periods does it take for a 12-gram sample of a radioactive substance to decay to just 0.75 grams?

Number of half-life periods = the number of times the original mass sample is cut in half to get to the remaining mass

12 g   →   6   →   3 →   1.5   →   **0.75 g**
Start with   Stop at
original mass   remaining mass

Each arrow cuts the mass in half

4 arrows = 4 Half-life periods

Example 5: Length of Time from Half-life and Masses

How long will it take for potassium–42 to decay from 100 g to 12.5 g?

Step 1: Determine number of half-life periods from masses. See previous example.

100 g →   50   →   25   →   12.5 g   3 arrows   = 3 half-life periods

Step 2: **Length of Time** = Number of half-life Periods   x   Half-life
Length of time =   3   x   12.4 hrs. =   **37.2 hrs.** *(answer)*

Example 6:   Original Mass from Half-life Periods and Remaining Mass

After 6 half-life periods, 15 grams of an unknown radioisotope remains. What was the original mass of the unknown radioisotope?

Original mass = Double the remaining mass as many times as the given half-life periods.

15 g   → 30 → 60 → 120   →   240   →   480   → **960 g** *(answer)*
start with   stop after
remaining mass   6 Doubling-arrows = 6 Half-life periods   6 arrows

Example 7:   Remaining Mass from Length of Time and Half-life

In approximately 4800 years, how many grams of a 100-gram sample of Radon – 226 will remain unchanged?

Step 1: Determine Number of Half-life Periods $= \dfrac{\text{Length of Time}}{\text{Half-life}} = \dfrac{4800 \text{ yrs}}{1600 \text{ yrs}} = 3$

(Table N for Rn-226)

Step 2: Cut 100 grams in half 3 times: 100 g   →   50 g   →   25 g   →   **12.5 g** *(answer)*

Topic 12   Nuclear Chemistry

Practice 61
A radioisotope undergoes 2 half-life periods in 180 ms. What is the half-life of this radioisotope?
1) 90 ms   3) 180 ms
2) 360 ms   4) 2 ms

Practice 62
A sample of francium-220 was allowed to decay for 165 seconds. How many half-life periods did the sample decayed?
1) 1.33   3) 5
2) 2   4) 6

Practice 63
The half-life of a radioisotope is 30 seconds. Which set up is correct for calculating the total length of time it takes for a 50-g sample of this isotope to decay to 3.125 g?
1) 30 x 3.125   3) 30 x 4
2) 30 ÷ 3.125   4) 30 ÷ 4

Practice 64
A 20-gram sample of ^{99}Tc decaying for 6.4 x 10^5 years will undergo how many life-periods?
1) 1   3) 3
2) 2   4) 4

Practice 65
After 4 half-life periods, 1.5 mg of a radioactive isotope remained. What was the mass of the original sample of the isotope?
1) 6.0 mg   3) 3.0 mg
2) 0.375 mg   4) 24 mg

Practice 66
Approximately how many grams of a 50-g sample of radium-226 will remain unchanged after 6400 years?
1) 25 g   3) 128 g
2) 6.25 g   4) 3.13 g

Practice 67
A radioisotope of element X has a half-life of 1.5 days. How many grams of a 5-gram sample of this isotope will remain unchanged after 3.0 days?
1) 1.25 grams   3) 2.5 grams
2) 7.5 grams   4) 4.5 grams

Practice 68
Cobalt-60 is an artificially produced radioisotope that emits gamma rays and beta particles. One hospital keeps a 100.0-gram sample of cobalt-60 in an appropriate, secure storage container for future cancer treatment. Determine the total time that will have elapsed when 12.5 grams of the original Co-60 sample at the hospital remains unchanged.

Practice 69
Determine the half-life of krypton-92 if only 6.0 milligrams of an original 96.0-milligram sample remains unchanged after 7.36 seconds.

E3Chemistry.com   279

Fraction Remaining Calculations

Fraction remaining expresses the remaining mass of a radioisotope in the form of ratio.

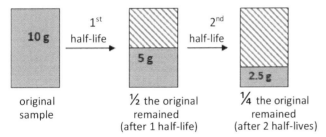

| original sample | ½ the original remained (after 1 half-life) | ¼ the original remained (after 2 half-lives) |

Fraction remaining of a radioisotope can be calculated when certain information is known of a decaying process.

Example 8: Fraction Remaining from Half-life Periods (n)

What fraction of Au-198 will remain unchanged after 4 half-life periods?

1) $\frac{1}{8}$ 2) $\frac{1}{2}$ 3) $\frac{1}{16}$ 4) $\frac{1}{4}$

$$\text{Fraction remaining} = \frac{1}{2^n} \quad n = \text{number of half-life periods}$$

$$\text{Fraction remaining} = \frac{1}{2^4} = \frac{1}{2 \times 2 \times 2 \times 2} = \frac{1}{16}$$

choice 3

Example 9:   Fraction Remaining from Length of time and Half-life

What fraction of ^{19}Ne will remain unchanged after 86 seconds?

1) $\frac{1}{32}$ 2) $\frac{1}{5}$ 3) $\frac{1}{2}$ 4) $\frac{1}{16}$

$$\text{Fraction remaining} = \frac{1}{(2)^{t/T}} \quad \begin{array}{l} t = \text{length of time} \\ T = \text{half-life} \\ t/T = n = \text{half-life periods} \end{array}$$

$$\text{Fraction remaining} = \frac{1}{(2)^{86/17.2}} = \frac{1}{2^5} = \frac{1}{2 \times 2 \times 2 \times 2 \times 2}$$

$$\text{Fraction remaining} = \frac{1}{32} \quad \text{choice 1}$$

Practice 70
What fraction of the radioactive waste Strontium-90 will remain unchanged after 5 half-life periods of decaying?
1) $\frac{1}{32}$ 3) $\frac{1}{16}$
2) $\frac{1}{8}$ 4) $\frac{1}{5}$

Practice 71
If the half-life of a radioactive element is 2.5 years, what fraction of this element will remain unchanged after 15 years?
1) $\frac{1}{32}$ 3) $\frac{1}{2}$
2) $\frac{1}{16}$ 4) $\frac{1}{64}$

Practice 72
After 1.42 x 10^9 years, what fraction of a 6-gram sample of U-235 will remain unchanged?
1) $\frac{1}{4}$ 3) $\frac{1}{2}$
2) $\frac{1}{6}$ 4) $\frac{1}{8}$

Practice 73
A sample of a radioisotope Cr-51 decays to $\frac{1}{8}$th in 84 days. what is the half-life of Cr-51?
1) 14 days   3) 56 days
2) 28 days   4) 84 days

Practice 74
A radioisotope has a half-life of 16 years. In how many years would a given sample of this isotope decays to $\frac{1}{32}$th of its original mass?
1) 8 years   3) 80 years
2) 2 years   4) 512 years

Base your answers to practice questions 75 and 76 on in the information below.

The radioisotopes carbon-14 and nitrogen-16 are present in a living organism. Carbon-14 is commonly used to date a once-living organism.

75. A sample of wood is found to contain 1/8 as much C-14 as is present in the wood of a living tree. What is the approximate age, in years, of this sample of wood?

76. Complete the nuclear equation for the decay of C-14.

$$^{14}_{6}C \rightarrow \; ^{0}_{-1}e \; + \; \underline{\hspace{2cm}}$$

Identifying Radioisotopes

When certain information about a decaying process is known, you can identify which radioisotope on Table N the information is referring to.

^{16}N	7.13 s	β^-	nitrogen-16
^{19}Ne	17.22 s	β^+	neon-19

Keep the following in mind when comparing the radioisotopes given as choices.

Decays to greatest extent
- Shortest half-life (N-16)

Decays to least extent
- Longest half-life (N-19)

Smallest remaining %
- Shortest half-life
- Smallest mass

Greatest remaining %
- Longest half-life
- Greatest mass

Practice 77
A 10-gram sample of which radioisotope will decay to the greatest extent in 50 years?
1) Kr-85   3) Cs-137
2) H-3   4) Sr-90

Practice 78
Which radioisotope sample will have the smallest amount remaining after 10 years?
1) 2.0 g of Au-198   3) 4.0 g of P-32
2) 2.0 g of K-42   4) 4.0 g of Co-60

Practice 79
According to Reference Table N, which radioisotope will retain only $^1/_8{}^{th}$ its original mass after approximately 43 days?
1) Phosphorus-32   3) Radon-222
2) Gold-198   4) Iron-53

Decay Data, Tables and Graphs

The decaying process of a radioisotope can be shown with a graph, diagram or data table.
The graph and data below are both showing the mass of a radioisotope remaining as it decays over time.

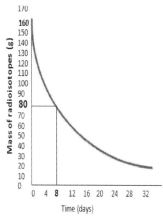

Time (days)	Mass of radioisotope sample remaining (g)
0	160
4	120
8	80 (half original mass)
12	60
16	40
20	30
24	20
28	15
32	10

The half-life of the radioisotope is 8 days.
This is the number of days half (80 g) of the original (160 g) of the radioisotope is unchanged.

The radioisotope is likely iodine-131.
According to Reference Table N, the half-life of I-131 is 8.07 day.

The graph below represents the decay of a radioactive material X into a stable decay product.

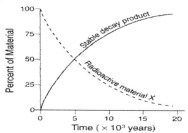

Practice 80
What is the half-life of radioactive material X?
1) 50 x 10^3 y   3) 20 x 10^3 y
2) 5 x 10^3 y   4) 10 x 10^3 y

Practice 81
Which graph best represents the relative percentages of the radioactive material X and its stable product after 15,000 years? (shaded area represents radioactive material while the non-shaded area represents stable products)

1)   3)

2)   4)

Radioactivity Applications and Wastes

Radioactivity Applications and Benefits
Radioactive isotopes have many useful and beneficial applications. Radioisotopes are used in the field of medicine for diagnosis and treatment of diseases. They are used in the field of science for research. They are used in the food industry to kill harmful bacteria in our food. In geological and archeological fields, radioisotopes are used in determining the age of rocks and fossils.

Tracers are radioisotopes that are used to follow the course or progress of a chemical reaction, medical diagnosis or treatment.

Tracers for diagnosis and treatments must have *short half-lives* and be *quickly eliminated* from the body.

Radioisotopes for dating usually have very long half-lives.

The table below lists selected radioisotopes and their common beneficial applications.

Radioisotope Name	Radioisotope Symbol	Common Applications and Benefits	Field of Application
Iodine-131	^{131}I	Thyroid disorder; diagnosis and treatment	Medical
Technetium-99	^{99}Tc	Cancer tumor diagnosis	Medical
Cobalt-60	^{60}Co	Cancer treatment	Medical
Iron-56	^{56}Fe	Blood disorder treatment	Medical
Carbon-14 *(alone)*	^{14}C	Tracer for chemical reactions	Research
Carbon-14	^{14}C	Fossil dating	Archeology
Carbon-12	^{12}C		
Uranium – 238	^{238}U	Rock dating	Geology
Lead - 206	^{206}Pb		

Radioactive Wastes and Radiations
Radiations and wastes produced from nuclear reactors can be very dangerous to life on earth. Prolonged and high dose exposures to radiation can cause serious health issues, and sometimes death.

• *Radiation* from nuclear power plants must be contained to protect humans and other living things.
• *Nuclear wastes* are equally dangerous because they are highly radioactive.
• *Nuclear wastes* have to be stored in safe areas to protect the public from being exposed to them.

Solid Wastes (Highly radioactive): Sr-90   Cs-137   **Gaseous Wastes:** Rn-222   Kr-85   N-16

Practice 82
A radioisotope is called a tracer when it is used to
1) determine the age of animal skeletal remains
2) determine the course of a chemical reaction
3) kill cancerous tissue
4) kill bacteria in food

Practice 83
Which procedure is based on the half-life of a radioisotope?
1) Accelerating to increase kinetic energy.
2) Counting to determine a level of radioactivity.
3) Dating to determine age.
4) Radiating to kill cancer cells.

Practice 84
Iodine-131 is used in diagnosing thyroid disorders because it is absorbed by the thyroid gland and
1) has a very short half-life   3) emits alpha particle
2) has a very long half-life   4) emits gamma radiation

Practice 85
A radioisotope that is sometimes used in pinpointing brain tumor is
1) technetium – 99   3) lead – 206
2) uranium – 238   4) carbon – 12

86. Explain why N-16 is a poor choice for radioactive dating of a bone.

 ©2017 E3 Scholastic Publishing. All Rights Reserved

Vocabulary

Lesson 1: Nuclear Chemistry Particles and Stability of the Nucleus
Alpha particle
Beta particle
Positron
Gamma ray
Accelerator
Radioisotope

Lesson 2:   Nuclear Reactions
Transmutation
Artificial transmutation
Natural transmutation
Alpha decay
Beta decay
Positron emission
Fission
Fusion

Lesson 3: Half-life
Half-life
Tracer

1. 4	7. 2	12. y	17. 2
2. 1	8. 3	13. 2	18. 3
3. 2	9. 2	14. 4	19. 3
4. 3	10. alpha particle, $_2^4He$	15. 1	
5. 4		16. 2	
6. 3	11. x, y, z		

20. Alpha particles have a positive charge so need to be accelerated to high speeds in order to overcome the repulsion forces of (+) to (+) particles for the nuclear reaction to occur. Neutrons have no charge so it's easier to accelerate them.

21. 9.7   22. neutron-to-proton ratio is 1:1.   23. 12 u, 12 amu

24. 3	28. 1	32. 4	36. 3
25. 3	29. 1	33. 2	37. $_{58}^{144}Ce$
26. 4	30. 4	34. 3	
27. 3	31. 1	35. 4	

38. FIssioned of plutonium-239 releases more energy than the combustion of methane.

39. It produces radioactive wastes.

40. 1   43. $_{92}^{235}U + _0^1n \rightarrow _{38}^{92}Sr + _{54}^{142}Xe + 2\,_0^1n$

41. 4

42. 2   44. $_{26}^{59}Fe \rightarrow _{-1}^0e + _{27}^{59}Co + energy$

45. Krypton – 85

$_{36}^{85}Kr \dashrightarrow _{-1}^0e + _{37}^{85}Rb$

46. Uranium – 233

$_{92}^{233}U \dashrightarrow _2^4He + _{90}^{229}Th$

47. Neon – 19

$_{10}^{19}Ne \dashrightarrow _{+1}^0e + _9^{19}F$

48. Radon – 222

$_{86}^{222}Rn \dashrightarrow _2^4He + _{84}^{218}Po$

49. Gold – 198

$_{79}^{198}Au \dashrightarrow _{-1}^0e + _{80}^{198}Hg$

50. Alpha emission by ^{214}Po

$_{84}^{214}Po \dashrightarrow _2^4He + _{82}^{210}Pb$

51. Electron absorption by ^{116}Sb

$_{51}^{116}Sb + _{-1}^0e \dashrightarrow _{50}^{116}Sn$

52. Neutron emission by ^{107}Ag

$_{47}^{107}Ag \dashrightarrow _0^1n + _{47}^{106}Ag$

53. Positron absorption by ^{40}Ar

$_{18}^{40}Ar + _{+1}^0e \dashrightarrow _{19}^{40}K$

54. Alpha absorption by ^{14}N with neutron emission

$_7^{14}N + _2^4He \dashrightarrow _1^0n + _8^{18}O$

55. Neutron absorption by ^{209}Bi with alpha emission

$_{83}^{209}Bi + _0^0n \dashrightarrow _2^4He + _{82}^{205}Pb$

56. 3	63. 3
57. 1	64. 3
58. 1	65. 4
59. 4	66. 4
60. 1	67. 1
61. 1	68. 15.813 years
62. 4	69. 1.84 seconds

70. 1	74. 3
71. 1	75. 17,145 years
72. 1	
73. 2	76. $_6^{14}C \rightarrow _{-1}^0e + _7^{14}N$

77. 1	82. 2
78. 4	83. 2
79. 1	84. 1
80. 2	85. 1
81. 3	

86. N-16 half-life is very short.
Very little, if any, N-16 will be left after a very short time.

Topic 13
Lab Safety and Measurements

Lesson 1: Lab Safety and Equipment

Lesson 2: Significant Figures

Lesson 3: Reading Measuring Instruments

Lesson 4: Percent Error

Lab Safety: *Always follow the instructions of your teacher.*

During a lab experiment, appropriate safety guidelines must be followed.

Safety Precautions
- Wear protective goggles at all times.
- Tie back long hair.
- Roll up long sleeves.
- No eating or drinking in the lab, or out of lab equipment.
- No running in the lab.

Safe Procedures
- When lighting a Bunsen burner, strike a match first, then turn on the gas.
- When diluting an acid, pour the acid slowly into water while stirring. Never add water to acid.

In Case of an Accident: *Report all accidents to your teacher immediately*
- Know the locations of all lab safety equipment and procedures for using them.
- Rinse skin with water if any chemical spills on your skin.
- Rinse eyes with water for 15 minutes if any chemical splashes in your eyes.
- A spilled acid or base should be neutralized first before cleaning it up.

Lab Equipment

	Beaker	Measuring volume of a liquid.
	Test Tube	Placing a substance for observation or to conduct experiment.
	Evaporating dish	Heating a substance.
	Crucible	Heating a substance.
	Watch glass	Drying a wet solid. Covering up glassware while heating.
	Tongs	Holding an object over heat, or removing heated glassware from heat.
	Buret	Dispensing an exact volume of a liquid. Often used in titration experiment.
	Erlenmeyer flask	Measuring volume of a liquid.
hottest part of a flame	**Bunsen burner**	A heat source for laboratory experiments. Requires natural gas such as propane.

                    ©2017 E3 Scholastic Publishing. All Rights Reserved

Lab Procedure, Safety and Equipment: Practice Problems

Practice 1
A student investigated the physical and chemical properties of a sample of an unknown gas and then identified the gas. Which statement represents a conclusion rather than an experimental observation?
1) The gas is colorless.
2) The gas is carbon dioxide.
3) When the gas is bubbled into limewater, the liquid becomes cloudy
4) When placed in the gas, a flaming splint stops burning

Practice 2
During a laboratory activity, a student combined two solutions. In the laboratory report, the student wrote "A yellow color appeared." The statement represents the student's recorded
1) conclusion   3) hypothesis
2) observation   4) inference

Practice 3
A student wishes to prepare approximately 100 mL of an aqueous solution of 6 M HCl using 12 M HCl. Which procedure is correct?
1) Adding 50 mL of 12 M HCl to 50 mL of water while stirring the mixture steadily.
2) Adding 50 mL of 12 M HCl to 50 mL of water, and then stir the mixture steadily.
3) Adding 50 mL of water to 50 mL of 12 M HCl while stirring the mixture steadily.
4) Adding 50 mL of water to 50 mL of 12 M HCl , and then stir the mixture steadily.

Practice 4
Which activity is considered a proper laboratory technique?
1) Heating the contents of an open test tube held vertically over a flame.
2) Heating the content of a test tube that has been closed with a stopper.
3) Adding water to a concentrated acid.
4) Striking a match first before turning on the gas valve to light a Bunsen burner.

Practice 5
Which set of laboratory equipment would most likely be used with a crucible?

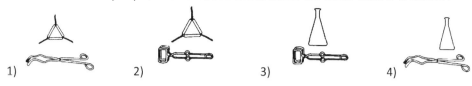

1)   2)   3)   4)

Practice 6
The two lab equipment shown below are

1) Round bottom flask and a crucible   3) Evaporated dish and a beaker
2) Round bottom flask and a watch glass   4) Evaporated dish and a watch glass

Significant Figures

Significant figures in a number include all digits that are known for certain plus one estimated digit.

Significant figures in a number can be determined using Atlantic – Pacific rule.

If a decimal point is Absent in a number
- Start counting with the first nonzero from the Atlantic (right) side of the number.

- Count toward the Pacific (left)
- Stop counting with the last nonzero digit.

How many you counted is the number of significant figures in that number.

If a decimal point is Present in a number
- Start counting with the first nonzero from the Pacific (left) side of the number.

- Count toward the Atlantic (right), and count all numbers (including zeros) once you've started counting.

How many you counted is the number of significant figures in that number.

In Summary:
All zeros to start a number are never counted as significant.

All zeros between two real numbers are always counted as significant.

Zeros at the end of a number are significant only *if* the number contains a decimal point.

405   has **3** significant figures

405**0**   has **3** significant figures

200   has **1** significant figure

0**2**   has **1** significant figure

0.00**36**   has **2** significant figures

0.0**936**   has **3** significant figures

0.0**9360** has **4** significant figures

200.   has **3** significant figures

0.0**13**   has **2** significant figures

10**40**   has **3** significant figures

1.040   has **4** significant figures

Practice 7
Which mass measurement contains four significant figures?
1) 0.086 g   2) 0.431 g   3) 1003 g   4) 3870 g

Practice 8
Which measurement contains three significant figures?
1) 0.03 g   2) 0.030 g   3) 0.035 g   4) 0.0351 g

Practice 9
Which volume measurement is expressed in two significant figures?
1) 20 mL   2) 202 mL   3) 220 mL   4) 0.2 mL

Practice 10
Which measurement has the greatest number of significant figures?
1) 44000 g   2) 404 g   3) 40.44 g   4) 0.40004 g

Practice 11
Which pressure measurement has the least number of significant figures?
1) 84 kPa   2) 34.1 kPa   3) 70.88 kPa   4) 90 kPa

                                    ©2017 E3 Scholastic Publishing. All Rights Reserved

Significant Figures in Calculations

Rules for leaving (or limited) a calculated result to the right number of significant figures vary depending on the type of mathematical operation that is involved in the calculation. These rules are described below.

Multiplying or Dividing
The answer should be limited or rounded to the same number of significant figures as the factor with the **least number** of significant figures.

Example 1
How much heat is absorbed by a 17-gram sample of ice to melt? Answer must have the correct number of significant figures.

Heat = (mass)(H_f)

Heat = (17)(334)

Heat = 5678 J

Heat = **5700 J**

17	factor with least number of sig fig.: **2**
5678	(calculator result) has 4 sig figures. It must be rounded to 2 sig figures.
5700	(answer) is rounded to 2 sig figures.

Example 2
What is the density of an unknown substance if a 42.6 cm³ sample has a mass of 22.43 g?

$$Density = \frac{22.43 \text{ g}}{42.6 \text{ cm}^3}$$

Density = **0.527 g/cm³**

42.6	factor with the least number of sig figures: **3**
0.527	(answer) also has 3 significant figures

Adding or Subtracting
The answer should be limited or rounded to the same number of decimal places as the factor with the *least number of decimal places*.

Example 3
A student measured out 0.31 g, 1.310 g and 1.3205 samples of sodium chloride. What is the total mass of the three samples of the salt?

0.31 + 1.310 + 1.3205 = 2.9405 = **2.94**

0.**31** is the factor with the least number of decimal places: **2**

2.**9405** (calculated result) has **4** decimal places. It must be rounded and limited to 2 decimal places.

2.**94** (answer) has **2** decimal places.

Practice 12
The mass of a solid is 3.60 g and its volume is 1.8 cm³. What is the density of the solid, expressed to the correct number of significant figures?
1) 12 g/cm³   3) 0.5 g/cm³
2) 2.0 g/cm³   4) 0.50 g/cm³

Practice 13
Which quantity expresses the sum of 22.1 g + 375.66 g + 5400.132 g to the correct number of significant figures?
1) 5800 g   3) 5797.9 g
2) 5798 g   4) 5797.892 g

Practice 14
The volume of a gas sample is 22 L at STP. The density of the gas is 1.35 g/L. What is the mass of the gas sample, expressed to the correct number of significant figures?
1) 30. g   3) 16.7 g
2) 30.0 g   4) 2.56 g

Practice 15
A student calculates the density of an unknown solid. The mass is 10.04 grams, and the volume is 8.21 cubic centimeters. How many significant figures should appear in the final answer?
1) 1   3) 3
2) 2   4) 4

Practice 16
The density of a solid is 1.9 g/mL and its volume is 40.2 mL. A student calculating the mass of the solid should have how many significant figures in the final answer?

1) 1   3) 3
2) 2   4) 4

Reading Measuring Equipment

- All laboratory measurements should include a value and unit.
- Measurements should be given to the correct number of significant figures.
- A measurement has the correct number of significant figures when it includes all digits known with certainty, and one estimated digit determined between two of the smallest unit markings on the measuring equipment.

Mass Measurement

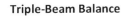	
Triple-Beam Balance	An equipment for measuring the mass of a substance.
Grams (g)	A unit of measurement for mass.
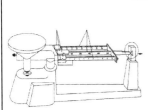	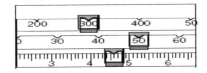 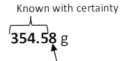 Known with certainty **354.58 g** Estimated based on the pointer position between two smallest markings.

Volume Measurement

Graduated Cylinder	An equipment for measuring the volume of a liquid.
Milliliters (mL)	A unit of measurement for volume.
Meniscus	The curved surface of a liquid in a graduated cylinder.
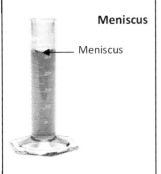	- Accurate volume of a liquid should be read at eye level with the bottom of the meniscus. 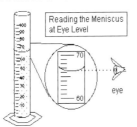 Known with certainty **66.1°C** Estimated based on the bottom of the meniscus level.

Temperature Measurement

Thermometer	An equipment for measuring the temperature of a liquid.
Celsius (°C)	A unit of measurement for temperature.
	- Accurate reading should be at eye level with the top of the red liquid inside the thermometer.  Known with certainty **44.7°C** Estimated based on the level between the two smallest markings.

                    ©2017 E3 Scholastic Publishing. All Rights Reserved

Reading Measuring Equipment: **Practice Problems**

Practice 17:
The diagram below represents a portion of a 100-milliliter graduated cylinder.

What is the reading of the meniscus?

1) 35.0 mL   3) 36.0 mL

2) 44.0 mL   4) 45.0 mL

Practice 18:   The diagram below shows a portion of a buret.

What is the meniscus reading in milliliters?

1) 16.00   3) 16.40

2) 17.00   4) 17.60

Practice 19:
The diagram below represents a Celsius thermometer recording a certain temperature.

What is the correct reading of the thermometer?

1) 5°C   3) 4.3°C

2) 0.3°C   4) 4°C

Practice 20:
The diagram below represents a portion of a triple beam balance.

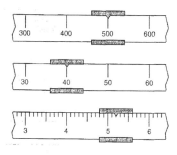

If the beams are in balance with the riders in the positions shown, what is the total mass of the object?

1) 540.20 g   3) 540.52 g

2) 545.20 g   4) 545.52 g

Practice 21
The diagram below represents a section of a buret containing acid used in acid-base titration.

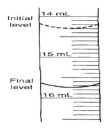

What is the total volume of acid that was used?

1) 1.10 mL

2) 1.30 mL

3) 1.40 mL

4) 1.45 mL

Percent Error

Percent error expresses the difference between the experimental (measured) and actual (accepted) values. The percent error equation is given on **Table T**.

• Percent error should always be positive.

• The smaller the percent error, the more accurate the measured value.
• Human errors and imprecision of measuring equipment are the common causes of high percent errors in a lab experiment.

$$\% \ error = \frac{measured \ value - accepted \ value}{accepted \ value} \times 100$$

The lower the percent error, the more accurate the lab result.

Reference Table T equation

Practice 22

A student determined the percentage of water of hydration in $BaCl_2 \bullet 2H_2O$ by using the data in the table below.

Quantity Measured	Value Obtained
Mass of $BaCl_2 \bullet 2H_2O$	3.80 grams
Mass of $BaCl_2$	3.20 grams
% of water calculated	15.79 %

The accepted percent of water of hydration is 14.75 %. What is the student's percent error?
1) 1.04 %   2) 6.00 %   3) 6.59 %   4) 7.05 %

Practice 23

A student determined in the laboratory that the percent by mass of water in $CuSO_4 \bullet 5H_2O$ is 40.0%. If the accepted value is 36%, what is the percent error?
1) 0.11 %   2) 1.1 %   3) 11 %   4) 4.0 %

Practice 24

A student calculated the percent by mass of water in a hydrate as 14.2 %. A hydrate is a compound that contains water as part of its crystal structure. If the accepted value is 14.7 %, the student's percent error was

1) $\dfrac{0.5}{14.2} \times 100$ 2) $\dfrac{14.7}{14.2} \times 100$ 3) $\dfrac{0.5}{14.7} \times 100$ 4) $\dfrac{14.2}{14.7} \times 100$

Practice 25

A student found the boiling point of a liquid to be 80.4°C . If the liquid's actual boiling point is 80.6°C, the experimental percent error is equal to

1) $\dfrac{80.6 - 80.4}{80.6} \times 100$

2) $\dfrac{80.5 - 80.4}{80.5} \times 100$

3) $\dfrac{80.6 - 80.4}{80.4} \times 100$

4) $\dfrac{80.5 - 80.4}{80.4} \times 100$

                                         ©2017 E3 Scholastic Publishing. All Rights Reserved

Base your answers to practice questions 26 through 28 on the information below.

    During a laboratory activity, a student places 25.0 mL of HCl(aq) of unknown concentration into a flask. The student adds four drops of phenolphthalein to the solution in the flask. The solution is titrated with 0.150 M KOH(aq) until the solution appears faint pink. The volume of KOH(aq) added is 18.5 mL.

26. Describe *one* laboratory safety procedure that should be used if a drop of the KOH(aq) is spilled on the arm of the student.

27. What number of significant figures is used to express the concentration of the KOH(aq)?

28. Calculate the concentration of the HCl solution in the flask that was titrated. Your response must include a correct numerical setup and the calculated result.

Base your answers to practice questions 29 and 30 on the information below.

    A method used by ancient Egyptians to obtain copper metal from copper(I) sulfide ore was heating the ore in the presence of air. Later, copper was mixed with tin to produce a useful alloy called bronze. Archeologist recently discovered a 129.5-gram piece of bronze artifact.

29. Calculate the density of the bronze artifact if its volume is 14.8 cubic centimeters. Your response must include a correct numerical setup and the calculated result.

30. A careful study of the 129.5-gram bronze artifact reveals that it is composed of approximately 110.0 grams of copper, and the rest tin. Calculate the percent composition of tin in the artifact.

Vocabulary

Significant figure

Percent error

Meniscus

_____ **Answers to Practice Questions** _____

1. 2
2. 2
3. 1
4. 4
5. 2
6. 4
7. 3
8. 4
9. 3

10. 4
11. 4
12. 2
13. 3
14. 1
15. 3
16. 2
17. 1

18. 3
19. 3
20. 2
21. 4
22. 1
23. 3
24. 3
25. 1

26. Rinse the arm with cold water for a long time.

27. 3, three

28. $M_a V_a \;=\; M_b V_b$

      $M_a (25.0) \;=\; (0.150)(18.5)$

$$M_a \;=\; \frac{2.775}{25.0} \;=\; \mathbf{0.111\ M}$$

29. $\text{Density} = \dfrac{\text{mass}}{\text{volume}} = \dfrac{129.5\ \text{g}}{14.8\ \text{cm}^3} = \mathbf{8.75\ g/cm^3}$

30. mass of tin $=$ $125.5\ \text{g} - 110.0\ \text{g} = 19.5\ \text{g}$

      $\text{Percent of tin} = \dfrac{19.5\ \text{g}}{129.5\ \text{g}} \times 100 = \mathbf{15.1\ \%}$

Regents Practice

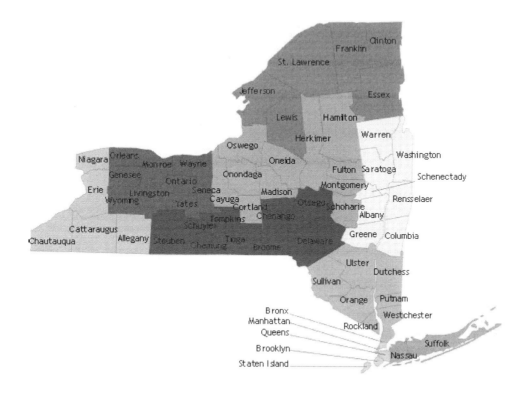

12 Topics of Regents Practice Questions

2 Regents Exams

for

NYS Regents Chemistry
The Physical Setting
Exam

1 Which sample of matter represents a mixture?
(1) aqueous ammonia (3) liquid mercury
(2) gaseous ethane   (4) solid iodine

2 Which type of matter is composed of two or more elements that are chemically combined in a fixed proportion?

(1) solution
(2) compound
(3) homogeneous mixture
(4) heterogeneous mixture

3 The ratio of chromium to iron to carbon varies among the different types of stainless steel. Therefore, stainless steel is classified as

(1) a compound   (3) a mixture
(2) an element   (4) a substance

4 Which statement defines the temperature of a sample of matter?

(1) Temperature is a measure of the total electromagnetic energy of the particles.
(2) Temperature is a measure of the total thermal energy of the particles.
(3) Temperature is a measure of the average potential energy of the particles.
(4) Temperature is a measure of the average kinetic energy of a particles.

5 According to the kinetic molecular theory for an ideal gas, all gas particles

(1) are in random, constant, straight-line motion
(2) are separated by very small distances relative to their sizes
(3) have strong intermolecular forces
(4) have collisions that decrease the total energy of the system

6 Equal amounts of ethanol and water are mixed at room temperature and at 101.3 kPa. Which process is used to separate ethanol frorn the mixture?

(1) distillation   (3) filtration
(2) reduction   (4) ionization

7 Which statement explains why water is classified as a compound?

(1) Water can be broken down by chemical means.
(2) Water is a liquid at room temperature.
(3) Water has a heat of fusion of 334 J/g.
(4) Water is a poor conductor of electricity.

8 Given four particle models:

Key
◯ = an atom of element T
⊙ = an atom of element X
◐ = an atom of element Z

   I   II   III   IV

Which two models can be classified as elements?

(1) I and II   (3) II and III
(2) I and IV   (4) II and IV

9 A sample of chlorine gas is at 300. K and 1.00 atmosphere. At which temperature and pressure would the sample behave more like an ideal gas?

(1) 0 K and 1.00 atm
(2) 150. K and 0.50 atm
(3) 273 K and 1.00 atm
(4) 600. K and 0.50 atm

10 Which rigid cylinder contains the same number of gas molecules at STP as a 2.0-liter rigid cylinder containing $H_2(g)$ at STP?

(1) 1.0-L cylinder of $O_2(g)$
(2) 2.0-L cylinder of $CH_4(g)$
(3) 1.5-L cylinder of $NH_3(g)$
(4) 4.0-L cylinder of $He(g)$

11 A rigid cylinder with a movable piston contains a sample of gas. At 300. K, this sample has a pressure of 240. kilopascals and a volume of 70.0 milliliters. What is the volume of this sample when the temperature is changed to 150. K and the pressure is changed to 160. kilopascals?

(1) 35.0 mL   (3) 70.0 mL
(2) 52.5 mL   (4) 105 mL

12 Which processes represent one chemical change and one physical change?

(1) freezing and melting
(2) freezing and vaporization
(3) decomposition and melting
(4) decomposition and combustion

13 Which equation represents sublimation?

(1) $Hg(\ell) \rightarrow Hg(s)$
(2) $H_2O(s) \rightarrow H_2O(g)$
(3) $NH_3(g) \rightarrow NH_3(\ell)$
(4) $CH_4(\ell) \rightarrow CH_4(g)$

14 What is the minimum amount of heat required to completely melt 20.0 grams of ice at its melting point?

(1) 20.0 J   (3) 6,680 J
(2) 83.6 J   (4) 45,200 J

15 Given the balanced particle-diagram equation:

Key	
○	= an atom of an element
●	= an atom of a different element

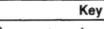 +  →

Which statement describes the type of change and the chemical properties of the product and reactants?

(1) The equation represents a physical change, with the product and reactants having different chemical properties.
(2) The equation represents a physical change, with the product and reactants having identical chemical properties.
(3) The equation represents a chemical change, with the product and reactants having different chemical properties.
(4) The equation represents a chemical change, with the product and reactants having identical chemical properties.

Base your answers to questions **16** and **17** on the information below and on your knowledge of chemistry.

A few pieces of dry ice, $CO_2(s)$, at $-78°C$ are placed in a flask that contains air at $21°C$. The flask is sealed by placing an uninflated balloon over the mouth of the flask. As the balloon inflates, the dry ice disappears and no liquid is observed in the flask.

16 Write the name of the process that occurs as the dry ice undergoes a phase change in the flask.

17 State the direction of heat flow that occurs between the dry ice and the air in the flask.

Base your answers to questions **18** through **20** on the information below and on your knowledge of chemistry.

Cylinder A has a movable piston and contains hydrogen gas. An identical cylinder, B, contains methane gas. The diagram below represents these cylinders and the conditions of pressure, volume, and temperature of the gas in each cylinder.

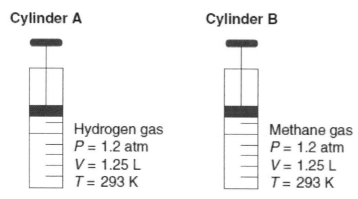

Cylinder A

Hydrogen gas
$P = 1.2$ atm
$V = 1.25$ L
$T = 293$ K

Cylinder B

Methane gas
$P = 1.2$ atm
$V = 1.25$ L
$T = 293$ K

18 Show a numerical setup for calculating the volume of the gas in cylinder B at STP.

19 State a change in temperature and a change in pressure that will cause the gas in cylinder A to behave more like an ideal gas.

20 Compare the total number of gas molecules in cylinder A to the total number of gas molecules in cylinder B.

Base your answers to questions **21** through **23** on the information below.

A student investigated heat transfer using a bottle of water. The student placed the bottle in a room at 20.5°C. The student measured the temperature of the water in the bottle at 7 a.m. and again at 3 p.m. The data from the investigation are shown in the table below.

Water Bottle Investigation Data

7 a.m.		3 p.m.	
Mass of Water (g)	Temperature (°C)	Mass of Water (g)	Temperature (°C)
800.	12.5	800.	20.5

21 Show a numerical setup for calculating the change in the thermal energy of the water in the bottle from 7 a.m. to 3 p.m.

22 State the direction of heat transfer between the surroundings and the water in the bottle from 7 a.m. to 3 p.m.

23 Compare the average kinetic energy of the water molecules in the bottle at 7 a.m. to the average kinetic energy of the water molecules in the bottle at 3 p.m.

Base your answers to questions **24** and **25** on the information below.

Starting as a gas at 206°C, a sample of a substance is allowed to cool for 16 minutes. This process is represented by the cooling curve below.

Cooling Curve for a Substance

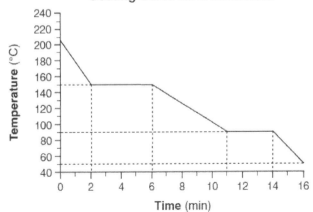

24 At what time do the particles of this sample have the *lowest* average kinetic energy?

25 What is the melting point of this substance?

Answers on Page 337

1 The elements on the Periodic Table are arranged in order of increasing

(1) mass number
(2) atomic number
(3) number of isotopes
(4) number of valence electrons

2 Which phrase describes the molecular structure and properties of two solid forms of carbon, diamond and graphite?

(1) the same molecular structures and the same properties
(2) the same molecular structures and different properties
(3) different molecular structures and the same properties
(4) different molecular structures and different properties

3 Which property can be defined as the ability of a substance to be hammered into thin sheets?

(1) conductivity   (3) melting point
(2) malleability   (4) solubility

4 The number of valence electrons in each atom of an element affects the element's

(1) chemical properties
(2) number of isotopes
(3) decay mode
(4) half-life

5 A solid element that is malleable, a good conductor of electricity, and reacts with oxygen is classified as a

(1) metal   (3) noble gas
(2) metalloid   (4) nonmetal

6 As the elements is Period 3 are considered in order of increasing atomic number, there is a general *decrease* in

(1) atomic mass
(2) atomic radius
(3) electronegativity
(4) first ionization energy

7 What is the total number of valence electrons in a germanium atom in the ground state?

(1) 22   (2) 2   (3) 32   (4) 4

8 Which term represents the attraction one atom has for the electrons in a bond with another atom?

(1) electronegativity
(2) electrical conductivity
(3) first ionization energy
(4) mechanical energy

9 In the ground state, an atom of each of the elements in Group 2 has a different

(1) oxidation state
(2) first ionization energy
(3) number of valence electrons
(4) number of electrons in the first shell

10 Which statement explains why neon is a Group 18 element?

(1) Neon is a gas at STP.
(2) Neon has a low melting point.
(3) Neon atoms have a stable valence electron configuration.
(4) Neon atoms have two electrons in the first shell.

11 Which elements have the most similar chemical properties?

(1) Si, As, and Te   (3) Mg, Sr, and Ba
(2) N_2, O_2, and F_2 (4) Ca, Cs, and Cu

12 Which list of elements contains a metal, a metalloid, and a nonmetal?

(1) B, Si, I_2 (3) Li, Mn, F_2
(2) Hg, Te, Ne   (4) H_2, Si, C

13 Which element is a liquid at STP?

(1) bromine   (3) francium
(2) cesium   (4) iodine

14 Which element is malleable and a good conductor of electricity at STP?

(1) argon   (3) iodine
(2) carbon   (4) silver

15 Which element has the highest melting point?

(1) tantalum   (3) osmium
(2) rhenium   (4) hafnium

16 Which element has the greatest density at STP?

(1) calcium   (3) chlorine
(2) carbon   (4) copper

17 Which atom has the largest atomic radius?

(1) potassium   (3) francium
(2) rubidium   (4) cesium

18 Which atom has the *weakest* attraction for electrons in a chemical bond?

(1) a boron atom   (3) a fluorine atom
(2) a calcium atom   (4) a nitrogen atom

19 Which atom in the ground state requires the *least amount of energy to remove its valence electron?*

(1) lithium atom   (3) rubidium atom
(2) potassium atom   (4) sodium atom

Base your answers to questions **20** and **21** on the information below and on your knowledge of chemistry.

There are six elements in Group 14 on the Periodic Table. One of these elements has the symbol Uuq, which is a temporary, systematic symbol. This element is now known as flerovium.

20 State the expected number of valence electrons in an atom of the element flerovium in the ground state.

21 Explain, in terms of electron shells, why each successive element in Group 14 has a larger atomic radius, as the elements are considered in order of increasing atomic number.

Base your answers to questions **22** through **25** on the information below and on your knowledge of chemistry.

The diagram below represents three elements in Group 13 and three elements in Period 3 and their relative positions on the Periodic Table.

Some elements in the solid phase exist in different forms that vary in their physical properties. For example, at room temperature, red phosphorus has a density of 2.16 g/cm^3 and white phosphorus has a density of 1.823 g/cm^3.

22 Identify *one* element from the diagram that will combine with phosphorus in the same ratio of atoms as the ratio in aluminum phosphide.

23 Compare the number of atoms per cubic centimeter in red phosphorus with the number of atoms per cubic centimeter in white phosphorus.

24 Consider the Period 3 elements in the diagram in order of increasing atomic number. State the trend in electronegativity for these elements.

25 Identify the element from the diagram that will react with chlorine to form a compound with the general formula XCl_4.

1 Which statement describes the distribution of charge in an atom?

(1) A neutral nucleus is surrounded by one or more negatively charged electrons.

(2) A neutral nucleus is surrounded by one or more positively charged electrons.

(3) A positively charged nucleus is surrounded by one or more negatively charged electrons.

(4) A positively charged nucleus is surrounded by one or more positively charged electrons.

2 In the wave-mechanical model of the atom, an orbital is defined as

(1) a region of the most probable proton location

(2) a region of the most probable electron location

(3) a circular path traveled by a proton around the nucleus

(4) a circular path traveled by an electron around the nucleus

3 Which phrase describes the charge and mass of a neutron?

(1) a charge of +1 and no mass

(2) a charge of +1 and an approximate mass of 1 u

(3) no charge and no mass

(4) no charge and an approximate mass of 1 u

4 Which quantity represents the number of protons in an atom?

(1) atomic number

(2) oxidation number

(3) number of neutrons

(4) number of valence electrons

5 The atomic mass of magnesium is the weighted average of the atomic masses of

(1) all of the artificially produced isotopes of Mg

(2) all of the naturally occurring isotopes of Mg

(3) the two most abundant artificially produced isotopes of Mg

(4) the two most abundant naturally occurring isotopes of Mg

6 A specific amount of energy is emitted when excited electrons in an atom in a sample of an element return to the ground state. This emitted energy can be used to determine the

(1) mass of the sample

(2) volume of the sample

(3) identity of the element

(4) number of moles of the element

7 Which particle has the *least mass?*

(1) alpha particle   (3) neutron

(2) beta particle   (4) proton

8 Which conclusion was a direct result of the gold foil experiment?

(1) An atom is mostly empty space with a dense, positively charged nucleus.

(2) An atom is composed of at least three types of subatomic particles.

(3) An electron has a positive charge and is located inside the nucleus.

(4) An electron has properties of both waves and particles.

9 An electron in a sodium atom gains enough energy to move from the second shell to the third shell. The sodium atom becomes

(1) a positive ion

(2) a negative ion

(3) an atom in an excited state

(4) an atom in the ground state

10 Which statement about one atom of an element identifies the element?

(1) The atom has 1 proton.

(2) The atom has 2 neutrons.

(3) The sum of the number of protons and neutrons in the atom is 3.

(4) The difference between the number of neutrons and protons in the atom is 1.

11 What is the charge of the nucleus of an oxygen atom?

(1) 0   (2) −2   (3) +8   (4) +16

12 The nuclides I-131 and I-133 are classified as

(1) isomers of the same element

(2) isomers of Xe-131 and Cs-133

(3) isotopes of the same element

(4) isotopes of Xe-131 and Cs-133

13 Given the particle diagram:

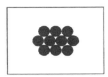

Key
● = an atom

Which substance at STP can be represented by this particle diagram?

(1) N_2 (2) H_2 (3) Mg (4) Kr

14 Which two notations represent different isotopes of the same element?

(1) $^{6}_{4}Be$ and $^{9}_{4}Be$ (2) $^{7}_{3}Li$ and $^{7}_{3}Li$ (3) $^{14}_{7}N$ and $^{14}_{6}C$ (4) $^{32}_{15}P$ and $^{32}_{16}S$

15 The table below gives the atomic mass and the abundance of the two naturally occurring isotopes of chlorine.

Naturally Occuring Isotopes of Chlorine

Isotopes	AtomicMassof theIsotopes (u)	Natural Abundance (%)
^{35}Cl	34.97	75.76
^{37}Cl	36.97	24.24

Which numerical setup can be used to calculate the atomic mass of the element chlorine?

(1) (34.97 u)(75.76) + (36.97 u)(24.24)

(2) (34.97 u)(0.2424) + (36.97 u)(0.7576)

(3) (34.97 u)(0.7576) + (36.97 u)(0.2424)

(4) (34.97 u)(24.24)   (36.97 u)(75.76)

16 Which electron configuration represents the electrons of an atom in an excited state?

(1) 2-1 (3) 2-8-7

(2) 2-7-4 (4) 2-4

17 A bromine atom in an excited state could have an electron configuration of

(1) 2-8-18-6 (3) 2-8-17-7

(2) 2-8-18-7 (4) 2-8-17-8

18 A sample of matter must be copper if

(1) each atom in the sample has 29 protons

(2) atoms in the sample react with oxygen

(3) the sample melts at 1768 K

(4) the sample can conduct electricity

19 Which atom in the ground state has an outermost electron with the most energy?

(1) Cs (2) K (3) Li (4) Na

Base your answers to questions **20** through **22** on the information below and on your knowledge of chemistry.

The bright-line spectra observed in a spectroscope for three elements and a mixture of two of these elements are represented in the diagram below.

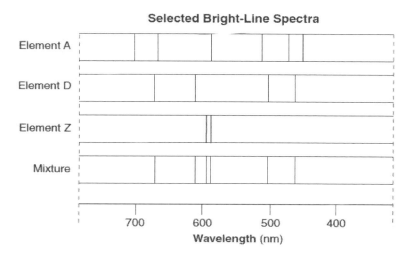

Selected Bright-Line Spectra

20 Describe, in terms of *both* electrons and energy state, how the light represented by the spectral lines is produced.

21 Explain why the spectrum produced by a 1-gram sample of element Z would have the same spectral lines at the same wavelengths as the spectrum produced by a 2-gram sample of element Z.

22 State evidence from the bright-line spectra that indicates element *A* is *not* present in the mixture.

23 Explain, in terms of electron configuration, why arsenic and antimony are chemically similar.

24 Copper has two naturally occurring isotopes. Information about the two isotopes is shown in the table below.

Naturally Occurring Isotopes of Copper

Isotope	Atomic Mass (atomic mass units, u)	Percent Natural Abundance (%)
Cu-63	62.93	69.17
Cu-65	64.93	30.83

In the space *in your answer booklet*, show a numerical setup for calculating the atomic mass of copper.

25 In the box below, draw a Lewis electron-dot diagram for an atom of boron.

307

1 Given the balanced equation representing a reaction:

$$O_2 \rightarrow O + O$$

What occurs during this reaction?

(1) Energy is absorbed as bonds are broken.
(2) Energy is absorbed as bonds are formed.
(3) Energy is released as bonds are broken.
(4) Energy is released as bonds are formed.

2 What occurs as two atoms of fluorine combine to become a molecule of fluorine?

(1) A bond is formed as energy is absorbed.
(2) A bond is formed as energy is released.
(3) A bond is broken as energy is absorbed.
(4) A bond is broken as energy is released.

3 Which term indicates how strongly an atom attracts the electrons in a chemical bond?

(1) alkalinity   (3) electronegativity
(2) atomic mass   (4) activation energy

4 Which type of bond results when one or more valence electrons are transferred from one atom to another?

(1) a hydrogen bond
(2) an ionic bond
(3) a nonpolar covalent bond
(4) a polar covalent bond

5 A solid substance is an excellent conductor of electricity. The chemical bonds in this substance are most likely

(1) ionic, because the valence electrons are shared between atoms
(2) ionic, because the valence electrons are mobile
(3) metallic, because the valence electrons are stationary
(4) metallic, because the valence electrons are mobile

6 Conductivity in a metal results from the metal atoms having

(1) high electronegativity
(2) high ionization energy
(3) highly mobile protons in the nucleus
(4) highly mobile electrons in the valence shell

7 Which element reacts with oxygen to form ionic bonds?

(1) calcium   (3) chlorine
(2) hydrogen   (4) nitrogen

8 Which formulas represent one ionic compound and one molecular compound?

(1) N_2 and SO_2 (3) $BaCl_2$ and N_2O_4
(2) Cl_2 and H_2S (4) $NaOH$ and $BaSO_4$

9 A sample of a substance has these characteristics:

• melting point of 984 K
• hard, brittle solid at room temperature
• poor conductor of heat and electricity as a solid
• good conductor of electricity as a liquid on in an aqueous solution

This sample is classified as

(1) a metallic element
(2) a radioactive element
(3) a molecular compound
(4) an ionic compound

10 Metallic bonding occurs between atoms of

(1) sulfur   (3) fluorine
(2) copper   (4) carbon

11 The electronegativity difference between the atoms in a molecule of HCl can be used to determine

(1) the entropy of the atoms
(2) the atomic number of the atoms
(3) the first ionization energy of the atoms
(4) the polarity of the bond between the two atoms

12 Which formula represents a molecule with the most polar bond?

(1) CO (2) NO (3) HI (4) HCl

13 Which molecule has a nonpolar covalent bond?

(1) H−H
(2) H∕N∖H with H below
(3) H∕O∖H
(4) H−Cl

14 Which phrase describes a molecule of CH_4, in terms of molecular polarity and distribution of charge?

(1) polar with an asymmetrical distribution of charge
(2) polar with a symmetrical distribution of charge
(3) nonpolar with an asymmetrical distribution of charge
(4) nonpolar with a symmetrical distribution of charge

15 Which symbol represents an atom in the ground state with the most stable valence electron configuration?

(1) B (2) O (3) Li (4) Ne

16 Which element has the *lowest* electronegativity value?

(1) F (2) Fr (3) Cl (4) Cr

17 Given the Lewis electron-dot diagram:

H
H:C:H
H

Which electrons are represented by all of the dots?

(1) the carbon valence electrons, only
(2) the hydrogen valence electrons, only
(3) the carbon and hydrogen valence electrons
(4) all of the carbon and hydrogen electrons

18 Which Lewis electron-dot diagram represents a nitrogen atom in the ground state?

(1) N
(2) ·N·
(3) ·N·
(4) :N:

19 Which Lewis electron-dot diagram represents a molecule having a nonpolar covalent bond?

(1) :Cl:Cl:
(2) H:Cl:
(3) K⁺[:Br:]⁻
(4) H:S: with H below

20 Which Lewis electron-dot diagram is correct for CO_2?

(1) :O· with C:O below
(2) :O:C:O:
(3) :O::C::O:
(4) ·O· with C:O below

21 At standard pressure, CH_4 boils at 112 K and H_2O boils at 373 K. What accounts for the higher boiling point of H_2O at standard pressure?

(1) covalent bonding
(2) ionic bonding
(3) hydrogen bonding
(4) metallic bonding

22 Hydrogen bonding is a type of

(1) strong covalent bond
(2) weak ionic bond
(3) strong intermolecular force
(4) weak intermolecular force

23 An ionic bond can be formed when one or more electrons are

(1) equally shared by two atoms
(2) unequally shared by two atoms
(3) transferred from the nucleus of one atom to the nucleus of another atom
(4) transferred from the valence shell of one atom to the valence shell of another atom

Base your answers to questions **24** and **25** on the information below.

Physical Properties of CF$_4$ and NH$_3$
at Standard Pressure

Compound	Melting Point (°C)	Boiling Point (°C)	Solubility in Water at 20.0°C
CF$_4$	−183.6	−127.8	insoluble
NH$_3$	−77.7	−33.3	soluble

24 In the space *in your answer booklet*, draw a Lewis electron-dot diagram for CF₄.

25 State evidence that indicates NH₃ has stronger intermolecular forces than CF₄.

_____

Base your answers to questions **26** through **28** on the information below and on your knowledge of chemistry.

Rubbing alcohol is a product available at most pharmacies and supermarkets. One rubbing alcohol solution contains 2-propanol and water. The boiling point of 2-propanol is 82.3°C at standard pressure.

26 Explain, in term of charge distribution, why a molecule of the 2-propanol is a polar molecule.

27 Identify a strong intermolecular force of attraction between an alcohol molecule and a water molecule in the solution.

28 Explain in terms of electronegativity differences, why a C–O bond is more polar than a C–H bond.

1 Which list includes three type of chemical formulas for organic compounds?

(1) covalent, metallic, isotopic
(2) covalent, metallic, molecular
(3) empirical, structural, isotopic
(4) empirical, structural, molecular

2 Which type of formula represents the simplest whole-number ratio of atoms of the elements in a compound?

(1) molecular formula
(2) condensed formula
(3) empirical formula
(4) structural formula

3 The coefficients in a balanced chemical equation represent

(1) the mass ratios of the substances in the reaction
(2) the mole ratios of the substances in the reaction
(3) the total number of electrons in the reaction
(4) the total number of elements in the reaction

4 A balanced equation representing a chemical reaction can be written using

(1) chemical formulas and mass numbers
(2) chemical formulas and coefficients
(3) first ionization energies and mass numbers
(4) first ionization energies and coefficients

5 Given the balanced equation representing a reaction:

$H^+(aq)$ $OH^-(aq) \rightarrow H_2O(\ell)$ 55.8 kJ
In this reaction there is conservation of

(1) mass, only
(2) mass and charge, only
(3) mass and energy, only
(4) mass, charge, and energy

6 Which formula is both a molecular and an empirical formula?

(1) $C_6H_{12}O_6$ (3) C_3H_8O
(2) $C_2H_4O_2$ (4) C_4H_8

7 Given the formula for a compound:

Which molecular formula and empirical formula represent this compound?

(1) C_2HNO_2 and CHNO
(2) C_2HNO_2 and C_2HNO_2
(3) $C_4H_2N_2O_4$ and CHNO
(4) $C_4H_2N_2O_4$ and C_2HNO_2

8 What is the empirical formula for a compound with the molecular formula $C_6H_{12}Cl_2O_2$?

(1) CHClO   (3) C_3H_6ClO
(2) CH_2Cl (4) $C_6H_{12}C_{12}O_2$

9 Which equation shows a conservation of mass?

(1) $Na + Cl_2 \rightarrow NaCl$
(2) $Al + Br_2 \rightarrow AlBr_3$
(3) $H_2O \rightarrow H_2 + O_2$
(4) $PCl_5 \rightarrow PCl_3 + Cl_2$

10 Which terms identify types of chemical reactions?

(1) decomposition and sublimation
(2) decomposition and synthesis
(3) deposition and sublimation
(4) deposition and synthesis

11 Which formula represents strontium phosphate?

(1) $SrPO_4$ (3) $Sr_2(PO_4)_3$
(2) Sr_3PO_8 (4) $Sr_3(PO_4)_2$

12 What is the IUPAC name for the compound ZnO?

(1) zinc oxide   (3) zinc peroxide
(2) zinc oxalate   (4) zinc hydroxide

13 What is the chemical formula of iron(III) sulfide?

(1) FeS   (3) $FeSO_3$
(2) Fe_2S_3 (4) $Fe_2(SO_3)_3$

14 Which formula represents copper(I) oxide?

(1) CuO   (3) Cu_2O

(2) CuO_2 (4) Cu_2O_2

15 In the formula X_2SO_4, the symbol X could represent the element

(1) Al   (2) Ar   (3) Mg   (4) Li

16 Given the incomplete equation representing a reaction:

$$2C_6H_{14} + \underline{\hspace{2cm}} O_2 \rightarrow 12CO_2 + 14H_2O$$

What is the coefficient of O_2 when the equation is completely balanced using the smallest whole-number coefficients?

(1) 13   (2) 14   (3) 19   (4) 26

17 Given the balanced equations representing two chemical reactions:

$$Cl_2 + 2NaBr \rightarrow 2NaCl + Br_2$$
$$2NaCl \rightarrow 2Na + Cl_2$$

Which type of chemical reactions are represented by these equations?

(1) single replacement and decomposition
(2) single replacement and double replacement
(3) synthesis and decomposition
(4) synthesis and double replacement

18 Which balanced equation represents a double replacement reaction?

(1) $Mg + 2AgNO_3 \rightarrow Mg(NO_3)_2 + 2Ag$
(2) $2Mg + O_2 \rightarrow 2MgO$
(3) $MgCO_3 \rightarrow MgO + CO_2$
(4) $MgCl_2 + 2AgNO_3 \rightarrow 2AgCl \quad Mg(NO_3)_2$

Base your answers to questions **19** through **22** on the information below.

The reaction between aluminum and an aqueous solution of copper(II) sulfate is represented by the unbalanced equation below.

$$Al(s) + CuSO_4(aq) \rightarrow Al_2(SO_4)_3(aq) + Cu(s)$$

19 Explain why the equation represents a chemical change.

20 Balance the equation below, using the smallest whole-number coefficients.

$$\underline{\hspace{1cm}}Al(s) + \underline{\hspace{0.5cm}}CuSO_4(aq) \rightarrow \underline{\hspace{1cm}}Al_2(SO_4)_3(aq) + \underline{\hspace{1cm}}Cu(s)$$

21 Identify the type of chemical reaction represented by the equation.

22 Determine the total mass of Cu produced when 1.08 grams of Al reacts completely with 9.58 grams of $CuSO_4$ to produce 6.85 grams of $Al_2(SO_4)_3$.

23 Base your answer to the following question on the information below.

In an experiment, 2.54 grams of copper completely reacts with sulfur, producing 3.18 grams of copper(I) sulfide.

Write the chemical formula of the compound produced.

314

1 The sum of the atomic masses of the atoms in one molecule of $C_3H_6Br_2$ is called the

   (1) formula mass
   (2) isotopic mass
   (3) percent abundance
   (4) percent composition

2 The gram-formula mass of NO_2 is defined as the mass of

   (1) one mole of NO_2
   (2) one molecule of NO_2
   (3) two moles of NO
   (4) two molecules of NO

3 Which sample contains a mole of atoms?

   (1) 23 g Na   (3) 42 g Kr
   (2) 24 g C   (4) 78 g K

4 What is the gram-formula mass of $(NH_4)_3PO_4$?

   (1) 112 g/mol   (3) 149 g/mol
   (2) 121 g/mol   (4) 242 g/mol

5 What is the mass of 1.5 moles of CO_2?

   (1) 66 g   (2) 44 g   (3) 33 g   (4) 29 g

6 The molar mass of $Ba(OH)_2$ is

   (1) 154.3 g   (3) 171.3 g
   (2) 155.3 g   (4) 308.6 g

7 Which compound has the greatest percent composition by mass of sulfur?

   (1) BaS   (2) CaS   (3) MgS   (4) SrS

8 What is the percent composition by mass of sulfur in the compound $MgSO_4$ (gram-formula mass = 120. grams per mole)?

   (1) 20%   (2) 27%   (3) 46%   (4) 53%

9 Given the balanced equation representing a reaction:

$$4NH_3(g) + 5O_2(g) \rightarrow 4NO(g) + 6H_2O(g)$$

What is the number of moles of $H_2O(g)$ formed when 2.0 moles of $NH_3(g)$ react completely?

   (1) 6.0 mol   (3) 3.0 mol
   (2) 2.0 mol   (4) 4.0 mol

10 Given the balanced equation representing the reaction between methane and oxygen:

$$CH_4 + 2O_2 \rightarrow CO_2 + 2H_2O$$

According to this equation, what is the mole ratio of oxygen to methane?

   (1) $\frac{1 \text{ gram } O_2}{2 \text{ grams } CH_4}$ (3) $\frac{2 \text{ grams } O_2}{1 \text{ gram } CH_4}$
   (2) $\frac{1 \text{ mole } O_2}{2 \text{ moles } CH_4}$ (4) $\frac{2 \text{ moles } O_2}{1 \text{ mole } CH_4}$

11 Given the balanced equation representing a reaction:

$$Al_2(SO_4)_3 + 6NaOH \rightarrow 2Al(OH)_3 + 3Na_2SO_4$$

The mole ratio of NaOH to $Al(OH)_3$ is

   (1) 1:1   (2) 1:3   (3) 3:1   (4) 3:7

Base your answers to questions **12** and **13** on the information below.

Vitamin C, also known as ascorbic acid, is water soluble and cannot be produced by the human body. Each day, a person's diet should include a source of vitamin C, such as orange juice. Ascorbic acid has a molecular formula of $C_6H_8O_6$ and a gram-formula mass of 176 grams per mole.

12 Show a numerical setup for calculating the percent composition by mass of oxygen in ascorbic acid.

13 Determine the number of moles of vitamin C in an orange that contains 0.071 gram of vitamin C.

_____

Base your answers to questions **14** and **15** on the information below.

A tablet of one antacid contains citric acid, $H_3C_6H_5O_7$, and sodium hydrogen carbonate, $NaHCO_3$. When the tablet dissolves in water, bubbles of CO_2 are produced. This reaction is represented by the incomplete equation below.

$H_3C_6H_5O_7(aq) + 3NaHCO_3(aq) \rightarrow Na_3C_6H_5O_7(aq) + 3CO_2(g) + 3$ _____ (ℓ)

14 Determine the total number of moles of sodium hydrogen carbonate that will completely react with 0.010 mole of citric acid.

15 Write the formula of the missing product.

_____

Base your answers to questions **16** through **18** on the information below.

Hydrogen peroxide, H_2O_2, is a water-soluble compound. The concentration of an aqueous hydrogen peroxide solution that is 3% by mass H_2O_2 is used as an antiseptic. When the solution is poured on a small cut in the skin, H_2O_2 reacts according to the balanced equation below.

$2H_2O_2 \rightarrow 2H_2O + O_2$

16 Determine the gram-formula mass of H_2O_2.

17 Calculate the total mass of H_2O_2 in 20.0 grams of an aqueous H_2O_2 solution that is used as an antiseptic. Your response must include both a numerical setup and the calculated result.

18 Identify the type of chemical reaction represented by the balanced equation.

1 Which property of an unsaturated solution of sodium chloride in water remains the same when more water is added to the solution?

(1) density of the solution
(2) boiling point of the solution
(3) mass of sodium chloride in the solution
(4) percent by mass of water in the solution

2 Under which conditions of temperature and pressure is a gas most soluble in water?

(1) high temperature and low pressure
(2) high temperature and high pressure
(3) low temperature and low pressure
(4) low temperature and high pressure

3 A change in pressure would have the greatest effect on the solubility of a

(1) solid in a liquid   (3) liquid in a liquid
(2) gas in a liquid   (4) liquid in a solid

4 Which phrase describes the molarity of a solution?

(1) liters of solute per mole of solution
(2) liters of solution per mole of solution
(3) moles of solute per liter of solution
(4) moles of solution per liter of solution

5 The concentration of a solution can be expressed in

(1) milliliters per minute
(2) parts per million
(3) grams per kelvin
(4) joules per gram

6 Two substances in a mixture differ in density and particle size. These properties can be used to

(1) separate the substances
(2) chemically combine the substances
(3) determine the freezing point of the mixture
(4) predict the electrical conductivity of the mixture

7 A solution consists of 0.50 mole of $CaCl_2$ dissolved in 100. grams of H_2O at 25°C. Compared to the boiling point and freezing point of 100. grams of H_2O at standard pressure, the solution at standard pressure has

(1) a lower boiling point and a lower freezing point
(2) a lower boiling point and a higher freezing point
(3) a higher boiling point and a lower freezing point
(4) a higher boiling point and a higher freezing point

8 According to Reference Table F, which of these compounds is most soluble at 298 K and 1 atm?

(1) $AgNO_3$ (3) $PbCrO_4$
(2) $AgCl$ (4) $PbCO_3$

9 Which ion, when combined with chloride ions, Cl^-, forms an insoluble substance in water?

(1) Fe^{2+} (3) Pb^{2+}
(2) Mg^{2+} (4) Zn^{2+}

10 Which substance is most soluble in water?

(1) $(NH_4)_3PO_4$ (3) Ag_2SO_4
(2) $Cu(OH)_2$ (4) $CaCO_3$

11 At standard pressure, which substance becomes *less* soluble in water as temperature increases from 10.°C to 80.°C?

(1) HCl   (3) NaCl
(2) KCl   (4) NH_4Cl

12 An unsaturated aqueous solution of NH_3 is at 90°C in 100. grams of water. According to Reference Table *G*, how many grams of NH_3 could this unsaturated solution contain?

(1) 5 g   (3) 15 g
(2) 10. g   (4) 20. g

13 What is the total mass of KNO_3 that must be dissolved in 50. grams of H_2O at 60.°C to make a saturated solution?

(1) 32 g   (3) 64 g
(2) 53 g   (4) 106 g

14 A 2400.-gram sample of an aqueous solution contains 0.012 gram of NH_3. What is the concentration of NH_3 in the solution, expressed as parts per million?

(1) 5.0 ppm   (3) 20. ppm
(2) 15 ppm   (4) 50. ppm

15 Which solution has the highest boiling point at standard pressure?

(1) 0.10 M KCl(aq)
(2) 0.10 M K_2SO_4(aq)
(3) 0.10 M K_3PO_4(aq)
(4) 0.10 M KNO_3(aq)

16 Which sample, when dissolved in 1.0 liter of water, produces a solution with the highest boiling point?

(1) 0.1 mole KI   (3) 0.1 mole $MgCl_2$
(2) 0.2 mole KI   (4) 0.2 mole $MgCl_2$

17 A student prepares four aqueous solutions, each with a different solute. The mass of each dissolved solute is shown in the table below.

Mass of Dissolved Solute
for Four Aqueous Solutions

Solution Number	Solute	Mass of Dissolved Solute (per 100. g of H_2O at 20.°C)
1	KI	120. g
2	$NaNO_3$	88 g
3	KCl	25 g
4	$KClO_3$	5 g

Which solution is saturated?

(1) 1   (2) 2   (3) 3   (4) 4

18 Base your answer to the following question on the information below and on your knowledge of chemistry.

Ethane, C_2H_6, has a boiling point of -89°C at standard pressure. Ethanol, C_2H_5OH, has a much higher boiling point than ethane at standard pressure. At STP, ethane is a gas and ethanol is a liquid.

A liquid boils when the vapor pressure of the liquid equals the atmospheric pressure on the surface of the liquid. Based on Table H, what is the boiling point of ethanol at standard pressure?

19 Base your answer to the following question on the information below and on your knowledge of chemistry

A 2.50-liter aqueous solution contains 1.25 moles of dissolved sodium chloride. The dissolving of NaCl(s) in water is represented by the equation below.

$$NaCl(s) \xrightarrow{H_2O} Na^+(aq) + Cl^-(aq)$$

Compare the freezing point of this solution to the freezing point of a solution containing 0.75 mole NaCl per 2.50 liters of solution.

20 Base your answer to the following question on the information below.

A scientist makes a solution that contains 44.0 grams of hydrogen chloride gas, HCl(g), in 200 grams of water, H2O(ℓ), at 20. °C. This process is represented by the balanced equation below.

$$HCl(g) \xrightarrow{H_2O} H^+(aq) + Cl^-(aq)$$

Based on Reference Table G, identify, in terms of saturation, the type of solution made by the scientist.

Base your answers to questions 21 through 23 on the information below.

The compounds NH4Br(s) and NH3(g) are soluble in water. Solubility data for NH4Br(s) in water are listed in the table below.

Solubility of NH$_4$Br in H$_2$O

Temperature (°C)	Mass of NH$_4$Br per 100. g of H$_2$O (g)
0	60.
20.	75
40.	90.
60.	105
80.	120.
100.	135

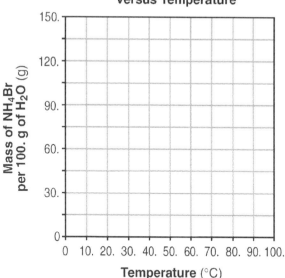

Solubility of NH$_4$Br in H$_2$O Versus Temperature

21 On the grid above, plot the data from the data table. Circle and connect the points.

22 Compare the solubilities of NH4Br(s) and NH3(g), each in 100. grams of H2O, as temperature increases at standard pressure. Your response must include *both* NH4Br(s) and NH3(g).

23 Determine the total mass of NH4Br(s) that must be dissolved in 200. grams of H2O at 60.°C to produce a saturated solution.

1 What can be explained by the Arrhenius theory?

(1) the behavior of many acids and bases
(2) the effect of stress on a phase equilibrium
(3) the operation of an electrochemical cell
(4) the spontaneous decay of some nuclei

2 Which statement describes one acid-base theory?

(1) An acid is an H^+ acceptor, and a base is an H^+ donor.
(2) An acid is an H^+ donor, and a base is an H^+ acceptor.
(3) An acid is an H^- acceptor, and a base is an H^- donor.
(4) An acid is an H^- donor, and a base is an H^- acceptor.

3 The reaction of an Arrhenius acid with an Arrhenius base produces water and

(1) a salt   (3) an aldehyde
(2) an ester   (4) a halocarbon

4 Potassium hydroxide is classified as an Arrhenius base because KOH contains

(1) OH^- ions   (3) K^+ ions
(2) O^{2-} ions   (4) H^+ ions

5 According to the Arrhenius theory, an acid is a substance that

(1) changes litmus from red to blue
(2) changes phenolphthalein from colorless to pink
(3) produces hydronium ions as the only positive ions in an aqueous solution
(4) produces hydroxide ions as the only negative ions in an aqueous solution

6 Which compounds are classified as Arrhenius acids?

(1) HCl and NaOH   (3) NH_3 and H_2CO_3
(2) HNO_3 and NaCl   (4) HBr and H_2SO_4

7 The pH of a solution is 7. When acid is added to the solution, the hydronium ion concentration becomes 100 times greater. What is the pH of the new solution?

(1) 1   (2) 5   (3) 9   (4) 14

8 When the pH of an aqueous solution is changed from 1 to 2, the concentration of hydronium ions in the solution is

(1) decreased by a factor of 2
(2) decreased by a factor of 10
(3) increased by a factor of 2
(4) increased by a factor of 10

9 Three samples of the same solution are tested, each with a different indicator. All three indicators, bromthymol blue, bromcresol green and thymol blue, appear blue if the pH of the solution is

(1) 4.7   (2) 6.0   (3) 7.8   (4) 9.9

10 What is the color of the indicator thymol blue in a solution that has a pH of 11?

(1) red   (3) pink
(2) blue   (4) yellow

11 Which solution reacts with LiOH(aq) to produce a salt and water?

(1) KCl(aq)   (3) NaOH(aq)
(2) CaO(aq)   (4) H_2SO_4(aq)

12 What are the products when potassium hydroxide reacts with hydrochloric acid?

(1) KH(s), Cl^+(aq), and OH^-(aq)
(2) K(s), Cl_2(g), and $H_2O(\ell)$
(3) KCl(aq) and $H_2O(\ell)$
(4) KOH(aq) and Cl_2(g)

13 Which process is used to determine the concentration of an acid?

(1) chromatography   (3) electrolysis
(2) distillation   (4) titration

14 Given the balanced equation representing a reaction:

$$HSO_4^-(aq) + H_2O(l) \rightarrow H_3O^+(aq) + SO_4^{2-}(aq)$$

According to one acid-base theory, the $H_2O(l)$ molecules act as

(1) a base because they accept H^+ ions   (3) an acid because they accept H^+ ions

(2) a base because they donate H^+ ions   (4) an acid because they donate H^+ ions

---

15 In a titration, 20.0 milliliters of a 0.150 M NaOH(aq) solution exactly neutralizes 24.0 milliliters of an HCl(aq) solution. What is the concentration of the HCl(aq) solution?

(1) 0.125 M   (3) 0.250 M

(2) 0.180 M   (4) 0.360 M

16 Which laboratory test result can be used to determine if KCl(s) is an electrolyte?

(1) pH of KCl(aq)

(2) pH of KCl(s)

(3) electrical conductivity of KCl(aq)

(4) electrical conductivity of KCl(s)

17 Which compound is an electrolyte?

(1) H_2O (3) H_3PO_4

(2) C_2H_6 (4) CH_3OH

18 Which substance is an electrolyte?

(1) O_2 (3) C_3H_8

(2) Xe   (4) KNO_3

Base your answers to questions **19** and **20** on the information below and on your knowledge of chemistry.

The pH of various aqueous solutions are shown in the table below.

pH of Various Aqueous Solutions

Aqueous Solution	pH
HCl(aq)	2
$HC_2H_3O_2$(aq)	3
NaCl(aq)	7
NaOH(aq)	12

19 State how many times greater the hydronium ion concentration in the HCl(aq) is than the hydronium ion concentration in the $HC_2H_3O_2$(aq).

20 Complete the table by writing the color of thymol blue in the NaCl(aq) and in the NaOH(aq) solutions.

Aqueous Solution	Color of Thymol Blue
NaCl(aq)	
NaOH(aq)	

Base your answers to questions **21** and **22** on the information below and on your knowledge of chemistry.

In a titration, 50.0 milliliters of 0.026 M HCl(aq) is neutralized by 38.5 milliliters of KOH(aq).

21 Complete the equation for the neutralization by writing the formula of the missing product.

$$KOH(aq) + HCl(aq) \rightarrow \underline{\hspace{3cm}} (aq) + H_2O(\ell)$$

22 Show a numerical setup for calculating the molarity of the KOH(aq).

1 A chemical reaction between iron atoms and oxygen molecules can only occur if

(1) the particles are heated
(2) the atmospheric pressure decreases
(3) there is a catalyst present
(4) there are effective collisions between the particle

2 A reaction is most likely to occur when reactant particles collide with

(1) proper energy, only
(2) proper orientation, only
(3) both proper energy and proper orientation
(4) neither proper energy nor proper orientation

3 The energy needed to start a chemical reaction is called

(1) potential energy   (3) activation energy
(2) kinetic energy   (4) ionization energy

4 Which factors have the greatest effect on the rate of a chemical reaction between $AgNO_3$(aq) and Cu(s)?

(1) solution concentration and temperature
(2) solution concentration and pressure
(3) molar mass and temperature
(4) molar mass and pressure

5 A catalyst lowers the activation energy of a reaction by

(1) providing an alternate reaction pathway
(2) decreasing the heat of reaction
(3) increasing the mass of the reactants
(4) changing the mole ratio of the reactants

6 Entropy is a measure of the

(1) acidity of a sample
(2) disorder of a system
(3) concentration of a solution
(4) chemical activity of an element

7 Which expression represents the heat of reaction for a chemical change in terms of potential energy, *PE*?

(1) $(PE_{products}) + (PE_{reactants})$
(2) $(PE_{products}) - (PE_{reactants})$
(3) $(PE_{products}) \times (PE_{reactants})$
(4) $(PE_{products}) \div (PE_{reactants})$

8 Which statement describes a reversible reaction at equilibrium?

(1) The activation energy of the forward reaction must equal the activation energy of the reverse reaction.
(2) The rate of the forward reaction must equal the rate of the reverse reaction.
(3) The concentration of the reactants must equal the concentration of the products.
(4) The potential energy of the reactants must equal the potential energy of the products.

9 Systems in nature tend to undergo changes toward

(1) lower energy and higher entropy
(2) lower energy and lower entropy
(3) higher energy and higher entropy
(4) higher energy and lower entropy

10 The entropy of a sample of CO_2 increases as the CO_2 changes from

(1) gas to liquid   (3) liquid to solid
(2) gas to solid   (4) solid to gas

11 At 101.3 kPa and 298 K, a 1.0-mole sample of which compound absorbs the greatest amount of heat as the entire sample dissolves in water?

(1) LiBr   (3) NaOH
(2) NaCl   (4) NH_4Cl

12 Which compound is formed from its elements by an exothermic reaction at 298 K and 101.3 kPa?

(1) C_2H_4(g)   (3) H_2O(g)
(2) HI(g)   (4) NO_2(g)

13 Given the balanced equation representing a reaction:

$$Fe(s) + 2HCl(aq) \rightarrow FeCl_2(aq) + H_2(g)$$

This reaction occurs more quickly when powdered iron is used instead of a single piece of iron of the same mass because the powdered iron

(1) acts as a better catalyst than the single piece of iron
(2) absorbs less energy than the single piece of iron
(3) has a greater surface area than the single piece of iron
(4) is more metallic than the single piece of iron

14 Given the potential energy diagram for a reaction:

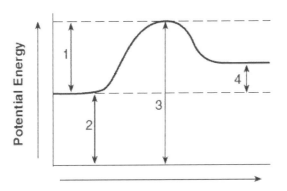

Reaction Coordinate

Which intervals are affected by the addition of a catalyst?

(1) 1 and 2   (3) 2 and 4
(2) 1 and 3   (4) 3 and 4

15 For a given chemical reaction, the addition of a catalyst provides a different reaction pathway that

(1) decreases the reaction rate and has a higher activation energy
(2) decreases the reaction rate and has a lower activation energy
(3) increases the reaction rate and has a higher activation energy
(4) increases the reaction rate and has a lower activation energy

16 Given the equation and potential energy diagram representing a reaction:

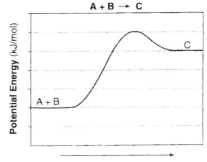

Reaction Coordinate

If each interval on the axis labeled "Potential Energy (kJ/mol)" represents 10. kJ/mol, what is the heat of reaction?   +

(1) +60. kJ/mol   (3) $^+$30. kJ/mol
(2) +20. kJ/mol   (4)   40. kJ/mol

17 Given the equation representing a system at equilibrium:

$$AgCl(s) \overset{H_2O}{\rightleftharpoons} Ag^+(aq) + Cl^-(aq)$$

When the concentration of Cl^- (aq) is increased, the concentration of Ag^+ (aq)

(1) decreases, and the amount of AgCl(s) increases
(2) decreases, and the amount of AgCl(s) decreases
(3) increases, and the amount of AgCl(s) increases
(4) increases, and the amount of AgCl(s) decreases

18 Given the equation representing a reaction at equilibrium:

$$2SO_2(g) + O_2(g) \rightleftharpoons 2SO_3(g) + heat$$

Which change causes the equilibrium to shift to the right?

(1) adding a catalyst
(2) adding more $O_2(g)$
(3) decreasing the pressure
(4) increasing the temperature

19 Given the equation representing a system at equilibrium:

$$N_2(g) + 3H_2(g) \leftrightarrow 2NH_3(g) + energy$$

Which changes occur when the temperature of this system is *decreased*?

(1) The concentration of $H_2(g)$ increases and the concentration of $N_2(g)$ increases.

(2) The concentration of $H_2(g)$ decreases and the concentration of $N_2(g)$ increases.

(3) The concentration of $H_2(g)$ decreases and the concentration of $NH_3(g)$ decreases.

(4) The concentration of $H_2(g)$ decreases and the concentration of $NH_3(g)$ increases.

Base your answers to questions **20** and **21** on the information below.

The chemical reaction between methane and oxygen is represented by the potential energy diagram and balanced equation below.

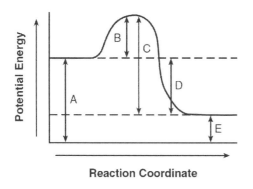

20 Explain, in terms of collision theory, why a lower concentration of oxygen gas *decreases* the rate of this reaction.

21 Which potential energy interval in the diagram represents the activation energy of the forward reaction?

$$CH_4(g) + 2O_2(g) \rightarrow CO_2(g) + 2H_2O(\ell) + 890.4 \text{ kJ}$$

Base your answers to questions **22** and **23** on the information below and on your knowledge of chemistry.

Carbon monoxide, $CO(g)$, is a toxic gas found in automobile exhaust. The concentration of $CO(g)$ can be decreased by using a catalyst in the reaction between $CO(g)$ and $O_2(g)$. This reaction is represented by the balanced equation below.

$$2CO(g) + O_2 \xrightarrow{catalyst} 2CO_2(g) + energy$$

22 On the labeled axes below, draw the potential energy curve for the reaction represented by this equation.

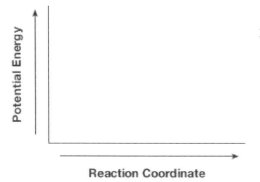

23 Explain, in terms of collision theory, why an increase in temperature increases the rate of the reaction.

Base your answers to questions **24** through **26** on the information below and on your knowledge of chemistry.

   Common household bleach is an aqueous solution containing hypochlorite ions. A closed container of bleach is an equilibrium system represented by the equation below.

$$Cl_2(g) + 2OH^-(aq) \rightleftharpoons ClO^-(aq) + Cl^-(aq) + H_2O(\ell)$$

24 State the effect on the concentration of the ClO^- ion when there is a *decrease* in the concentration of the OH^- ion.

25 Explain why the container must be closed to maintain equilibrium.

26 Compare the rate of the forward reaction to the rate of the reverse reaction for this system.

1 Hydrocarbons are compounds that contain

  (1) carbon, only
  (2) carbon and hydrogen, only
  (3) carbon, hydrogen, and oxygen, only
  (4) carbon, hydrogen, oxygen, and nitrogen, only

2 A molecule of an unsaturated hydrocarbon must have

  (1) at least one single carbon-carbon bond
  (2) at least one multiple carbon-carbon bond
  (3) two or more single carbon-carbon bonds
  (4) two or more multiple carbon-carbon bonds

3 Which element is present in all organic compounds?

  (1) nitrogen   (3) carbon
  (2) oxygen   (4) sulfur

4 Two types of organic reactions are

  (1) deposition and saponification
  (2) deposition and transmutation
  (3) polymerization and saponification
  (4) polymerization and transmutation

5 Which reaction produces ethanol?

  (1) combustion   (3) fermentation
  (2) esterification   (4) polymerization

6 When butane burns in an excess of oxygen, the principal products are

  (1) CO_2 and H_2O (3) CO and H_2O
  (2) CO_2 and H_2 (4) CO and H_2

7 Which compound is a saturated hydrocarbon?

  (1) propanal   (3) propene
  (2) propane   (4) propyne

8 Which formula represents an unsaturated hydrocarbon?

  (1) C_2H_4 (3) C_4H_{10}
  (2) C_3H_8 (4) C_5H_{12}

9 Which term identifies a type of organic reaction?

  (1) deposition   (3) esterification
  (2) distillation   (4) sublimation

10 Given the formula representing a compound:

$$H-\overset{\overset{\displaystyle H}{|}}{\underset{\underset{\displaystyle H}{|}}{C}}-\overset{\overset{\displaystyle H}{|}}{\underset{\underset{\displaystyle H}{|}}{C}}-\overset{\overset{\displaystyle H}{|}}{C}=\overset{}{C}-\overset{\overset{\displaystyle H}{|}}{\underset{\underset{\displaystyle H}{|}}{C}}-H$$

  What is a chemical name of this compound?

  (1) 2-pentene   (3) 3-pentene
  (2) 2-pentyne   (4) 3-pentyne

11 Which compound is classified as a hydrocarbon?

  (1) butanal   (3) 2-butanol
  (2) butyne   (4) 2-butanone

12 A carbon-carbon triple bond is found in a molecule of

  (1) butane   (3) butene
  (2) butanone   (4) butyne

13 Functional groups are used to classify

  (1) organic compounds
  (2) inorganic compounds
  (3) heterogeneous mixtures
  (4) homogeneous mixtures

14 The two isomers of butane have different

  (1) formula masses
  (2) empirical formulas
  (3) molecular formulas
  (4) structural formulas

15 Given a formula of a functional group:

$$-\overset{\overset{\displaystyle O}{\|}}{C}-OH$$

  An organic compound that has this functional group is classified as

  (1) an acid   (3) an ester
  (2) an aldehyde   (4) a ketone

327

16 Which class of organic compounds has molecules that contain nitrogen atoms?

(1) alcohol　　　　(3) ether
(2) amine　　　　(4) ketone

17 Given a formula representing a compound:

$$\begin{array}{ccccc} & O & H & H & H \\ & \| & | & | & | \\ H- & C- & C- & C- & C-H \\ & & | & | & | \\ & & H & H & H \end{array}$$

Which formula represents an isomer of this compound?

(1)
$$\begin{array}{ccccc} H & H & H & O \\ | & | & | & \| \\ H-C-C-C-C-H \\ | & | & | \\ H & H & H \end{array}$$

(2)
$$\begin{array}{ccccc} H & O & H & H \\ | & \| & | & | \\ H-C-C-C-C-H \\ | & & | & | \\ H & & H & H \end{array}$$

(3)
$$\begin{array}{ccccc} H & H & H & O \\ | & | & | & \| \\ H-C-C-C-C-OH \\ | & | & | \\ H & H & H \end{array}$$

(4)
$$\begin{array}{cccccc} H & H & O & & H \\ | & | & \| & & | \\ H-C-C-C-O-C-H \\ | & | & & & | \\ H & H & & & H \end{array}$$

18 Given the formula for a compound:

$$\begin{array}{cccc} H & H & & H \\ | & | & & | \\ H-C-C-C-C-H \\ | & | & \| & | \\ H & H & O & H \end{array}$$

A chemical name for this compound is

(1) butanal　　　　(3) butanone
(2) butanol　　　　(4) butanoic acid

19 Which class of compounds contains *at least one* element from Group 17 of the Periodic Table?

(1) aldehyde　　　　(3) ester
(2) amine　　　　(4) halide

20 Which formula represents the product of the addition reaction between ethene and chlorine, Cl_2 ?

(1)
$$\begin{array}{ccc} Cl & Cl \\ | & | \\ Cl-C-C-Cl \\ | & | \\ H & H \end{array}$$

(2)
$$\begin{array}{ccc} Cl & Cl \\ | & | \\ H-C-C-H \\ | & | \\ H & H \end{array}$$

(3)
$$\begin{array}{ccc} Cl & Cl \\ | & | \\ H-C=C-H \\ | & | \\ H & H \end{array}$$

(4)
$$\begin{array}{ccc} Cl & H \\ | & | \\ H-C-C-H \\ | & | \\ H & H \end{array}$$

21 Which equation represents fermentation?

(1) $C_2H_6 + Cl_2 \rightarrow C_2H_6Cl + HCl$
(2) $C_6H_{12}O_6 \rightarrow 2\ C_2H_5OH + 2\ CO_2$
(3) $CH_3COOH + CH_3OH \rightarrow CH_3COOCH_3 + H_2O$
(4) $nC_2H_4 \rightarrow (C_2H_4)n$

Base your answers to questions **22** through **24** on the information below and on your knowledge of chemistry.

The diagrams below represent ball-and-stick models of two molecules. In a ball-and-stick model, each ball represents an atom, and the sticks between balls represent chemical bonds.

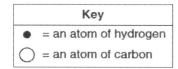

Key
● = an atom of hydrogen
○ = an atom of carbon

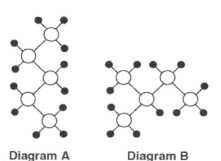

Diagram A   Diagram B

22 Explain why the molecules in diagrams A and B are isomers of each other.

23 Explain, in terms of carbon-carbon bonds, why the hydrocarbon represented in diagram B is saturated.

24 Draw a Lewis electron-dot diagram for an atom of the element present in all organic compounds.

Base your answers to questions **25** through **27** on information below.

One type of soap is produced when ethyl stearate and sodium hydroxide react. The soap produced by this reaction is called sodium stearate. The other product of the reaction is ethanol. This reaction is represented by the balanced equation below.

$$C_{17}H_{35}-\overset{\overset{\displaystyle O}{\|}}{C}-O-C_2H_5 \ + \ NaOH \ \longrightarrow \ C_{17}H_{35}-\overset{\overset{\displaystyle O}{\|}}{C}-O^-\ Na^+ \ + \ C_2H_5OH$$

Ethyl stearate   Sodium hydroxide   Sodium stearate   Ethanol

25 Identify the *two* types of bonds in the compound sodium stearate.

26 To which class of organic compounds does ethyl stearate belong?

27 Identify the type of organic reaction used to make soap.

Base your answers to questions **28** and **29** on the information below.

A reaction between bromine and a hydrocarbon is represented by the balanced equation below.

$$Br_2 \ + \ H-\overset{\overset{\displaystyle H}{|}}{C}=\overset{\overset{\displaystyle H}{|}}{\underset{\underset{\displaystyle H}{|}}{C}}-\overset{\overset{\displaystyle H}{|}}{\underset{\underset{\displaystyle H}{|}}{C}}-H \ \longrightarrow \ H-\overset{\overset{\displaystyle H}{|}}{\underset{\underset{\displaystyle Br}{|}}{C}}-\overset{\overset{\displaystyle H}{|}}{\underset{\underset{\displaystyle Br}{|}}{C}}-\overset{\overset{\displaystyle H}{|}}{\underset{\underset{\displaystyle H}{|}}{C}}-H$$

28 Write the name of the homologous series to which the hydrocarbon belongs.

29 Identify the type of organic reaction.

329

1 In an oxidation-reduction reaction, the number of electrons lost is

(1) equal to the number of electrons gained
(2) equal to the number of protons gained
(3) less than the number of electrons gained
(4) less than the number of protons gained

2 The chemical process in which electrons are gained by an atom or an ion is called

(1) addition   (3) reduction
(2) oxidation   (4) substitution

3 Which process occurs in an operating voltaic cell?

(1) Electrical energy is converted to chemical energy.
(2) Chemical energy is converted to electrical energy.
(3) Oxidation takes place at the cathode.
(4) Reduction takes place at the anode.

4 Which energy conversion must occur in an operating electrolytic cell?

(1) electrical energy to chemical energy
(2) electrical energy to nuclear energy
(3) chemical energy to electrical energy
(4) chemical energy to nuclear energy

5 Which term identifies the half-reaction that occurs at the anode of an operating electrochemical cell?

(1) oxidation   (3) neutralization
(2) reduction   (4) transmutation

6 Which reaction occurs at the cathode in an electrochemical cell?

(1) combustion   (3) oxidation
(2) neutralization   (4) reduction

7 When a voltaic cell operates, ions move through the

(1) anode   (3) salt bridge
(2) cathode   (4) external circuit

8 What is the oxidation state of nitrogen in the compound NH_4Br?

(1) –1   (2) +2   (3) –3   (4) +4

9 Reduction occurs at the cathode in

(1) electrolytic cells, only
(2) voltaic cells, only
(3) both electrolytic cells and voltaic cells
(4) neither electrolytic cells nor voltaic cells

10 What is the oxidation number of manganese in $KMnO_4$?

(1) +7   (2) +2   (3) +3   (4) +4

11 Which half-reaction correctly represents oxidation?

(1) $Mn^{4+} \rightarrow Mn^{3+} + e^-$
(2) $Mn^{4+} \rightarrow Mn^{7+} + 3e^-$
(3) $Mn^{4+} + e^- \rightarrow Mn^{3+}$
(4) $Mn^{4+} + 3e^- \rightarrow Mn^{7+}$

12 Given the balanced ionic equation below:

$$2Al(s) + 3Cu^{2+}(aq) \rightarrow 2Al^{3+}(aq) + 3Cu(s)$$

Which half-reaction represents the reduction that occurs?

(1) $Al \rightarrow Al^{3+} + 3e$ (3) $Cu \rightarrow Cu^{2+} + 2e$
(2) $Al^{3+} + 3e \rightarrow Al$ (4) $Cu^{2+} + 2e \rightarrow Cu$

13 Which metal will spontaneously react with Zn^{2+} (aq), but will *not* spontaneously react with Mg^{2+} (aq)?

(1) Mn(s)   (3) Ni(s)
(2) Cu(s)   (4) Ba(s)

14 Given the balanced equation representing a reaction:

$$2Al(s) + 3Cu^{2+}(aq) \rightarrow 2Al^{3+}(aq) + 3Cu(s)$$

Which particles are transferred in this reaction?

(1) electrons   (3) positrons
(2) neutrons   (4) protons

Base your answers to questions **15** through **17** on the information below and on your knowledge of chemistry.

An operating voltaic cell has zinc and iron electrodes. The cell and the unbalanced ionic equation representing the reaction that occurs in the cell are shown below.

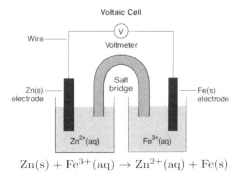

$$Zn(s) + Fe^{3+}(aq) \rightarrow Zn^{2+}(aq) + Fe(s)$$

15 Explain, in terms of Zn atoms and Zn ions, why the mass of the Zn electrode *decreases* as the cell operates.

16 Describe the direction of electron flow in the external circuit in this operating cell.

17 State the purpose of the salt bridge in this voltaic cell.

Base your answers to questions **18** through **20** on the information below.

The diagram below represents an operating electrolytic cell used to plate silver onto a nickel key. As the cell operates, oxidation occurs at the silver electrode and the mass of the silver electrode decreases.

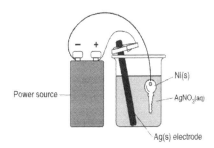

18 Explain, in terms of Ag atoms and $Ag^+(aq)$ ions, why the mass of the silver electrode *decreases* as the cell operates.

19 State the purpose of the power source in the cell.

20 Identify the cathode in the cell.

Base your answers to questions **21** through **24** on the information below.

In a laboratory investigation, a student constructs a voltaic cell with iron and copper electrodes. Another student constructs a voltaic cell with zinc and iron electrodes. Testing the cells during operation enables the students to write the balanced ionic equations below.

Cell with iron and copper electrodes: $Cu^{2+}(aq) + Fe(s) \rightarrow Cu(s) + Fe^{2+}(aq)$

Cell with zinc and iron electrodes: $Fe^{2+}(aq) + Zn(s) \rightarrow Fe(s) + Zn^{2+}(aq)$

21 State the relative activity of the three metals used in these two voltaic cells.

22 Write a balanced half-reaction equation for the reduction that takes place in the cell with zinc and iron electrodes.

23 Identify the particles transferred between Fe^{2+} and Zn during the reaction in the cell with zinc and iron electrodes.

24 State evidence from the balanced equation for the cell with iron and copper electrodes that indicates the reaction in the cell is an oxidation-reduction reaction.

25 Explain, in terms of activity, why HCl(aq) reacts with Mg(s), but HCl(aq) does *not* react with Cu(s).

1 Which nuclear emission is negatively charged?

(1) an alpha particle   (3) a neutron
(2) a beta particle   (4) a positron

2 Positrons and beta particles have

(1) the same charge and the same mass
(2) the same charge and different masses
(3) different charges and the same mass
(4) different charges and different masses

3 Compared to the mass and the penetrating power of an alpha particle, a beta particle has

(1) less mass and greater penetrating power
(2) less mass and less penetrating power
(3) more mass and greater penetrating power
(4) more mass and less penetrating power

4 The dating of geological formations is an example of a beneficial use of

(1) isomers
(2) electrolytes
(3) organic compounds
(4) radioactive nuclides

5 Which term identifies a type of nuclear reaction?

(1) transmutation   (3) deposition
(2) neutralization   (4) reduction

6 What occurs in both fusion and fission reactions?

(1) Small amounts of energy are converted into large amounts of matter.
(2) Small amounts of matter are converted into large amounts of energy.
(3) Heavy nuclei are split into lighter nuclei.
(4) Light nuclei are combined into heavier nuclei.

7 Which reaction releases the greatest amount of energy per mole of reactant?

(1) decomposition   (3) fermentation
(2) esterification   (4) fission

8 The energy released by a nuclear reaction results primarily from the

(1) breaking of bonds between atoms
(2) formation of bonds between atoms
(3) conversion of mass into energy
(4) conversion of energy into mass

9 Which radioisotope is used in dating geological formations?

(1) I-131   (3) Ca-37
(2) U-238   (4) Fr-220

10 Which nuclides are used to date the remains of a once-living organism?

(1) C-14 and C-12
(2) Co-60 and Co-59
(3) I-131 and Xe-131
(4) U-238 and Pb-206

11 Which radioisotope is used for diagnosing thyroid disorders?

(1) U-238   (3) I-131
(2) Pb-206   (4) Co-60

12 Which risk is associated with using nuclear fission to produce energy in a power plant?

(1) depletion of hydrocarbons
(2) depletion of atmospheric oxygen
(3) exposure of workers to radiation
(4) exposure of workers to sulfur dioxide

13 Given the equation representing a nuclear reaction in which X represents a nuclide:

$$^{232}_{90}\text{Th} \rightarrow \,^{4}_{2}\text{He} + X$$

Which nuclide is represented by X?

(1) $^{236}_{92}\text{Ra}$ (3) $^{236}_{92}\text{U}$
(2) $^{228}_{88}\text{Ra}$ (4) $^{228}_{88}\text{U}$

14 Which balanced equation represents a spontaneous radioactive decay?

(1) $14\text{C} + \text{Ca}_3(\text{PO}_4)_2 \rightarrow 3\text{CaC}_2 + 2\text{P} + 8\text{CO}$
(2) $^{14}_{7}\text{N} + \,^{1}_{0}\text{n} \rightarrow \,^{14}_{6}\text{C} + \,^{1}_{1}\text{P}$
(3) $\text{H}_2\text{CO}_3 \rightarrow \text{H}_2\text{O} + \text{CO}_2$
(4) $^{14}_{6}\text{C} \rightarrow \,^{14}_{7}\text{N} + \,^{0}_{-1}\text{e}$

15 Which nuclear emission has the greatest penetrating power?

(1) proton   (3) gamma radiation

(2) beta particle   (4) positron

16 In which reaction is mass converted to energy by the process of fission?

(1) $^{14}_{7}N + ^{1}_{0}n \rightarrow ^{14}_{6}C + ^{1}_{1}H$

(2) $^{235}_{92}U + ^{1}_{0}n \rightarrow ^{87}_{35}Br + ^{146}_{57}La + 3^{1}_{0}n$

(3) $^{226}_{88}Ra \rightarrow ^{222}_{86}Ra + ^{4}_{2}He$

(4) $^{2}_{1}H + ^{2}_{1}H \rightarrow ^{4}_{2}He$

17 Which balanced equation represents nuclear fusion?

(1) $^{3}_{1}H \rightarrow ^{3}_{2}He + ^{0}_{-1}e$

(2) $^{235}_{92}U \rightarrow ^{231}_{90}Th + ^{4}_{2}He$

(3) $^{2}_{1}H + ^{2}_{1}H \rightarrow ^{4}_{2}He$

(4) $^{235}_{92}U + ^{1}_{0}n \rightarrow ^{90}_{38}Sr + ^{143}_{54}Xe + 3^{1}_{0}n$

18 Given the equation representing a reaction where the masses are expressed in atomic mass units:

hydrogen-2 + hydrogen-1 $\rightarrow$ helium-3 + 8.814×10^{-16} kJ
2.014 102 u   1.007 825 u   3.016 029 u

Which phrase describes this reaction?

(1) a chemical reaction and mass being converted to energy

(2) a chemical reaction and energy being converted to mass

(3) a nuclear reaction and mass being converted to energy

(4) a nuclear reaction and energy being converted to mass

19 What fraction of a Sr-90 sample remains unchanged after 87.3 years?

(1) 1/2   (3) 1/4

(2) 1/3   (4) 1/8

20 After decaying for 48 hours, $\frac{1}{16}$ of the original mass of a radioisotope sample remains unchanged. What is the half-life of this radioisotope?

(1) 3.0 h   (3) 12 h

(2) 9.6 h   (4) 24 h

Base your answers to questions **21** through **24** on the information below.

Nuclear fission has been used to produce electricity. However, nuclear fusion for electricity production is still under development. The notations of some nuclides used in nuclear reactions are shown in the table below.

Some Nuclides Used in Nuclear Reactions

Reaction	Nuclides
nuclear fission	$^{233}_{92}U$, $^{235}_{92}U$
nuclear fusion	$^{1}_{1}H$, $^{3}_{1}H$

21 State *one* potential benefit of using nuclear fusion instead of the current use of nuclear fission to produce electricity.

22 Complete the table below that compares the total number of protons and the total number of neutrons for the hydrogen nuclides used for fusion.

Nuclide	Total Number of Protons	Total Number of Neutrons
$^{1}_{1}H$		
$^{3}_{1}H$		

23 Compare the atomic masses of nuclides used in fusion to the atomic masses of nuclides used in fission

24 Complete the nuclear equation below for the fission of $^{235}_{92}U$ by writing the notation of the missing product.

$^{235}_{92}U + ^{1}_{0}n \rightarrow ^{142}_{56}Ba + ^{91}_{36}Kr + 3$ _____ + energy

Base your answers to questions **25** through **27** on the information below.

Nuclear radiation is harmful to living cells, particularly to fast-growing cells, such as cancer cells and blood cells. An external beam of the radiation emitted from a radioisotope can be directed on a small area of a person to destroy cancer cells within the body.

Cobalt-60 is an artificially produced radioisotope that emits gamma rays and beta particles. One hospital keeps a 100.0-gram sample of cobalt-60 in an appropriate, secure storage container for future cancer treatment.

25 Determine the total time that will have elapsed when 12.5 grams of the original Co-60 sample at the hospital remains unchanged.

26 Compare the penetrating power of the two emissions from the Co-60.

27 State *one* risk to human tissue associated with the use of radioisotopes to treat cancer.

Base your answers to questions **28** through **30** on the information below.

Polonium-210 occurs naturally, but is scarce. Polonium-210 is primarily used in devices designed to eliminate static electricity in machinery. It is also used in brushes to remove dust from camera lenses.

Polonium-210 can be created in the laboratory by bombarding bismuth-209 with neutrons to create bismuth-210. The bismuth-210 undergoes beta decay to produce polonium-210. Polonium-210 has a half-life of 138 days and undergoes alpha decay.

28 Determine the total mass of an original 28.0-milligram sample of Po-210 that remains unchanged after 414 days.

29 Complete the nuclear equation for the decay of Po-210, by writing a notation for the missing product.

$$_{84}^{210}\text{Po} \rightarrow {}_{2}^{4}\text{He} + \underline{\hspace{3cm}}$$

30 State *one beneficial use of Po-210.*

Base your answers to questions **31** and **32** on the information below.

Some radioisotopes used as tracers make it possible for doctors to see the images of internal body parts and observe their functions. The table below lists information about three radioisotopes and the body part each radioisotope is used to study.

Medical Uses of Some Radioisotopes

Radioisotope	Half-life	Decay Mode	Body Part
^{24}Na	15 hours	beta	circulatory system
^{59}Fe	44.5 days	beta	red blood cells
^{131}I	8.1 days	beta	thyroid

32 It could take up to 60. hours for a radioisotope to be delivered to the hospital from the laboratory where it is produced. What fraction of an original sample of ^{24}Na remains unchanged after 60. hours?

31 Write the equation for the nuclear decay of the radioisotope used to study red blood cells. Include *both* the atomic number and the mass number for *each* missing particle.

$$^{59}\text{Fe} \rightarrow \underline{\hspace{1.5cm}} + \underline{\hspace{1.5cm}} + \text{energy}$$

Topic 1 Regents Practice (Pg 299 - 302)

1. 1   2. 2   3. 3   4. 4   5. 1   6. 1   7. 1   8. 3   9. 4   10. 2   11. 2

12. 3   13. 2   14. 3   15. 3   16. sublimation

17. Heat flows from the air in the flask to the dry ice.   From air to ice.

18. $$\frac{(1.2\,\text{atm})(1.25\,\text{L})}{293\,\text{K}} = \frac{(1.0\,\text{atm})(V_2)}{273\,\text{K}}$$

$$\frac{(273)(1.2)(1.25)}{293}$$

19. Temperature: above 293K   Temperature: higher
    Pressure : below 1.2 atm   Pressure: lower

20. The number of gas molecules in cylinder A is the same as the number of gas molecules in cylinder B

21. q = (800. g)(4.18 J/g •°C)(20.5°C − 12.5°C)

    (800)(4.18)(8)

22. Heat was transferred from the surroundings to the water in the bottle.
    The water absorbed energy from the surroundings.

23. The average kinetic energy of the water molecules at 7 a.m. is less than the average kinetic energy of the water molecules at 3 p.m.
    The average kinetic energy of the molecules is greater at 3 p.m.

24. minute 16 or at 16 minutes   25. 90°±2°C

Topic 2 Regents Practice (Pg 303 - 304)

1. 2   2. 4   3. 2   4. 1   5. 1   6. 2   7. 4   8. 1   9. 2   10. 3

11. 3   12. 2   13. 1   14. 4   15. 2   16. 4   17. 3   18. 2   19.3

20. 4 valence electrons   4 e-

21. As atomic number increases, the number of electron shells increases.
    Each successive element has one more electron shell.

22. Ga   Gallium   Element 31   23. White phosphorous has fewer atoms per cm^3.
    In   Indium   Element 41   Red has more.

24. As atomic number increases, the electronegativity increases.   25. Si Silicon   Element 14
    Electronegativity increases from left to right.
    Electronegativity increases.

Topic 3 Regents Practice (Pg 305 - 307)

1. 3   2. 2   3. 4   4. 1   5. 2   6. 3   7. 2   8. 1   9. 3   10. 1

11. 3   12. 3   13. 3   14. 1   15. 3   16. 2   17. 4   18. 1   19. 1

20. Different colors of light are produced when electrons return from higher energy states to lower energy states.
    Light energy can be emitted when electrons in excited atoms return to lower shells.
    Electrons release energy as they move toward the ground state.

21. The wavelengths of the spectral lines for element Z are independent of the mass of the sample.
    All atoms of element Z have the same electron configuration in the ground state.
    The intensive properties of an element remain constant.

22. Not all of the wavelengths of element A are shown in the wavelengths of the mixture.
    The mixture has no spectral line at 700 nm.

23. Arsenic atoms and antimony atoms each have 5 valence electrons.
    An As atom and a Sb atom both have five outermost electrons.
    same number of valence e−

24. Acceptable responses include, but are not limited to:
    $(62.93 \text{ u})(0.6917) + (64.93 \text{ u})(0.3083)$

25. $\dot{\text{B}}\!:$
    $\cdot\dot{\text{B}}\cdot$

Topic 4 Regents Practice (Pg 309 - 311)

1. 1   2. 2   3. 3   4. 2   5. 4   6. 4   7. 1   8. 3   9. 4   10. 2   11. 4   12. 4

13. 1   14. 4   15. 4   16. 2   17. 3   18. 3   19. 4   20. 3   21. 3   22. 3   23. 4

24.

25. At standard pressure, NH_3 has a higher boiling point than CF_4.

The melting point of CF_4 is lower.

26. A 2-proponal molecule is polar because it has an asymmetrical distribution of charge.
    The charge distribution is uneven.
    The center of positive charge and the center of negative charge do not coincide.

27. hydrogen bonding   dipole-dipole

28. There is a greater electronegativity difference in a CO bond than in a CH bond.
    The CO bond is more polar because the electronegativity difference for a CO bond is 0.8, and the electronegativity difference for a CH bond is 0.4.
    The CH bond has a smaller difference.
    The CO is .8 and the CH is .4

Topic 5 Regents Practice (Pg 313 - 314)

1. 4   2. 3   3. 2   4. 2   5. 4   6. 3   7. 4   8. 3   9. 4   10. 2

11. 4   12. 1   13. 2   14. 3   15. 4   16. 3   17. 1   18. 4

19. The products are different substances with different properties from the reactants.
    There is a loss and gain of electrons by substances in the reaction.

20. $\underline{2}Al(s) + \underline{3}CuSO_4(aq) \rightarrow \_Al_2(SO_4)_3(aq) + \underline{3}Cu(s)$

21. single replacement   redox   22. 3.81 g   23. Cu_2S

Topic 6 Regents Practice (Pg 315 - 316)

1. 1   2. 1   3. 1   4. 3   5. 1   6. 3   7. 3   8. 2   9. 3   10. 4   11. 3

12. $\dfrac{6(16 \text{ g/mol})}{176 \text{ g/mol}} \times 100$

$\dfrac{(96)(100)}{176}$

13. 4.0×10^{-4} mol or 0.00040 mol

14. 0.030 mol. Significant figures do not need to be shown.

15. H_2O 16. 34 g/mol.

17    $3 = \dfrac{x}{20} \times 100$ or $(20)(0.03)$ 18. decomposition, redox

Topic 7 Regents Practice (Pg 317 - 319)

1. 3   2. 4   3. 2   4. 3   5. 2   6. 1   7. 3   8. 1   9. 3   10. 1

11. 1   12. 1   13. 2   14. 1   15. 3   16. 4   17. 2   18. 78°C to 80.°C

19. The solution that contains 1.25 moles of NaCl has a lower freezing point.
   lower for the first one
   higher for the solution with 0.75 mol
   The 0.30 M solution has a higher freezing point than the 0.50 M solution.
   This solution has a lower f.p.

20. unsaturated solution

21

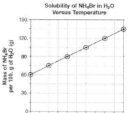

22. As temperature increases, the solubility of $NH_4Br(s)$
   in H_2O increases and the solubility of $NH_3(g)$ in H_2O decreases.
   NH_4Br becomes more soluble and NH_3 becomes less soluble.

23. 210. g

Topic 8 Regents Practice (Pg 321 - 322)

1. 1   2. 2   3. 1   4. 1   5. 3   6. 4   7. 2   8. 2   9. 4   10. 2

11. 4   12. 3   13. 4   14. 1   15. 1   16. 3   17. 3   18. 4

19. 10
   ten tenfold
   10 times

20.

Aqueous Solution	Color of Thymol Blue
NaCl(aq)	yellow
NaOH(aq)	blue

21. KCl
   K^+ Cl^-
   ClK

22. $(0.026 \text{ M})(50.0 \text{mL}) = M_B (38.5 \text{ mL})$

$$\frac{(0.026)(50)}{38.5} = M_B$$

Topic 9 Regents Practice (Pg 323 - 326)

1. 4   2. 3   3. 3   4. 1   5. 1   6. 2   7. 2   8. 2   9. 1   10. 4

11. 4   12. 3   13. 3   14. 2   15. 4   16. 3   17. 1   18. 2   19. 4

20. A lower concentration of oxygen gas decreases the number of effective collisions between
   O_2 molecules and CH_4 molecules.

21. B   22. 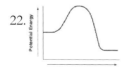   The product end (right) of your diagram must be lower than
            the reactant end (left).

23. The rate of the chemical reaction increases because the reactant molecules move faster and collide
   with more kinetic energy.
   Increasing the temperature causes more frequent collisions.
   As molecules acquire more kinetic energy, the probability of effective collisions increases.
   More reactant molecules collide with sufficient energy.

24. The concentration of the ClO⁻ ion decreases.
   [ClO⁻] decreases.   lower ClO⁻ concentration.   less ClO⁻

25. The container must be closed so that no matter can enter or leave, thus distributing the equilibrium.
   If the container is open, Cl_2 gas escapes.
   To keep the concentration of the reactants and products constant.

26. The rate of the forward reaction is equal to the rate of the reverse reaction.
   They are the same.
   equal

Topic 10 Regents Practice (Pg 327 - 329)

1. 2   2. 2   3. 3   4. 3   5. 3   6. 1   7. 2   8. 1   9. 3   10. 1   11. 2

12. 4   13. 1   14. 4   15. 1   16. 2   17. 2   18. 3   19. 4   20. 2   21. 2

22. Both molecules have the same molecular formula, but have different structural formulas.
   Both molecules are composed of 5 carbon atoms and 12 hydrogen atoms, but differ in the
   arrangement of their atoms.

23. The molecule in diagram B has only single carbon-carbon bonds.
   There are no multiple bonds between the carbon atoms.
   Cannot add more H atoms to the C atoms because all C—C bonds are single.

24.

25. covalent bonds and ionic bonds
   polar and nonpolar
   single and double

26. ester or esters

27. saponification

28. alkene
   alkenes

29. addition
   halogenation
   bromination

Topic 11 Regents Practice (Pg 331 - 332)

1. 1   2. 3   3. 2   4. 1   5. 1   6. 4   7. 3   8. 3   9. 3   10. 1

11. 2   12. 4   13. 1   14. 1

15. Zinc atoms from the electrode are oxidized to zinc ions in the solution, decreasing the
   mass of the electrode.
   Zinc atoms become Zn^{2+}(aq).
   The atoms become ions dissolved in the water.
   Zn atoms lose electrons, producing ions in solution.

16. Electrons flow from the zinc electrode to the iron electrode through the wires and voltmeter.
   The e- flow is from Zn to Fe in the external circuit.
   from anode to cathode

17. The salt bridge allows for the migration of ions between the half-cells.
   The salt bridge prevents polarization of the half-cells maintains electrical neutrality

18. Silver atoms lose electrons and become silver ions in the solution.
   Some of the Ag atoms become Ag^+ ions.
   Silver atoms are oxidized to silver ions.

19. The cell requires electrical energy for the non-spontaneous reaction to occur.
The power source causes some Ag(s) atoms to oxidize.

20. Ni(s)   nickel   key

21. Zinc is more reactive than iron, and iron is more reactive than copper.
The order of decreasing activity is Zn, Fe, Cu.
Copper is least active and zinc is most active.

22. $Fe^{2+} + 2e^- \rightarrow Fe$ 23. e- electrons

24. The oxidation number of Cu^{2+} changes to 0.
Iron's oxidation state changes from zero to +2.
Oxidation numbers change during the reaction because electrons are transferred.

25. Magnesium is more active than hydrogen, but copper is less active than hydrogen.
On Table J, Mg is above H_2, and Cu is below H_2.

Topic 12 Regents Practice (Pg 333 - 335)

1. 2   2. 3   3. 1   4. 4   5. 1   6. 2   7. 4   8. 3   9. 2   10. 1

11 3   12. 3   13. 2   14. 4   15. 3   16. 2   17. 3   18. 3   19. 4   20. 3

21. Fusion produces more energy per gram of reactant.
The fusion process produces less radioactive waste.
The fusion reactant material is more readily available.

22.

Nuclide	Total Number of Protons	Total Number of Neutrons
$^{1}_{1}H$	1	0
$^{3}_{1}H$	1	2

23. The nuclides used for fusion have smaller atomic masses than nuclides used for fission.
The nuclides used in fission are many times more massive.
Fusion particles are lighter.

24. $^{1}_{0}n$ 25. 15.813 years   15.8 y

26. Gamma radiation has greater penetrating power.
Beta particles have weaker penetrating power.

27. Nuclear radiation is harmful to all living cells.
Radioisotopes can cause gene mutations.
Treatments can cause stomach problems, such as nausea.

28. **3.5 mg**   29. $^{206}_{82}Pb$ lead-206   Pb-206

30. Polonium-210 is used to eliminate static electricity in machinery.
removes dust from camera lenses

31. $^{59}_{26}Fe \rightarrow \underline{\quad ^{0}_{-1}e \quad} + \underline{\quad ^{59}_{27}Co \quad} +$ energy   32. $^{1}/_{6}$ or 0.0625

Physical Setting/Chemistry
Regents Exam - January 2017

Part A

Answer all questions in this part.

Directions (1–30): For *each* statement or question, record on your separate answer sheet the *number* of the word or expression that, of those given, best completes the statement or answers the question. Some questions may require the use of the *2011 Edition Reference Tables for Physical Setting/Chemistry*.

1 Which statement describes the location of two types of subatomic particles in a helium atom?

   (1) Protons and neutrons are located in the nucleus.
   (2) Protons and neutrons are located outside the nucleus.
   (3) Protons and electrons are located in the nucleus.
   (4) Protons and electrons are located outside the nucleus.

2 An atom that contains six protons, six neutrons, and six electrons has a mass of approximately

   (1) 12 u   (3) 18 u
   (2) 12 g   (4) 18 g

3 Which term identifies the most probable location of an electron in the wave-mechanical model of the atom?

   (1) anode   (3) nucleus
   (2) orbital   (4) cathode

4 Which element has atoms in the ground state with the greatest number of valence electrons?

   (1) tin   (3) arsenic
   (2) sulfur   (4) fluorine

5 Which group on the Periodic Table has two elements that exist as gases at STP?

   (1) Group 1   (3) Group 16
   (2) Group 2   (4) Group 17

6 Which list of elements contains a metal, a metalloid, and a nonmetal?

   (1) Ag, Si, I_2 (3) K, Cu, Br_2
   (2) Ge, As, Ne   (4) S, Cl_2, Ar

7 What is the charge of the nucleus of a copper atom?

   (1) +1   (3) +29
   (2) +2   (4) +64

8 At STP, $O_2(g)$ and $O_3(g)$ have different properties because $O_3(g)$ has

   (1) more dense nuclei than in $O_2(g)$
   (2) more protons per atom than in $O_2(g)$
   (3) molecules with a different structure than in $O_2(g)$
   (4) molecules with fewer covalent bonds than in $O_2(g)$

9 A compound is a substance composed of two or more elements that are

   (1) physically mixed in a fixed proportion
   (2) physically mixed in a variable proportion
   (3) chemically combined in a fixed proportion
   (4) chemically combined in a variable proportion

10 Which element has the highest boiling point at standard pressure?

   (1) Mg   (3) Rb
   (2) Na   (4) Sr

11 How many pairs of electrons are shared between the nitrogen atoms in a molecule of N_2?

   (1) 5   (3) 3
   (2) 2   (4) 6

12 A molecule must be nonpolar if the molecule

   (1) is linear
   (2) is neutral
   (3) has ionic and covalent bonding
   (4) has a symmetrical charge distribution

13 Which property is used to determine the degree of polarity between two bonded atoms?

(1) density   (3) pressure
(2) electronegativity   (4) temperature

14 In a chemical reaction, a catalyst provides an alternate reaction pathway that

(1) decreases the concentration of the products
(2) increases the concentration of the reactants
(3) has a lower activation energy
(4) has a higher activation energy

15 Which substance can be decomposed by chemical means?

(1) cobalt   (3) methane
(2) krypton   (4) zirconium

16 Which sample of matter represents a mixture?

(1) aqueous ammonia   (3) liquid mercury
(2) gaseous ethane   (4) solid iodine

17 Differences in which property allow the separation of a sample of sand and seawater by filtration?

(1) concentration of ions
(2) volume of sample
(3) mass of sample
(4) particle size

18 Which process is a chemical change?

(1) evaporating an alcohol
(2) subliming of iodine
(3) melting an ice cube
(4) rusting of iron

19 Which term represents an intermolecular force in a sample of water?

(1) hydrogen bonding
(2) covalent bonding
(3) metallic bonding
(4) ionic bonding

20 Which sample of matter has particles arranged in a crystalline structure?

(1) $Ne(g)$ (3) $NaCl(aq)$

(2) $Br_2(\ell)$ (4) $CuSO_4(s)$

21 Which term is defined as a measure of the randomness of a system?

(1) heat   (3) pressure
(2) entropy   (4) temperature

22 Which formula represents an alkane?

(1) C_2H_2 (3) C_3H_4
(2) C_2H_4 (4) C_3H_8

23 Which term represents a chemical reaction?

(1) deposition   (3) sublimation
(2) combustion   (4) vaporization

24 Which type of reaction includes esterification and polymerization?

(1) decomposition   (3) organic
(2) neutralization   (4) nuclear

25 In a redox reaction, the total number of electrons lost is

(1) less than the total number of electrons gained
(2) greater than the total number of electrons gained
(3) equal to the total number of electrons gained
(4) unrelated to the total number of electrons gained

26 Which type of equation can represent the oxidation occurring in a reaction?

(1) a double-replacement reaction equation
(2) a half-reaction equation
(3) a neutralization reaction equation
(4) a transmutation reaction equation

27 The electrical conductivity of an aqueous solution depends on the concentration of which particles in the solution?

(1) molecules   (3) atoms
(2) electrons   (4) ions

28 An electrolytic cell differs from a voltaic cell because an electrolytic cell

(1) generates its own energy from a spontaneous physical reaction
(2) generates its own energy from a nonspontaneous physical reaction
(3) requires an outside energy source for a spontaneous chemical reaction to occur
(4) requires an outside energy source for a nonspontaneous chemical reaction to occur

29 A sample of which radioisotope emits particles having the greatest mass?

(1) ^{137}Cs   (3) ^{220}Fr
(2) ^{53}Fe   (4) ^{3}H

30 Which term represents a nuclear reaction?

(1) combustion   (3) transmutation
(2) fermentation   (4) saponification

Part B–1

Answer all questions in this part.

Directions (31–50): For *each* statement or question, record on your separate answer sheet the *number* of the word or expression that, of those given, best completes the statement or answers the question. Some questions may require the use of the *2011 Edition Reference Tables for Physical Setting/Chemistry*.

31 Which electron configuration represents the distribution of electrons in a potassium atom in the ground state?

(1) 2-8-8-1   (3) 2-8-5
(2) 2-8-7-2   (4) 2-7-6

32 At STP, which element is malleable and a good conductor of electricity?

(1) xenon   (3) platinum
(2) silicon   (4) hydrogen

33 Which general trends in atomic radius and electronegativity are observed as the elements in Period 3 are considered in order of increasing atomic number?

(1) Atomic radius decreases and electronegativity increases.
(2) Atomic radius increases and electronegativity decreases.
(3) Both atomic radius and electronegativity increase.
(4) Both atomic radius and electronegativity decrease.

34 What is the chemical name for Na_2SO_3?

(1) sodium sulfite   (3) sodium sulfide
(2) sodium sulfate   (4) sodium thiosulfate

35 Which molecular formula is also an empirical formula?

(1) C_6H_6 (3) N_2H_4
(2) H_2O_2 (4) N_2O_5

36 Given the balanced equation representing a reaction:

$$2H_2 + O_2 \rightarrow 2H_2O + energy$$

Which mass of oxygen completely reacts with 4.0 grams of hydrogen to produce 36.0 grams of water?

(1) 8.0 g   (3) 32.0 g
(2) 16.0 g   (4) 40.0 g

37 What is the gram-formula mass of $Ca(OH)_2$?

(1) 29 g/mol   (3) 57 g/mol
(2) 54 g/mol   (4) 74 g/mol

38 Given the equation representing a reaction:

$$H_2(g) + I_2(g) \rightarrow 2HI(g)$$

Which statement describes the energy changes that occur in this reaction?

(1) Energy is absorbed as bonds are formed, only.
(2) Energy is released as bonds are broken, only.
(3) Energy is absorbed as bonds are formed, and energy is released as bonds are broken.
(4) Energy is absorbed as bonds are broken, and energy is released as bonds are formed.

39 Based on Table *F*, which compound is *least* soluble in water?

(1) $AlPO_4$ (3) $Ca(OH)_2$
(2) Li_2SO_4 (4) $AgC_2H_3O_2$

40 How many joules of heat are absorbed to raise the temperature of 435 grams of water at 1 atm from 25°C to its boiling point, 100.°C?

(1) 4.5×10^4 J   (3) 2.5×10^7 J
(2) 1.4×10^5 J   (4) 7.4×10^7 J

41 Which temperature represents the highest average kinetic energy of the particles in a sample of matter?

(1) 298 K   (3) 27°C
(2) 267 K   (4) 12°C

42 Which change in the H^+ ion concentration of an aqueous solution represents a *decrease* of one unit on the pH scale?

(1) a tenfold increase
(2) a tenfold decrease
(3) a hundredfold increase
(4) a hundredfold decrease

43 Which particle diagram represents a mixture of three substances?

Key
= an atom of one element
● = an atom of a different element

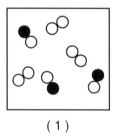

(1)

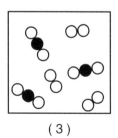

(3)

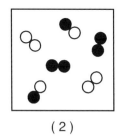

(2)

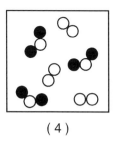

(4)

44 Given the equation representing a system at equilibrium:

$$PCl_5(g) \rightleftharpoons PCl_3(g) + Cl_2(g)$$

Which statement describes this system?

(1) The concentration of $PCl_5(g)$ is increasing.
(2) The concentration of $PCl_5(g)$ is decreasing.
(3) The concentrations of $PCl_5(g)$ and $PCl_3(g)$ are equal.
(4) The concentrations of $PCl_5(g)$ and $PCl_3(g)$ are constant.

45 Given the formula representing a compound:

$$H-\overset{\overset{\displaystyle H}{|}}{\underset{\underset{\displaystyle H}{|}}{C}}-\overset{\overset{\displaystyle H}{|}}{\underset{\underset{\displaystyle H}{|}}{C}}-\overset{\overset{\displaystyle H}{|}}{\underset{\underset{\displaystyle H}{|}}{C}}-\overset{\overset{\displaystyle H}{|}}{\underset{\underset{\displaystyle H}{|}}{C}}-\overset{\overset{\displaystyle H}{|}}{\underset{\underset{\displaystyle H}{|}}{C}}-\overset{\overset{\displaystyle Cl}{|}}{\underset{\underset{\displaystyle Cl}{|}}{C}}-\overset{\overset{\displaystyle H}{|}}{\underset{\underset{\displaystyle H}{|}}{C}}-H$$

What is the IUPAC name of this compound?

(1) 2-chloroheptane
(2) 6-chloroheptane
(3) 2,2-dichloroheptane
(4) 6,6-dichloroheptane

46 Given the equation representing a reaction:

$$Sn^{4+}(aq) + 2e^- \rightarrow Sn^{2+}(aq)$$

Which term best describes this reaction?

(1) ionization   (3) oxidation
(2) neutralization   (4) reduction

47 Which ionic equation represents a spontaneous reaction that can occur in a voltaic cell?

(1) $Cu(s) + Zn(s) \rightarrow Cu^{2+}(aq) + Zn^{2+}(aq)$
(2) $Cu(s) + Zn^{2+}(aq) \rightarrow Cu^{2+}(aq) + Zn(s)$
(3) $Cu^{2+}(aq) + Zn(s) \rightarrow Cu(s) + Zn^{2+}(aq)$
(4) $Cu^{2+}(aq) + Zn^{2+}(aq) \rightarrow Cu(s) + Zn(s)$

48 Given the formulas representing two compounds at standard pressure:

$$H-\underset{\underset{H}{|}}{\overset{\overset{H}{|}}{C}}-\underset{\underset{H}{|}}{\overset{\overset{H}{|}}{C}}-\underset{\underset{H}{|}}{\overset{\overset{H}{|}}{C}}-O-H \qquad H-\underset{\underset{H}{|}}{\overset{\overset{H}{|}}{C}}-O-\underset{\underset{H}{|}}{\overset{\overset{H}{|}}{C}}-\underset{\underset{H}{|}}{\overset{\overset{H}{|}}{C}}-H$$

1 – propanol   methyl ethyl ether

The compounds can be differentiated by their

(1) boiling points
(2) gram-formula masses
(3) numbers of hydrogen atoms
(4) percent compositions by mass of carbon

49 The table below shows the atomic mass and natural abundance of the two naturally occurring isotopes of lithium.

Naturally Occurring Isotopes of Lithium

Isotope	Atomic Mass (u)	Natural Abundance (%)
Li-6	6.015	7.6
Li-7	7.016	92.4

Which numerical setup can be used to determine the atomic mass of naturally occurring lithium?

(1) $(7.6)(6.015 \text{ u}) + (92.4)(7.016 \text{ u})$

(2) $(0.076)(6.015 \text{ u}) + (0.924)(7.016 \text{ u})$

(3) $\dfrac{(7.6)(6.015 \text{ u}) + (92.4)(7.016 \text{ u})}{2}$

(4) $\dfrac{(0.076)(6.015 \text{ u}) + (0.924)(7.016 \text{ u})}{2}$

50 Given the equation representing a reaction at equilibrium:

$$H_2S(aq) + CH_3NH_2(aq) \rightleftharpoons HS^-(aq) + CH_3NH_3{}^+(aq)$$

According to one acid-base theory, the forward reaction is classified as an acid-base reaction because

(1) H_2S is a H^+ donor and CH_3NH_2 is a H^+ acceptor
(2) CH_3NH_2 is a H^+ donor and H_2S is a H^+ acceptor
(3) HS^- and $CH_3NH_3{}^+$ are both H^+ donors
(4) $CH_3NH_3{}^+$ and HS^- are both H^+ acceptors

Answer Key

Regents Exam January 2017

Part A

1 . . . . . **1**	9 . . . . . **3**	17 . . . . . **4**	25 . . . . . **3** . . . .
2 . . . . . **1**	10 . . . . . **4**	18 . . . . . **4**	26 . . . . . **2** . . . .
3 . . . . . **2**	11 . . . . . **3**	19 . . . . . **1**	27 . . . . . **4** . . . .
4 . . . . . **4**	12 . . . . . **4**	20 . . . . . **4**	28 . . . . . **4** . . . .
5 . . . . . **4**	13 . . . . . **2**	21 . . . . . **2**	29 . . . . . **3** . . . .
6 . . . . . **1**	14 . . . . . **3**	22 . . . . . **4**	30 . . . . . **3** . . . .
7 . . . . . **3**	15 . . . . . **3**	23 . . . . . **2**	
8 . . . . . **3**	16 . . . . . **1**	24 . . . . . **3**	

Part B–1

31 . . . . . **1**	36 . . . . . **3**	41 . . . . . **3** . . .	46 . . . . . **4** . . . .
32 . . . . . **3**	37 . . . . . **4**	42 . . . . . **1**	47 . . . . . **3** . . . .
33 . . . . . **1**	38 . . . . . **4**	43 . . . . . **2**	48 . . . . . **1** . . . .
34 . . . . . **1**	39 . . . . . **1**	44 . . . . . **4**	49 . . . . . **2** . . . .
35 . . . . . **4**	40 . . . . . **2**	45 . . . . . **3**	50 . . . . . **1** . . . .

Part B–2

Answer all questions in this part.

Directions (51–65): Record your answers in the spaces provided in your answer booklet. Some questions may require the use of the *2011 Edition Reference Tables for Physical Setting/Chemistry.*

51 Explain, in terms of electron configuration, why arsenic and antimony are chemically similar. [1]

52 Identify the element in Period 3 that is an unreactive gas at STP. [1]

53 Compare the energy of an electron in the first shell of a cadmium atom to the energy of an electron in the third shell of the same atom. [1]

Base your answers to questions 54 and 55 on the information below and on your knowledge of chemistry.

The densities for two forms of carbon at room temperature are listed in the table below.

Densities of Two Forms of Carbon

Element Form	Density (g/cm³)
carbon (graphite)	2.2
carbon (diamond)	3.513

54 Compare the number of carbon atoms in a 0.30-cm³ sample of graphite and a 0.30-cm³ sample of diamond. [1]

55 A student calculated the density of a sample of graphite to be 2.3 g/cm³. Show a numerical setup for calculating the student's percent error for the density of graphite. [1]

Base your answers to questions 56 and 57 on the information below and on your knowledge of chemistry.

A sample of calcium carbonate, $CaCO_3$, has a mass of 42.2 grams. Calcium carbonate has a gram-formula mass of 100. g/mol.

56 Show a numerical setup for calculating the number of moles in the sample of $CaCO_3$. [1]

57 Determine the percent composition by mass of oxygen in the $CaCO_3$. [1]

Base your answers to questions 58 and 59 on the information below and on your knowledge of chemistry.

Carbon monoxide, $CO(g)$, is a toxic gas found in automobile exhaust. The concentration of $CO(g)$ can be decreased by using a catalyst in the reaction between $CO(g)$ and $O_2(g)$. This reaction is represented by the balanced equation below.

$$2CO(g) + O_2(g) \xrightarrow{\text{catalyst}} 2CO_2(g) + \text{energy}$$

58 Explain, in terms of collision theory, why an increase in temperature increases the rate of the reaction. [1]

59 On the labeled axes *in your answer booklet*, draw the potential energy curve for the reaction represented by this equation. [1]

Base your answers to questions 60 and 61 on the information below and on your knowledge of chemistry.

The diagram and data below represent a gas and the conditions of pressure, volume, and temperature of the gas in a rigid cylinder with a moveable piston.

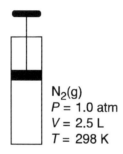

$N_2(g)$
$P = 1.0$ atm
$V = 2.5$ L
$T = 298$ K

60 Determine the volume of the gas in the cylinder at STP. [1]

61 State *one* change in temperature and *one* change in pressure that will cause the gas in the cylinder to behave more like an ideal gas. [1]

Base your answers to questions 62 through 65 on the information below and on your knowledge of chemistry.

During a titration, 10.00 mL of acetic acid, $HC_2H_3O_2$(aq), is completely neutralized by adding 12.50 mL of 0.64 M sodium hydroxide, NaOH(aq).

62 Identify the only positive ion in the $HC_2H_3O_2$(aq). [1]

63 State the number of significant figures used to express the volume of the acetic acid. [1]

64 Determine the molarity of the acetic acid. [1]

65 Explain why it is better to use data from multiple trials to determine the molarity of acetic acid, rather than data from a single trial. [1]

Part C

Answer all questions in this part.

Directions (66–85): Record your answers in the spaces provided in your answer booklet. Some questions may require the use of the *2011 Edition Reference Tables for Physical Setting/Chemistry*.

Base your answers to questions 66 through 68 on the information below and on your knowledge of chemistry.

Carbon dioxide, CO_2, changes from the solid phase to the gas phase at 1 atm and 194.5 K. In the solid phase, CO_2 is often called dry ice. When dry ice sublimes in air at 298 K, the water vapor in the air can condense, forming a fog of small water droplets. This fog is often used for special effects at concerts and in movie-making.

66 State the direction of heat flow between the dry ice and the water vapor in the air. [1]

67 At 1 atm and 298 K, compare the potential energies of the water molecules before and after the water vapor condenses. [1]

68 At 1 atm and 190. K, compare the amount of thermal energy in a 1.0-kilogram block of dry ice to the amount of thermal energy in a 2.0-kilogram block of dry ice. [1]

Base your answers to questions 69 through 72 on the information below and on your knowledge of chemistry.

A solution of ethylene glycol and water can be used as the coolant in an engine-cooling system. The ethylene glycol concentration in a coolant solution is often given as percent by volume. For example, 100. mL of a coolant solution that is 40.% ethylene glycol by volume contains 40. mL of ethylene glycol diluted with enough water to produce a total volume of 100. mL. The graph below shows the freezing point of coolants that have different ethylene glycol concentrations.

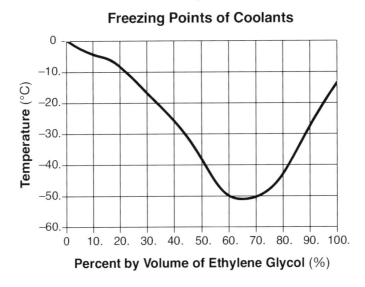

Freezing Points of Coolants

69 Explain, in terms of particle distribution, why a coolant solution is a homogeneous mixture. [1]

70 Explain, in terms of the molecular polarity, why ethylene glycol dissolves in water to form a solution. [1]

71 Identify the percent by volume of ethylene glycol in a solution that freezes at −10.°C. [1]

72 One engine-cooling system has a volume of 6400 mL. Determine the volume of ethylene glycol in the completely filled engine-cooling system when the concentration of ethylene glycol is 50.% by volume. [1]

Base your answers to questions 73 through 77 on the information below and on your knowledge of chemistry.

Molecules containing two carbon atoms and a functional group have many home and industrial uses. These compounds can be produced by a variety of reactions, as shown by the equations below.

$$\text{Equation 1: } C_2H_4 + H_2O \rightarrow CH_3CH_2OH$$

$$\text{Equation 2: } 2CH_3CH_2OH + O_2 \rightarrow 2CH_3CHO + 2H_2O$$

$$\text{Equation 3: } 2CH_3CHO + O_2 \rightarrow 2CH_3COOH$$

73 Explain, in terms of bonding, why the hydrocarbon reactant in equation 1 is unsaturated. [1]

74 Draw a structural formula of the ethanal molecule in equation 2. [1]

75 Explain, in terms of atoms, why CH_3CH_2OH and CH_3CHO are *not* isomers of each other. [1]

76 Identify the class of organic compounds to which the product in equation 3 belongs. [1]

77 Determine the number of moles of oxygen required to completely react with six moles of CH_3CHO in equation 3. [1]

Base your answers to questions 78 and 79 on the information below and on your knowledge of chemistry.

The hydrangea is a flowering plant. The color of the flowers it produces can change depending on the pH value of the soil in which the plant grows. Adding aluminum sulfate makes the soil more acidic and adding calcium hydroxide makes the soil more basic.

A student performed an experiment by varying soil pH and recording the color of the flowers. The following table summarizes the results of the experiment.

Hydrangea Soil pH and Flower Color

Soil pH	Flower Color
5.5 and below	blue
between 5.5 and 6.5	purple
6.5 and above	pink

78 Identify the independent variable in this experiment. [1]

79 Hydrangea plants can be grown in soil that turns litmus red. What color are the flowers of the plants grown in this soil? [1]

Base your answers to questions 80 through 82 on the information below and on your knowledge of chemistry.

The diagram and balanced ionic equation below represent two half-cells connected to produce an operating voltaic cell in a laboratory investigation. The half-cells are connected by a salt bridge.

Voltaic Cell

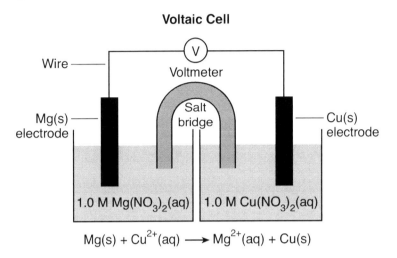

$$Mg(s) + Cu^{2+}(aq) \longrightarrow Mg^{2+}(aq) + Cu(s)$$

80 Determine the oxidation number of nitrogen in the negative ion in the aqueous solutions. [1]

81 State the purpose of the salt bridge in this voltaic cell. [1]

82 Explain, in terms of atoms and ions, why the mass of the Mg(s) electrode decreases as the cell operates. [1]

Base your answers to questions 83 through 85 on the information below and on your knowledge of chemistry.

The radioisotope Mo-99 naturally decays to produce the metastable isotope Tc-99m, which is used in medical diagnosis. A doctor can obtain images of organs and bones by injecting a patient with a solution of Tc-99m. The half-life of the metastable Tc-99m is six hours.

83 Complete the nuclear equation *in your answer booklet* for the nuclear decay of Mo-99. [1]

84 State *both* the number of protons and the number of neutrons in a Tc-99 nuclide. [1]

85 Determine the fraction of an original sample of metastable Tc-99m that remains unchanged after 24 hours. [1]

PHYSICAL SETTING
CHEMISTRY

Wednesday, January 25, 2017 — 9:15 a.m. to 12:15 p.m., only

ANSWER BOOKLET

☐ Male

Student . . . . Sex: ☐ Female

Teacher . . . .

School . . . . Grade . . . .

Record your answers for Part B–2 and Part C in this booklet.

Part B–2

51 _____

52 _____

53 _____

54 _____

55

56

57 _____ %

58 _____

_____

_____

59

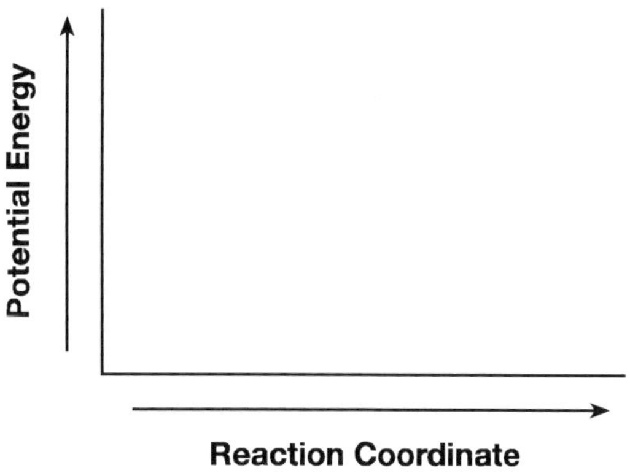

60 _____ **L**

61 Temperature: _____

Pressure: _____

62 _____

63 _____

64 _____ **M**

65 _____

_____

_____

Part C

66 From_____ to _____

67 _____

_____

_____

68 _____

_____

_____

69 _____

_____

_____

70 _____

_____

_____

71 _____ %

72 _____ mL

73 _____

_____

_____

74

75 _____

_____

_____

76 _____

77 _____ mol

78 _____

79 _____

80 _____

81 _____

_____

_____

82 _____

_____

_____

83 $^{99}_{42}\text{Mo} \rightarrow$ _____ $+ \, ^{99\text{m}}_{43}\text{Tc}$

84 Protons: _____

Neutrons: _____

85 _____

The University of the State of New York

REGENTS HIGH SCHOOL EXAMINATION

PHYSICAL SETTING
CHEMISTRY

Wednesday, January 25, 2017 — 9:15 a.m. to 12:15 p.m., only

ANSWER BOOKLET

Student . . . . Sex: ☐ Male ☐ Female

Teacher . . . .

School . . . . Grade . . . .

Record your answers for Part B–2 and Part C in this booklet.

Part B–2

51 [1] Allow 1 credit. Acceptable responses include, but are not limited to:

Arsenic atoms and antimony atoms each have 5 valence electrons.

An As atom and a Sb atom both have five outermost electrons.

same number of valence e$^-$

52 [1] Allow 1 credit. Acceptable responses include, but are not limited to:

Argon   Ar   element 18

53 [1] Allow 1 credit. Acceptable responses include, but are not limited to:

An electron in the first shell has less energy than an electron in the third shell.

The third shell electron has higher energy.

3rd shell > 1st shell

54 [1] Allow 1 credit. Acceptable responses include, but are not limited to:

The 0.30-cm^3 sample of graphite has fewer carbon atoms than the 0.30-cm^3 sample of diamond.

The diamond sample has more atoms.

more C atoms in the diamond

---

55 [1] Allow 1 credit. Acceptable responses include, but are not limited to:

$$\frac{2.3 \text{ g/cm}^3 - 2.2 \text{ g/cm}^3}{2.2 \text{ g/cm}^3} \times 100$$

$$\frac{2.3 - 2.2}{2.2} \times 100$$

$$\frac{0.1(100)}{2.2}$$

56 [1] Allow 1 credit. Acceptable responses include, but are not limited to:

$$\frac{42.2 \text{ g}}{100. \text{ g/mol}}$$

$$42.2 \text{ g} \times \frac{1.00 \text{ mol}}{100. \text{ g}}$$

$$\frac{x}{42.2} = \frac{1}{100}$$

57 [1] Allow 1 credit for 48.0% *or* for any value from 47.9% to 48%, inclusive.

58 [1] Allow 1 credit. Acceptable responses include, but are not limited to:

The rate of the chemical reaction increases because the reactant molecules move faster and collide with more kinetic energy.

Increasing the temperature causes more frequent collisions.

As molecules acquire more kinetic energy, the probability of effective collisions increases.

More reactant molecules collide with sufficient energy.

59 [1] Allow 1 credit for showing that the potential energy of the products is lower than the potential energy of the reactants.

Example of a 1-credit response:

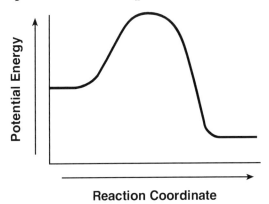

60 [1] Allow 1 credit for 2.3 L *or* for any value from 2.29 L to 2.3 L, inclusive.

61 [1] Allow 1 credit. Acceptable responses include, but are not limited to:

Temperature: higher/increase

Pressure: lower/decrease

Temperature: above 298 K

Pressure: below 1.0 atm

62 [1] Allow 1 credit. Acceptable responses include, but are not limited to:

$H^+(aq)$

H_3O^+

hydrogen ions

hydronium

63 [1] Allow 1 credit for 4 *or* four.

64 [1] Allow 1 credit. Acceptable responses include, but are not limited to:

0.80 M

8.0×10^{-1} M

.8 M

65 [1] Allow 1 credit. Acceptable responses include, but are not limited to:

Multiple trials may improve the precision of results.

Each trial may involve errors either above or below the acceptable value. Therefore, an average value may be more accurate.

Results can be shown to be reproducible.

Multiple trials help cancel random errors.

Part C

66 [1] Allow 1 credit. Acceptable responses include, but are not limited to:

from water vapor to the dry ice

from $H_2O(g)$ to $CO_2(s)$

from water to CO_2

67 [1] Allow 1 credit. Acceptable responses include, but are not limited to:

The potential energy of the $H_2O(g)$ molecules is higher than the potential energy of the $H_2O(\ell)$ molecules.

The water vapor has greater PE.

There is less PE in the liquid water.

68 [1] Allow 1 credit. Acceptable responses include, but are not limited to:

The block of dry ice with less mass contains less thermal energy.

There is more thermal energy in the 2.0-kg block.

69 [1] Allow 1 credit. Acceptable responses include, but are not limited to:

The particles are distributed uniformly throughout the coolant mixture.

There is an even distribution of molecules in the solution.

The water and ethylene glycol molecules mix uniformly.

All particles are evenly dispersed.

70 [1] Allow 1 credit. Acceptable response include, but are not limited to:

Water molecules and ethylene glycol molecules are both polar.

Water and the glycol have similar polarities.

71 [1] Allow 1 credit for any value from 21% to 23%, inclusive.

72 [1] Allow 1 credit. Acceptable responses include, but are not limited to:

3200 mL

3.2×10^3 mL

73 [1] Allow 1 credit. Acceptable responses include, but are not limited to:

In ethene, there is a double bond between the two carbon atoms, which makes the compound unsaturated.

More H atoms can bond with C atoms.

has C=C

Two carbons share four electrons.

74 [1] Allow 1 credit.

Examples of 1-credit responses:

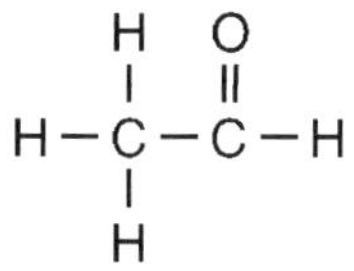

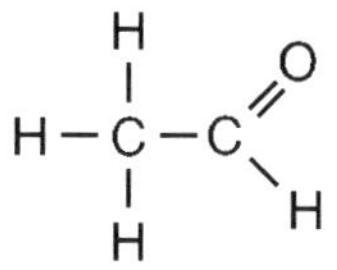

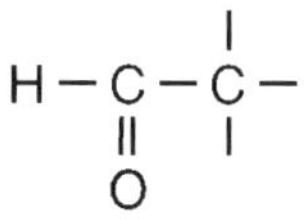

```
      H   O
      |   ||
  H − C − C − H
      |
      H


      H
      |        O
  H − C − C ⫽
      |       \
      H        H


              |
  H − C − C −
      ||    |
      O
```

75 [1] Allow 1 credit. Acceptable responses include, but are not limited to:

The CH_3CH_2OH has 2 carbon atoms, 6 hydrogen atoms, and 1 oxygen atom, while the CH_3CHO has 2 carbon atoms, 4 hydrogen atoms, and 1 oxygen atom.

They don't have the same number of H atoms.

different molecular formulas

76 [1] Allow 1 credit. Acceptable responses include, but are not limited to:

organic acid

carboxylic acid

acids

77 [1] Allow 1 credit for 3 mol *or* three mol.

78 [1] Allow 1 credit. Acceptable responses include, but are not limited to:

pH value of the soil

soil pH

79 [1] Allow 1 credit for blue.

80 [1] Allow 1 credit for +5 *or* 5 *or* five.

81 [1] Allow 1 credit. Acceptable responses include, but are not limited to:

The salt bridge allows ions to flow between the two half-cells.

It maintains the electrical neutrality of the solutions.

prevents polarization of the half-cells

82 [1] Allow 1 credit. Acceptable responses include, but are not limited to:

Magnesium atoms lose electrons and become magnesium ions in the solution.

Some of the Mg atoms oxidize to Mg^{2+} ions, decreasing the electrode mass.

Atoms become aqueous Mg^{2+} ions.

83 [1] Allow 1 credit. Acceptable responses include, but are not limited to:

$_{-1}^{0}e$

$_{-1}^{0}\beta$

β^{-}

84 [1] Allow 1 credit for 43 protons and 56 neutrons.

85 [1] Allow 1 credit. Acceptable responses include, but are not limited to:

$\frac{1}{16}$

0.0625

6.25%

Determine Your January 2017 Regents Exam Score

Part A and B1 (out of 50) : _____

Part B2 and C (out of 35) : _____

Total Raw Score (out of 85): _____

Regents (Scale) Score: _____
Use the chart below.

Regents Examination in Physical Setting/Chemistry – January 2017

Chart for Converting Total Test Raw Scores to Final Examination Scores (Scale Scores)

Raw Score	Scale Score	Raw Score	Scale Score	Raw Score	Scale Score	Raw Score	Scale Score
85	100	62	74	39	57	16	34
84	98	61	73	38	57	15	32
83	97	60	72	37	56	14	30
82	95	59	71	36	55	13	29
81	93	58	71	35	54	12	27
80	92	57	70	34	53	11	25
79	91	56	69	33	53	10	24
78	89	55	68	32	52	9	22
77	88	54	68	31	51	8	20
76	87	53	67	30	50	7	18
75	86	52	66	29	49	6	15
74	85	51	66	28	48	5	13
73	83	50	65	27	47	4	11
72	82	49	64	26	46	3	8
71	81	48	64	25	45	2	6
70	80	47	63	24	44	1	3
69	79	46	62	23	43	0	0
68	79	45	62	22	42		
67	78	44	61	21	40		
66	77	43	60	20	39		
65	76	42	60	19	38		
64	75	41	59	18	36		
63	74	40	58	17	35		

Physical Setting/Chemistry
Regents Exam - August 2016

Part A

Answer all questions in this part.

Directions (1–30): For *each* statement or question, record on your separate answer sheet the *number* of the word or expression that, of those given, best completes the statement or answers the question. Some questions may require the use of the *2011 Edition Reference Tables for Physical Setting/Chemistry*.

1 Which change occurs when an atom in an excited state returns to the ground state?

(1) Energy is emitted.
(2) Energy is absorbed.
(3) The number of electrons decreases.
(4) The number of electrons increases.

2 The valence electrons in an atom of phosphorus in the ground state are all found in

(1) the first shell   (3) the third shell
(2) the second shell   (4) the fourth shell

3 Which two elements have the most similar chemical properties?

(1) beryllium and magnesium
(2) hydrogen and helium
(3) phosphorus and sulfur
(4) potassium and strontium

4 Which phrase describes a compound that consists of two elements?

(1) a mixture in which the elements are in a variable proportion
(2) a mixture in which the elements are in a fixed proportion
(3) a substance in which the elements are chemically combined in a variable proportion
(4) a substance in which the elements are chemically combined in a fixed proportion

5 The formula mass of a compound is the

(1) sum of the atomic masses of its atoms
(2) sum of the atomic numbers of its atoms
(3) product of the atomic masses of its atoms
(4) product of the atomic numbers of its atoms

6 The arrangement of the elements from left to right in Period 4 on the Periodic Table is based on

(1) atomic mass
(2) atomic number
(3) the number of electron shells
(4) the number of oxidation states

7 Which diatomic molecule is formed when the two atoms share six electrons?

(1) H_2 (3) O_2
(2) N_2 (4) F_2

8 Which formula represents a polar molecule?

(1) O_2 (3) NH_3
(2) CO_2 (4) CH_4

9 Which element is *least* likely to undergo a chemical reaction?

(1) lithium   (3) fluorine
(2) carbon   (4) neon

10 Which element has a melting point higher than the melting point of rhenium?

(1) iridium   (3) tantalum
(2) osmium   (4) tungsten

11 Which property can be defined as the ability of a substance to be hammered into thin sheets?

(1) conductivity   (3) melting point
(2) malleability   (4) solubility

12 Which list of elements consists of a metal, a metalloid, and a noble gas?

(1) aluminum, sulfur, argon
(2) magnesium, sodium, sulfur
(3) sodium, silicon, argon
(4) silicon, phosphorus, chlorine

13 Which sample of matter has a crystal structure?

(1) $Hg(\ell)$ (3) $NaCl(s)$
(2) $H_2O(\ell)$ (4) $CH_4(g)$

14 One mole of liquid water and one mole of solid water have *different*

(1) masses
(2) properties
(3) empirical formulas
(4) gram-formula masses

15 Which substance can *not* be broken down by a chemical change?

(1) butanal   (3) gold
(2) propene   (4) water

16 Which statement describes particles of an ideal gas, based on the kinetic molecular theory?

(1) Gas particles are separated by distances smaller than the size of the gas particles.
(2) Gas particles do not transfer energy to each other when they collide.
(3) Gas particles have no attractive forces between them.
(4) Gas particles move in predictable, circular motion.

17 Which expression could represent the concentration of a solution?

(1) 3.5 g   (3) 3.5 mL
(2) 3.5 M   (4) 3.5 mol

18 Which form of energy is associated with the random motion of the particles in a sample of water?

(1) chemical energy   (3) nuclear energy
(2) electrical energy   (4) thermal energy

19 Which change is most likely to occur when a molecule of H_2 and a molecule of I_2 collide with proper orientation and sufficient energy?

(1) a chemical change, because a compound is formed
(2) a chemical change, because an element is formed
(3) a physical change, because a compound is formed
(4) a physical change, because an element is formed

20 Which changes can reach dynamic equilibrium?

(1) nuclear changes, only
(2) chemical changes, only
(3) nuclear and physical changes
(4) chemical and physical changes

21 What occurs when a reaction reaches equilibrium?

(1) The concentration of the reactants increases.
(2) The concentration of the products increases.
(3) The rate of the forward reaction is equal to the rate of the reverse reaction.
(4) The rate of the forward reaction is slower than the rate of the reverse reaction.

22 In terms of potential energy, *PE*, which expression defines the heat of reaction for a chemical change?

(1) $PE_{products} - PE_{reactants}$

(2) $PE_{reactants} - PE_{products}$

(3) $\dfrac{PE_{products}}{PE_{reactants}}$

(4) $\dfrac{PE_{reactants}}{PE_{products}}$

23 Systems in nature tend to undergo changes that result in

(1) lower energy and lower entropy
(2) lower energy and higher entropy
(3) higher energy and lower entropy
(4) higher energy and higher entropy

24 What occurs when Cr^{3+} ions are reduced to Cr^{2+} ions?

(1) Electrons are lost and the oxidation number of chromium increases.
(2) Electrons are lost and the oxidation number of chromium decreases.
(3) Electrons are gained and the oxidation number of chromium increases.
(4) Electrons are gained and the oxidation number of chromium decreases.

374

25 Where do reduction and oxidation occur in an electrolytic cell?

(1) Both occur at the anode.
(2) Both occur at the cathode.
(3) Reduction occurs at the anode, and oxidation occurs at the cathode.
(4) Reduction occurs at the cathode, and oxidation occurs at the anode.

26 Which compound is an electrolyte?

(1) H_2O (3) H_3PO_4
(2) C_2H_6 (4) CH_3OH

27 When the hydronium ion concentration of an aqueous solution is increased by a factor of 10, the pH value of the solution

(1) decreases by 1   (3) decreases by 10
(2) increases by 1   (4) increases by 10

28 The stability of isotopes is related to the ratio of which particles in the atoms?

(1) electrons and protons
(2) electrons and positrons
(3) neutrons and protons
(4) neutrons and positrons

29 Which radioisotope has the fastest rate of decay?

(1) ^{14}C (3) ^{53}Fe
(2) ^{37}Ca (4) ^{42}K

30 The atomic mass of an element is the weighted average of the atomic masses of

(1) the least abundant isotopes of the element
(2) the naturally occurring isotopes of the element
(3) the artificially produced isotopes of the element
(4) the natural and artificial isotopes of the element

Part B–1

Answer all questions in this part.

Directions (31–50): For *each* statement or question, record on your separate answer sheet the *number* of the word or expression that, of those given, best completes the statement or answers the question. Some questions may require the use of the *2011 Edition Reference Tables for Physical Setting/Chemistry*.

31 Which list of elements is arranged in order of increasing electronegativity?

(1) Be, Mg, Ca   (3) K, Ca, Sc
(2) F, Cl, Br   (4) Li, Na, K

32 The table below gives the masses of two different subatomic particles found in an atom.

Subatomic Particles and Their Masses

Subatomic Particle	Mass (g)
X	1.67×10^{-24}
Z	9.11×10^{-28}

Which of the subatomic particles are each paired with their corresponding name?

(1) X, proton and Z, electron
(2) X, proton and Z, neutron
(3) X, neutron and Z, proton
(4) X, electron and Z, proton

33 Which electron configuration represents an excited state for an atom of calcium?

(1) 2-8-7-1   (3) 2-8-7-3
(2) 2-8-7-2   (4) 2-8-8-2

34 At STP, graphite and diamond are two solid forms of carbon. Which statement explains why these two forms of carbon differ in hardness?

(1) Graphite and diamond have different ionic radii.
(2) Graphite and diamond have different molecular structures.
(3) Graphite is a metal, but diamond is a nonmetal.
(4) Graphite is a good conductor of electricity, but diamond is a poor conductor of electricity.

35 Which equation shows conservation of charge?

(1) $Cu + Ag^+ \rightarrow Cu^{2+} + Ag$
(2) $Mg + Zn^{2+} \rightarrow 2Mg^{2+} + Zn$
(3) $2F_2 + Br^- \rightarrow 2F^- + Br_2$
(4) $2I^- + Cl_2 \rightarrow I_2 + 2Cl^-$

36 What occurs when potassium reacts with chlorine to form potassium chloride?

(1) Electrons are shared and the bonding is ionic.
(2) Electrons are shared and the bonding is covalent.
(3) Electrons are transferred and the bonding is ionic.
(4) Electrons are transferred and the bonding is covalent.

37 Given the balanced equation representing a reaction:

$$H_2 + energy \rightarrow H + H$$

What occurs as bonds are broken in one mole of H_2 molecules during this reaction?

(1) Energy is absorbed and one mole of unbonded hydrogen atoms is produced.
(2) Energy is absorbed and two moles of unbonded hydrogen atoms are produced.
(3) Energy is released and one mole of unbonded hydrogen atoms is produced.
(4) Energy is released and two moles of unbonded hydrogen atoms are produced.

38 Which pair of atoms has the most polar bond?

(1) H–Br   (3) I–Br
(2) H–Cl   (4) I–Cl

39 Which two notations represent isotopes of the same element?

(1) $^{14}_{7}N$ and $^{18}_{7}N$ (3) $^{14}_{7}N$ and $^{17}_{10}Ne$

(2) $^{20}_{7}N$ and $^{20}_{10}Ne$ (4) $^{19}_{7}N$ and $^{16}_{10}Ne$

40 The graph below shows the volume and the mass of four different substances at STP.

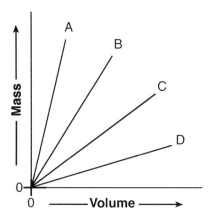

Which of the four substances has the *lowest* density?

(1) *A*   (3) *C*

(2) *B*   (4) *D*

41 What is the total amount of heat required to completely melt 347 grams of ice at its melting point?

(1) 334 J   (3) 116 000 J

(2) 1450 J   (4) 784 000 J

42 As the temperature of a reaction increases, it is expected that the reacting particles collide

(1) more often and with greater force
(2) more often and with less force
(3) less often and with greater force
(4) less often and with less force

43 Given the formula representing a compound:

$$\begin{array}{ccccccc} H & H & H & O & H & H \\ | & | & | & \| & | & | \\ H-C & -C & -C & -C & -C & -C-H \\ | & | & | & & | & | \\ H & H & H & & H & H \end{array}$$

What is an IUPAC name for this compound?

(1) ethyl propanoate   (3) 3-hexanone
(2) propyl ethanoate   (4) 4-hexanone

44 A voltaic cell converts chemical energy to

(1) electrical energy with an external power source
(2) nuclear energy with an external power source
(3) electrical energy without an external power source
(4) nuclear energy without an external power source

45 Which acid and base react to form water and sodium sulfate?

(1) sulfuric acid and sodium hydroxide
(2) sulfuric acid and potassium hydroxide
(3) sulfurous acid and sodium hydroxide
(4) sulfurous acid and potassium hydroxide

46 Given the equation representing a reaction:

$$H_2CO_3 + NH_3 \rightarrow NH_4^+ + HCO_3^-$$

According to one acid-base theory, the compound NH_3 acts as a base because it

(1) accepts a hydrogen ion
(2) donates a hydrogen ion
(3) accepts a hydroxide ion
(4) donates a hydroxide ion

47 Which statement describes characteristics of a 0.01 M KOH(aq) solution?

(1) The solution is acidic with a pH less than 7.
(2) The solution is acidic with a pH greater than 7.
(3) The solution is basic with a pH less than 7.
(4) The solution is basic with a pH greater than 7.

48 Four statements about the development of the atomic model are shown below.

    A: Electrons have wavelike properties.
    B: Atoms have small, negatively charged particles.
    C: The center of an atom is a small, dense nucleus.
    D: Atoms are hard, indivisible spheres.

Which order of statements represents the historical development of the atomic model?

(1) $C \rightarrow D \rightarrow A \rightarrow B$ (3) $D \rightarrow B \rightarrow A \rightarrow C$
(2) $C \rightarrow D \rightarrow B \rightarrow A$ (4) $D \rightarrow B \rightarrow C \rightarrow A$

49 Five cubes of iron are tested in a laboratory. The tests and the results are shown in the table below.

Iron Tests and the Results

Test	Procedure	Result
1	A cube of Fe is hit with a hammer.	The cube is flattened.
2	A cube of Fe is placed in 3 M HCl(aq).	Bubbles of gas form.
3	A cube of Fe is heated to 1811 K.	The cube melts.
4	A cube of Fe is left in damp air.	The cube rusts.
5	A cube of Fe is placed in water.	The cube sinks.

Which tests demonstrate chemical properties?

(1) 1, 3, and 4   (3) 2 and 4
(2) 1, 3, and 5   (4) 2 and 5

50 A rigid cylinder with a movable piston contains a sample of helium gas. The temperature of the gas is held constant as the piston is pulled outward. Which graph represents the relationship between the volume of the gas and the pressure of the gas?

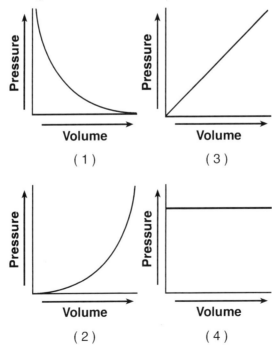

378

Answer Key   Regents Exam August 2016

Part A

1 . . . . . 1	9 . . . . . 4	17 . . . . . 2	25 . . . . . 4 . . . .
2 . . . . . 3	10 . . . . . 4	18 . . . . . 4	26 . . . . . 3 . . . .
3 . . . . . 1	11 . . . . . 2	19 . . . . . 1	27 . . . . . 1 . . . .
4 . . . . . 4	12 . . . . . 3	20 . . . . . 4	28 . . . . . 3 . . . .
5 . . . . . 1	13 . . . . . 3	21 . . . . . 3	29 . . . . . 2 . . . .
6 . . . . . 2	14 . . . . . 2	22 . . . . . 1	30 . . . . . 2 . . . .
7 . . . . . 2	15 . . . . . 3	23 . . . . . 2	
8 . . . 3	16 . . . . . 3	24 . . . . . 4	

Part B–1

31 . . . . . 3	36 . . . . . 3	41 . . . . . 3	46 . . . . . 1 . . . .
32 . . . . . 1	37 . . . . . 2	42 . . . . . 1	47 . . . . . 4 . . . .
33 . . . . . 3	38 . . . . . 2	43 . . . . . 3	48 . . . . . 4 . . . .
34 . . . . . 2	39 . . . . . 1	44 . . . . . 3	49 . . . . . 3 . . . .
35 . . . . . 4	40 . . . . . 4	45 . . . . . 1	50 . . . . . 1 . . . .

Answer all questions in this part.

Directions (51–65): Record your answers in the spaces provided in your answer booklet. Some questions may require the use of the *2011 Edition Reference Tables for Physical Setting/Chemistry.*

51 What is the empirical formula for C_6H_{12}? [1]

52 Using Table *G*, determine the minimum mass of NaCl that must be dissolved in 200. grams of water to produce a saturated solution at 90.°C. [1]

53 State the physical property that makes it possible to separate a solution by distillation. [1]

Base your answers to questions 54 and 55 on the information below and on your knowledge of chemistry.

A beaker contains a liquid sample of a molecular substance. Both the beaker and the liquid are at 194 K. The graph below represents the relationship between temperature and time as the beaker and its contents are cooled for 12 minutes in a refrigerated chamber.

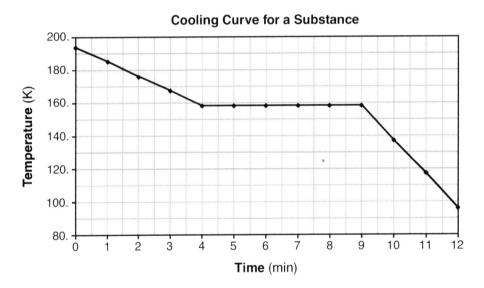

54 State what happens to the average kinetic energy of the molecules in the sample during the first 3 minutes. [1]

55 Identify the physical change occurring during the time interval, minute 4 to minute 9. [1]

Base your answers to questions 56 through 59 on the information below and on your knowledge of chemistry.

The equation below represents a reaction between propene and hydrogen bromide.

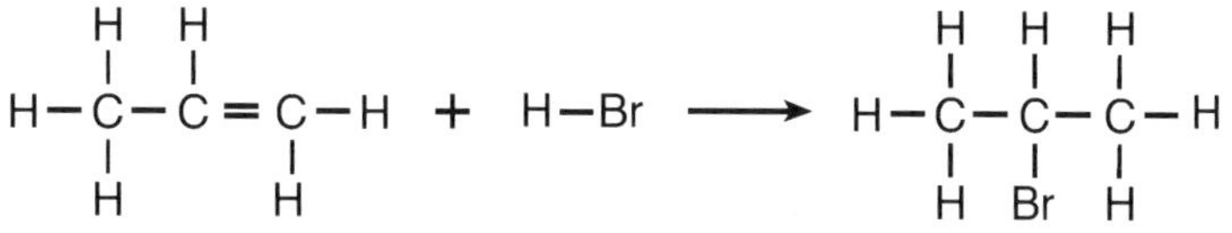

$$
\begin{array}{ccccc}
& H \ \ H & & & H \ \ H \ \ H \\
& | \ \ \ | & & & | \ \ \ | \ \ \ | \\
H-C-C=C-H & + & H-Br & \longrightarrow & H-C-C-C-H \\
& | \ \ \ \ \ \ | & & & | \ \ \ | \ \ \ | \\
& H \ \ \ \ \ H & & & H \ \ Br \ \ H
\end{array}
$$

Cyclopropane, an isomer of propene, has a boiling point of $-33°C$ at standard pressure and is represented by the formula below.

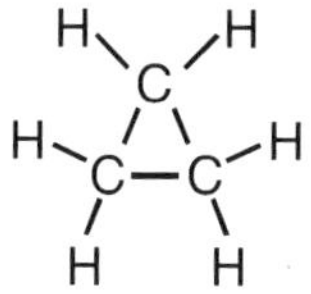

$$
\begin{array}{c}
H \diagdown \ \ \diagup H \\
C \\
H \diagup \diagdown \\
\diagup C - C \diagdown \\
H \diagdown \ \ \diagup H \\
H \ \ \ \ \ \ H
\end{array}
$$

56 Explain why this reaction can be classified as a synthesis reaction. [1]

57 Identify the class of organic compounds to which the product of this reaction belongs. [1]

58 Explain, in terms of molecular formulas and structural formulas, why cyclopropane is an isomer of propene. [1]

59 Convert the boiling point of cyclopropane at standard pressure to kelvins. [1]

Base your answers to questions 60 through 63 on the information below and on your knowledge of chemistry.

The radius of a lithium atom is 130. picometers, and the radius of a fluorine atom is 60. picometers. The radius of a lithium ion, Li^+, is 59 picometers, and the radius of a fluoride ion, F^-, is 133 picometers.

60 Compare the radius of a fluoride ion to the radius of a fluorine atom. [1]

61 Explain, in terms of subatomic particles, why the radius of a lithium ion is smaller than the radius of a lithium atom. [1]

62 In the space *in your answer booklet*, draw a Lewis electron-dot diagram for a fluoride ion. [1]

63 Describe the general trend in atomic radius as each element in Period 2 is considered in order from left to right. [1]

Base your answers to questions 64 and 65 on the information below and on your knowledge of chemistry.

Nuclear fission reactions can produce different radioisotopes. One of these radioisotopes is Te-137, which has a half-life of 2.5 seconds. The diagram below represents one of the many nuclear fission reactions.

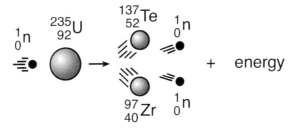

64 State evidence that this nuclear reaction represents transmutation. [1]

65 Complete the nuclear equation *in your answer booklet* for the beta decay of Zr-97, by writing an isotopic notation for the missing product. [1]

Part C

Answer all questions in this part.

Directions (66–85): Record your answers in the spaces provided in your answer booklet. Some questions may require the use of the *2011 Edition Reference Tables for Physical Setting/Chemistry*.

Base your answers to questions 66 through 69 on the information below and on your knowledge of chemistry.

Stamping an identification number into the steel frame of a bicycle compresses the crystal structure of the metal. If the number is filed off, there are scientific ways to reveal the number.

One method is to apply aqueous copper(II) chloride to the number area. The Cu^{2+} ions react with some iron atoms in the steel frame, producing copper atoms that show the pattern of the number. The ionic equation below represents this reaction.

$$Fe(s) + Cu^{2+}(aq) \rightarrow Fe^{2+}(aq) + Cu(s)$$

Another method is to apply hydrochloric acid to the number area. The acid reacts with the iron, producing bubbles of hydrogen gas. The bubbles form faster where the metal was compressed, so the number becomes visible. The equation below represents this reaction.

$$2HCl(aq) + Fe(s) \rightarrow FeCl_2(aq) + H_2(g)$$

66 Explain why the Fe atoms in the bicycle frame react with the Cu^{2+} ions. [1]

67 Determine the number of moles of hydrogen gas produced when 0.001 mole of HCl(aq) reacts completely with the iron metal. [1]

68 Write a balanced half-reaction equation for the reduction of the hydrogen ions to hydrogen gas. [1]

69 Describe *one* change in the HCl(aq) that will increase the rate at which hydrogen bubbles are produced when the acid is applied to the steel frame. [1]

Base your answers to questions 70 through 73 on the information below and on your knowledge of chemistry.

In an investigation, aqueous solutions are prepared by completely dissolving a different amount of NaCl(s) in each of four beakers containing 100.00 grams of $H_2O(\ell)$ at room temperature. Each solution is heated and the temperature at which boiling occurred is measured. The data are recorded in the table below.

Boiling Point Data for Four NaCl(aq) Solutions

Beaker Number	Mass of $H_2O(\ell)$ (g)	Mass of NaCl(s) Dissolved (g)	Boiling Point of Solution (°C)
1	100.00	8.76	101.5
2	100.00	17.52	103.1
3	100.00	26.28	104.6
4	100.00	35.04	106.1

70 Identify the solute and the solvent used in this investigation. [1]

71 Show a numerical setup for calculating the percent by mass of NaCl in the solution in beaker 4. [1]

72 Explain, in terms of ions, why the ability to conduct an electric current is greater for the solution in beaker 4 than for the solution in beaker 1. [1]

73 State the relationship between the concentration of ions and the boiling point for these solutions. [1]

Base your answers to questions 74 through 76 on the information below and on your knowledge of chemistry.

One type of voltaic cell, called a mercury battery, uses zinc and mercury(II) oxide to generate an electric current. Mercury batteries were used because of their miniature size, even though mercury is toxic. The overall reaction for a mercury battery is given in the equation below.

$$Zn(s) + HgO(s) \rightarrow ZnO(s) + Hg(\ell)$$

74 Determine the change in the oxidation number of zinc during the operation of the cell. [1]

75 Compare the number of moles of electrons lost to the number of moles of electrons gained during the reaction. [1]

76 Using information in the passage, state *one* risk and *one* benefit of using a mercury battery. [1]

Base your answers to questions 77 through 80 on the information below and on your knowledge of chemistry.

A company produces a colorless vinegar that is 5.0% $HC_2H_3O_2$ in water. Using thymol blue as an indicator, a student titrates a 15.0-milliliter sample of the vinegar with 43.1 milliliters of a 0.30 M NaOH(aq) solution until the acid is neutralized.

77 Based on Table *M*, what is the color of the indicator in the vinegar solution before any base is added? [1]

78 Identify the negative ion in the NaOH(aq) used in this titration. [1]

79 The concentration of the base used in this titration is expressed to what number of significant figures? [1]

80 Determine the molarity of the $HC_2H_3O_2$ in the vinegar sample, using the titration data. [1]

Base your answers to questions 81 through 85 on the information below and on your knowledge of chemistry.

In industry, ethanol is primarily produced by two different reactions. One process involves the reaction of glucose in the presence of an enzyme that acts as a catalyst. The equation below represents this reaction.

$$\text{Equation 1:} \quad \underset{\text{glucose}}{C_6H_{12}O_6} \xrightarrow{\text{enzyme}} \underset{\text{ethanol}}{2CH_3CH_2OH} + 2CO_2$$

In another reaction, ethanol is produced from ethene and water. The equation below represents this reaction in which H_2SO_4 is a catalyst.

$$\text{Equation 2:} \quad CH_2CH_2 + H_2O \xrightarrow{H_2SO_4} CH_3CH_2OH$$

Industrial ethanol can be oxidized using a catalyst to produce ethanal. The equation representing this oxidation is shown below.

$$\text{Equation 3:} \quad CH_3CH_2OH \xrightarrow{\text{catalyst}} CH_3CHO + H_2$$

81 Identify the element that causes the reactant in equation 1 to be classified as an organic compound. [1]

82 Identify the type of organic reaction represented by equation 1. [1]

83 Explain why the hydrocarbon in equation 2 is unsaturated. [1]

84 Explain, in terms of intermolecular forces, why ethanol has a much higher boiling point than ethene, at standard pressure. [1]

85 Draw a structural formula for the organic product in equation 3. [1]

386

The University of the State of New York

REGENTS HIGH SCHOOL EXAMINATION

PHYSICAL SETTING CHEMISTRY

Wednesday, August 17, 2016 — 8:30 to 11:30 a.m., only

ANSWER BOOKLET

☐ Male

Student .... Sex: ☐ Female

Teacher ....

School .... Grade ....

Record your answers for Part B–2 and Part C in this booklet.

Part B–2

51 ______________________________

52 __________ **g**

53 ______________________________

54 ____

____

____

55 ______________________________

56 _____

_____

_____

57 _____

58 _____

_____

_____

59 _____ **K**

60 _____

_____

_____

61 _____

_____

_____

62

63 _____

_____

_____

64 _____

_____

_____

65 $^{97}_{40}\text{Zr} \rightarrow\ ^{0}_{-1}\text{e} +$ _____

Part C

66 _____

_____

_____

67 _____ **mol**

68 _____

69 _____

_____

_____

70 Solute: _____

Solvent: _____

71

72 _____

_____

_____

73 _____

_____

_____

74 From _____ to _____

75 _____

_____

_____

76 Risk: _____

Benefit: _____

77 _____

78 _____

79 _____

80 _____ **M**

81 _____

82 _____

83 _____

_____

_____

84 _____

_____

_____

85

Part B–2

51 [1] Allow 1 credit for CH_2. The order of the elements can vary.

52 [1] Allow 1 credit for any value from 78 g to 82 g inclusive.

53 [1] Allow 1 credit. Acceptable responses include, but are not limited to:

boiling point

boiling temperature

54 [1] Allow 1 credit. Acceptable responses include, but are not limited to:

The average kinetic energy decreases.

The average KE goes down.

55 [1] Allow 1 credit. Acceptable responses include, but are not limited to:

freezing

solidification

liquid to solid

56 [1] Allow 1 credit. Acceptable responses include, but are not limited to:

Two substances react to produce one substance.

This product is formed by chemically combining two substances.

Two molecules produce a more complex molecule.

One compound is formed from two compounds.

57 [1] Allow 1 credit. Acceptable responses include, but are not limited to:

halide   halocarbon

alkyl halide   halogenalkane

58 [1] Allow 1 credit. Acceptable responses include, but are not limited to:

The molecular formulas for the two compounds are the same, but the structural formulas are different.

Both molecules have the same number of C atoms and the same number of H atoms, but have a different arrangement of atoms.

Both compounds are C_3H_6, but have different structures.

Both compounds are C_3H_6, but one has a ring and one has a double bond.

59 [1] Allow 1 credit for 240. K. Significant figures need *not* be shown.

60 [1] Allow 1 credit. Acceptable responses include, but are not limited to:

The radius of a fluoride ion is larger than the radius of a fluorine atom.

The radius of F_- is 73 pm greater than the radius of an F atom.

The F atom is 60 pm, the F_- is 133 pm.

The F atom is smaller.

61 [1] Allow 1 credit. Acceptable responses include, but are not limited to:

A lithium atom loses its second-shell electron, so the lithium ion has only one shell of electrons.

A lithium ion has one fewer electron.

The Li atom has 3 electrons and the Li^+ ion has 2 electrons.

A Li ion has one less electron.

62 [1] Allow 1 credit. The positions of the dots may vary.

Examples of 1-credit responses:

$$\left[\ddot{\overset{..}{\underset{..}{\text{F}}}} \times \right]^{-}$$

$$\ddot{\underset{..}{\text{F}}}^{\,-}$$

$$\ddot{\underset{..}{\text{F}}}^{\,-1}$$

63 [1] Allow 1 credit. Acceptable responses include, but are not limited to:

As the elements in Period 2 are considered from left to right, the atomic radius generally decreases.

The atomic radius goes down except for Neon.

The atomic radius gets smaller.

64 [1] Allow 1 credit. Acceptable responses include, but are not limited to:

In this reaction, uranium is changing to other elements.

Different elements are formed.

One element becomes two new elements.

Two atoms are formed with different atomic numbers from the U-235.

65 [1] Allow 1 credit. Acceptable responses include, but are not limited to:

$^{97}_{41}\text{Nb}$

^{97}Nb

Nb–97

niobium–97

Part C

Allow a total of 20 credits for this part. The student must answer all questions in this part.

66 [1] Allow 1 credit. Acceptable responses include, but are not limited to:

Fe oxidizes in the presence of Cu^{2+} ions.

Iron is a more active metal than copper.

Cu^2 ions act as an oxidizing agent.

Fe is above Cu on Table J.

67 [1] Allow 1 credit. Acceptable responses include, but are not limited to:

5×10^{-4} mol   0.0005 mol

68 [1] Allow 1 credit. Acceptable responses include, but are not limited to:

$2H^+(aq) + 2e^- \rightarrow H_2(g)$

$2H^+ + 2e^- \rightarrow H_2$

$2e^- + 2H^{+1} \rightarrow H_2$

69 [1] Allow 1 credit. Acceptable responses include, but are not limited to:

Increase the concentration of the HCl(aq).

Increase the temperature.

70 [1] Allow 1 credit. Acceptable responses include, but are not limited to:

Solute: NaCl   Solute: sodium chloride
Solvent: H_2O Solvent: water

71 [1] Allow 1 credit. Acceptable responses include, but are not limited to:

$$\frac{35.04 \text{ g}}{100.00 \text{ g} + 35.04 \text{ g}} \times 100 \qquad \frac{35}{135} \times 100 \qquad \frac{35 \text{ g }(100)}{35 \text{ g} + 100 \text{ g}}$$

72 [1] Allow 1 credit. Acceptable responses include, but are not limited to:

The solution in beaker 4 has a greater ability to conduct an electric current because it has a greater concentration of aqueous ions than the solution in beaker 1.

There are fewer charged particles free to move in beaker 1.

There are more ions in beaker 4.

73 [1] Allow 1 credit. Acceptable responses include, but are not limited to:

The greater the concentration of ions, the higher the boiling point of the solution.

The boiling point is lower with fewer dissolved particles.

The boiling point goes up with more aqueous ions.

74 [1] Allow 1 credit. Acceptable responses include, but are not limited to:

From 0 to +2

From 0 to 2+

From zero to two

75 [1] Allow 1 credit. Acceptable responses include, but are not limited to:

The number of moles of electrons lost is equal to the number of moles of electrons gained.

The number of moles is the same.

e^- lost = e^- gained.

76 [1] Allow 1 credit. Acceptable responses include, but are not limited to:

Risk: Mercury is toxic.
Benefit: Mercury batteries are miniature.

Risk: harmful to humans
Benefit: producing electricity

77 [1] Allow 1 credit for yellow.

78 [1] Allow 1 credit for OH^- *or* hydroxide.

79 [1] Allow 1 credit for 2 *or* two.

80 [1] Allow 1 credit for 0.86 M *or* 0.862 M.

81 [1] Allow 1 credit for carbon *or* C.

82 [1] Allow 1 credit. Acceptable responses include, but are not limited to:

fermentation

fermenting

83 [1] Allow 1 credit. Acceptable responses include, but are not limited to:

There is a double carbon-carbon bond in an ethene molecule.

Molecules of the compound contain a multiple C to C bond.

More H atoms can be added to the molecule.

Each molecule has C = C.

84 [1] Allow 1 credit. Acceptable responses include, but are not limited to:

The alcohol functional group, $-OH$, allows for hydrogen bonding between ethanol molecules, so ethanol has a higher boiling point than ethene.

The boiling point of ethene is lower because its intermolecular forces are weaker than the intermolecular forces in the alcohol.

IMF for ethanol is stronger.

85 [1] Allow 1 credit.

Examples of 1-credit responses:

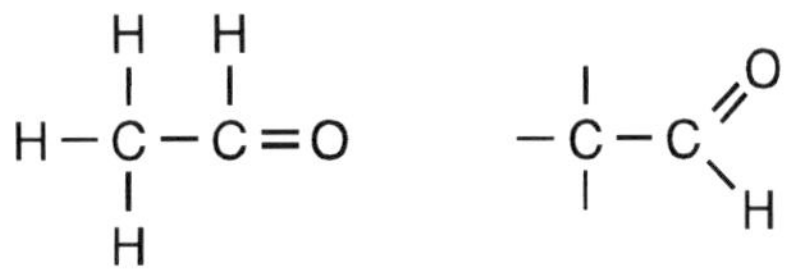

Determine Your August 2016 Regents Exam Score

Part A and B1 (out of 50) : _____

Part B2 and C (out of 35) : _____

Total Raw Score (out of 85): _____

Regents (Scale) Score: _____
Use the chart below.

Regents Examination in Physical Setting/Chemistry – August 2016

Chart for Converting Total Test Raw Scores to Final Examination Scores (Scale Scores)

Raw Score	Scale Score	Raw Score	Scale Score	Raw Score	Scale Score	Raw Score	Scale Score
85	100	62	74	39	57	16	33
84	98	61	73	38	56	15	31
83	97	60	72	37	56	14	29
82	95	59	71	36	55	13	28
81	94	58	71	35	54	12	26
80	92	57	70	34	53	11	24
79	91	56	69	33	52	10	22
78	90	55	68	32	51	9	20
77	88	54	68	31	50	8	18
76	87	53	67	30	49	7	16
75	86	52	66	29	49	6	14
74	85	51	66	28	48	5	12
73	84	50	65	27	46	4	10
72	83	49	64	26	45	3	8
71	82	48	64	25	44	2	5
70	81	47	63	24	43	1	3
69	80	46	62	23	42	0	0
68	79	45	61	22	41		
67	78	44	61	21	40		
66	77	43	60	20	38		
65	76	42	59	19	37		
64	75	41	59	18	35		
63	74	40	58	17	34		

Reference Tables for Physical Setting/CHEMISTRY
2011 Edition

Table A
Standard Temperature and Pressure

Name	Value	Unit
Standard Pressure	101.3 kPa 1 atm	kilopascal atmosphere
Standard Temperature	273 K 0°C	kelvin degree Celsius

Table B
Physical Constants for Water

Heat of Fusion	334 J/g
Heat of Vaporization	2260 J/g
Specific Heat Capacity of $H_2O(\ell)$	4.18 J/g•K

Table C
Selected Prefixes

Factor	Prefix	Symbol
10^3	kilo-	k
10^{-1}	deci-	d
10^{-2}	centi-	c
10^{-3}	milli-	m
10^{-6}	micro-	μ
10^{-9}	nano-	n
10^{-12}	pico-	p

Table D
Selected Units

Symbol	Name	Quantity
m	meter	length
g	gram	mass
Pa	pascal	pressure
K	kelvin	temperature
mol	mole	amount of substance
J	joule	energy, work, quantity of heat
s	second	time
min	minute	time
h	hour	time
d	day	time
y	year	time
L	liter	volume
ppm	parts per million	concentration
M	molarity	solution concentration
u	atomic mass unit	atomic mass

Table E
Selected Polyatomic Ions

Formula	Name	Formula	Name
H_3O^+	hydronium	CrO_4^{2-}	chromate
Hg_2^{2+}	mercury(I)	$Cr_2O_7^{2-}$	dichromate
NH_4^+	ammonium	MnO_4^-	permanganate
$C_2H_3O_2^-$ } CH_3COO^- }	acetate	NO_2^-	nitrite
		NO_3^-	nitrate
CN^-	cyanide	O_2^{2-}	peroxide
CO_3^{2-}	carbonate	OH^-	hydroxide
HCO_3^-	hydrogen carbonate	PO_4^{3-}	phosphate
$C_2O_4^{2-}$	oxalate	SCN^-	thiocyanate
ClO^-	hypochlorite	SO_3^{2-}	sulfite
ClO_2^-	chlorite	SO_4^{2-}	sulfate
ClO_3^-	chlorate	HSO_4^-	hydrogen sulfate
ClO_4^-	perchlorate	$S_2O_3^{2-}$	thiosulfate

Table F
Solubility Guidelines for Aqueous Solutions

Ions That Form *Soluble* Compounds	Exceptions	Ions That Form *Insoluble* Compounds*	Exceptions
Group 1 ions (Li^+, Na^+, etc.)		carbonate (CO_3^{2-})	when combined with Group 1 ions or ammonium (NH_4^+)
ammonium (NH_4^+)		chromate (CrO_4^{2-})	when combined with Group 1 ions, Ca^{2+}, Mg^{2+}, or ammonium (NH_4^+)
nitrate (NO_3^-)			
acetate ($C_2H_3O_2^-$ or CH_3COO^-)		phosphate (PO_4^{3-})	when combined with Group 1 ions or ammonium (NH_4^+)
hydrogen carbonate (HCO_3^-)		sulfide (S^{2-})	when combined with Group 1 ions or ammonium (NH_4^+)
chlorate (ClO_3^-)		hydroxide (OH^-)	when combined with Group 1 ions, Ca^{2+}, Ba^{2+}, Sr^{2+}, or ammonium (NH_4^+)
halides (Cl^-, Br^-, I^-)	when combined with Ag^+, Pb^{2+}, or Hg_2^{2+}		
sulfates (SO_4^{2-})	when combined with Ag^+, Ca^{2+}, Sr^{2+}, Ba^{2+}, or Pb^{2+}		

*compounds having very low solubility in H_2O

Table G
Solubility Curves at Standard Pressure

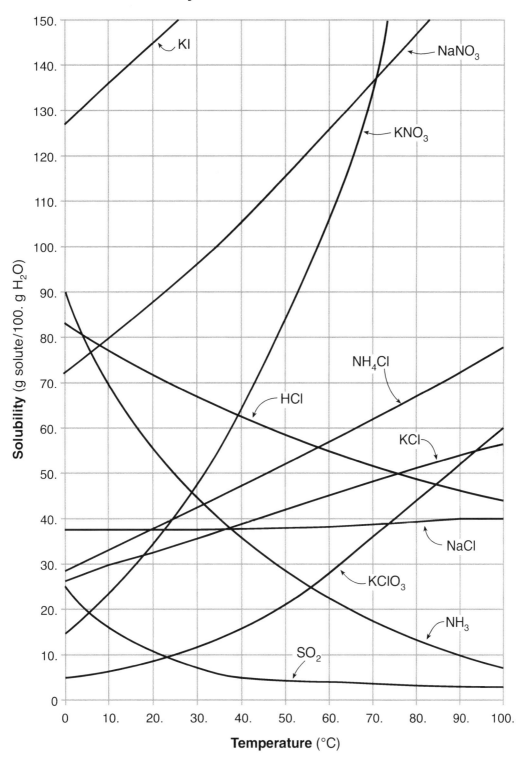

Table H
Vapor Pressure of Four Liquids

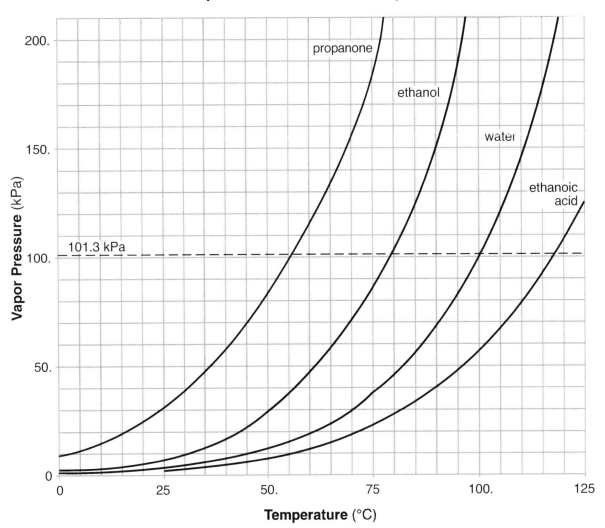

Table I
Heats of Reaction at 101.3 kPa and 298 K

Reaction	ΔH (kJ)*
$CH_4(g) + 2O_2(g) \longrightarrow CO_2(g) + 2H_2O(\ell)$	-890.4
$C_3H_8(g) + 5O_2(g) \longrightarrow 3CO_2(g) + 4H_2O(\ell)$	-2219.2
$2C_8H_{18}(\ell) + 25O_2(g) \longrightarrow 16CO_2(g) + 18H_2O(\ell)$	-10943
$2CH_3OH(\ell) + 3O_2(g) \longrightarrow 2CO_2(g) + 4H_2O(\ell)$	-1452
$C_2H_5OH(\ell) + 3O_2(g) \longrightarrow 2CO_2(g) + 3H_2O(\ell)$	-1367
$C_6H_{12}O_6(s) + 6O_2(g) \longrightarrow 6CO_2(g) + 6H_2O(\ell)$	-2804
$2CO(g) + O_2(g) \longrightarrow 2CO_2(g)$	-566.0
$C(s) + O_2(g) \longrightarrow CO_2(g)$	-393.5
$4Al(s) + 3O_2(g) \longrightarrow 2Al_2O_3(s)$	-3351
$N_2(g) + O_2(g) \longrightarrow 2NO(g)$	$+182.6$
$N_2(g) + 2O_2(g) \longrightarrow 2NO_2(g)$	$+66.4$
$2H_2(g) + O_2(g) \longrightarrow 2H_2O(g)$	-483.6
$2H_2(g) + O_2(g) \longrightarrow 2H_2O(\ell)$	-571.6
$N_2(g) + 3H_2(g) \longrightarrow 2NH_3(g)$	-91.8
$2C(s) + 3H_2(g) \longrightarrow C_2H_6(g)$	-84.0
$2C(s) + 2H_2(g) \longrightarrow C_2H_4(g)$	$+52.4$
$2C(s) + H_2(g) \longrightarrow C_2H_2(g)$	$+227.4$
$H_2(g) + I_2(g) \longrightarrow 2HI(g)$	$+53.0$
$KNO_3(s) \xrightarrow{H_2O} K^+(aq) + NO_3^-(aq)$	$+34.89$
$NaOH(s) \xrightarrow{H_2O} Na^+(aq) + OH^-(aq)$	-44.51
$NH_4Cl(s) \xrightarrow{H_2O} NH_4^+(aq) + Cl^-(aq)$	$+14.78$
$NH_4NO_3(s) \xrightarrow{H_2O} NH_4^+(aq) + NO_3^-(aq)$	$+25.69$
$NaCl(s) \xrightarrow{H_2O} Na^+(aq) + Cl^-(aq)$	$+3.88$
$LiBr(s) \xrightarrow{H_2O} Li^+(aq) + Br^-(aq)$	-48.83
$H^+(aq) + OH^-(aq) \longrightarrow H_2O(\ell)$	-55.8

*The ΔH values are based on molar quantities represented in the equations. A minus sign indicates an exothermic reaction.

Table J
Activity Series**

Most Active	Metals	Nonmetals	Most Active
	Li	F_2	
	Rb	Cl_2	
	K	Br_2	
	Cs	I_2	
	Ba		
	Sr		
	Ca		
	Na		
	Mg		
	Al		
	Ti		
	Mn		
	Zn		
	Cr		
	Fe		
	Co		
	Ni		
	Sn		
	Pb		
	H_2		
	Cu		
	Ag		
Least Active	Au		Least Active

**Activity Series is based on the hydrogen standard. H_2 is *not* a metal.

Table K
Common Acids

Formula	Name
$HCl(aq)$	hydrochloric acid
$HNO_2(aq)$	nitrous acid
$HNO_3(aq)$	nitric acid
$H_2SO_3(aq)$	sulfurous acid
$H_2SO_4(aq)$	sulfuric acid
$H_3PO_4(aq)$	phosphoric acid
$H_2CO_3(aq)$ or $CO_2(aq)$	carbonic acid
$CH_3COOH(aq)$ or $HC_2H_3O_2(aq)$	ethanoic acid (acetic acid)

Table L
Common Bases

Formula	Name
$NaOH(aq)$	sodium hydroxide
$KOH(aq)$	potassium hydroxide
$Ca(OH)_2(aq)$	calcium hydroxide
$NH_3(aq)$	aqueous ammonia

Table M
Common Acid–Base Indicators

Indicator	Approximate pH Range for Color Change	Color Change
methyl orange	3.1–4.4	red to yellow
bromthymol blue	6.0–7.6	yellow to blue
phenolphthalein	8–9	colorless to pink
litmus	4.5–8.3	red to blue
bromcresol green	3.8–5.4	yellow to blue
thymol blue	8.0–9.6	yellow to blue

Source: *The Merck Index*, 14th ed., 2006, Merck Publishing Group

Table N
Selected Radioisotopes

Nuclide	Half-Life	Decay Mode	Nuclide Name
^{198}Au	2.695 d	β^-	gold-198
^{14}C	5715 y	β^-	carbon-14
^{37}Ca	182 ms	β^+	calcium-37
^{60}Co	5.271 y	β^-	cobalt-60
^{137}Cs	30.2 y	β^-	cesium-137
^{53}Fe	8.51 min	β^+	iron-53
^{220}Fr	27.4 s	α	francium-220
^3H	12.31 y	β^-	hydrogen-3
^{131}I	8.021 d	β^-	iodine-131
^{37}K	1.23 s	β^+	potassium-37
^{42}K	12.36 h	β^-	potassium-42
^{85}Kr	10.73 y	β^-	krypton-85
^{16}N	7.13 s	β^-	nitrogen-16
^{19}Ne	17.22 s	β^+	neon-19
^{32}P	14.28 d	β^-	phosphorus-32
^{239}Pu	2.410×10^4 y	α	plutonium-239
^{226}Ra	1599 y	α	radium-226
^{222}Rn	3.823 d	α	radon-222
^{90}Sr	29.1 y	β^-	strontium-90
^{99}Tc	2.13×10^5 y	β^-	technetium-99
^{232}Th	1.40×10^{10} y	α	thorium-232
^{233}U	1.592×10^5 y	α	uranium-233
^{235}U	7.04×10^8 y	α	uranium-235
^{238}U	4.47×10^9 y	α	uranium-238

Source: *CRC Handbook of Chemistry and Physics*, 91st ed., 2010–2011, CRC Press

Table O
Symbols Used in Nuclear Chemistry

Name	Notation	Symbol
alpha particle	$^{4}_{2}\text{He}$ or $^{4}_{2}\alpha$	α
beta particle	$^{0}_{-1}\text{e}$ or $^{0}_{-1}\beta$	β^{-}
gamma radiation	$^{0}_{0}\gamma$	γ
neutron	$^{1}_{0}\text{n}$	n
proton	$^{1}_{1}\text{H}$ or $^{1}_{1}\text{p}$	p
positron	$^{0}_{+1}\text{e}$ or $^{0}_{+1}\beta$	β^{+}

Table P
Organic Prefixes

Prefix	Number of Carbon Atoms
meth-	1
eth-	2
prop-	3
but-	4
pent-	5
hex-	6
hept-	7
oct-	8
non-	9
dec-	10

Table Q
Homologous Series of Hydrocarbons

Name	General Formula	Examples	
		Name	Structural Formula
alkanes	C_nH_{2n+2}	ethane	H H | | H—C—C—H | | H H
alkenes	C_nH_{2n}	ethene	H H \\ / C=C / \\ H H
alkynes	C_nH_{2n-2}	ethyne	H—C≡C—H

Note: n = number of carbon atoms

Table R
Organic Functional Groups

Class of Compound	Functional Group	General Formula	Example
halide (halocarbon)	$-F$ (fluoro-) $-Cl$ (chloro-) $-Br$ (bromo-) $-I$ (iodo-)	$R-X$ (X represents any halogen)	$CH_3CHClCH_3$ 2-chloropropane
alcohol	$-OH$	$R-OH$	$CH_3CH_2CH_2OH$ 1-propanol
ether	$-O-$	$R-O-R'$	$CH_3OCH_2CH_3$ methyl ethyl ether
aldehyde	$-\overset{\overset{\textstyle O}{\|\|}}{C}-H$	$R-\overset{\overset{\textstyle O}{\|\|}}{C}-H$	$CH_3CH_2\overset{\overset{\textstyle O}{\|\|}}{C}-H$ propanal
ketone	$-\overset{\overset{\textstyle O}{\|\|}}{C}-$	$R-\overset{\overset{\textstyle O}{\|\|}}{C}-R'$	$CH_3\overset{\overset{\textstyle O}{\|\|}}{C}CH_2CH_2CH_3$ 2-pentanone
organic acid	$-\overset{\overset{\textstyle O}{\|\|}}{C}-OH$	$R-\overset{\overset{\textstyle O}{\|\|}}{C}-OH$	$CH_3CH_2\overset{\overset{\textstyle O}{\|\|}}{C}-OH$ propanoic acid
ester	$-\overset{\overset{\textstyle O}{\|\|}}{C}-O-$	$R-\overset{\overset{\textstyle O}{\|\|}}{C}-O-R'$	$CH_3CH_2COCH_3$ methyl propanoate
amine	$-\overset{\overset{\textstyle \|}{\vphantom{}}}{N}-$	$R-\overset{\overset{\textstyle R'}{\|}}{N}-R''$	$CH_3CH_2CH_2NH_2$ 1-propanamine
amide	$-\overset{\overset{\textstyle O}{\|\|}}{C}-\overset{\overset{\textstyle \|}{\vphantom{}}}{N}H$	$R-\overset{\overset{\textstyle O}{\|\|}}{C}-\overset{\overset{\textstyle R'}{\|}}{N}H$	$CH_3CH_2\overset{\overset{\textstyle O}{\|\|}}{C}-NH_2$ propanamide

Note: R represents a bonded atom or group of atoms.

Periodic Table of the Elements

KEY

Atomic Mass → 12.011
Symbol → **C**
Atomic Number → 6
Electron Configuration → 2-4

−4 +2 +4 ← Selected Oxidation States

Relative atomic masses are based on $^{12}C = 12$ (exact)

Note: Numbers in parentheses are mass numbers of the most stable or common isotope.

Group 1

1.00794 +1 −1	
H	
1 1	

Group 2

Period

Period 2: 6.941 +1 **Li** 3 2-1 | 9.01218 +2 **Be** 4 2-2

Period 3: 22.98977 +1 **Na** 11 2-8-1 | 24.305 +2 **Mg** 12 2-8-2

Period 4: 39.0983 +1 **K** 19 2-8-8-1 | 40.08 +2 **Ca** 20 2-8-8-2

Period 5: 85.4678 +1 **Rb** 37 2-8-18-8-1 | 87.62 +2 **Sr** 38 2-8-18-8-2

Period 6: 132.905 +1 **Cs** 55 2-8-18-18-8-1 | 137.33 +2 **Ba** 56 2-8-18-18-8-2

Period 7: (223) +1 **Fr** 87 -18-32-18-8-1 | (226) +2 **Ra** 88 -18-32-18-8-2

*denotes the presence of (2-8-) for elements 72 and above

**The systematic names and symbols for elements of atomic numbers 113 and above will be used until the approval of trivial names by IUPAC.

Source: *CRC Handbook of Chemistry and Physics*, 91st ed., 2010–2011, CRC Press

Table S
Properties of Selected Elements

Atomic Number	Symbol	Name	First Ionization Energy (kJ/mol)	Electro-negativity	Melting Point (K)	Boiling* Point (K)	Density** (g/cm³)	Atomic Radius (pm)
1	H	hydrogen	1312	2.2	14	20.	0.000082	32
2	He	helium	2372	—	—	4	0.000164	37
3	Li	lithium	520.	1.0	454	1615	0.534	130.
4	Be	beryllium	900.	1.6	1560.	2744	1.85	99
5	B	boron	801	2.0	2348	4273	2.34	84
6	C	carbon	1086	2.6	—	—	—	75
7	N	nitrogen	1402	3.0	63	77	0.001145	71
8	O	oxygen	1314	3.4	54	90.	0.001308	64
9	F	fluorine	1681	4.0	53	85	0.001553	60.
10	Ne	neon	2081	—	24	27	0.000825	62
11	Na	sodium	496	0.9	371	1156	0.97	160.
12	Mg	magnesium	738	1.3	923	1363	1.74	140.
13	Al	aluminum	578	1.6	933	2792	2.70	124
14	Si	silicon	787	1.9	1687	3538	2.3296	114
15	P	phosphorus (white)	1012	2.2	317	554	1.823	109
16	S	sulfur (monoclinic)	1000.	2.6	388	718	2.00	104
17	Cl	chlorine	1251	3.2	172	239	0.002898	100.
18	Ar	argon	1521	—	84	87	0.001633	101
19	K	potassium	419	0.8	337	1032	0.89	200.
20	Ca	calcium	590.	1.0	1115	1757	1.54	174
21	Sc	scandium	633	1.4	1814	3109	2.99	159
22	Ti	titanium	659	1.5	1941	3560.	4.506	148
23	V	vanadium	651	1.6	2183	3680.	6.0	144
24	Cr	chromium	653	1.7	2180.	2944	7.15	130.
25	Mn	manganese	717	1.6	1519	2334	7.3	129
26	Fe	iron	762	1.8	1811	3134	7.87	124
27	Co	cobalt	760.	1.9	1768	3200.	8.86	118
28	Ni	nickel	737	1.9	1728	3186	8.90	117
29	Cu	copper	745	1.9	1358	2835	8.96	122
30	Zn	zinc	906	1.7	693	1180.	7.134	120.
31	Ga	gallium	579	1.8	303	2477	5.91	123
32	Ge	germanium	762	2.0	1211	3106	5.3234	120.
33	As	arsenic (gray)	944	2.2	1090.	—	5.75	120.
34	Se	selenium (gray)	941	2.6	494	958	4.809	118
35	Br	bromine	1140.	3.0	266	332	3.1028	117
36	Kr	krypton	1351	—	116	120.	0.003425	116
37	Rb	rubidium	403	0.8	312	961	1.53	215
38	Sr	strontium	549	1.0	1050.	1655	2.64	190.
39	Y	yttrium	600.	1.2	1795	3618	4.47	176
40	Zr	zirconium	640.	1.3	2128	4682	6.52	164

Atomic Number	Symbol	Name	First Ionization Energy (kJ/mol)	Electro-negativity	Melting Point (K)	Boiling* Point (K)	Density** (g/cm³)	Atomic Radius (pm)
41	Nb	niobium	652	1.6	2750.	5017	8.57	156
42	Mo	molybdenum	684	2.2	2896	4912	10.2	146
43	Tc	technetium	702	2.1	2430.	4538	11	138
44	Ru	ruthenium	710.	2.2	2606	4423	12.1	136
45	Rh	rhodium	720.	2.3	2237	3968	12.4	134
46	Pd	palladium	804	2.2	1828	3236	12.0	130.
47	Ag	silver	731	1.9	1235	2435	10.5	136
48	Cd	cadmium	868	1.7	594	1040.	8.69	140.
49	In	indium	558	1.8	430.	2345	7.31	142
50	Sn	tin (white)	709	2.0	505	2875	7.287	140.
51	Sb	antimony (gray)	831	2.1	904	1860.	6.68	140.
52	Te	tellurium	869	2.1	723	1261	6.232	137
53	I	iodine	1008	2.7	387	457	4.933	136
54	Xe	xenon	1170.	2.6	161	165	0.005366	136
55	Cs	cesium	376	0.8	302	944	1.873	238
56	Ba	barium	503	0.9	1000.	2170.	3.62	206
57	La	lanthanum	538	1.1	1193	3737	6.15	194
Elements 58–71 have been omitted.								
72	Hf	hafnium	659	1.3	2506	4876	13.3	164
73	Ta	tantalum	728	1.5	3290.	5731	16.4	158
74	W	tungsten	759	1.7	3695	5828	19.3	150.
75	Re	rhenium	756	1.9	3458	5869	20.8	141
76	Os	osmium	814	2.2	3306	5285	22.587	136
77	Ir	iridium	865	2.2	2719	4701	22.562	132
78	Pt	platinum	864	2.2	2041	4098	21.5	130.
79	Au	gold	890.	2.4	1337	3129	19.3	130.
80	Hg	mercury	1007	1.9	234	630.	13.5336	132
81	Tl	thallium	589	1.8	577	1746	11.8	144
82	Pb	lead	716	1.8	600.	2022	11.3	145
83	Bi	bismuth	703	1.9	544	1837	9.79	150.
84	Po	polonium	812	2.0	527	1235	9.20	142
85	At	astatine	—	2.2	575			148
86	Rn	radon	1037	—	202	211	0.009074	146
87	Fr	francium	393	0.7	300.	—	—	242
88	Ra	radium	509	0.9	969	—	5	211
89	Ac	actinium	499	1.1	1323	3471	10.	201
Elements 90 and above have been omitted.								

* boiling point at standard pressure
** density of solids and liquids at room temperature and density of gases at 298 K and 101.3 kPa
— no data available

Source: CRC Handbook for Chemistry and Physics, 91st ed. 2010–2011, CRC Press

Table T
Important Formulas and Equations

Density	$d = \dfrac{m}{V}$	d = density m = mass V = volume
Mole Calculations	number of moles = $\dfrac{\text{given mass}}{\text{gram-formula mass}}$	
Percent Error	% error = $\dfrac{\text{measured value} - \text{accepted value}}{\text{accepted value}} \times 100$	
Percent Composition	% composition by mass = $\dfrac{\text{mass of part}}{\text{mass of whole}} \times 100$	
Concentration	parts per million = $\dfrac{\text{mass of solute}}{\text{mass of solution}} \times 1\,000\,000$ molarity = $\dfrac{\text{moles of solute}}{\text{liter of solution}}$	
Combined Gas Law	$\dfrac{P_1 V_1}{T_1} = \dfrac{P_2 V_2}{T_2}$	P = pressure V = volume T = temperature
Titration	$M_A V_A = M_B V_B$	M_A = molarity of H^+ M_B = molarity of OH^- V_A = volume of acid V_B = volume of base
Heat	$q = mC\Delta T$ $q = mH_f$ $q = mH_v$	q = heat H_f = heat of fusion m = mass H_v = heat of vaporization C = specific heat capacity ΔT = change in temperature
Temperature	K = °C + 273	K = kelvin °C = degree Celsius

Glossary and Index

Absolute Zero (9)

0 K or -273°C; the temperature at which all molecular movements stop

Accelerator (263)

a device which gives charged particles sufficient kinetic energy to penetrate the nucleus

Acid, Arrhenius (161)

a substance that produces H^+ (hydrogen ion, proton) or H_3O^+ (hydronium) ion as the only positive ion in solutions

Acid , Alternate Theory (162)

a substance that donates H+ (hydrogen ion, proton) in acid-base reactions

Activated complex (188)

a high energy substance formed during the course of a chemical reaction

Activation energy (179)

minimal amount of energy needed to start a reaction

Addition reaction (224, 228)

organic reaction that involves the adding of hydrogen atoms (or halogen atoms) to a double or a triple bond

Addition polymerization (226, 228)

the joining of monomers (small unit molecules) with double bonds to form a polymer (a larger unit) molecule

Alcohol (213)

an organic compound containing the hydroxyl group (-OH) as the functional group

Aldehyde (215)

an organic compound containing the $-\overset{\overset{\text{O}}{\|}}{\text{C}}\text{-H}$ as the functional group

Alkali metal (36)

an element in Group 1 of the Periodic Table

Alkaline Earth metal (36)

an element in Group 2 of the Periodic Table

Alkane (190, 200)

a saturated hydrocarbon with all single bonds and general formula of C_nH_{2n+2}

Alkene (209, 210)

an unsaturated hydrocarbon with a double bond and general formula of C_nH_{2n}

Alkyl group (220)

a hydrocarbon group (found as a side chain) that contains one less H atom than an alkane with the same number of C atoms

Alkyne (209, 211)

an unsaturated hydrocarbon with a triple (≡) bond and general formula of C_nH_{2n-2}

Allotropes (39)

two or more different forms of the same element that have different formulas, structures, and properties

Alloy

a homogeneous mixture of a metal with another element (often another metal)

Alpha decay (267, 273)

a nuclear decay that releases an alpha particle

Alpha emitter (265)

a radioisotope that releases alpha particles as it decays or undergoes radioactivity

Alpha particle (263)

a helium nucleus, ^4_2He

Amide (217)

an organic compound formed from a reaction of an organic acid with an amine

Amine (217)

an organic compound that has $-\overset{|}{N}-$ (nitrogen) as its functional group

A cont

Amino acid   (217)
        an organic compound containing an amine (-NH$_2$-) and a carboxyl (-COOH) functional group

Amphoteric
        a species that can act either as an acid or as a base in acid-base reactions

Anhydrous solid   (121)
        the solid that remained after a hydrate is heated and the water of hydration is driven off

Anode   (246)
        an electrode (site) where oxidation occurs in electrochemical (voltaic and electrolytic) cells
        In voltaic cells, the anode is negative.
        In electrolytic cells, the anode is positive.

Aqueous solution   (4, 134)
        a homogeneous mixture made with water as the solvent

Artificial Transmutation   (269, 273)
        changing one atom to another by bombarding or hitting the nucleus with high-speed particles

Asymmetrical molecule   (75)
        a molecule that has a polarized structure because of an uneven charge distribution

Atom   (50, 53)
        the basic or the smallest unit of an element that can be involved in chemical reactions

Atomic mass   (60)
        the weighted average mass of an element's naturally occurring isotopes

Atomic mass unit   (60, 110)
        one-twelfth (1/12th) the mass of a carbon-12 atom

Atomic number   (55)
        the number of protons in the nucleus of an atom

Atomic radius (size)   (33, 41)
        half the distance between adjacent nuclei of identical bonded atoms

Avogadro's law (hypothesis)   (24)
        equal volumes of all gases under the same pressure and temperature contain equal numbers of
        molecules

Avogadro's number   (110, 117)
        the amount or quantity of particles in one mole of a substance; 6.02 x 10^{23}

B

Base, Arrhenius   (161)
        a substance that produces OH$^-$ (hydroxide) ions as the only negative ions in solutions

Base, Alternate Theory   (162)
        a substance that accepts H$^+$ (hydrogen ion, proton) in acid-base reactions

Battery (245, 246)
        an example of a voltaic cell It uses a redox reaction to produce electricity

Beta decay   (268)
        a nuclear decay that releases a beta particle

Beta emitter (265)
        a radioisotope that releases beta particles as it decays or undergoes radioactivity

Beta particle   (263)
        a high-speed electron ($_{-1}^{0}$e) released from an atomic nucleus during a nuclear decay

Binary compound   (96)
        a chemical substance composed of two different elements chemically combined

Boiling point   (33, 45, 150)
        the temperature of a liquid at which the vapor pressure of the liquid is equal to the
        atmospheric pressure
        The boiling point of water is 100°C at 1 atm.

Boyle's law   (21)
        describes behavior of a gas at constant temperature:
        At constant temperature, volume of a gas varies indirectly with the pressure.

Brittle   (33)
        a physical property of a substance to shatter easily when struck

C

Calorimeter (14)

a device used in measuring heat energy change during a physical and a chemical process

Catalyst (178, 180)

a substance that speeds up a reaction by providing an alternate, lower activation energy pathway

Cathode (246)

an electrode (site) where reduction occurs in electrochemical (voltaic and electrolytic) cells
In voltaic cells, the cathode is positive.
In electrolytic cells, the cathode is negative.

Cathode ray experiment (51)

experiment conducted by J.J. Thompson that confirms the existence of negative particles in atoms

Charles' Law (22)

describes behavior of gases at constant pressure:
At constant pressure, the volume of a gas is directly proportional to its Kelvin (absolute) temperature.

Chemical bonding (74)

the simultaneous attraction of two nuclei to electrons

Chemical change (26, 102)

a change in the composition of one or more substances during a chemical reaction

Chemical equation (102)

a way of using chemical symbols to show changes in chemical composition of substances

Chemical formula (92)

expression of qualitative and quantitative composition of pure substances

Chemical property (26)

a characteristic of a substance based on its interaction with other substances

Chemistry (2)

the study of the composition, properties, changes, and energy of matter

Chromatography (5)

the process of separating and analyzing the components of an ink or a pigment by how far they travel with the solvent

Coefficient (100, 124)

a number (usually a whole number) in front of a formula that indicates how many moles (or unit) of a substance

Collision theory (71)

for a chemical reaction to occur, reacting particles must collide effectively

Combustion (101, 227, 228)

an exothermic reaction of a substance with oxygen to release energy and produce CO_2 and H_2O

Compound (3)

a substance composed of two or more different elements chemically combined in a definite ratio
a substance that can be separated (decomposed) only by chemical methods

Concentrated solution (142)

a solution containing a large amount of dissolved solute relative to the amount of solvent

Condensation (9)

exothermic phase change of a substance from gas (vapor) to a liquid

Condensation polymerization (226, 228)

the joining of monomers (small unit molecules) into a polymer (a large unit molecule) by the removal of water

Conductivity (33)

ability of an electrical current to flow through a substance
Conductivity of electrolytes (soluble substances) in aqueous and liquid states is due to mobile ions.
Conductivity of metallic substances is due to mobile or free-moving valence electrons.

Covalent bond (75, 209)

a bond formed by the sharing of electrons between nonmetal atoms

Cracking (228)

the breaking of a large hydrocarbon molecule into smaller molecules

Crystallization (5, 135)

a process of recovering a solute from a solution (mixture) by evaporation (or boiling)

D

Decantation   (5)
> the process of removing layers of liquids that do not dissolve well in each other.

Decomposition   (101)
> a chemical reaction in which a compound is broken down into simpler substances

Density   (33, 45)
> mass per unit volume of a substance ;   Density = $\dfrac{\text{Mass}}{\text{Volume}}$

Deposition   (9)
> an exothermic phase change by which a gas changes to a solid

Diatomic molecules (element)
> a molecule consisting of two identical atoms (ex O_2)

Dihydroxy alcohol   (?13)
> an alcohol with two attached −OH (hydroxyl) groups

Dilute solution   (142)
> a solution containing very little dissolved solute in comparison to the amount of solvent

Dipole (aka polar)   (81)
> a molecule with positive and negative ends due to uneven charge distributions

Dipole-dipole interaction   (81)
> the force of attraction that holds polar molecules together in a polar substance

Distillation   (5, 31)
> a process by which components of a homogeneous mixture can be separated by differences
> in boiling points

Double covalent bond (=)   (190, 191)
> the sharing of two pairs of electrons (four total electrons) between two atoms

Double replacement   (101)
> a chemical reaction that involves the exchange of ions

Ductile   (33)
> ability (property) of a metal to be drawn into a thin wire

E

Effective collision   (179)
> a collision in which the particles collide with sufficient kinetic energy, and at appropriate angles

Electrochemical cell   (245)
> a system in which there is a flow of electrical current while a chemical reaction is taking place
> Voltaic and Electrolytic cells are the two most common types of electrochemical cells.

Electrode   (246)
> site at which oxidation or reduction can occur in electrochemical cells
> The anode (oxidation site) and cathode (reduction site) are the two electrodes of electrochemical cells.

Electrolysis   (250)
> a process by which electrical current forces a nonspontaneous redox reaction to occur
> Electrolysis of water: $2H_2O$ + electricity $\rightarrow$ $2H_2$ + O_2

Electrolyte   (171)
> a substance that dissolves in water to produce aqueous solution that conducts electricity
> Conductivity of electrolytes is due to the mobile ions in the solution.

Electrolytic cell   (245, 250)
> an electrochemical cell that requires an electrical current to cause a nonspontaneous redox
> reaction to occur

Electron   (54)
> a negatively charged subatomic particle found surrounding the nucleus (in orbitals) of an atom

Electron configuration   (62)
> distribution of electrons in electron shells (energy levels) of an atom

Electron-dot diagram   (85)
> a diagram showing the symbol of an atom and dots equal to the number of valence electrons

Electronegativity   (31, 4)
          a measure of an atom's ability (tendency) to attract electrons during chemical bonding

Electrolytic reduction   (250)
          the use of an electrolytic cell to force an ion to gain electrons and form a neutral atom

Electroplating   (250)
          the use of an electrolytic cell to coat a thin layer of a metal onto another surface

Element   (2)
          a substance composed of atoms of the same atomic number
          A substance that CANNOT be decomposed or broken down into simpler substances.

Empirical formula   (94)
          a formula showing atoms combined in the simplest whole number ratio

Endothermic   (9, 14, 73, 184)
          a process that absorbs energy
          Products of endothermic reactions always have more energy than the reactants.

Energy
          ability to do work; can be measured in joules or calories

Entropy   (192)
          a measure of the disorder or randomness of a system
          Entropy increases from solid to liquid to gas, and with an increase in temperature

Equilibrium   (194)
          a state of a system by which the rate (speed) of opposing processes (reactions) are equal

Ester   (216)
          an organic compound with $-\overset{\overset{\text{O}}{\|}}{\text{C}}-\text{O}$ ($-COO-$) as the functional group

Esterification   (225, 228)
          an organic reaction between an alcohol and organic acid to produce an ester

Ether   (214)
          an organic compound with $-O-$ as the functional group

Evaporation   (9, 135)
          an endothermic phase change by which a liquid change to gas (vapor)

Excited state   (64)
          a state of an atom in which electrons have "jumped" to higher electron shells (energy levels)

Exothermic   (9, 14, 181, 184)
          a process that releases energy
          Products of exothermic reactions always have less energy than the reactants.

F

Family (Group)   (31)
          the vertical column of the Periodic Table
          Elements in the same family have the same number of valence electrons and have similar chemical properties.

Fermentation   (204, 207)
          an organic reaction in which sugar is converted to alcohol (ethanol, C_2H_5OH) and carbon dioxide

Filtration   (5)
          a process that is used to separate a heterogeneous mixture that is composed of substances with different particle sizes

Flame test   (65)
          a lab procedure used for identifying metallic ions in compounds

F

Fission   (270, 273)

the splitting of a large nucleus into smaller nuclei fragments in a nuclear reaction

Mass is converted to huge amounts of energy during fission

Formula   (91)

symbols and subscripts used to represent the composition of a substance

Formula mass   (112)

the total mass of all the atoms in one unit of a formula

Freezing (solidification)   (9)

an exothermic phase change by which a liquid change to a solid

Freezing point (solid/liquid equilibrium)

the temperature at which both solid and liquid phases of a substance can exist at equilibrium

The freezing point and melting point of a substance are the same.

Functional group   (212)

an atom or a group of atoms that replaces a hydrogen atom in a hydrocarbon

Fusion (nuclear change)   (270, 273)

the joining of two small nuclei to make a larger nucleus in a nuclear reaction

Mass is converted to energy during nuclear fusion.

G

Gamma ray   (263)

high-energy rays similar to X-rays that are released during nuclear decay

Gamma rays have zero mass and zero charge ($_{0}^{0}\gamma$)

Gas phase   (9)

a phase of matter with no definite shape and no definite volume

Gay-Lussac's Law   (21)

describes behavior of a gas at constant volume: At constant volume, pressure of a gas varies directly with the Kelvin temperature

Geological dating   (282)

determining the age of a rock or mineral by comparing amounts of Uranium-238 to Lead-206 in a sample

Gold Foil experiment   (51)

an experiment conducted by Earnest Rutherford that led him to propose the "**Empty Space**" theory of atoms

Gram-formula mass   (112)

the mass of one mole of a substance expressed in grams

The total mass of all atoms in one mole of a substance.

Ground state   (64)

a state of an atom in which all electrons of the atom occupy the lowest available electron shell

Group   (31)

the vertical column of the Periodic Table

elements in the same group have the same number of valence electrons and share similar chemical properties

H

Haber process   (197)

a chemical reaction that produces ammonia from nitrogen and hydrogen

$$N_2 + 3H_2 \rightarrow 2NH_3$$

Half-life   (276, 277)

the length of time it takes for a sample of a radioisotope to decay to half its original mass (or atoms)

Half-reaction (240, 241)
a reaction that shows either the oxidation or the reduction part of a redox reaction

Halide (214)
a compound that contains a halogen (Group 17) atom

Halogen (37)
an element found in Group 17 of the Periodic Table

Halogenation (224, 228)
an organic reaction that adds halogen atoms to the double bond of an alkene

Heat (14)
a form of energy that can flow (or transfer) from one substance (or area) to another
Joules and calories are two units commonly used to measure the quantity of heat

Heat of fusion (16)
the amount of heat needed to change a unit mass of a solid to a liquid at its melting point
Heat of fusion for water is 334 Joules per gram

Heat of reaction (Δ H) (183)
the amount of heat absorbed or released during a reaction
the difference between the heat energy of the products and the heat energy of the reactants
ΔH = heat of products − heat of reactants

Heat of vaporization (16)
the amount of heat needed to change a unit mass of a liquid to vapor (gas) at its boiling point
Heat of vaporization for water is 2260 Joules per gram.

Heterogeneous (4)
a type of mixture in which the substances in the mixture are not uniformly or evenly mixed

Homogeneous (4)
a type of mixture in which the substances in the mixture are uniformly and evenly mixed
Solutions are homogeneous mixtures.

Homologous series (199)
a group of related compounds in which one member differs from the next member by a set number of atoms

Hydrate (120)
an ionic compound containing a set number of water molecules within its crystal structures
$CuSO_4 \cdot 5H_2O$ is an example of a hydrate. This hydrate contains five moles of water.

Hydrocarbon (209)
an organic compound containing only hydrogen and carbon atoms

Hydrogen bond (81, 82)
the attraction of a hydrogen atom to oxygen, nitrogen, or fluorine atom of another molecule
hydrogen bonding exists (or is strongest) in H_2O (water), NH_3 (ammonia), and HF (hydrogen fluoride)

Hydrogen ion (H^+) (161)
a hydrogen atom that has lost its only electron H^+ is similar to a proton
The only positive ion produced by all Arrhenius acids in solutions.

Hydrogenation (224, 228)
an organic reaction that adds hydrogen atoms to the double bond of an alkene

Hydrolysis
a reaction of a salt in water to produce a solution that is either acidic, basic, or neutral

Hydronium ion (H_3O^+) (161)
a polyatomic ion formed when H_2O (a water molecule) combines with H^+ (hydrogen ion)
Ion formed by all Arrhenius acids in solutions

Hydroxide ion (OH⁻) (161)
the only negative ion produced by Arrhenius bases in solutions

Hydroxyl group (−OH) (213)
a functional group found in compounds of alcohols NOTE: Hydroxyl groups do not ionize in water.

I

Ideal gas   (18)
  a theoretical gas that possesses all the characteristics described by the kinetic molecular theory

Immiscible liquids   (137)
  two liquids that do not mix well with each other

Indicator   (163)
  any substance that changes color in the presence of another substance
  An indicator can also be used to determine the completion of a chemical reaction.
  An acid-base indicator is used to determine if a substance is an acid or a base.

Insoluble   (134)
  a solute substance with low solubility (doesn't dissolve well) in a given solvent

Intramolecular forces   (74)
  bonding between the atoms of a substance; ionic, covalent, and metallic

Intermolecular forces   (81)
  weak forces holding molecules together in the solid and liquid states; dipole-dipole, hydrogen
  bond, and London dispersion forces

Ion   (67)
  a charged (+ or -) particle

Ionic bond   (74)
  a bond formed by the transfer of one or more electrons from one atom to another
  An ionic bond is formed by the electrostatic attraction of a positive ion to a negative ion

Ionic compound (substance)   (74)
  compounds that are composed of positive and negative particles
  $NaCl$, $NaNO_3$, and ammonium chloride are examples of ionic substances.

Ionic radius   (33)
  the size of an ion as measured from the nucleus to the outer energy level of that ion

Ionization energy   (33, 42)
  the amount of energy needed to remove the most loosely bound valence electron from an atom

Isomers   (220)
  organic compounds with the same molecular formula but different structural formulas
  isomers also have different properties

Isotopes   (57)
  atoms of the same element with the same number of protons but different numbers of neutrons
  atoms of the same element with the same atomic number but different mass numbers

J

Joules   (14)
  a unit for measuring the amount of heat energy

K

Kelvin (K)   (9)
  a unit for measuring temperature
  a Kelvin temperature unit is always 273 higher than the equivalent temperature in Celsius.
  $K = {}^\circ C + 273$

Ketone   (216)
  an organic compound containing $-\overset{\overset{\text{O}}{\|}}{\text{C}}- \; (-CO-)$, a carbonyl group) as the functional group

Kinetic energy   (10)
  energy due to motion or movement of particles in a substance
  The average kinetic energy of particles in a substance determines its temperature.

Kinetic molecular theory (of an ideal gas)   (18)
  a theory that is used to explain behavior of gas particles

Kinetics   (178)
  the study of rates and mechanisms of reactions

L

Law of conservation (102)
>In a chemical reaction, mass, atoms, charges, and energy are conserved. They are neither created nor destroyed.

Law of definite proportion (3)
>the ratio of atoms in all samples of a compound is always the same or fixed

Le Chatelier's principle (198)
>a chemical or physical process will shift at equilibrium to compensate for added stress

Lewis electron-dot diagram (85)
>a diagram showing the symbol of an atom and dots equal to the number of its valence electrons

Liquid phase (7)
>a phase of matter with definite volume but no definite shape (takes the shape of the container)

London-dispersion forces (81)
>weak intermolecular force that hold molecules of nonpolar substances together in the liquid and gas states

Luster (33)
>a property that describes the shininess of a metallic element

M

Malleable (33)
>ability (or property) of a metal to be hammered into a thin sheet

Mass number (55)
>the total number of protons and neutrons in the nucleus of an atom

Matter (2)
>anything that has mass and volume (occupied space)

Melting point (33, 45)
>the temperature at which both the solid and the liquid phases of a substance can co-exist
>The melting point of water is 0°C or 273 K

Meniscus (290)
>the curve surface of a liquid in a test tube or graduated cylinder

Metal (4)
>an element that tends to lose electrons and form a positive ion during chemical reactions
>The majority of the elements (about 75%) are metals

Metallic bond (76)
>a bond due to the attraction of valence electrons of a metallic atom to its positive nucleus
>Metallic bonding is described as "positive ions immersed in a sea of mobile electrons."

Metalloid (34)
>an element with both metallic and nonmetallic properties (characteristics)

Miscibility (137)
>the extent to which two liquids will mix

Miscible (137)
>two liquids that mix very well together

Mixture (4)
>a physical combination of two or more substances in varying ratio, and can be physically separated

Molar mass (112)
>the mass in grams of one mole of a substance

Molar volume (116)
>the volume of one mole of a gas at STP; 22.4 liters

Molarity (147)
>concentration of a solution expressed in moles of solute per liter of solution

$$Molarity = \frac{moles\ of\ solute}{liter\ of\ solution}$$

Mole (110)
>a unit for measuring the number of particles (atoms, molecules, ions, electrons) in a substance

Molecular formula   (94)
>   a formula showing the actual composition (or ratio of atoms) in a substance

Molecule   (75)
>   the smallest unit of a covalent (molecular) substance that has all properties of the substance

Molecular substance (covalent substance)   (75)
>   a substance composed of molecules

Monohydroxy alcohol   (213)
>   an alcohol with one attached −OH (hydroxyl) group

Monomer   (226)
>   an individual unit of a polymer

Multiple covalent bond   (75, 209)
>   a double or a triple covalent bond formed by the sharing of more than two electrons

N

Negative ion   (67)
>   a charged atom with more electrons than protons

Network solid covalent   (76)
>   a bond in network solid substances with absence of discrete particles

Neutral atom   (67)
>   an atom with equal number of protons to electrons

Neutralization   (168)
>   a reaction of an acid with a base to produce water and a salt

Neutron   (54, 263)
>   a subatomic particle with no charge, found in the nucleus of an atom

Noble gas   (38)
>   an element found in Group 18 of the Periodic Table

Nonmetal   (34)
>   an element that tends to gain electrons and forms negative ions, or shares electrons to form a covalent bond

Nonpolar covalent bond   (75)
>   a bond formed by the equal sharing of electrons between two identical nonmetal atoms (or atoms with the same electronegativity)

Nonpolar substance   (75)
>   a type of molecular substance with symmetrical charge distribution within its molecules

Nucleons   (55)
>   particles in the nucleus of atoms Protons and neutrons

Nucleus   (53)
>   the small, dense, positive core of an atom containing protons and neutrons

O

Octet of electrons   (72)
>   when an atom has a stable electron configuration with eight electrons in the valence shell

Orbital   (50, 62)
>   a region in an atom where electrons are likely to be found (or located)

Organic acid   (215)
>   a compound containing −COOH   or $-\overset{\overset{\displaystyle O}{\displaystyle \|}}{C}-OH$ as its functional group

Organic compounds   (206)
>   carbon based compounds

Oxidation   (237 240)
>   the loss of electrons by an atom during a redox reaction

Oxidized substance (Reducing agent)   (240)
>   a substance that loses electrons in a redox reaction
>   a substance whose oxidation number (state) increases after a redox reaction

Oxidizing agent (Reduced substance)   (240)
>   a substance that is reduced (gains electrons) in a redox reaction
>   a substance whose oxidation number (state) decreases after a redox reaction

Oxidation number/ Oxidation state   (240)
>   a charge an atom has or appears to have during a redox reaction

Ozone   (39)
> O_3, an allotrope (a different molecular form) of oxygen

P

Parts per million   (148)

concentration of a solution expressed as the ratio of mass of solute per million parts of a solution

Part per million (ppm)   = $\dfrac{\text{mass of solute}}{\text{mass of solution}}$ x   1 000 000

Percent composition   (119)

composition of a compound as the percentage by mass of each element compared to the total mass of the compound

Percent composition   = $\dfrac{\text{mass of parts}}{\text{mass of whole}}$ x   100

Percent error   (292)

the difference between an approximate or measured value and an exact or known value

Period   (31)

the horizontal row of the Periodic Table

Elements within a Period have the same number of occupied electron shells (or energy levels)

Periodic law   (31)

states that properties of elements are periodic functions of their atomic numbers

pH   (156)

values that indicate the strength of an acid or a base pH value ranges from 0 – 14

pH value is determined from how much H^+ ions are in a solution

Phase equilibrium   (194)

a state of balance when the rates of two opposing (opposite) phase changes are equal

Physical change   (25)

a change that does not change the composition of a substance

Phase changes and dissolving are examples of physical changes

Physical properties   (25)

characteristics of a substance that can be observed or measured without changing the chemical composition of the substance

Polar covalent bond   (75)

a bond formed by the unequal sharing of electrons between two different nonmetal atoms

Polar substance   (75)

a type of molecular substance with asymmetrical charge distribution within its molecules

Polyatomic ion   (96)

a group of two or more atoms with excess positive or negative charges (See Reference Table E)

Polymer   (226)

an organic compound composed of chains of monomers (smaller units)

Polymerization   (226, 228)

an organic reaction by which monomers (small units of molecules) are joined together to make a polymer (a larger unit molecule)

Positron   (263)

a positively charge particle similar in mass to an electron $_{+1}^{0}e$

Positive ion   (67)

a charged atom containing more protons than electrons

Positron decay (emission)   (268)

a nuclear decay that releases a positron

Positron emitter (251)

a radioisotope that releases positrons as it decays or undergoes radioactivity

Potential energy   (73, 183)

stored energy in chemical substances

Amount of potential energy depends on composition and the structure of a substance.

Potential energy diagram   (183)

a diagram showing the changes in potential energy of substances during a reaction

Precipitate   (146)

a solid that forms out of a solution

Primary alcohol   (213)

an alcohol with an –OH functional group attached to an end carbon

P cont

Product (100, 188)
a substance that remains (or forms) after a chemical reaction is completed
products are placed to the right of an arrow in equations

Proton (53)
a subatomic particle with a positive charge found in the nucleus of an atom
The number of protons in an atom is equal to the atomic number of the element

Pure substance (2)
a type of matter with the same composition and properties in all samples
Elements and compounds are pure substances

Q

Quanta
a specific amount of energy absorbed or released by an electron as it changes from one level to another

Qualitative (92)
indicates the type of atom that is in a chemical formula

Quantitative (92)
indicates the number of each atom in a formula

R

Radioisotope (265)
an unstable isotope of an element that is radioactive and can decay

Rate (178)
a measure of the speed (how fast) a reaction occurs

Reactant (100, 188)
the starting substance in a chemical reaction
Reactants are shown (or placed) to the left of the arrow in equations

Redox (236, 245)
a reaction that involves oxidation and reduction

Reduction (236, 245)
the gaining of electrons during a redox reaction
Reduction leads to a decrease in oxidation number (state) of a substance

Reduced substance (oxidizing agent) (236)
a substance that gains electrons during a redox reaction
a substance whose oxidation number (state) decreases after a reaction

Reducing agent (oxidized substance) (236)
the substance that is oxidized (loses electrons) in a redox reaction
a substance whose oxidation number (state) increases after a redox reaction

Rutherford, Earnest (50, 51)
proposed the "empty space" theory of atom based on the result of his Gold Foil experiment

S

Saponification (227, 228)
an organic reaction that produces soap and glycerol (a trihydroxy alcohol)

Salt (165)
a product of a neutralization reaction
an ionic substance

Salt bridge (246, 248)
allows for ions to flow (migrate) between the two half cells of voltaic cells

S cont

Saturated hydrocarbon   (209)
    alkane hydrocarbon with only single bonds between the carbon atoms
Saturated solution   (142)
    a solution containing the maximum amount of dissolved solute possible at a given temperature
Secondary alcohol   (213)
    an alcohol in which the −OH is bonded to a carbon atom that is already bonded to two other carbon atoms
Single covalent bond   (75, 209)
    a covalent bond formed by the sharing of just two electrons (or one pair of electrons)
Single replacement   (101)
    a reaction in which a more reactive element replaces the less reactive element of a compound
Significant figures (288)
    digits in a value that include all digits that are known for certain plus one estimated digit

Solid phase   (8)
    a phase of matter with definite shape and definite volume
Solubility   (137)
    a measure of the extent to which a solute will dissolve in a given solvent at a specified temperature
Soluble   (137)
    a substance with high solubility
Solute   (137)
    the substance that is being dissolved
    When a salt is dissolved in water, the solute is the salt.
Solution   (137)
    a homogeneous mixture of substances in the same physical state
Solvent   (137)
    the substance (usually a liquid) that is dissolving the solute
    Water is the solvent in all aqueous solutions.
Specific heat capacity   (15)
    the amount of heat needed to change the temperature of a 1-grams sample of a substance by one degree Celsius or one Kelvin
Spectral lines (65)
    bands of colors produced at specific wavelength as excited electrons return to the ground state
Spontaneous reaction (254)
    a reaction that will occur under a given set of conditions
    a reaction that proceed in the direction of lower energy and greater entropy
Stress   (189)
    a change in temperature, pressure, or concentration in a reaction at equilibrium

Stock system   (97)
    the use of a Roman numeral in a chemical name to indicate the positive oxidation state of an atom in the substance
Structural formula   (94)
    a formula showing how atoms of a substance are bonded together
Sublimation   (9)
    an endothermic phase change from solid to gas
Subscript   (91)
    a whole number written next to a chemical symbol to indicate the number of atoms
Substitution reaction   (223)
    an organic reaction of an alkane with a halogen to produce a halide
    A reaction in which a halogen atom replaces a hydrogen atom of an alkane.
Surface area   (156)
    amount of exposed area where reactions can occur in a   set mass of a solid substance
Supersaturated solution   (142)
    a solution containing more solute than would normally dissolve at that given temperature
Symmetrical molecule   (75)
    a molecule that has a nonpolarized structure due to an even charge distribution
Synthesis   (101)
    a chemical reaction in which two or more substances combine to make one substance

T

Temperature (10)
the measure of the average kinetic energy of particles in a substance
Temperature and average kinetic energy are directly related. As one increases, so does the other.

Tertiary alcohol (213)
an alcohol in which the –OH is bonded to a carbon atom that is already bonded to three other carbon atoms

Thermal energy (14)
energy produced by the random motion of particles (atoms, molecules, or ions) in a sample of matter

Titration (169)
a process used in determining the concentration of an unknown solution by reacting it with a solution of known concentration

Thomson, J.J. (50, 51)
conducted "Cathode Ray" experiment that confirmed the existence of negative particles in atoms

Tracer (282)
a radioisotope used to track a chemical reaction

Transition element (37)
an element found in Groups 3 – 12 of the Periodic Table

Transmutation (267)
the changing or converting of a nucleus of one atom into a nucleus of a different atom

Trihydroxy alcohol (213)
an alcohol with three –OH (hydroxyl) groups

Triple covalent bond (75, 209)
a covalent bond resulting from the sharing of three pairs of electrons (six total electrons)

U

Unsaturated hydrocarbon (209)
organic compound containing double or triple bonded carbon atoms

Unsaturated solution (142)
a solution containing less dissolved solute than can be dissolved at a given temperature

V

Valence electrons (62)
the electrons in the outermost electron shell (energy level) of an atom

Vapor (150)
a gas form of a substance that is normally a liquid at room temperature

Vapor pressure (150)
the pressure exerted by vapor (evaporated particles) on the surface of the liquid

Voltaic cell (245)
an electrochemical cell in which electrical energy is produced from a spontaneous redox chemical reaction

Van der Waals forces (see London-dispersion forces) (81)

W

Wave-mechanical model (electron-cloud model) (50)
the current model of an atom that places electrons in orbital
The orbital is described as the most probable location (region) of finding electrons in an atom.